lonely planet W9-CDJ-787

Discover
New Zealand

Contents ➡

Throughout this book, we use these icons to highlight special recommendations:

 The Best...
Lists for everything from bars to wildlife – to make sure you don't miss out

 Don't Miss
A must-see – don't go home until you've been there

Local Knowledge Local experts reveal their top picks and secret highlights

 Detour
Special places a little off the beaten track

 If you like...
Lesser-known alternatives to world-famous attractions

These icons help you quickly identify reviews in the text and on the map:

 Sights

 Eating

 Drinking

 Sleeping

 Information

This edition written and researched by

Charles Rawlings-Way
Brett Atkinson, Sarah Bennett,
Peter Dragicevich, Lee Slater

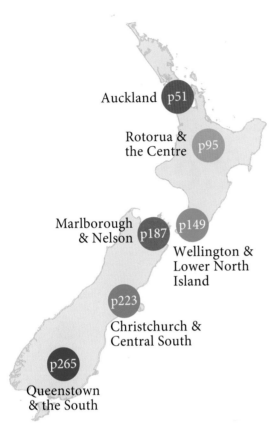

Wellington & Lower North Island

Marlborough & Nelson

Auckland

Rotorua & the Centre

Christchurch & Central South

Contents

Contents

On the Road

The Best of the Rest · 311

This Is New Zealand

You probably already know how ludicrously photogenic New Zealand is. You may also know that adventure sports rule here (bungy jumping, skiing, skydiving, white-water rafting etc). Then there's NZ's antinuclear stance, its rich Maori culture, its passion for rugby, its abundant sheep...

But one pleasant surprise is the Kiwi culinary scene. Local chefs plunge into Pacific Rim cookbooks for inspiration, organic farmers markets are everywhere, and Maori faves such as paua (abalone) and kina (sea urchin) make regular menu appearances. Thirsty? Locally made sauvignon blanc has been collecting trophies for decades now, and the country's booming craft-beer scene also deserves your attention. And caffeine cravers can rest assured: coffee culture is firmly entrenched.

Indeed, the nation is well fed and watered, but NZ has had a few setbacks lately. The Christchurch earthquakes, the Greymouth mine disaster and the grounding of the MV *Rena* in the Bay of Plenty have caused a lot of heartache. But shining through the gloom are the All Blacks, NZ's deified rugby team, who won the World Cup on home soil in 2011. Don't expect locals to stop talking about it any time soon...

Of course, the All Blacks could never have become world-beaters without their awesome Maori players. This is just one example of how Maori culture impresses itself on contemporary Kiwi life. Across NZ you can join in a *hangi* (Maori feast), visit a *marae* (meeting house) or catch a cultural performance, usually involving a blood-curdling *haka* (war dance).

Also for your consideration is the fact that NZ is a remarkably easy place to visit. On-the-road frustrations are rare: buses and trains are punctual, roads are in good nick, ATMs proliferate, pickpockets are practically nonexistent and the food is unlikely to send you running for the nearest public toilets. This decent nation is a place where you can relax and enjoy (rather than endure) your holiday.

> "
> NZ is a remarkably easy place to visit
> "

Thermal lake at Wai-o-Tapu Thermal Wonderland (p109)

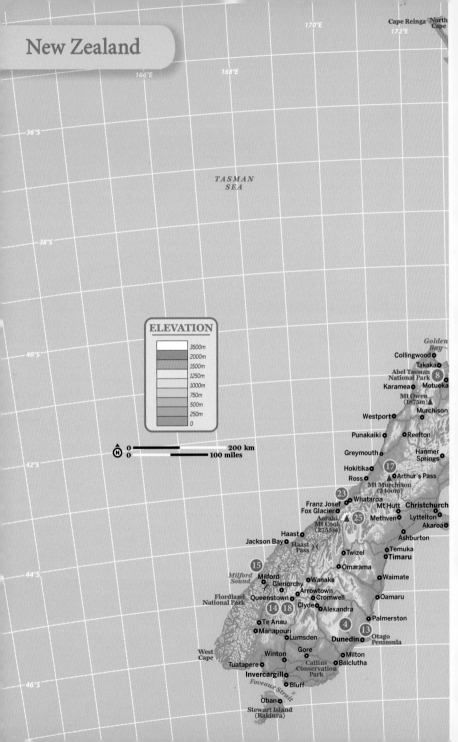

25

Top Experiences

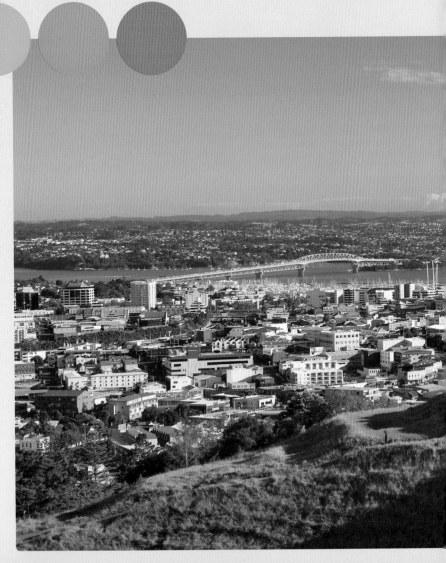

25 New Zealand's Top Experiences

Urban Auckland

Held in the embrace of two harbours and liberally sprinkled with volcanoes, Auckland (p62) isn't your average metropolis. It's regularly rated one of the world's most liveable cities, and while it's never going to challenge Sydney or London in the excitement stakes, it's blessed with good beaches, is flanked by wine regions and has a large enough population to support a thriving dining, drinking and live-music scene. Cultural festivals are celebrated with gusto in this ethnically diverse city, which has the world's largest Pacific Island population. View of Auckland from Mt Eden

MICAH WRIGHT / LONELY PLANET IMAGES ©

②

Auckland Harbour & Hauraki Gulf

Island-studded Hauraki Gulf is Auckland's aquatic playground, providing ample room for the City of Sails' pleasure fleet. Despite the maritime traffic, the gulf has resident pods of whales and dolphins. Rangitoto Island is an icon, its volcanic cone providing the backdrop for many a tourist snapshot. Yet Waiheke Island (p83), with its beaches, wineries and upmarket eateries, is Auckland's most popular island escape. Vineyard, Waiheke Island

Geothermal Rotorua

The first thing you'll notice about Rotorua (p106) is the sulphur smell: this geothermal hot spot whiffs like old socks! But as locals point out, volcanic by-products are what everyone is here to see: geysers, bubbling mud, boiling pools of mineral-rich water... And you don't have to spend a fortune to see it – there are plenty of affordable (even free!) volcanic encounters to be had in parks, Maori villages or just along the roadside. Pohutu geyser, Te Puia

The Best...
Museums

TE PAPA
Interactive Kiwi culture, history and performance, plus Maori artefacts and a *marae* (meeting house). (p167)

CANTERBURY MUSEUM
Brilliant collection of Kiwi artefacts, both Maori and Pakeha. (p236)

AUCKLAND MUSEUM
This shiny Greek temple is a great introduction to Maori culture. (p67)

OTAGO MUSEUM
Otago culture and landscapes: dinosaurs, geology, wildlife and Maori heritage. (p296)

ROTORUA MUSEUM
An amazing old building with an amazing new wing dedicated to local Maori culture. (p110)

WIBOWO RUSLI / LONELY PLANET IMAGES ©

The Best...
Geothermal Hot Springs

HOT WATER BEACH
Dig your own spa pool in the Coromandel sand. (p92)

POLYNESIAN SPA
Rotorua's long-running bathhouse has lake-edge hot pools. (p111)

HANMER SPRINGS
Let it all hang out at this subalpine hot spot. (p248)

SPA PARK HOT SPRING
Free-and-easy swimming at Taupo's thermal swimming hole. (p138)

TOKAANU THERMAL POOLS
Low-key hot springs and a mud-pool boardwalk. (p142)

4 Central Otago

Here's your chance to balance virtue and vice, all with a background of some of NZ's most starkly beautiful landscapes. Take to two wheels to negotiate the easygoing Otago Central Rail Trail (p304), cycling into heritage South Island towns such as Clyde and Naseby. Tuck into well-earned beers in laid-back country pubs, or linger for a classy lunch in the vineyard restaurants of Bannockburn. Other foodie diversions include Cromwell's weekly farmers market, and the summer stonefruit harvest of the country's best orchards.

Otago Rail Trail

5 Bay of Islands

Turquoise waters in pretty bays, dolphins at the bows of boats, pods of orcas gliding by: the chances are these are just the kind of images that drew you to New Zealand in the first place, and these are exactly the kind of experiences that the Bay of Islands (p312) delivers so well. Whether you're a hardened seadog or a confirmed landlubber, there are myriad options to tempt you out onto the water to explore the 150-odd islands that dot this beautiful bay.

Beach view, Russell

Tongariro Alpine Crossing

At the centre of the North Island, Tongariro National Park (p143) presents an alien landscape of alpine desert punctuated by three smouldering volcanoes. This track skirts the base of two of the mountains and provides views of craters, brightly coloured lakes and the vast Central Plateau beyond. It's rated as one of the world's best single-day wilderness walks. Emerald Lakes and Blue Lake

IGNACIO PALACIOS / LONELY PLANET IMAGES ©

OCEAN / CORBIS ©

Kaikoura

Kaikoura (p206), meaning 'eat crayfish' in Maori, is now NZ's best spot for both consuming and communing with marine life. Whales are definitely off the menu, but you're almost guaranteed a good gander at Moby's mates on a whale-watching tour, or there's swimming with seals and dolphins, or spotting some of the many birds – including albatross – that wheel around the shore. When it comes to 'sea food and eat it', crayfish is still king, but on fishing tours you can hook into other edible wonders of the unique Kaikoura deep. Dusky dolphins off Kaikoura

Abel Tasman National Park

Here's nature at its most seductive: lush green hills fringed with golden sandy coves, slipping gently into warm shallows before meeting a crystal-clear sea of cerulean blue. Abel Tasman National Park (p218) is the quintessential postcard paradise, where you can put yourself in the picture assuming an endless number of poses: tramping, kayaking, swimming, sunbathing or even makin' whoopee in the woods. This sweet-as corner of NZ raises the bar and keeps it there.

DAVID WALL / / LONELY PLANET IMAGES ©

The Best...
Tramps

ABEL TASMAN COAST TRACK
Walk through Abel Tasman National Park. Three to five days, 51km. (p218)

TONGARIRO ALPINE CROSSING
Tramp Tongariro National Park and see volcanic vents, alpine vegetation and lush forest. One day, 18km. (p146)

MILFORD TRACK
Rainforest and towering mountains at Milford Sound. Five days, 54km. (p307)

QUEEN CHARLOTTE TRACK
Hike through the scenic Marlborough Sounds. Three to five days, 71km. (p202)

RAKIURA TRACK
Play 'spot the kiwi' along this spectacular, isolated three-day tramp on Stewart Island. (p323)

Wellington

Voted the 'coolest little capital in the world' by Lonely Planet in 2011, windy Wellington (p162) lives up to the mantle by keeping things fresh and dynamic. Long famed for a vibrant arts and music scene – fuelled by excellent espresso and more restaurants per head than New York – a host of craft-beer bars have now elbowed in on the action. Edgy yet sociable, colourful yet often dressed in black, Wellington is big on the unexpected and unconventional. Erratic weather only adds to the excitement. City and harbour from Mt Victoria Lookout

The Best...
Foodie Experiences

EATING OUT IN AUCKLAND
Fine dining, cafes, delicatessens – Auckland takes the cake (and the steak, the pasta sauce, the bouillabaisse...). (p72)

BAY OF PLENTY KIWIFRUIT
Bag yourself a dozen delicious kiwifruit from a roadside stall anywhere between Tauranga and Whakatane. (p118)

HOKITIKA WILDFOODS FESTIVAL
You're a big baby, Bear Grylls – eating insects is fun! Detour to Hokitika on the West Coast in March. (p43)

ORIGINAL KAIKOURA SEAFOOD BARBECUE
Fabulous outdoor fish shack serving whitebait, mussels, paua (abalone) and crayfish. (p210)

OLIVER STREWE / LONELY PLANET IMAGES ©

AMOS CHAPPLE / LONELY PLANET IMAGES ©

Waitomo Caves

10

Waitomo (p133) is a must-see: an astonishing maze of subterranean caves, canyons and rivers perforating the northern King Country limestone. Black-water rafting is the big lure here (like white-water rafting, but through a dark cave!), plus glowworm grottos, underground abseiling and more stalactites and stalagmites than you'll ever see in one place again. Above ground, Waitomo township is a quaint collection of businesses, but don't linger in the sunlight – it's party time downstairs!

Akaroa & Banks Peninsula

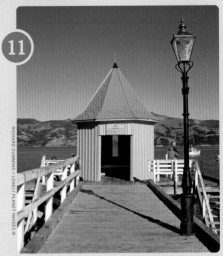

11

RICHARD CUMMINS / LONELY PLANET IMAGES ©

Infused with a healthy dash of Gallic ambience, French-themed Akaroa (p246) bends languidly around one of the prettiest harbours on Banks Peninsula. Sleek dolphins and plump penguins inhabit clear waters perfect for sailing and exploring. Elsewhere on the peninsula, the spidery Summit Rd traces the rim of an ancient volcano while winding roads descend to hidden bays and coves. Spend your days tramping and kayaking amid the improbable landscape and seascape, and relax at night in chic bistros or cosy B&B accommodation. Daly's Wharf, Akaroa

ROSS BARNETT / / LONELY PLANET IMAGES ©

12

Art Deco Napier

Like a cross between a film set and a 1930s time capsule, Napier (p179) was levelled by an earthquake in 1931, and was then rebuilt in high art-deco style (the architectural flavour of the decade). Must-sees include a sculpted live-music shell, the suburb of Marewa and the National Tobacco Company and Daily Telegraph buildings. There are some great places to eat and drink here too: wine and welcome are right on time, even if the architecture is firmly rooted in the past.

GRANT DIXON / / LONELY PLANET IMAGES ©

13 ## Otago Peninsula

The Otago Peninsula (p303) is stunning proof there's more to the South Island than alpine and lake scenery. Among coastal vistas that combine rugged beaches with an expansive South Pacific horizon, it's very easy to spot penguins, seals and sea lions. Fascinating avian residents include the rare yellow-eyed penguin and the royal albatross. Otago Peninsula's Taiaroa Head is the world's only mainland royal albatross colony: visit in January or February to see these magnificent birds. Yellow-eyed penguin

Queenstown

Queenstown (p278) may be world-renowned as the birth-place of bungy jumping, but there's more to NZ's adventure hub than leaping off a bridge wearing a giant rubber band. Against the scenic backdrop of the jagged indigo profile of the Remarkables mountain range, travellers can spend days skiing, tramping or mountain biking, before dining in cosmo-politan restaurants or partying in some of NZ's best bars. Next-day options include hang gliding, kayaking or river raft-ing, or easing into your Kiwi holiday with sleepier detours to Arrowtown or Glenorchy. Bungy jumping from Kawarau Bridge

The Best...
Extreme Activities

BUNGY JUMPING
Hurl yourself off a perfectly good bridge/canyon/high-wire in Queenstown. (p279)

SKYDIVING
Head to Taupo, the sky-diving capital of the world. (p139)

SKIING
Hit the perfect powder on South Island slopes. (p349)

RAFTING, ABSEILING & ROCK CLIMBING
Visit Waitomo Caves for black-water rafting, abseil-ing and rock climbing. (p134)

MOUNTAIN BIKING
For 100km of NZ's best mountain-bike tracks, get to the Redwoods Whakarewarewa Forest. (p117)

The Best...
Beaches

KAREKARE
Classic black-sand beach west of Auckland, with wild surf. (p87)

HAHEI
Iconic Kiwi beach experience on the Coromandel Peninsula. (p92)

ABEL TASMAN NATIONAL PARK
Warm, clear waters and golden sand beaches (try Marahau). (p218)

MANU BAY
NZ's most famous surf break (seen *Endless Summer*?) peels ashore south of Raglan. (p131)

ST KILDA & ST CLAIR
Chilly or refreshing, depending on your mood, Dunedin's twin beaches have fab rolling surf. (p297)

Milford Sound

Fingers crossed you'll be lucky enough to see Milford Sound (p307) on a clear, sunny day. That's definitely when the world-beating collage of water-falls, verdant cliffs and peaks, and dark cobalt waters is at its best. More likely though is the classic Fiordland combination of mist and drizzle, with the iconic snow-capped profile of Mitre Peak revealed slowly through shimmering sheets of precipitation. Either way, keep your eyes peeled for seals and dolphins, especially if you're exploring NZ's most famous fiord by kayak. Left: Ferry cruising Milford Sound; Above: Fur seal

ABOVE: GARETH MCCORMACK / LONELY PLANET IMAGES © LEFT: GERARD WALKER / LONELY PLANET IMAGES ©

Maori Culture

NZ's indigenous Maori culture is accessible and engaging: join in a *haka* (war dance); chow down at a traditional *hangi* (Maori feast cooked in the ground); carve a pendant from bone or *pounamu* (jade); learn some Maori language; or check out an authentic cultural performance with song, dance, legends, arts and crafts. Big-city and regional museums around NZ are crammed with Maori artefacts and historical items (Rotorua Museum has a fabulous display; p110), but this is a living culture: vibrant, potent and contemporary.

PETER BENNETTS / LONELY PLANET IMAGES ©

DAVID WALL / LONELY PLANET IMAGES ©

TranzAlpine

In less than five hours, the *TranzAlpine* (p256) crosses from the Pacific to the Tasman Sea. Leaving Christchurch, the train speeds across the Canterbury Plains to the foothills of the Southern Alps. After a cavalcade of tunnels and viaducts, it enters broad Waimakariri Valley. A stop at Arthur's Pass Village is followed by the 8.5km-long Otira tunnel through NZ's alpine spine. Then it's down through the Taramakau valley, past Lake Brunner and into Greymouth.

TranzAlpine, Arthur's Pass

Skiing & Snowboarding

NZ is studded with some massive mountains, and you're guaranteed to find decent snow right through the winter season (June to October). Most of the famous slopes are on the South Island: hip Queenstown (p278) and hippie Wanaka are where you want to be, with iconic ski runs such as Coronet Peak, the Remarkables and Treble Cone close at hand. There are also dedicated snowboarding and cross-country (Nordic) snow parks here. And on the North Island, Mt Ruapehu offers the chance to ski down a volcano! Skiing, Treble Cone

The Best...
Maori Experiences

WHAKAREWAREWA THERMAL VILLAGE
Opportunities to check out weaving, carving and cultural performances abound in Rotorua. (p107)

ONE TREE HILL (MAUNGAKIEKIE)
This volcanic cone (one of the many in Auckland) is an important historical site. (p66)

TE PAPA
Maori *marae* (meeting house), galleries and guided tours at NZ's national museum. (p167)

RAGLAN BONE CARVING STUDIO
One of several hands-on bone-carving studios around NZ. (p130)

The Best...
Wine Regions

MARLBOROUGH
The country's biggest and best. Don't be picky, just drink some sauvignon blanc (or some pinot gris, chardonnay, gewürz-traminer...). (p207)

MARTINBOROUGH
A small-but-sweet wine region a day trip from Wellington: easy cycling and easy-drinking pinot noir. (p176)

WAIHEKE ISLAND
Auckland's favourite weekend playground produces Bordeaux-style reds and rosé. (p83)

GIBBSTON VALLEY
A valley with a meandering river (of wine?) near Queenstown. (p289)

Marlborough Wine Region

19

It's hard to avoid Marlborough sauvignon blanc in the world's liquor stores these days – crisp, zesty and drinkable. Whether it's on a minibus, a bicycle or the back seat of someone's car, touring the cellar doors of the Marlborough Wine Region (p207) near Blenheim is a decadent delight. And it's not just sav blanc on offer: there's also plenty of cool-climate pinot noir, chardonnay, riesling and pinot gris to swill around the back of your palate. Vineyard near Renwick

/LONELY PLANET IMAGES ©

AMOS CHAPPLE / LONELY PLANET IMAGES ©

20 Rugby

Rugby is NZ's national game and governing preoccupation. If your timing's good you might catch the revered national team (and reigning world champions), the All Blacks, in action. The 'ABs' are resident gods: mention Richie McCaw or Dan Carter in any conversation and you'll win friends for life! Or just watch some Saturday-morning kids chasing a ball around a suburban field, or yell along with the locals in a small-town pub as the big men collide on the big screen. The New Zealand Rugby Museum (p176) in Palmerston North is well worth a detour.

Raglan Surf Safari

Laid-back, hippified and surprisingly multicultural, little Raglan (p129) is the mythical surf village you always knew was there but could never find. A few kilometres south of town are some of the best point breaks on the planet: join the hordes of floating rubber people at Manu Bay, Whale Bay and Indicators. We can't guarantee the perfect wave, but when a southwesterly swell is running, you'll be in line for some seriously *looong* rides.

PAUL KENNEDY / LONELY PLANET IMAGES ©

JOHN ELK III / LONELY PLANET IMAGES ©

Te Papa

Dominating the Wellington waterfront, Te Papa (p167) is New Zealand's national museum. It's an inspiring, high-tech, interactive repository of historical and cultural artefacts...and best of all, it's free! Expect plenty of Maori artefacts and culture (including a *marae*), engaging tours (a great way to see a lot in a short time), plenty of kid-friendly exhibits and a slew of innovative displays celebrating all things Kiwi. Don't miss the earthquake simulator, and the national art collection.

Franz Josef Glacier

The spectacular glaciers of Franz Josef (p257) and Fox are remarkable for many reasons, including their rates of accumulation and descent, and their improbable proximity to both the loftiest peaks of the Southern Alps and the Tasman Sea about 10km away. Get almost face to face with them on one of several short walks, or take a hike on the ice with Franz Josef or Fox Glacier Guides. The ultimate encounter is on a scenic flight, which often also provides grandstand views of Mt Cook, Westland forest and a seemingly endless ocean.

Walkers on Franz Josef Glacier

The Best...
City Life

LIVE MUSIC IN DUNEDIN
Reggae, garage, dub, hip-hop...Dunedin rocks. (p301)

WELLINGTON'S CAFFEINE SCENE
Wide-awake Wellington cranks out serious coffee. (p166)

SHOP IN AUCKLAND
Buy up big brands, rummage for retro or browse the bookshelves. (p78)

PARTY IN QUEENSTOWN
Cuddle-up with après-ski drinkers. (p284)

CHRISTCHURCH ON THE REBOUND
Resourceful and inspirational, 'Chch' is reinventing itself postquake. (p236)

Hot Water Beach

Get yourself into hot water on the Coromandel Peninsula at the legendary Hot Water Beach (p92), where warm geothermal springs bubble up through the sand. If you time your arrival to within a couple of hours either side of low tide, with some creative digging you can kick back in your custom-made spa pool and watch the surf lap along the beach. If you don't carry a shovel around with you in your luggage, you can hire one from a local cafe.

The Best...
Markets

DUNEDIN FARMERS MARKET
Organic fruit and veg, Green Man beer, robust coffee and homemade pies. (p300)

OTARA MARKET
Auckland's multicultural Otara Market brims with buskers, arts and crafts, fashions and food. (p79)

ROTORUA NIGHT MARKET
Gourmet night-bites, plus buskers and local crafts. (p114)

WELLINGTON FARMERS MARKET
Wellington's obligatory fruit-and-veg pit stop. (p166)

25

Aoraki/Mt Cook

At a cloud-piercing 3754m, Aoraki (p251) is New Zealand's crowning peak. Unless you're a professional mountaineer it's unlikely you'll be scaling the summit, but there are plenty of other ways to experience this massive mount: take a walk around the rumbling glaciers and moody lakes dappling its flanks, carve up the snow on a ski trip, or get closer to the top on an eye-popping scenic flight. Afterwards, retreat to your accommodation and warm up by an open fire.

New Zealand's
Top Itineraries

Auckland to the Bay of Islands
City to the Sea

5 DAYS

If you're on a tight, five-day schedule with jetlag bending your mind, focus on Auckland's must-see sights, eat and drink your way around town, ferry across Auckland Harbour to Waiheke Island, then maybe take an overnight trip north to the Bay of Islands.

① Central Auckland (p62)

One of the world's great nautical cities, **Auckland** offers islands, beaches and access to both an ocean and a sea, plus stellar bars and restaurants. Don't miss the Maori and South Pacific Islander exhibits at **Auckland Museum**, a stroll across the **Domain** to **K Rd** for lunch, a visit to the grand **Auckland Art Gallery** (architecture boffins will enjoy the new extension) and the iconic **Sky Tower**.

CENTRAL AUCKLAND ❍ PONSONBY

🚗 **10 minutes** From central Auckland via Pitt St to Ponsonby Rd. 🚌 **15 minutes** Inner Link bus Queen St to Ponsonby Rd.

② Ponsonby (p73)

Auckland is a city of enclaves, each with its own flavour. **Parnell** fosters an affluent 'village' vibe; **Newmarket** is festooned with boutiques; and across the harbour, **Devonport** resembles a 19th-century maritime village...but **Ponsonby** wins on the foodie front. Head straight for Ponsonby Rd: Thai, Japanese and Italian, plus cafes and wine bars – perfect for a meal any time of day.

Harbour and Sky Tower, Auckland (p51)
PHOTOGRAPHER: BLAINE HARRINGTON III/CORBIS ©

PONSONBY ❍ WAIHEKE ISLAND

🚌 **15 minutes** Inner Link bus Ponsonby Rd to central Auckland, then ⛴ **50 minutes** from Quay St to Waiheke Island.

③ Waiheke Island (p83)

Steeped in ocean-going credibility, Auckland Harbour is awash with yachts and ferries. Take the ferry over to **Rangitoto Island**, then chug into **Devonport** for a meal: if the weather's good check out **Cheltenham Beach** while you're in the 'hood. Afterwards, ferry-hop to **Waiheke Island** for some fabulous wineries and beaches.

WAIHEKE ISLAND ❍ BAY OF ISLANDS

⛴ **50 minutes** From Waiheke Island to Quay St, then 🚗 or 🚌 **three hours** From Auckland to Bay of Islands via SH1 and SH11.

④ Bay of Islands (p312)

A few hours' drive north of Auckland (make it an overnighter) is the utterly photogenic **Bay of Islands**. Like a tourism brochure in 3D, the area is a **yachting**, **snorkelling** and beach-bumming paradise. If you've never swum with **dolphins** or set-sail for an uninhabited island (take your pick from 150 of them!), this is the place to fulfil your sea-salty fantasies.

5 DAYS

Queenstown to Kaikoura
Winter Wanderer

Yes, we know a whole bunch of you are here for one thing only: snow! Hit Queenstown on the South Island for perfect powder, and great bars and restaurants. Further north, Kaikoura's winter days are crisp, the whales are wallowing and the crowds are absent.

TASMAN SEA

③ KAIKOURA

○ CHRISTCHURCH

PACIFIC OCEAN

② WANAKA

① QUEENSTOWN

① Queenstown (p278)

Take a direct flight to **Queenstown** and get ready for some seriously snowy fun, with access to world-class skiing, cool bars and restaurants, and a kickin' nocturnal scene. If you're here in late June or early July, the **Queenstown Winter Festival** goes berserk, with live music, comedy, parades and lots of family fun. When you've had your fill of snowy slopes, the **extreme activities** on offer in Queenstown will keep the winter chills at bay: try kayaking, paragliding, jetboating, white-water rafting, skydiving or mountain biking.

On the ski front, **Coronet Peak** is the region's oldest ski field, with a multimillion dollar snow-making system, treeless slopes, consistent gradient and excellent skiing for all levels (great for snowboarders, too). The visually remarkable **Remarkables** are more family-friendly – look for the sweeping run called 'Homeward Bound'.

QUEENSTOWN ⭢ WANAKA

🚌 or 🚗 **One hour** From Queenstown to Wanaka along Cardrona Valley Rd.

② Wanaka (p290)

As an alternative to Queenstown, head to **Wanaka**. It's like Queenstown's little brother – all the benefits without the hype. Ski fields near here include **Treble Cone**, with steep intermediate and advanced slopes, plus snowboarding half-pipes and a terrain park; **Cardrona**, with high-capacity chairlifts, beginners' tows and extreme snowboarding terrain; **Snow Farm New Zealand**, the country's only commercial Nordic (cross-country) ski area; and **Snow Park**, the only dedicated freestyle ski and board area in New Zealand, with pipes, terrain parks, boxes and rails. Want something different? Take an overnight trip to Westland Tai Poutini National Park on the West Coast to check out **Franz Josef Glacier** and **Fox Glacier**.

WANAKA ⭢ KAIKOURA

✈ **One hour** From Wanaka to Christchurch, then
🚌 **2½ hours** or 🚗 **three hours** Christchurch to Kaikoura.

③ Kaikoura (p206)

From Wanaka, fly north to **Christchurch**, a city rebuilding and reinventing itself after the 2010 earthquakes – peek out the aeroplane window as you pass massive, brooding **Aoraki/Mt Cook**. From Christchurch, drive for a few hours north to **Kaikoura**, a photogenic town on the South Island's northwest coast. In winter (especially), migrating humpback and sperm whales come close to the shore – check them out up close on a whale-watching tour while the summer crowds are a million miles (or at least a few months) away.

Snowboarding at Coronet Peak (p279)

Auckland to Queenstown
Kiwi Classics

Classy cities, geothermal eruptions, fantastic wine, Maori culture, glaciers, extreme activities, isolated beaches and forests. These are just a few of NZ's favourite things, and what you'll want to see if you're a first-time, short-trip visitor. It's the best of the country, north and south.

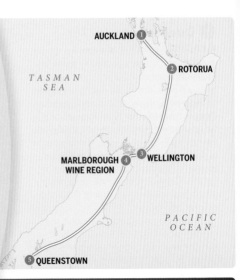

TASMAN SEA

AUCKLAND ①

② ROTORUA

MARLBOROUGH WINE REGION ④ — ③ WELLINGTON

PACIFIC OCEAN

⑤ QUEENSTOWN

① Auckland & Around (p62)

The City of Sails, **Auckland** is a South Pacific melting pot – spend a few days shopping, eating, drinking and experiencing NZ at its most cosmopolitan. Need a night out of town? Truck north to the winterless **Bay of Islands** for sailing, surfing, kayaking and scuba-diving, or scoot southeast to explore the forests and beaches of the **Coromandel Peninsula**.

AUCKLAND ➡ ROTORUA

🚗 or 🚌 **Three hours** From Auckland to Rotorua via SH1. ✈ **40 minutes** From Auckland to Rotorua.

② Rotorua (p106)

Further south is **Rotorua**, a real geothermal hot spot: giggle at volcanic mud bubbles, gasp as geothermal geysers blast boiling water into the sky, and get a nose full of rotten-egg gas. Rotorua is also a great place to experience Maori culture via a *haka* (war dance), *hangi* (feast) or legend-loaded cultural performance.

ROTORUA ➡ WELLINGTON

🚗 **Six hours** From Rotorua to Wellington via SH1. ✈ **1¼ hours** From Rotorua to Wellington.

③ Wellington (p162)

Way down in **Wellington**, the coffee's hot, the beer's cold and wind from the politicians generates its own low-pressure system. Clinging to the hillsides like a mini San Francisco, NZ's capital city is the place for serious arts, live music and hip street culture. Don't miss the boutiques, bars and cafes on Cuba St.

WELLINGTON ➡ MARLBOROUGH WINE REGION

⛴ **3¼ hours** From Wellington to Picton, then 🚗 or 🚌 **25 minutes** from Picton to Blenheim.

④ Marlborough Wine Region (p207)

Swan over to the South Island for a few days (even the ferry trip is scenic) and experience the best the south has to offer. Start with a tour through the **Marlborough Wine Region** – the sauvignon blanc they produce in this cool microclimate is world class. The mirror-perfect inlets and tree-cloaked headlands of the **Marlborough Sounds** make a great day-trip from here.

MARLBOROUGH WINE REGION ➡ QUEENSTOWN

🚌 **Five hours** From Blenheim to Christchurch, then 🚗 **Six hours** Christchurch to Queenstown. ✈ **Three hours** From Blenheim to Queenstown via Christchurch.

⑤ Queenstown (p278)

Further south is **Christchurch**: the South Island's biggest city is being born again after the 2010 earthquakes. From here you can meander southwest to bungy- and ski-obsessed party town **Queenstown**, a must-visit for adrenaline junkies. Hop on a flight directly back to Auckland to round out your Kiwi adventure.

Queenstown (p278)

Auckland to Auckland
Northern Exposure

Three-quarters of New Zealanders live on the North Island – time to find out why! Auckland is the obvious launch pad, but beyond the big smoke you'll discover ancient forests, erupting geothermal geysers, art-deco architecture, caves, islands and salubrious wine regions.

① Auckland (p62)

Begin in **Auckland**, NZ's biggest city. There's not much you can't see, eat or buy here (prime your credit card). Eat streets abound: our faves are **Ponsonby Rd** in Ponsonby, **K Rd** in Newton, and **New North Rd** in Kingsland. Hike up **Maungakiekie (One Tree Hill)** to burn off resultant calories, and don't miss **Auckland Art Gallery** and **Auckland Museum**.

AUCKLAND ◯ BAY OF ISLANDS

🚗 or 🚌 **Three hours** From Auckland to Bay of Islands via SH1 and SH11.

② Bay of Islands (p312)

Heading north, you'll reach the magnificent **Bay of Islands**: spend a day bobbing around on a yacht, snorkelling or dolphin-swimming. Adventurous, road-eager types might want to continue to the rugged northern tip of NZ: **Cape Reinga** is shrouded in solitude and Maori lore.

BAY OF ISLANDS ◯ NAPIER

🚗 **8½ hours** From Bay of Islands to Napier via Rotorua, Mt Maunganui or Coromandel Peninsula.
✈ **Three hours** From Whangarei to Napier via Auckland.

③ Napier (p179)

It's a long haul from the Bay of Islands to Napier on the East Coast: break up the journey with a night in geothermal **Rotorua**, surfie **Mt Maunganui** in the Bay of Plenty, or one of the laid-back beach towns on the **Coromandel Peninsula**. Once you roll into **Napier**, check out the amazing art-deco architecture and the surrounding chardonnay vineyards of **Hawke's Bay Wine Country**.

NAPIER ◯ WELLINGTON

🚗 or 🚌 **4½ hours** From Napier to Wellington via SH2. ✈ **One hour** From Napier to Wellington.

④ Wellington (p162)

Boot it south into the sheepy/winey **Wairarapa** region (try the superb pinot noir produced around Martinborough), before soaring over the cloud-wrapped Rimutaka Range into hipper-than-hip **Wellington**. Don't miss **Te Papa**, NZ's national museum, and a night on the tiles along **Cuba St** or **Courtenay Pl**.

WELLINGTON ◯ AUCKLAND

🚗 **10 hours** From Wellington to Auckland via Mt Taranaki, Raglan, Hamilton or Waitomo Caves.
✈ **One hour** From Wellington to Auckland.

⑤ Auckland (p62)

Take the northwesterly route back to Auckland slow and easy, passing the epic volcanic cone of **Mt Taranaki** en route. Hit the point breaks near **Raglan** if you're into surfing, or go underground at **Waitomo Caves** for glorious glow-worms and black-water rafting. **Hamilton**, NZ's fourth-biggest town, has a happening nocturnal scene if you're craving some city-sized action.

Mt Taranaki (p321)

Auckland to Christchurch
Icons & Beyond

Check some big-ticket attractions off your list on this trip, with some kayaking, caving and tramping breaking up the road trip. With a couple of weeks at your disposal, you'll really be able to switch into holiday mode, embrace nature and savour the flavours of dual-island travel.

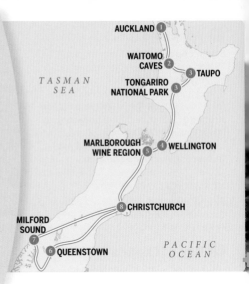

TASMAN SEA

AUCKLAND ①
WAITOMO CAVES ②
③ TAUPO
TONGARIRO NATIONAL PARK ③
MARLBOROUGH WINE REGION ⑤ ④ WELLINGTON
⑧ CHRISTCHURCH
MILFORD SOUND ⑦
⑥ QUEENSTOWN
PACIFIC OCEAN

① Auckland (p62)

Cruise the hip, inner-city streets of **Auckland**: hike up **One Tree Hill (Maungakiekie)**, ride a bike along **Tamaki Dr** then take your pick of myriad lunch spots along **K Rd** or in **Kingsland**. Dinner at **Ponsonby** will attune your tastebuds to NZ's brand of 'Pacific fusion' cooking. Afterwards, hit the bars around **Viaduct Harbour** or **Vulcan La**.

AUCKLAND ➔ WAITOMO CAVES

 or 🚌 **Three hours** From Auckland to Waitomo Caves via SH1 and SH39.

② Waitomo Caves (p133)

The amazing **Waitomo Caves** are an underground labyrinth of glow-worm-filled caverns. Don a wet suit and headlamp and dive in for black-water rafting, abseiling or floating along on an inner-tube in the inky darkness. There are a couple of good eateries to refuel at afterwards.

WAITOMO CAVES ➔ TONGARIRO NATIONAL PARK

🚗 **Two hours** From Waitomo Caves to Taupo via SH30.

③ Taupo & Tongariro National Park (p143)

From Waitomo, hook southeast to progressive **Taupo** and try skydiving (you know you want to) or go tramping around the triple-peaked, volcanic wilderness of **Tongariro National Park**. The **Tongariro Alpine Crossing** is one of the best day walks in NZ.

TONGARIRO NATIONAL PARK ➔ WELLINGTON

🚗 or 🚌 **Five hours** From Taupo to Wellington via SH1.

④ Wellington (p162)

Watch the nocturnal freak show pass by in late-night, caffeinated **Wellington** (a great place to prop up the bar and try some NZ craft beers). Spend a few hours wandering through NZ's national museum, **Te Papa**, then roll onto the ferry for the trip across Cook Strait to the South Island.

WELLINGTON ➔ MARLBOROUGH WINE REGION

⚓ **3¼ hours** From Wellington to Picton, then 🚗 or 🚌 **25 minutes** From Picton to Blenheim.

Marlborough region vinyeard (p207)
PHOTOGRAPHER: MICHAEL GEBICKI / LONELY PLANET IMAGES ©

Josef Glacier or impressive **Fox Glacier**. Hike around the icy valleys, or take a helicopter up onto the glaciers themselves: a sure-fire way to develop feelings of insignificance. Drive up over Haast Pass to adrenaline-addicted **Queenstown** for a night or two of partying Kiwi-style.

QUEENSTOWN ○ MILFORD SOUND

🚗 **3½ hours** From Queenstown to Milford Sound via Te Anau.

⑦ Milford Sound (p307)

Mix and match highways to Te Anau for the beguiling side-road to **Milford Sound** – you might want to do a bit of kayaking here, or take a boat trip around the craggy inlets and mirror-topped waterways. This is NZ at its most pure, pristine and perfect.

MILFORD SOUND ○ CHRISTCHURCH

🚗 **3½ hours** From Milford Sound to Queenstown, then ✈ **One hour** From Queenstown to Christchurch.

⑧ Christchurch & Around (p236)

Veer back east to Queenstown and hop a flight to the southern capital of **Christchurch**, where you can while away a day or two exploring, shopping and gallery-hopping. Take an afternoon to explore the quirky harbour town of **Lyttelton** or the amazing **Banks Peninsula** south of the city, with its French-influenced town of **Akaroa**.

⑤ Marlborough Wine Region (p207)

Track west from pretty **Picton** and disappear into the leafy vine-rows and welcoming cellar-door tasting rooms of the **Marlborough Wine Region**. If you have an extra day, explore the waterways and woodlands of the **Marlborough Sounds**, or continue west to the golden-sand bays of **Abel Tasman National Park**.

MARLBOROUGH WINE REGION ○ QUEENSTOWN

🚗 **11 hours** From Marlborough Wine Region to Queenstown via SH6.

⑥ Queenstown (p278)

Time to get your skates on: track down the rain-swept, lonesome **West Coast** and spend a night at either iconic **Franz**

New Zealand Month by Month

January

Festival of Lights
New Plymouth's Pukekura Park really sparkles during this festival. It's a magical scene: pathways glow and trees are impressively lit with thousands of lights. Live music, dance and kids' performances too.

World Buskers Festival
Christchurch could use a little cheering up: jugglers, musos, tricksters, puppeteers, mime artists, dancers... Avoid if you're scared of audience participation!

February

Waitangi Day
On 6 February 1840, the Treaty of Waitangi was first signed between Maori and the British Crown. The day remains a public holiday across NZ, but in Waitangi itself there's guided tours, concerts, market stalls and family entertainment.

Marlborough Wine Festival
NZ's biggest and best wine festival features tastings from around 50 Marlborough wineries, plus fine food and entertainment. It's usually on a Saturday early in the month.

New Zealand International Arts Festival
Feeling artsy? This month-long spectacular happens in Wellington in February–March in even-numbered years. NZ's cultural capital exudes artistic enthusiasm with theatre, dance, music, visual arts and international acts aplenty.

Te Matatini National Kapa Haka Festival
This engrossing Maori *haka* (war dance) competition happens in February in odd-numbered years.

Top Events

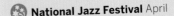

National Jazz Festival April

New Zealand International Sevens February

World of WearableArt Award Show September

Marlborough Wine Festival February

World Buskers Festival January

Venues vary: 2013 is Rotorua. It's not just the *haka*: expect traditional song, dance, storytelling and other performing arts.

Fringe NZ

Music, theatre, comedy, dance, visual arts... but not the mainstream stuff. These are the unusual, emerging, controversial, low-budget and/or downright weird acts that don't seem to fit in anywhere else, all on show in Wellington.

Splore

Explore Splore, a cutting-edge outdoor summer fest in Tapapakanga Regional Park, southeast of Auckland. There's contemporary live music, performance, visual arts, safe swimming and pohutukawa trees!

New Zealand International Sevens

February sees the world's top seven-a-side rugby teams crack heads in Wellington: everyone from stalwarts such as Australia, Wales and South Africa to minnows such as the Cook Islands, Kenya and Canada.

March

Wildfoods Festival

Eat some worms, hare testicles or crabs at Hokitika's comfort-zone-challenging food fest. There are usually plenty of quality NZ brews available, too, which help subdue any difficult tastes.

WOMAD

Local and international music, arts and dance performances fill New Plymouth's Brooklands Bowl. An evolution of the original world-music festival dreamed up by Peter Gabriel. Perfect for families.

Auckland International Boat Show

Auckland harbour blooms with sails and churns with outboard motors. It doesn't command the instant nautical recognition of Sydney or San Diego, but Auckland really is one of the world's great sailing cities.

Pasifika Festival

With around 140,000 Maori and notable communities of Tongans, Samoans, Cook Islanders, Niueans, Fijians and other South Pacific Islanders, Auckland has the largest Polynesian community in the world. These vibrant cultures come together at this annual fiesta in Western Springs Park.

April

National Jazz Festival

Every Easter Tauranga hosts the longest-running jazz fest in the southern hemisphere. The line up is invariably impressive (Kurt Elling, Keb Mo), and there's plenty of fine NZ food and wine to accompany the finger-snappin' sonics.

May

New Zealand International Comedy Festival

Three-week laugh-fest with venues across Auckland, Wellington and various regional centres: International gag-merchants (Arj Barker, Danny Bhoy) line up next to home-grown talent.

June

Matariki

Maori New Year is heralded by the rise of Matariki (aka Pleiades star cluster) in May and the sighting of the new moon in June. Remembrance, education, music, film, community days and tree planting take place, mainly around Auckland and Northland.

screenings in regional towns from July to November.

 Russell Birdman

Birdman rallies are just so '80s... but they sure are funny. This one in Russell features the usual cast of costumed contenders propelling themselves off a jetty in pursuit of weightlessness.

 # August

 Taranaki International Arts Festival

Beneath the snowy slopes of Mt Taranaki, August used to be a time of quiet repose. Not anymore: this arts festival now shakes the winter from the city (New Plymouth) with music, theatre, dance, visual arts and parades.

 Jazz & Blues Festival

You might think that the Bay of Islands is all about sunning yourself on a yacht, but in the depths of winter, this jazzy little festival will give you something else to do.

 New Zealand Gold Guitar Awards

We like both kinds of music: country and western! These awards in Gore cap off a week of boot-scootin' good times, with plenty of concerts and buskers.

July

 # September

 World of WearableArt Award Show

A bizarre (in the best way) two-week Wellington event featuring amazing hand-crafted garments. Entries are displayed at the World of WearableArt & Classic Cars Museum in Nelson afterwards.

Queenstown Winter Festival

This southern snow-fest has been running since 1975, and now attracts around 45,000 snowbunnies. It's a 10-day party, studded with fireworks, jazz, street parades, comedy, a Mardi Gras, a masquerade ball and lots of snow-centric activities.

October

New Zealand International Film Festival

After separate film festivals in Wellington, Auckland, Dunedin and Christchurch, a selection of flicks hits the road for

Seafest Kaikoura

Kaikoura is a town built on crayfish, many of which find themselves on plates at

Seafest (also a great excuse to drink a lot and dance around).

November

 ## Toast Martinborough

Bound for a day of boozy indulgence, wine-swilling Wellingtonians head over Rimutaka Hill and roll into upmarket Martinborough. The Wairarapa region produces some seriously good pinot noir: don't go home without trying some.

 ## Pohutukawa Festival

Markets, picnics, live music, kite-flying, cruises, snorkelling, poetry...not everything has to be about drinking, dancing and decadence. And just look at those pohutukawa trees.

BikeFest & Lake Taupo Cycle Challenge

Feeling fit? Try cycling 160km around Lake Taupo. In the week prior to the big race, BikeFest celebrates all things bicycular: BMX, mountain bike, unicycle, tandem...

 ## Oamaru Victorian Heritage Celebrations

Ahhh, the good old days, when Queen Vic sat dourly on the throne, when hems were low, collars were high... Old Oamaru thoroughly enjoys this tongue-in-cheek historic homage: dress-ups, penny-farthing races, choirs and guided tours.

December

 ## Rhythm & Vines

Wine, music and song (all the good things) in sunny east-coast Gisborne on New Year's Eve. Top DJs, hip-hop acts, bands and singer-songwriters compete for your attentions.

Far left: November Martinborough vineyards **Left: February** Waitangi Day celebrations

What's New

For this new edition of Discover New Zealand, our authors have hunted down the fresh, the transformed, the hot and the happening. These are some of our favourites. For up-to-the-minute recommendations, see lonelyplanet.com/new-zealand.

1 MOUNTAIN BIKING, QUEENSTOWN
With new trails and the opening of the gondola-assisted Queenstown Bike Park, the South Island's adventure capital is now a southern-hemisphere hub for two-wheeled downhill thrills (p282).

2 AUCKLAND ART GALLERY
This wonderful gallery – housing more than 15,000 works – has just reopened after a major refurbishment, a sexy new wing emerging from the original heritage building (p68).

3 WALLACE ARTS CENTRE, AUCKLAND
A brilliant new (and free!) contemporary art gallery in a historic mansion in Hillsborough, a few kilometres south of the city centre (p66).

4 ADDINGTON, CHRISTCHURCH
Welcome to Christchurch's most exciting and funkiest postearthquake neighbourhood. Previously sleepy Addington is now being transformed with new cafes, restaurants, theatres and live-music venues (p226).

5 DON STAFFORD WING, ROTORUA MUSEUM
Named after a former curator, this amazing new museum extension houses eight intricate, interactive galleries dedicated to Rotorua's Te Arawa people (p110).

6 CRAFT BEER TRAIL, NELSON
Sunny Nelson claims the crown of NZ Brewing Capital, and summons its subjects with a Craft Beer Trail that hops around the region. (www.craftbrewingcapital.co.nz)

7 HAWKE'S BAY COASTAL CYCLE TRAIL
What Hawke's Bay lacks in golden sand it now makes up for with new cycle trails, including a coastal run from Bayview to Clifton (p184).

8 WYNYARD QUARTER, AUCKLAND
Formerly the 'Western Reclamation', this waterside precinct has been reinvented as the far hipper Wynyard Quarter, with bars, cafes and public spaces, linking up with the Viaduct (p62).

9 STEAMPUNK HQ, OAMARU
Forging an eccentric combination of Victoriana and an industrial future, Oamaru's new Steampunk HQ gallery adds a quirky layer to the town's fascinating heritage ambience. (www.steampunkoamaru.co.nz; 1 Itchen St; ⊙10am-4pm)

10 NEW ZEALAND RUGBY MUSEUM
Yeah, we know, this museum has been a Palmerston North fixture for years, but the shiny new premises are really worth barracking for (p176).

11 WEST COAST WILDLIFE CENTRE, FRANZ JOSEF
Get up close to a kiwi (a bird, not a person) and see conservation in action in the amazing hatchery and nursery (p257).

12 TE MANUKA TUTAHI MARAE, WHAKATANE
Laid-back Whakatane has a beautiful new *marae* (meeting house), right on the main street. Actually, it dates from 1875 but travelled for many years to get here! (p123)

Get Inspired

Books

- **Mister Pip** (Lloyd Jones, 2007) Reflections of *Great Expectations* in an isolated Bougainville community. Booker Prize shortlisted.

- **The Carpathians** (Janet Frame, 1989) A New Yorker in rural New Zealand; disturbing interplay between reality and imagination.

- **The 10pm Question** (Kate De Goldi, 2009) Frankie is 12 and has many questions; Sydney has some difficult answers.

- **In My Father's Den** (Maurice Gee, 1972) A harrowing homecoming; made into a film in 2004.

Films

- **The Piano** (1993, director Jane Campion) Betrayal and passion on an 1850s NZ frontier: a mute woman, her daughter and her piano.

- **The Lord of the Rings trilogy** (2001–03, director Peter Jackson) *The Fellowship of the Ring*, *The Two Towers* and the Oscar-winning *The Return of the King*.

- **Whale Rider** (2002, director Niki Caro) Maori on the North Island's East Coast are torn between tradition and today's world.

- **Boy** (2010, director Taika Waititi) Coming-of-age poignancy and self-deprecation. The highest-grossing NZ-made film of all time!

Music

- **Slice of Heaven** (David Dobbyn with Herbs, 1986) South Pacific smash hit from veteran Dave.

- **Not Many** (Scribe, 2003) Hot Kiwi hip-hop: 'How many dudes you know flow like this?'

- **Home Again** (Shihad, 1997) Riff-driven power from NZ's guitar-rock kings.

- **Somebody That I Used To Know** (Gotye, 2011) He's from Melbourne, but co-vocalist Kimbra is a Hamilton gal.

Websites

- **Department of Conservation** (www.doc.govt.nz) Parks, recreation and conservation info.

- **DineOut** (www.dineout.co.nz) Restaurant reviews across NZ.

- **Living Landscapes** (www.livinglandscapes.co.nz) Maori tourism operator listings.

- **Muzic.net** (www.muzic.net.nz) Gigs, reviews, band bios and charts.

Short on time?

This list will give you an instant insight into the country.

Read *The Bone People* (Keri Hulme, 1984) Maori legends, isolation and violence: this Booker Prize–winning novel explores traumatic family interactions.

Watch *Once Were Warriors* (1994, director Lee Tamahori) Brutal, tragic, gritty: Jake 'the Muss' Heke in urban Auckland.

Listen *Don't Dream it's Over* (Crowded House, 1986) Neil Finn tries to catch a deluge in a paper cup – timeless melancholia.

Log on *100% Pure New Zealand* (www.newzealand.com) Info-central for all things NZ.

Mountain biking at Queenstown Bike Park (p282)

Need to Know

Currency
New Zealand dollars ($)

Language
English and Maori

ATMs
In cities and most towns

Credit Cards
Visa /MasterCard widely accepted; Amex less so

Visas
Citizens of Australia, the UK and 56 other countries don't need visas (see www.immigration.govt.nz). Other nationalities do.

Mobile Phones
European phones will work in NZ, but not most American or Japanese phones. Use global roaming or a local SIM card.

Wi-Fi
Often available in hotels, hostels, cafes and pubs

Internet Access
Internet cafes in most cities and large towns, plus public libraries; around $6 per hour

Driving
Drive on the left; the steering wheel is on the right (in case you can't find it...)

Tipping
Not expected, but tip 5–10% for good restaurant service.

When to Go

Auckland
GO Feb–Apr

Rotorua
GO Oct–Dec

Wellington
GO Dec–Feb

Christchurch
GO Jan–Mar

Queenstown
GO Jun–Aug

High Season
(Dec–Feb)
- Summertime: local holidays, busy beaches, festivals and sporting events.
- Pay up to 25% more for city hotels.
- High season in the ski towns (Queenstown, Wanaka) is June–August.

Shoulder
(Mar–Apr)
- Prime travelling time: fine weather, short queues and warm(ish) ocean.
- Long evenings supping Kiwi wines and craft beers.
- Spring (September–November) is shoulder season too.

Low Season
(Jun–Aug)
- Head for the Southern Alps for brilliant skiing.
- No crowds, good accommodation deals and a seat in any restaurant.
- Warm-weather beach towns might be half asleep.

Advance Planning

- **Three months before** Read a Kiwi novel: Keri Hulme, Lloyd Jones, Janet Frame, Maurice Gee...
- **One month before** Book accommodation and regional flights, trains, ferries etc.
- **One week before** Book a bungy jump, surf lesson, caving tour or Maori cultural experience.
- **Day before** Reserve a table at a top Auckland/Wellington restaurant and make sure you've packed your hiking boots.

Your Daily Budget

Budget less than $130

o Dorm beds or campsites: $25 to $35 per night

o Big-city food markets for self-catering bargains

o Explore NZ with a money-saving bus pass

Midrange $130–250

o Hotel/motel doubles: $100 to $180

o Midrange restaurants, a movie or a live band, and a few beers at the pub

o Hire a car and explore further

Top End more than $250

o Top-end hotel doubles: from $180

o Three-course meal in a classy restaurant: $70

o Take a guided tour, go shopping or hit some ritzy bars

Exchange Rates		
Australia	A$1	NZ$1.30
Canada	C$1	NZ$1.23
Euro zone	€1	NZ$1.59
Japan	¥100	NZ$1.62
UK	UK£1	NZ$1.92
US	US$1	NZ$1.25

For current exchange rates see www.xe.com

What to Bring

o **Driver's licence** The best way to see NZ is under your own steam.

o **Insect repellent** Kiwi sandfly bites just keep on giving.

o **Power-plug adaptor** Keep your gadgets charged.

o **Travel insurance** Ensure you're covered for 'high-risk' activities (skiing, white-water rafting, surfing etc).

o **Visa** Confirm current visa situation.

Arriving in New Zealand

o **Auckland Airport**

Buses 24-hour Airbus Express at least half-hourly

Shuttle Buses Prebooked, 24-hour door-to-door services

Taxis Around $70; 45 minutes to the city

o **Wellington Airport**

Buses Every 15 minutes 5.50am to 9.30pm

Shuttle Buses Prebooked, 24-hour door-to-door services

Taxis Around $30; 20 minutes to the city

o **Christchurch Airport**

Buses Every 30 minutes 7.15am to 9.15pm

Shuttle Buses Prebooked, 24-hour door-to-door services

Taxis Around $50; 25 minutes to the city

Getting Around

o **Bus** Well-organised links between towns.

o **Drive** Car hire from major cities and airports.

o **Ferry** Daily between the North and South Islands.

o **Fly** Domestic carriers fly between cities.

o **Train** Scenic railways cross the Southern Alps and link some major cities.

o **Walk** Long and short tracks, sublime scenery.

Accommodation

o **B&Bs** Bed (and breakfast) down in a locally run cabin/house/mansion (DB&B means dinner too!).

o **Camping & holiday parks** Camp in spectacular isolation or park your campervan at a holiday park.

o **Farmstays** Work on a farm, eat with the family.

o **Hostels** Spartan and decent or beery and oversexed – backpacker bonanza!

o **Hotels** From cheap pub rooms to five-star hotels.

o **Motels** Cookie-cutter sameness, but reliable.

Be Forewarned

o **Summertime blues** December to February bring crowds and steep accommodation prices.

o **Winter** Beaches are empty but mountains are full: ski season runs June to August (and beyond).

o **Take the long way home** Getting from A to B takes time: many roads are wiggly, two-lane affairs.

Auckland

Paris may be the city of love, but Auckland is the city of many lovers according to its Maori name, Tamaki Makaurau. Those lovers so desired this place that they fought over it for centuries.

It's hard to imagine a more geographically blessed city. Its two harbours frame a narrow isthmus punctuated by volcanic cones and surrounded by fertile farmland. From any of its numerous vantage points you'll be astounded at how close the Tasman Sea and Pacific Ocean come to kissing and forming a new island.

As a result, water's never far away – whether it's the ruggedly beautiful west-coast surf beaches or the glistening Hauraki Gulf with its myriad islands.

And within 90 minutes' drive from the high-rise heart of the city there are the forests, beaches and gold-mining towns of the Coromandel Peninsula. Don't miss a trip to Hot Water Beach, offering a hint of NZ's famed geothermal hubbub.

Looking across Waitemata Harbour to Auckland and the Sky Tower (p62)

Auckland

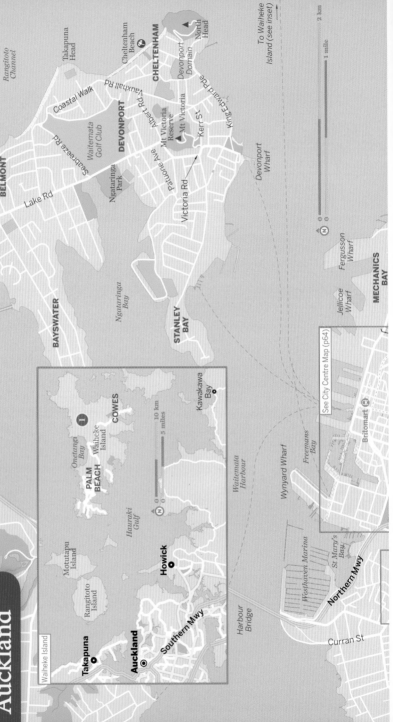

Rangitoto Channel

Takapuna Head

Cheltenham Beach

CHELTENHAM

North Head

Coastal Walk

Vauxhall Rd

Devonport Domain

DEVONPORT

Waitemata Golf Club

Seabreeze Rd

Albert Rd

Mt Victoria Reserve

Mt Victoria

King Edward Pde

Devonport Wharf

BELMONT

Lake Rd

Ngataringa Park

Patuone Ave

Kerr St

Victoria Rd

Ngataringa Bay

BAYSWATER

Fergusson Wharf

STANLEY BAY

Jellicoe Wharf

MECHANICS BAY

To Waiheke Island (see inset)

See City Centre Map (p64)

Britomart

COWES

Kawakawa Bay

Onetangi Bay

Waiheke Island

PALM BEACH

Hauraki Gulf

Waitemata Harbour

Wynyard Wharf

Freemans Bay

Howick

Motutapu Island

Rangitoto Island

Westhaven Marina

St Mary's Bay

Northern Mwy

Harbour Bridge

Southern Mwy

Takapuna

Auckland

Curran St

Waiheke Island

2 km
1 mile

10 km
5 miles

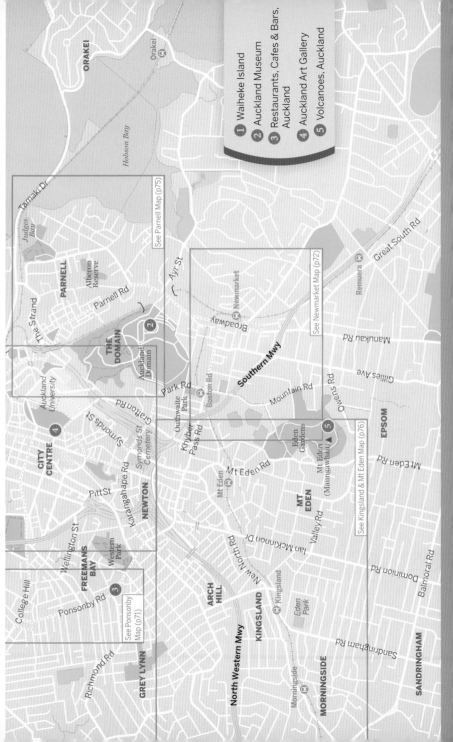

1 Waiheke Island
2 Auckland Museum
3 Restaurants, Cafes & Bars, Auckland
4 Auckland Art Gallery
5 Volcanoes, Auckland

Auckland's Highlights

1 Waiheke Island

Just a short ferry ride from the centre of Auckland, Waiheke may well be the highlight of your entire trip to New Zealand. You can arrive from Sydney or Los Angeles at breakfast time, then be on Waiheke for a vineyard-restaurant lunch with eye-popping views. Finish off with a swim on an uncrowded beach.

Need to Know

BOOKINGS ESSENTIAL Lunch on summer weekends at vineyard restaurants **BEST ADVICE** The sign for cars off the ferry: 'Slow down. You're here.' **For further coverage, see p83**

Waiheke Island Don't Miss List

BY STEVE & NIGEL ROBINSON, ANANDA TOURS

1 THE ARTS SCENE

There are lots of artists on Waiheke, and the *Waiheke Art Map* brochure is a good guide to the island's galleries. The gallery at the Artworks Complex (p83) in Oneroa showcases local artists, while the sculpture park at Connells Bay (p84) features a two-hour walk through installations on a former sheep farm.

2 WINE

Waiheke wine is all about quality over quantity: wines from Goldwater Estate (now Goldie Vineyard), Te Motu and Stonyridge (p83) all made the grade in the 2008 book *1001 Wines You Must Taste Before You Die.* You can take a tour (p84) of a few island wineries, meet the winemakers and learn about the local wines.

3 BEACHES

On beaches such as Onetangi, Oneroa, and Palm Beach (p83), we think it's crowded if there are more than 20 people on the sand! Visitors arrive and say, 'Where is everybody?' Even in the height of summer, it's easy to find quiet stretches of beach.

4 STONY BATTER HISTORIC RESERVE

This amazing landscape is strewn with huge boulders thrown up by volcanic eruptions 20 million years ago. It's also a historic reserve: the Stony Batter Fort (p83) was built in WWII to defend against a naval invasion that never happened. There's more than a kilometre of tunnels 7.5m underground to be explored.

5 WALKING THE COAST

Because the island is so hilly, around every corner there's a new view – usually with sea in it. The local council has put lots of resources into bush and coastal walkways, and there's public access to most parts of the coast. Other activities include horse riding and sea kayaking.

Auckland Museum

If you have the slightest interest in Maori and Pacific Islander culture, your first stop should be the Auckland Museum (p67). The Maori galleries are loaded with artefacts from around the country, and there are cultural performances daily – see why NZ's All Blacks rugby team uses the *haka* (war dance) to put the fear of God into their opposition. There's plenty of natural history, war history and kids stuff, too.

2

JOHN ELK III / LONELY PLANET IMAGES ©

3

Restaurants, Cafes & Bars

Dress up for the classy restaurants and bars around Viaduct Harbour (p72), browse the eateries along Ponsonby Rd (p73), or order some fast sushi in the city centre. Breakfast and coffee are big business in Auckland – the cafes are kickin' around Parnell and Newmarket (p74). Later on, you'll find plenty of places to wet your whistle: Vulcan Lane, Ponsonby Rd and K Rd are drinking (p74) hot spots. Left: Dining on Vulcan Lane

ANDREW WATSON / GETTY IMAGES ©

Auckland Art Gallery

Renovated in fine style in 2011, Auckland Art Gallery (p68) provides a hushed, cultured escape from the streets. The Main Gallery and the New Gallery (predictably) focus on the old and the new respectively: look for European masters and early colonial works in the former, and contemporary Kiwi creations and temporary exhibitions in the latter.

Volcanoes

Feel the heat! There's a huge reservoir of molten magma 100km below the streets of Auckland, and there are 50 volcanic peaks around the city. But don't sweat – there hasn't been an eruption here for 600 years, and most of the cones are dormant. Take a hike up Mt Eden (Maungawhau; p79) or One Tree Hill (Maungakiekie; p66) and see what you can see. Above: The volcanic crater of Mt Eden (p79)

Coromandel Beaches

Pack your swimsuit and get up early for a day trip to the Coromandel Peninsula (or book a B&B and stay overnight). Explore the heritage streetscapes of Thames (p87) and Coromandel Town (p89), and make sure you dedicate some time to the beach! The legendary geothermal springs of Hot Water Beach (p92) are near Hahei, and there are some gorgeous stretches of sand around Whitianga (p90). Above: Lonely Bay (p90)

Auckland's Best...

Points of View

○ **Mt Eden** (Maungawhau; p79) Killer views from Auckland's highest volcanic cone (196m)

○ **Sky Tower** (p62) The southern hemisphere's tallest structure

○ **One Tree Hill** (Maungakiekie; p66) Historic volcanic cone: 182m tall with a 360-degree outlook

○ **On the water** (p82) Take a ferry out onto the harbour and see Auckland from the water

Fresh-air Factories

○ **The Domain** (p63) Eighty city-centre hectares of recreational greenery and themed gardens

○ **Tamaki Drive** (p63) Tree-lined runway for joggers and the generically good looking

○ **Eden Garden** (p70) Burgeoning blooms on the slopes of Mt Eden

○ **Albert Park** (p62) A formal Victorian-era garden full of canoodling students

Eat Streets & Drinking Dens

○ **Ponsonby Rd, Ponsonby** (p73) Auckland's hippest strip (www.ponsonbyroad.co.nz)

○ **Karangahape Rd (K Rd), Newton** (p73) Edgy strip of affordable restaurants and bars

○ **New North Rd, Kingsland** (p73) Emerging eat street with great Thai and French

○ **Viaduct Harbour, Central Auckland** (p72) Upmarket waterfront eating and drinking (dress up!)

○ **Vulcan Lane, Central Auckland** (p74) Photogenic city-centre collation of cafes and bars

Need to Know

Festivals

○ **Devonport Food & Wine Festival** (www.devonportwinefestival.co.nz) Sassy two-day sip-fest in mid-February

○ **Auckland Arts Festival** (www.aucklandfestival.co.nz) Auckland's biggest arts party: three weeks in March, odd-numbered years

○ **Pasifika Festival** (www.aucklandcouncil.govt.nz) Giant Polynesian party in March: performances, food and arts and crafts

○ **New Zealand International Film Festival** (www.nzff.co.nz) Beat a retreat from the cold July streets for art-house treats

ADVANCE PLANNING

○ **One month before** Book your bed in the city (and on the Coromandel Peninsula if it's summer), plus transport, accommodation and activities on the Hauraki Gulf Islands.

○ **Two weeks before** Book tickets for concerts, the rugby and maybe a Cathedral Cove sea-kayak tour on the Coromandel Peninsula.

○ **One week before** Book tickets for a harbour cruise and a table at one of Auckland's premier restaurants.

RESOURCES

○ **Auckland NZ** (www.aucklandnz.com) The city's official tourist site

○ **Destination Coromandel** (www.thecoromandel.com) Tourist info for the Coromandel

○ **Auckland i-SITEs** (www.aucklandnz.com) Central tourist info, at the SkyCity complex and the Princes Wharf ferries on Quay St

○ **New Zealand Herald** (www.nzherald.co.nz) NZ's biggest daily newspaper is based in Auckland

○ **MAXX Regional Transport** (www.maxx.co.nz) Public transport details: bus, train and ferry

GETTING AROUND

○ **Walk** Around Central Auckland and along the waterfront

○ **Ferry** To the Hauraki Gulf islands (Waiheke, Rangitoto) and Devonport on the North Shore

○ **Bus** All around the city

○ **Hire a car** When you want to leave town (the Coromandel Peninsula is 90 minutes away)

○ **Airbus Express** Buses pinball between the airport and the city

○ **Train** To access the southwestern suburbs

BE FOREWARNED

○ **Crowds** Summer (December to February) is the busy season: expect queues at Auckland's big-ticket sights, lots of beach-bums on the Coromandel Peninsula and elevated accommodation prices

Left: Tongans taking part in Pasifika festivities; **Above:** Morning meditation in Albert Park (p62)

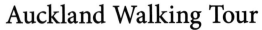

Auckland Walking Tour

Auckland's CBD can feel a little scrappy and disorienting: this walk aims to shed some light by taking you through the best bits, with a few hidden nooks and architectural treats thrown in for good measure.

WALK FACTS

- **Start** St Kevin's Arcade, Karangahape Rd
- **Finish** Wynyard Quarter
- **Distance** 4.5km
- **Duration** Around three hours

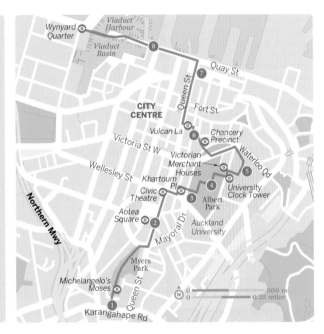

① St Kevin's Arcade

Start among the second-hand boutiques of **St Kevin's Arcade**, then take the stairs down to Myers Park: look out for the reproduction of **Michelangelo's Moses** at the bottom of the stairs. Continue through the park, taking the stairs on the right just before the overpass to head up to street level.

② Auckland Town Hall

Heading down Queen St, you'll pass the noble **Auckland Town Hall** and sprawling, paved **Aotea Square**, the civic heart of the city. On the next corner is the wonderfully art deco **Civic Theatre**. It was built in 1929, and reopened in 2000 after a major overhaul. Don't miss the amazing Indian-inspired lobby.

③ Auckland Art Gallery

Turn right on Wellesley St and then left onto Lorne St. Immediately to your right is **Khartoum Pl**, a pretty little square with tiling celebrating the suffragettes; NZ women were the first in the world to win the vote. Head up the stairs to the fabulously renovated **Auckland Art Gallery**: free tours kick-off at 11.30am, 12.30pm and 1.30pm daily.

4 Albert Park

Behind the gallery is **Albert Park**, a Victorian formal garden. Cross through it and turn left into Princes St, where a row of **Victorian merchant's houses** faces the intricately styled **University Clock Tower**.

5 Old Government House

Cut around behind the clock tower to the restrained grandeur of **Old Government House**, and then follow the diagonal path back to Princes St. The good-looking building on the corner of Princes and Bowen Ave was once the city's main **synagogue**.

6 High St

Head down Bowen Ave and cut through the park to the **Chancery precinct**, an upmarket area of designer shops and cafes. A small square connects it to **High St**, Auckland's main fashion strip. Take a left onto **Vulcan La**, lined with historical pubs and cool cafes.

7 Britomart Train Station

Turn right onto Queen St and follow it down to the **Britomart Train Station**, housed in the former Central Post Office. You're now standing on reclaimed land – the original shoreline was at Fort St, about 200m behind you (to the south).

8 Viaduct Harbour

Turn left on Quay St and head to **Viaduct Harbour**, bustling with bars, cafes and lunching types, and then continue over the bridge to the rejuvenated **Wynyard Quarter**.

Auckland In…

TWO DAYS

Start by acquainting yourself with the inner city. Take our walking tour from **Karangahape Rd (K Rd)** to the **Wynyard Quarter**, stopping to check out the NZ section of the **Auckland Art Gallery**. Catch a ferry to **Devonport**, head up **North Head** and cool down at **Cheltenham Beach** (weather permitting), before heading back for dinner.

On day two, head up **One Tree Hill**, wander around **Cornwall Park** and then visit the **Auckland Museum** and **Domain**. Take a trip along **Tamaki Drive**, stopping at Bastion or Achilles Point to enjoy the harbour views. Spend the evening dining and bar hopping in **Ponsonby**.

FOUR DAYS

On the third day, get out on the **Hauraki Gulf**. Catch the ferry to **Waiheke Island** and spend your time between the beaches and the wineries.

On the final day, head west. Breakfast in **Titirangi** before exploring the **Waitakere Ranges Regional Park**, **Karekare** and **Piha**. Then have a night out on K Rd or **Britomart**.

One Tree Hill (p66)
DAVID WALL / ALAMY ©

Discover Auckland

Passenger ferry at Auckland's waterfront
OLIVER STREWE / LONELY PLANET IMAGES ©

Sights

City Centre

ALBERT PARK & AUCKLAND UNIVERSITY   Park, University
(Map p64) Hugging the hill on the city's eastern flank, Albert Park is a charming Victorian formal garden overrun by students during term time, the more radical of whom have been known to deface the statues of Governor Grey and Queen Victoria. Auckland University's campus stretches over several streets and incorporates a row of stately **Victorian merchant houses** (Princes St) and **Old Government House** (Waterloo Quadrant). The **University Clock Tower** is Auckland's architectural triumph. It's usually open, so wander inside.

SKY TOWER   Landmark
(www.skycityauckland.co.nz; cnr Federal & Victoria Sts; adult/child $25/8; ⊙8.30am-10.30pm) The impossible-to-miss Sky Tower looks like a giant hypodermic giving a fix to the heavens. Spectacular lighting renders it space-age at night. At 328m it is the tallest structure in the southern hemisphere. A lift takes you up to the observation decks in 40 stomach-lurching seconds; look down through the glass floor panels if you're after an extra kick. It costs $3 extra to catch the skyway lift to the ultimate viewing level. See also SkyWalk and SkyJump.

VOYAGER – NEW ZEALAND MARITIME MUSEUM   Museum
(☎09-373 0800; www.maritimemuseum.co.nz; 149-159 Quay St; adult/child $17/9; ⊙9am-5pm) This well-presented museum traces NZ's seafaring history from Maori voyaging

canoes to the America's Cup. Recreations include a tilting 19th-century steerage-class cabin and a fab 1950s beach store and bach (holiday home).

Parnell & Newmarket

AUCKLAND DOMAIN — Park

(Map p75) Covering about 80 hectares, this green swathe contains sports fields, interesting sculpture, formal gardens, wild corners and the **Wintergarden** (admission free; ☺9am-5.30pm Mon-Sat, 9am-7.30pm Sun Nov-Mar, 9am-4.30pm Apr-Oct), with its fernery, tropical house, cool house, cute cat statue and neighbouring cafe. The mound in the centre of the park is all that remains of Pukekaroa, one of Auckland's volcanoes.

Tamaki Drive

This scenic, pohutukawa-lined road heads east from the city, hugging the waterfront. In summer it's a jogging/cycling/roller-blading blur offering plenty of eye candy.

A succession of child-friendly, peaceful swimming beaches starts at Ohaku Bay. Around the headland is Mission Bay, a popular beach with an iconic art-deco fountain, historic mission house, restaurants and bars. Safe swimming beaches Kohimarama and St Heliers follow. Further east along Cliff Rd, the Achilles Point lookout offers panoramic views. At its base is Ladies Bay, where nudists put up with mud and shells for the sake of relative seclusion.

Buses 745 to 769 from Britomart follow this route.

KELLY TARLTON'S — Aquarium

(Antarctic Encounter; ☎09-531 5065; www.kellytarltons.co.nz; 23 Tamaki Dr; adult/child $34/17; ☺9.30am-5.30pm) In the **Underwater World**, sharks and stingrays swim around and over you as you're shunted on a conveyor belt through transparent tunnels in what were once stormwater and sewage holding tanks.

In a post Happy Feet world, Kelly Tarlton's biggest attraction is the permanent winter wonderland known as **Antarctic Encounter**. It includes a walk through a replica of Scott's 1911 Antarctic hut, and a ride aboard a heated snowcat

through a frozen environment where a colony of king and gentoo penguins lives.

Book online for a shorter wait (queues can be horrendous) and a 10% discount. There's a free shark-shaped shuttle bus that departs from 172 Quay St (opposite the ferry terminal) on the hour between 9am and 4pm.

Devonport

Nestling at the bottom of the North Shore, Devonport is a short ferry trip from the city. Quaint without being sickeningly twee, it retains a village atmosphere, with many well-preserved Victorian and Edwardian buildings and loads of cafes.

For a self-guided tour of historic buildings, pick up the Old Devonport Walk pamphlet from the i-SITE.

Ferries to Devonport (adult/child return $11/5.80, 12 minutes) depart from the Auckland Ferry Building every 30 minutes (hourly after 8pm) from 6.15am to 11.15pm (until 1am Friday and Saturday), and from 7.15am to 10pm on Sundays and public holidays. Some Waiheke Island and Rangitoto ferries also stop here.

FREE NAVY MUSEUM — Museum

(www.navymuseum.mil.nz; Torpedo Bay; ☺10am-5pm) The navy has been in Devonport since the earliest days of the colony. Its history is on display at this well-presented and often moving museum, focussing on the stories of the sailors themselves.

Western Springs

AUCKLAND ZOO — Zoo

(Map p76; www.aucklandzoo.co.nz; Motions Rd; adult/child $21/11; ☺9.30am-5pm, last entry 4.15pm) At this modern, spacious zoo, the big foreigners tend to steal the attention from the timid natives, but if you can wrestle the kids away from the tigers, there's a well-presented NZ section. Called Te Wao Nui, it's divided into seven zones: Coast (seals, penguins), Islands (mainly lizards, including NZ's pint-sized dinosaur, the tuatara), Wetlands (ducks, herons, eels), Night (kiwi, frogs, native owls and weta), Forest (birds) and High Country (cheekier birds and lizards).

City Centre

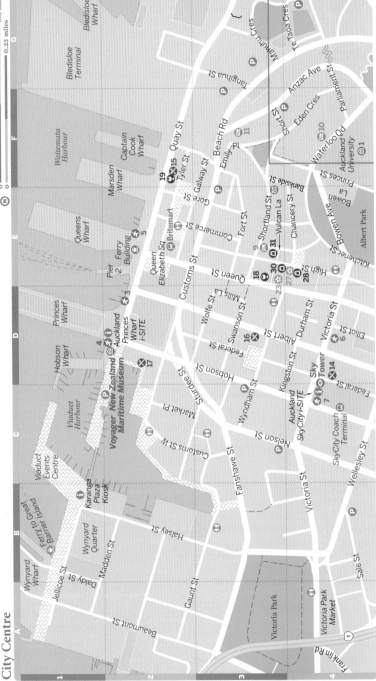

0 0.25 miles
0 0.5 km

Waitemata Harbour

Bledisloe Wharf

Bledisloe Terminal

Captain Cook Wharf

Marsden Wharf

Queens Wharf

Princes Wharf

Hobson Wharf

Viaduct Harbour

Viaduct Events Centre

Wynyard Wharf

Wynyard Quarter

Ferry to Great Barrier Island

Karanga Plaza Kiosk

Voyager New Zealand Maritime Museum

Auckland Princes Wharf i-SITE

Ferry Building

Pier 2

Queen Elizabeth Sq

Britomart

Quay St

Tyler St

Gore St

Galway St

Tangihua St

Te Taoa Cres

Manukau Cres

Anzac Ave

Eden Cres

Parliament St

Shortt St

Waterloo Qd

Auckland University

Bowen La

Princes St

Albert Park

Kitchener St

Bowen Ave

Chancery St

Vulcan La

Shortland St

Fort St

Commerce St

Customs St

Queen St

Emily Pl

Beach Rd

Bankside St

Wolfe St

Mills La

Swanson St

Albert St

Durham St

High St

Victoria St

Elliott St

Federal St

Kingston St

Wyndham St

Hobson St

Nelson St

Fanshawe St

Customs St W

Market Pl

Sturdee St

Halsey St

Madden St

Daldy St

Jellicoe St

Beaumont St

Gaunt St

Victoria Park

Victoria Park Market

Franklin Rd

Sale St

Wellesley St

Victoria St

SkyCity Coach Terminal

Sky Tower

Auckland SkyCity i-SITE

Franklin Rd

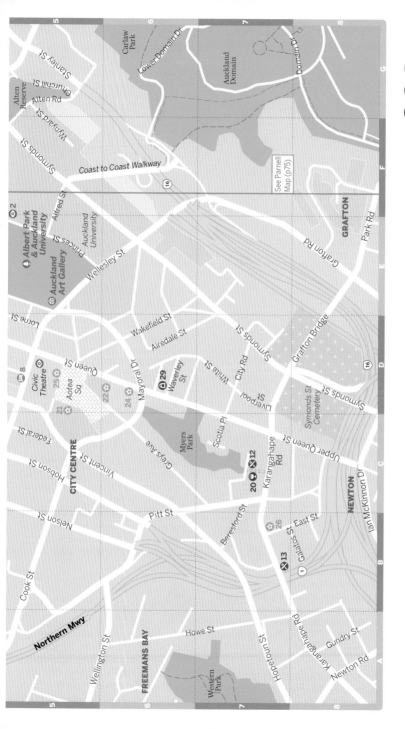

City Centre map labels:

Carlaw Park

Lower Domain Dr

Auckland Domain

Domain Dr

Stanley St

Churchill St

Alten Rd

Alten Reserve

Wynyard St

Symonds St

Coast to Coast Walkway

16

See Parnell Map (p75)

GRAFTON

Park Rd

Alfred St

Albert Park & Auckland University

Princes St

Auckland University

Auckland Art Gallery

Wellesley St

Grafton Rd

Lorne St

Wakefield St

Airedale St

Symonds St

Grafton Bridge

16

Civic Theatre

Aotea Sq

Queen St

Mayoral Dr

Waverley St

White St

City Rd

Symonds St

Symonds St Cemetery

Symonds St

Federal St

CITY CENTRE

Vincent St

Greys Ave

Myers Park

Scotia Pl

Liverpool St

Upper Queen St

Hobson St

Nelson St

Pitt St

Beresford St

Karangahape Rd

NEWTON

Ian McKinnon Dr

Cook St

Northern Mwy

Wellington St

FREEMANS BAY

Howe St

Western Park

Hopetoun St

Galatos St

East St

Karangahape Rd

Gundry St

Newton Rd

65

City Centre

Other Suburbs

ONE TREE HILL (MAUNGAKIEKIE) Volcano, Park
(www.cornwallpark.co.nz) This volcanic cone was the isthmus's key *pa* (fortified village) and the greatest fortress in the country. It's easy to see why: a drive or walk to the top (182m) offers 360-degree views. At the summit is the grave of John Logan Campbell, who when gifting the land to the city in 1901 requested that a memorial (the imposing obelisk and statue above the grave) be built to the Maori people. Nearby is the stump of the last 'one tree'.

To get here from the city, take a train to Greenlane and walk 1km along Green Lane West. By car, take the Greenlane exit of the Southern Motorway and turn right into Green Lane West.

FREE WALLACE ARTS CENTRE Gallery
(www.tsbbankwallaceartscentre.org.nz; Pah Homestead, 72 Hillsborough Rd, Hillsborough;

⏱10am-3pm Tue-Fri, 10am-5pm Sat & Sun) Housed in a gorgeous 1879 mansion with views to One Tree Hill and the Manakau Harbour, the Wallace Arts Centre is lavishly endowed with contemporary New Zealand art from a private collection, generously offered for free public viewing.

Bus 299 (Lynfield) departs every 15 minutes from Wellesley St in the city (near the Civic Theatre) and heads to Hillsborough Rd ($4.50, about 40 minutes).

# Activities

Visitors centres and public libraries stock the city council's *Auckland City's Walkways* pamphlet, which has a good selection of urban walks, including the Coast to Coast Walkway (p68).

TRAVELSCAPE IMAGES / ALAMY ©

Don't Miss **Auckland Museum**

Dominating the Domain is this imposing neoclassical temple (1929), capped with an impressive copper-and-glass dome (2007). Its comprehensive display of Pacific Island and Maori artefacts on the ground floor deserves to be on your 'must see' list. Highlights include a 25m war canoe and an extant carved meeting house (remove your shoes before entering). There's also an Egyptian mummy (a sure-fire hit with the kids) and a fascinating display on the volcanic field, including an eruption simulation.

Hour-long museum highlights tours (adult/child $20/8) are held daily at 10.30am, 12.30pm and 2pm. Half-hour Maori cultural performances (adult/child $25/13) take place at 11am and 1.30pm, with Maori gallery tours (adult/child $10/5) departing immediately afterwards.

NEED TO KNOW

Map p75; ☎09-309 0443; www.aucklandmuseum.com; adult/child $10/free; ◷10am-5pm

---

SAIL NZ　　　Sailing
(☎0800 397 567; www.explorenz.co.nz; Viaduct Harbour) Shoot the breeze on a genuine America's Cup yacht (adult/child $160/115) or head out on a Whale and Dolphin Safari (adult/child $160/105; dolphins are spotted 90% of the time and whales 75%. The *Pride of Auckland* fleet of glamorous large yachts offers 90-minute Harbour Sailing Cruises (adult/child $75/55), 2½-hour Dinner Cruises ($120/85) and full-day Sailing Adventures ($165/125).

SKYWALK　　　Extreme Sports
(Map p64; ☎0800 759 925; www.skywalk.co.nz; Sky Tower; adult/child $145/115; ◷10am-4.30pm) The Sky Tower offers an ever-expanding selection of pant-wetting activities. If you thought the observation deck was for pussies, SkyWalk involves circling the 192m-high, 1.2m-wide outside halo of the tower without rails or a balcony – but with

67

MICHAEL SNELL / ALAMY ©

Don't Miss **Auckland Art Gallery**

Reopened in 2011 after a $121-million refurbishment, Auckland's premier art repository now has a gorgeous glass-and-wood atrium grafted onto its already impressive 1887 French-chateau frame. It's a worthy receptacle for important works by the likes of Pieter Bruegel the Younger, Guido Reni, Picasso, Cezanne, Gauguin and Matisse. It also showcases the best of NZ art: from the intimate 19th-century portraits of tattooed Maori subjects by Charles Goldie, to the text-scrawled canvasses of Colin McCahon, and beyond.

Free tours depart from the main entrance at 11.30am, 12.30pm and 1.30pm.

NEED TO KNOW

Map p64; www.aucklandartgallery.com; cnr Kitchener & Wellesley Sts; admission free; ⊙10am-5pm

a safety harness (they're not completely crazy).

SKYJUMP Extreme Sports
(Map p64; ☏0800 759 586; www.skyjump. co.nz; adult/child $225/175; ⊙10am-5pm) This 11-second, 85km/h base wire leap from the observation deck of the Sky Tower is more like a parachute jump than a bungy and it's a rush and a half. Combine it with the SkyWalk in the Look 'n Leap package ($290).

COAST TO COAST WALKWAY Walking
(www.aucklandcity.govt.nz) Heading clear across the country from the Tasman to the Pacific (actually, that's only 16km), this walk encompasses One Tree Hill, Mt Eden, the Domain and the University, keeping as much as possible to reserves rather than city streets. You can do it in either direction: we recommend catching the train to Onehunga, the least impressive trailhead, and finishing up at one of the Viaduct's bars. From Onehunga Station, take Onehunga Mall up to Princes

St, turn left and pick up the track at the inauspicious park by the motorway.

FERGS KAYAKS Kayaking
(☏ 09-529 2230; www.fergskayaks.co.nz; 12 Tamaki Dr, Okahu Bay; ⏰10am-5pm) Hires out kayaks and paddleboards (per hour/day from $15/50), bikes (per hour/day $20/120) and inline skates (per hour/day $15/30). Day and night guided kayak trips are available to Devonport ($95, three hours, 8km) or Rangitoto Island ($120, six hours, 13km).

PARNELL BATHS Swimming
(Map p75; www.parnellbaths.co.nz; Judges Bay Rd; adult/child $6.30/4.20; ⏰6am-8pm Mon-Fri, 8am-8pm Sat & Sun Nov-Apr) Outdoor saltwater pools with an awesome 1950s mural.

BALLOON EXPEDITIONS Ballooning
(☏ 09-416 8590; www.balloonexpeditions.co.nz; flight $340) Offers hour-long hot-air balloon flights at sunrise, including breakfast and a bottle of bubbles.

 Tours

Cultural Tours

TORU TOURS Cultural Tour
(☏ 027 457 0011; www.torutours.com; with/without performance $213/178) Maori cultural tours stopping in at a *marae* (meeting house complex), Auckland Museum (with an optional cultural show), the native critter section of the zoo, Mt Eden, One Tree Hill and Bastion Point. Three-hour Express Tours ($69) are also available.

NZ WINEPRO Wine Tasting
(☏ 09-575 1958; www.nzwinepro.co.nz; tours $119-325) Offers a range of highly rated tours to all of Auckland's wine regions, combining tastings with sightseeing.

EXPLORER BUS Bus Tour
(☏ 0800 439 756; www.explorerbus.co.nz; adult/child $40/20) This hop-on, hop-off service departs from the Ferry Building every

hour from 10am to 3pm (more frequently in summer), heading to 14 tourist sites around the central city.

FULLERS Cruise
(Map p64; ☏ 09-367 9111; www.fullers.co.nz; Ferry Building, 99 Quay St; adult/child $38/19; ⏰10.30am & 1.30pm) As well as ferry services, Fullers has daily 1½-hour harbour cruises which include a stop on Rangitoto, a complimentary cuppa and a free return ticket to Devonport.

 Sleeping

City Centre

HOTEL DE BRETT Boutique Hotel $$$
(Map p64; ☏ 09-925 9000; www.hoteldebrett.com; 2 High St; r $300-600; @ 🛜) Supremely

69

If You Like…
Parks & Gardens

If you like wandering through Albert Park, we think you'll enjoy these other Auckland green zones.

1 **AUCKLAND BOTANICAL GARDENS**
(www.aucklandbotanicgardens.co.nz; 102 Hill Rd, Manurewa; ⊙8am-6pm mid-Mar–mid-Oct, 8am-8pm mid-Oct–mid-Mar) These 64-hectare gardens have themed areas, threatened plants and an infestation of wedding parties.

2 **EDEN GARDEN**
(Map p72; www.edengarden.co.nz; 24 Omana Ave; adult/child $8/6; ⊙9am-4pm) On the eastern slopes of Mt Eden, this horticultural showpiece is noted for its collections of camellia, rhododendron and azalea.

3 **PARNELL ROSE GARDENS**
(Map p75; 85-87 Gladstone Rd; ⊙7am-7pm) These formal gardens are blooming excellent from November to March.

4 **BASTION POINT**
(Hapimana St) Politics, harbour views and lush lawns combine on this pretty headland with a chequered history. Follow the lawn to a WWII gun embankment.

5 **WESTERN SPRINGS PARK**
(Map p76; Great North Rd) Formed by a confluence of lava flows, the lake here was once Auckland's water supply. It's a great spot for a picnic (watch out for the geese).

hip, this lavishly refurbished historic hotel has been zooshed up with stripey carpets and clever designer touches in every nook of the extremely comfortable rooms. Prices include breakfast, free broadband and a predinner drink.

🏷 **WALDORF CELESTION**　　　Apartment Hotel $$
(Map p64; ☎09-280 2200; www.celestion -waldorf.co.nz; 19-23 Anzac Ave; apt $137-239) A rash of Waldorfs has opened in recent

years, all presenting similar symptoms: affordable, modern, inner-city apartments in city fringe locations. We prefer this one for its stylish red, black and grey colour palette, and the sumptuous velvet curtains in reception.

ELLIOTT HOTEL　　　Apartment Hotel $$
(Map p64; ☎09-308 9334; www.theelliott hotel.com; cnr Elliott & Wellesley Sts; apt $139-219; [P]) Housed in a grand historic building (1880s), this apartment-style hotel is much plusher than the price implies. Rooms may not be huge but the high ceilings will let your spirits rise.

🏷 **QUADRANT**　　　Hotel $$
(Map p64; ☎09-984 6000; www.the quadrant.com; 10 Waterloo Quadrant; apt $165-600; 🛜) Slick, central and full of all the whiz-bang gadgets, this apartment-style complex is an excellent option. The only catch is that the units are tiny and the bathrooms beyond small.

Ponsonby & Grey Lynn

🏷 **HENRY'S**　　　B&B $$$
(Map p71; ☎09-360 2700; www.henrysonpeel. co.nz; 33 Peel St; r/apt $220/275; @🛜🏊) These beautiful wooden villas are what Auckland's inner suburbs are all about. Henry's has been stylishly renovated, adding en suites to the downstairs rooms and a self-contained harbour-view apartment above.

ABACO ON JERVOIS　　　Motel $$
(Map p71; ☎09-360 6850; www.abaco.co.nz; 57 Jervois Rd; r $125-165, ste $184-205; [P]) A neutral-toned motel, with a contemporary fit-out, including slick stainless-steel kitchenettes (with dish drawers and proper ovens) and fluffy white towels for use in the spa. The darker rooms downstairs are priced accordingly.

Mt Eden

🏷 **EDEN PARK B&B**　　　B&B $$$
(Map p76; ☎09-630 5721; www.bedandbreakfast nz.com; 20 Bellwood Ave; s $135-150, d $235-250; 🛜) If you know any rugby fans who

require chandeliers in their bathrooms, send them here. The hallowed turf of Auckland's legendary rugby ground is only a block away and while the rooms aren't overly large for the prices, they mirror the Edwardian elegance of this fine wooden villa.

BAVARIA Guesthouse $$

(Map p76; ☏09-638 9641; www.bavariabandb hotel.co.nz; 83 Valley Rd; s $95-110, d $145-175; P@🛜) Sitting somewhere between a B&B and a small hotel, this spacious villa offers large, airy rooms and a buffet breakfast. The communal TV lounge, dining room and deck all encourage mixing and mingling.

Parnell & Newmarket

PARNELL INN Motel $$

(Map p75; ☏09-358 0642; www.parnellinn.co.nz; 320 Parnell Rd; r $105-140; P@🛜) You'll get a chipper welcome from the friendly folks at this good-looking, revamped motel with local photography on the walls. Rooms 3 and 4 have great harbour views and some rooms have kitchenettes.

QUALITY HOTEL BARRYCOURT Hotel $$

(Map p75; ☏09-303 3789; www.barrycourt.co.nz; 20 Gladstone Rd; units $113-283, r $131-179, ste $188-283; P🛜) A mixed bag of more than 100 motel rooms and units are available in this large, well-maintained complex with friendly multilingual staff. The newer north wing has some fantastic harbour views.

Devonport

HAMPTON BEACH HOUSE B&B $$$

(☏09-445 1358; www.hamptonbeachhouse. co.nz; 4 King Edward Pde; s $195, r $235-305; @🛜) One of a fine strip of waterside mansions, this upmarket, gay-friendly, Edwardian B&B has rooms opening onto the rear garden. It's all very tastefully done; expect quality linen and gourmet breakfasts.

DEVONPORT MOTEL Motel $$

(☏09-445 1010; www.devonportmotel.co.nz; 11 Buchanan St; r $150; 🛜; 🚢Devonport) This minimotel has just two units in the tidy back garden. They're modern, clean,

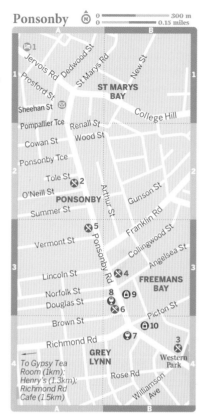

Ponsonby

Newmarket

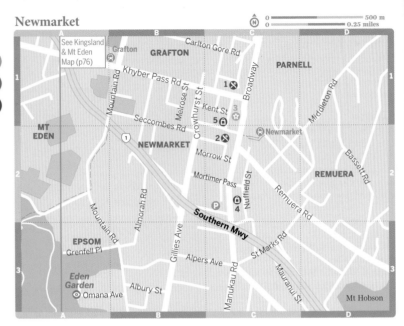

Newmarket

N 0 ——————— 500 m
0 ——————— 0.25 miles

See Kingsland & Mt Eden Map (p76)

Grafton
GRAFTON
Carlton Gore Rd
PARNELL
Khyber Pass Rd
Mountain Rd
Melrose St
Crownhurst St
Kent St
Seccombes Rd
Broadway
Middleton Rd
1
3
5
Newmarket
2
MT EDEN
NEWMARKET
Morrow St
Mortimer Pass
Nuffield St
REMUERA
Bassett Rd
Mountain Rd
Almorah Rd
Southern Mwy
4
Remuera Rd
St Marks Rd
Maurani St
EPSOM
Grenfell Pl
Gilles Ave
Alpers Ave
Manukau Rd
Eden Garden
Omana Ave
Albury St
Mt Hobson

Newmarket

◎ Top Sights
Eden Garden..A3

✷ Eating
1 Basque Kitchen Bar..............................C1
2 Teed St Larder C2

◎ Entertainment
3 Rialto...C1

ⓖ Shopping
4 Texan Art Schools C2
5 Zambesi C1

self-contained and in a nice quiet location that's still close to Devonport's action (such as it may be).

 Eating

Because of its size and ethnic diversity, Auckland tops the country when it comes to dining options and quality.

Aucklanders demand good coffee, so you never have to walk too far to find a decent cafe.

City Centre

GROVE Modern NZ **$$$**
(Map p64; ☎09-368 4129; www.thegrove restaurant.co.nz; St Patrick's Sq, Wyndham St; mains $43; ☺lunch Mon-Fri, dinner Mon-Sat) Romantic fine dining at its best: the room is cosy and moodily lit, the menu encourages sensual experimentation and the service is effortless. If you can't find anything to break the ice on the extensive wine list, give it up – it's never going to happen.

DEPOT Modern NZ **$$**
(Map p64; www.eatatdepot.co.nz; 86 Federal St; dishes $14-32; ☺7am-late) Opened to instant acclaim in 2011, TV chef Al Brown's first Auckland eatery offers first-rate comfort food in informal surrounds (communal tables, butcher tiles and a constant buzz). Dishes are divided into 'small' and 'a little bigger' and are designed to be shared. A pair of clever shuckers are kept busy serving up the city's freshest oysters.

O'CONNELL STREET BISTRO French **$$$**
(Map p64; ☎09-377 1884; www.oconnellstbistro. com; 3 O'Connell St; lunch $28-38, dinner $34-45;

lunch Mon-Fri, dinner Mon-Sat) O'Connell St is a grown-up treat, with elegant decor and truly wonderful food and wine, satisfying lunchtime powerbrokers and dinnertime daters alike. If you're dining before 7.30pm, a fixed-price menu is available (two-/three-courses $33/40).

SOUL BAR   Modern NZ $$
(Map p64; ✆09-356 7249; www.soulbar.co.nz; Viaduct Harbour; mains $20-42; ⌚11am-late) Eating seafood by the water is a must in Auckland and this modernist gastrodome boasts an unbeatable see-and-be-seen location (Jay-Z and Beyoncé dined not-at-all-inconspicuously on the deck) and some of the best seafood in town.

EBISU   Japanese $$
(Map p64; www.ebisu.co.nz; 116-118 Quay St; large plates $28-35; ⌚lunch Mon-Fri, dinner daily) Auckland's food-lovers are in the midst of a minicraze for *izakaya*, a style of drinking and eating that eschews Japanese formality, yet doesn't involve food being flung around the room or chugging along on a conveyor belt. This large bar gets it exactly right, serving exquisite plates, large and small, designed to be shared.

Ponsonby & Grey Lynn

MOOCHOWCHOW   Thai $$
(Map p71; ✆09-360 6262; www.moochowchow. co.nz; 23 Ponsonby Rd; dishes $18-30; ⌚lunch Tue-Fri, dinner Tue-Sat) It's Thai, Nahm Jim, but not as we know it. Bangkok's street food has been channelled into this supremely Ponsonby mooching spot without missing a piquant note. We haven't had a bad dish here, and we've sampled most of the menu.

⌀ PQR   Italian $$
(Map p71; www.spqrnz.co.nz; 150 Ponsonby Rd; mains $25-39; ⌚noon-late) This Ponsonby Rd hot spot is well known for Roman-style, thin, crusty pizzas and excellent Italian-influenced mains. The surrounds are a stylish blend of the industrial and the chic, the lights low (bring your reading glasses!), the buzz constant and the smooth staff aren't beyond camping it up.

PONSONBY ROAD
BISTRO   International $$
(Map p71; ✆09-360 1611; www.ponsonbyroad bistro.co.nz; 165 Ponsonby Rd; mains $23-36; ⌚lunch Mon-Fri, dinner Mon-Sat) Portions are large at this modern, upmarket restaurant with an Italian/French sensibility and first-rate service. Imported cheese and wine are a highlight, and the crispy-based pizzas make a delicious shared snack.

DIZENGOFF   Cafe $
(Map p71; 256 Ponsonby Rd; mains $7-19; ⌚6.30am-5pm; ▢Link) This stylish shoebox crams in a mixed crowd of corporate and fashion types, gay guys, Jewish families, Ponsonby denizens and travellers. Mouth-watering scrambled eggs, tempting counter food, heart-starting coffee, plus a great stack of reading material if you tire of eavesdropping and people-watching.

Newton

COCO'S CANTINA   Italian $$
(Map p64; www.cocoscantina.co.nz; 376 Karanga-hape Rd; mains $27-31; ⌚5pm-late Tue-Sat) Rub shoulders with Auckland's hipsters and foodsters at this bustling cantina where the wait for a table is part of the experience. Propping up the bar is hardly a hardship: the ambience and drinks list see to that. The rustic menu is narrowly focussed, seasonal and invariably delicious.

ALLELUYA   Cafe $
(Map p64; St Kevin's Arcade, Karangahape Rd; mains $10-19; ⌚8am-3pm; 📶📱) To the bohemian denizens of K Rd, Alleluya means good coffee, moreish cakes and lots of vegetarian options. It's situated at the end of the city's hippest arcade, with windows offering a wonderful snapshot of the city skyline.

Kingsland

ATOMIC ROASTERY   Cafe $
(Map p76; www.atomiccoffee.co.nz; 420c New North Rd; snacks $9-10; ⌚8am-3pm) Coffee hounds should follow their noses to this, one of the country's best-known coffee roasters. Tasty accompaniments include pies served in mini-frypans, rolls, salads and cakes.

Mt Eden

MEREDITHS
Modern NZ $$$

(Map p76; 📞09-623 3140; www.merediths.co.nz; 365 Dominion Rd; 6-9 course degustation $90-130; ⏱lunch Fri, dinner Tue-Sat) Dining at Merediths is the culinary equivalent of black-water rafting – tastes surprise you at every turn, you never know what's coming next and you're left with a sense of breathless exhilaration.

Parnell & Newmarket

LA CIGALE
Market, French $$

(Map p75; 📞09-366 9361; www.lacigale.co.nz; 69 St Georges Bay Rd; cafe $8-18, bistro $30; ⏱ market 9am-1.30pm Sat & Sun, cafe 9am-4pm Mon-Fri, bistro dinner Wed-Fri) Catering to Francophiles, foodies and homesick Gauls, this warehouse stocks French imports (wine, cheese, tinned snails etc) and has a patisserie-laden cafe. Yet it's during the weekend farmers markets that this *cigale* (cicada) really chirps, with stalls laden with produce and all manner of tasty eats. Three nights a week the space is converted into a quirky bistro, where mains are ordered three days in advance and served in large communal bowls.

BASQUE KITCHEN BAR
Tapas $$

(Map p72; 📞09-523 1057; 61 Davies Cres; tapas $7-15; ⏱4pm-late Mon-Thu & Sat, noon-late Fri) It doesn't look like much but this dark little bar serves delectable tapas accompanied by a large range of Spanish wine and sherry. The stuffed squid is sublime.

TEED ST LARDER
Cafe $

(Map p72; www.teedstreetlarder.co.nz; 7 Teed St; ⏱8am-4pm) Polished concrete floors, beer crate tables and colourful oversized lampshades set the scene at Newmarket's best cafe. There are plenty of enticing cooked items on the menu but it's hard to go past the delicious sandwiches and tarts beckoning from the counter.

Northcote

ENGINE ROOM
Modern NZ $$$

(📞09-480 9502; www.engineroom.net.nz; 115 Queen St, Northcote; meals $32-35; ⏱dinner Tue-Sat) One of Auckland's best restaurants, this informal eatery serves up lighter-than-air goat's cheese soufflés, inventive whiteboard mains and oh-my-God chocolate truffles. It's worth booking ahead and catching the ferry.

 # Drinking

Auckland's nightlife tends to be quiet during the week – if you're looking for some vital signs, head to Ponsonby Rd, Britomart or the Viaduct. K Rd wakes up late on Friday and Saturday; don't even bother staggering this way before 11pm.

City Centre

HOTEL DE BRETT
Bars

(Map p64; www.hoteldebrett.com; 2 High St; ⏱noon-late) Grab a beer in the cornerbar, a cocktail in the chic art-deco housebar or nab a spot by the fire in the atrium, an interesting covered space fashioned from the alleyway between the old buildings.

OCCIDENTAL
Pub

(Map p64; www.occidentalbar.co.nz; 6 Vulcan Lane; ⏱7.30am-late Mon-Fri, 9am-late Sat & Sun) Belgian beer, Belgian food (plenty of *moules* and *frites* – mussels and chips) and live music are on offer at this historic 1870 pub.

TYLER STREET GARAGE
Bar

(Map p64; www.tylerstreetgarage.co.nz; 120 Quay St, Britomart; ⏱11.30am-late) Just in case you were in any doubt that this was actually a garage, they've left the parking lines painted on the concrete floor. It's still an excellent place to get well lubricated, with on-to-it staff and a little roof terrace facing over the wharves.

Ponsonby & Grey Lynn

GOLDEN DAWN
Bar

(Map p71; http://thegoldendawntavernofpower.blogspot.com/; 134b Ponsonby Rd (enter Richmond Rd); ⏱4pm-late Tue-Sun) Here be where Ponsonby's hipsters hide. Occupying an old shop front and an inviting stables yard, this late-night drinking den regularly hosts random happenings: live bands, burlesque, drag and the like.

Parnell

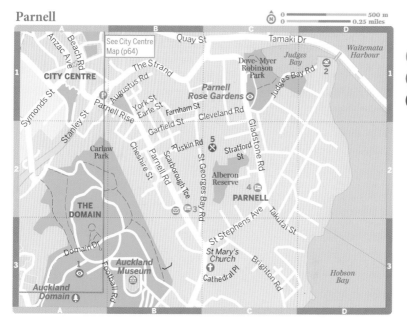

GYPSY TEA ROOM   Cocktail Bar
(Map p71; www.gypsytearoom.co.nz; 455 Richmond Rd; ⏰4-11.30pm Sun-Thu, 3pm-2am Fri & Sat) No one comes here for tea. This cute wine/cocktail bar has dishevelled charm in bucketloads.

PONSONBY SOCIAL CLUB   Bar
(Map p71; www.ponsonbysocialclub.com; 152 Ponsonby Rd; ⏰5pm-late) Half-and-half alleyway and bar, the back end of this long, narrow space heaves on the weekends when the DJs crank out classic funk and hip-hop.

Newton

WINE CELLAR & WHAMMY BAR   Bar
(Map p64; St Kevin's Arcade, K Rd; ⏰5pm-midnight Mon-Thu, 5.30pm-2am Fri & Sat) Secreted down some stairs in an arcade, this is the kind of bar that Buffy the Vampire Slayer would have hung out in on Auckland-based assignments. It's dark, grungy and very cool, with regular live music in the neighbouring Whammy Bar.

GALBRAITH'S ALEHOUSE   Brewery, Pub
(Map p76; www.alehouse.co.nz; 2 Mt Eden Rd; ⏰noon-11pm) Brewing up real ales and

lagers on-site, this English-style pub offers bliss on tap. The backdoor beer garden trumps the brightly lit bar.

Kingsland

WINEHOT   Wine Bar
(Map p76; www.winehot.co.nz; 605 New North Rd, Morningside; ⏰5pm-late Tue-Sat) Behind an unlikely-looking doorway, this tiny

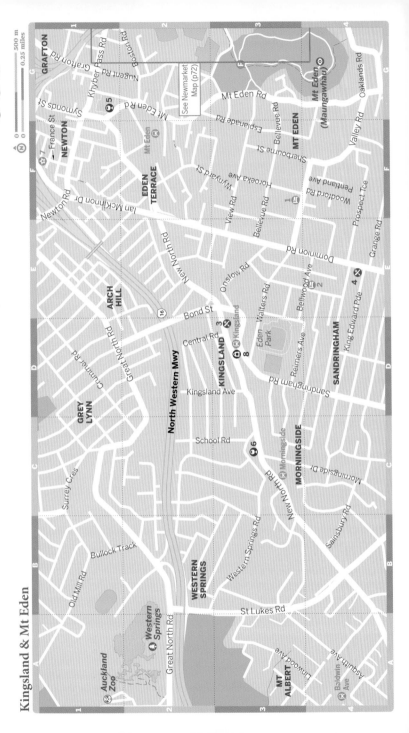

Kingsland & Mt Eden

500 m
0.25 miles

GRAFTON

NEWTON

EDEN
TERRACE

NolsoN Rd

ARCH
HILL

GREY
LYNN

North Western Mwy

KINGSLAND

MORNINGSIDE

WESTERN
SPRINGS

MT
ALBERT

SANDRINGHAM

MT EDEN

Mt Eden
(Maungawhau)

See Newmarket
Map (p72)

Auckland
Zoo

Western
Springs

Great North Rd

St Lukes Rd

Surrey Cres

Bullock Track

Old Mill Rd

Cnuminer Rd

Great North Rd

Ian McKinnon Dr

New North Rd

School Rd

Kingsland Ave

Central Rd

Bond St

Onslow Rd

Eden
Walters Rd

Reimers Ave

Sandringham Rd

New North Rd

Morningside Dr

Sainsbury Rd

Linwood Ave

Asquith Ave

Baldwin Ave

Western Springs Rd

Newton Rd

France St

Symonds St

Khyber Pass Rd

Nugent Rd

Boston Rd

Grafton Rd

Mt Eden Rd

Mt Eden Rd

Esplanade Rd

Bellevue Rd

Sherbourne St

Horoeka Ave

Wynyard St

View Rd

Bellevue Rd

Dominion Rd

Bellwood Ave

King Edward Pde

Prospect Tce

Pentland Ave

Woodford Rd

Grange Rd

Valley Rd

Oaklands Rd

Kingsland

Morningside

Eden Park

7

5

6

3

8

2

4

1

16

Kingsland & Mt Eden

black-painted and chandelier-festooned hideaway serves an impressive selection of both beer and wine, along with delicious platters of French goodies (terrines, pâtés, baguettes).

 Entertainment

The *NZ Herald* has an in-depth run down of the coming week's happenings in its *Time Out* magazine on Thursday and again in its Saturday edition. If you're planning a big night along K Rd, then visit www.kroad.co.nz for a detailed list of bars and clubs.

Live Music & Nightclubs

The Viaduct, Britomart and K Rd are the main late-night hangouts, but some of the Ponsonby Rd bars continue into the wee smalls.

RAKINOS   DJ
(Map p64; www.rakinos.com; Level 1, 35 High St) By day it's a cafe but only head here after dark, when the DJs are spinning old-school hip-hop, funk, Motown and R&B like it's, well, anytime between 1968 and the present. When the mood takes, it's hands-down our favourite place to bust a move.

CASSETTE NINE   Club
(Map p64; www.cassettenine.com; 9 Vulcan Lane, City; ⊙noon-late Tue-Sat) Auckland's most out-there hipsters gravitate to this eccentric bar-club where swishy boys rub shoulders with beardy dudes and girls in very short dresses, and the music ranges from live indie to international DJ sets.

KINGS ARMS TAVERN   Live Music
(Map p76; www.kingsarms.co.nz; 59 France St, Newton) Auckland's leading small venue for local and international bands, which play four or five nights per week. It's a rite of passage if you want to get your band noticed.

Cinema

RIALTO   Cinema
(Map p72; ☎ 09-369 2417; www.rialto.co.nz; 167 Broadway, Newmarket; adult/child $16.50/10) Screens art-house and international films, plus some of the better mainstream fare.

EVENT CINEMAS   Cinema
(Map p64; ☎ 09-369 2400; www.eventcinemas. co.nz; Level 3, 297 Queen St, City; adult/child $16.50/10.50) Part of Aotea Square's futuristic Metro mall, which also includes bars and a food court.

NZ FILM ARCHIVES   Cinema
(Map p64; ☎ 09-379 0688; www.filmarchive.org. nz; 300 Karangahape Rd, Newton; ⊙11am-5pm Mon-Sat) A wonderful resource of more than 150,000 Kiwi feature films, documentaries and TV shows which you can watch for free on a TV screen.

Theatre, Classical Music & Comedy

Auckland's main arts and entertainment complex is grouped around Aotea Sq. Branded the **Edge** (☎ 09-357 3355; www. the-edge.co.nz), it comprises the Town Hall, Civic Theatre and Aotea Centre.

AUCKLAND TOWN HALL
Classical Music

(Map p64; 305 Queen St) This elegant Edwardian venue (1911) hosts concert performances by the likes of the NZ Symphony Orchestra (www.nzso.co.nz) and Auckland Philharmonia (www.apo.co.nz).

AOTEA CENTRE
Theatre

(Map p64; 50 Mayoral Dr) Auckland's largest venue for theatre, dance, ballet and opera, with two main stages: the cavernous ASB Auditorium and the tiny Herald Theatre. NZ Opera (www.nzopera.com) regularly performs here.

CLASSIC COMEDY CLUB
Comedy

(Map p64; 09-373 4321; www.comedy.co.nz; 321 Queen St; tickets $5-27) Auckland's top venue for comedy, with performances from Wednesday through to Saturday.

 ## Shopping

Followers of fashion should head to High St in the city, Newmarket's Teed and Nuffield Sts, and Ponsonby Rd. For second-hand boutiques try K Rd or Ponsonby Rd.

Auckland Volcanic Field

Some cities think they're tough just by living in the shadow of a volcano. Auckland's built on 55 of them and, no, they're not all extinct. The last one to erupt was Rangitoto about 600 years ago and no one can predict when the next eruption will occur. But relax: this has only happened 19 times in the last 20,000 years.

Some of Auckland's volcanoes are cones, some are filled with water and some have been completely quarried away. The most interesting to explore are Mt Eden, One Tree Hill and Rangitoto.

City Centre

REAL GROOVY
Music

(Map p64; www.realgroovy.co.nz; 438 Queen St; ⏰9am-7pm Sat-Wed, 9am-9pm Thu & Fri) A music-lovers' nirvana, this huge store has masses of new, second-hand and rare releases, as well as concert tickets, giant posters, DVDs, books, magazines and clothes.

PAUANESIA
Gifts

(Map p64; www.pauanesia.co.nz; 35 High St; ⏰9:30am-6:30pm Mon-Fri, 10am-4.30pm Sat & Sun) A treasure-trove of homewares and gifts with a pronounced Polynesian influence.

UNITY BOOKS
Books

(Map p64; www.unitybooks.co.nz; 19 High St; ⏰8.30am-7pm Mon-Thu, 8.30am-9pm Fri, 9am-6pm Sat, 11am-6pm Sun) Excellent independent bookshop with knowledgeable staff.

ZAMBESI
Clothing

(Map p64; www.zambesi.co.nz; cnr Vulcan Lane & O'Connell St); Ponsonby (Map p71; 169 Ponsonby Rd); Newmarket (Map p72; 38 Osborne St) The most famous fashion label to come out of NZ, and much sought after by local and international celebs.

Ponsonby & Grey Lynn

MARVEL
Clothing

(Map p71; www.marvelmenswear.co.nz; 143 Ponsonby Rd) Smart, tailored shirts and trousers in interesting fabrics and quirky partywear are the mainstays of this local menswear designer.

TEXAN ART SCHOOLS
Art & Crafts

(Map p71; www.texanartschools.co.nz; 95 Ponsonby Rd; ⏰9.30am-5.30pm); Newmarket (Map p72; 366 Broadway) Despite the name, it's got nothing to do with the Lone Star State. A collective of 200 local artists sell their wares here.

Kingsland

ROYAL JEWELLERY STUDIO
Jewellery

(Map p76; www.royaljewellerystudio.com; 486 New North Rd; ⏰10am-5pm) Displaying interesting work by local artisans, including some beautiful Maori designs,

AMOS CHAPPLE / LONELY PLANET IMAGES ©

Don't Miss **Mt Eden (Maungawhau)**

From the top of Auckland's highest volcanic cone (196m) the entire isthmus and both harbours are laid bare. The symmetrical crater (50m deep) is known as Te Ipu Kai a Mataaho (the Food Bowl of Mataaho, the god of things hidden in the ground) and is highly *tapu* (sacred); don't enter it, but feel free to explore the remainder of the mountain. The remains of *pa* (fortified village) terraces and storage pits are clearly visible.

You can drive to the very top or you can join the legions of fitness freaks jogging or trudging up.

NEED TO KNOW
Map p76; ⊙ road access 7am-11pm

this is a great place to pick up authentic *pounamu* (greenstone) jewellery.

Otara

OTARA MARKET   Market
(Newbury St; ⊙ 6am-noon Sat) Held in the car park between the Manukau Polytech and the Otara town centre, this market has a palpable Polynesian atmosphere and is a good place to stock up on South Pacific food, music and fashions. Take bus 497 from Britomart ($6.80, 50 minutes).

ℹ **Information**

Auckland City Hospital (✆ 09-367 0000; www. adhb.govt.nz; Park Rd, Grafton; ⊙ 24hr) The city's main hospital has a dedicated accident and emergency (A&E) service.

Auckland Domestic Airport i-SITE (✆ 09-256 8480; ⊙ 7am-9pm) In the Air New Zealand terminal.

Auckland International Airport i-SITE (✆ 09-275 6467; ⊙ 24hr) Located on your left as you exit the customs hall.

Below: Native rata blossom; **Right:** Glasshouse in the Wintergarden, Auckland Domain (p63)

(BELOW) PAUL KENNEDY / LONELY PLANET IMAGES ©; (RIGHT) OZIMAGES / ALAMY ©

Auckland Princes Wharf i-SITE (☎ 09-307 0612; www.aucklandnz.com; 137 Quay St; ☺ 9am-5.30pm)

Auckland SkyCity i-SITE (☎ 09-363 7182; www.aucklandnz.com; SkyCity Atrium, cnr Victoria & Federal Sts; ☺ 8am-8pm)

🛈 Getting There & Away

Air

Auckland International Airport (AKL; ☎ 09-275 0789; www.aucklandairport.co.nz; Ray Emery Dr, Mangere) is 21km south of the city centre. It has separate international and domestic terminals, each with a tourist information centre. A free shuttle service operates every 15 minutes (5am to 10.30pm) between the terminals and there's also a signposted footpath (about a 10-minute walk). Domestic airlines flying from Auckland and the destinations they serve:

Air New Zealand (☎ 09-357 3000; www.airnewzealand.co.nz) Flys to Kaitaia, Kerikeri, Whangarei, Hamilton, Tauranga, Whakatane, Gisborne, Rotorua, Taupo, New Plymouth, Napier, Whanganui, Palmerston North, Masterton, Wellington, Nelson, Blenheim, Christchurch, Queenstown and Dunedin.

Jetstar (☎ 0800 800 995; www.jetstar.com) Flies to Wellington, Christchurch, Queenstown and Dunedin.

Bus

Coaches depart from 172 Quay St, opposite the Ferry Building, except for InterCity services, which depart from SkyCity Coach Terminal (☎ 09-913 6220; 102 Hobson St).

Go Kiwi (☎ 07-866 0336; www.go-kiwi.co.nz) Has daily Auckland City–International Airport – Thames–Tairua–Whitianga shuttles.

InterCity (☎ 09-583 5780; www.intercity.co.nz)

Naked Bus (☎ 0900 62533; www.nakedbus.com) Naked Buses travel along SH1 as far north as Kerikeri (four hours) and as far south as Wellington (12 hours), as well as heading to Tauranga (3½ hours) and Napier (12 hours).

Car, Caravan & Campervan

Apex Car Rentals (☎09-307 1063; www.apexrentals.co.nz; 156 Beach Rd)

Budget (☎09-976 2270; www.budget.co.nz; 163 Beach Rd)

Go Rentals (☎09-257 5142; www.gorentals.co.nz; Auckland Airport)

Hertz (☎09-367 6350; www.hertz.co.nz; 154 Victoria St)

Omega (☎09-377 5573; www.omegarentals.com; 75 Beach Rd)

Thrifty (☎09-309 0111; www.thrifty.co.nz; 150 Khyber Pass Rd)

Train

Overlander (☎0800 872 467; www.tranzscenic.co.nz) trains depart from Britomart station (Map p64), the largest underground diesel train station in the world. They depart from Auckland at 7.25am (daily late September to April, Friday to Sunday otherwise) and arrive in Wellington at 7.25pm (the return train from Wellington departs and arrives at the same time). A standard fare to Wellington is $129, but a limited number of discounted seats are available for each journey at $79 and $99 (first-in, first-served).

ℹ Getting Around

To & From the Airport

A taxi between the airport and the city usually costs between $60 and $80, more if you strike traffic snarls.

Airbus Express (☎09-366 6400; www.airbus.co.nz; 1-way/return adult $16/26, child $6/12) Runs between the terminals and the city, every 10 minutes from 7am to 7pm and at least hourly through the night.

Super Shuttle (☎0800 748 885; www.supershuttle.co.nz) This convenient door-to-door shuttle charges $28 for one person heading between the airport and a city hotel; the price increases for outlying suburbs.

Public Transport

The Auckland Council runs the Maxx (☎09-366 6400; www.maxx.co.nz) information service, covering buses, trains and ferries, which has an excellent trip-planning feature. The Discovery Pass provides a day's transport on most trains and buses and on North Shore ferries ($15); buy it on the bus or train or at Fullers offices.

Bus Bus routes spread their tentacles throughout the city and you can purchase a ticket from the driver. Many services terminate around Britomart station. Single-ride fares in the inner city are 50c for an adult and 30c for a child (free for HOP users).

Perhaps the most useful services are the environmentally friendly Link Buses that loop in both directions around three routes (taking in many of the major sights) from 7am to 11pm:

○ City Link (50c, every seven to 10 minutes) – Britomart, Queen St, Karangahape Rd, with some buses connecting to Wynyard Quarter.

○ Inner Link (maximum $1.80, every 10 to 15 minutes) – Queen St, SkyCity, Victoria Park, Ponsonby Rd, Karangahape Rd, Museum, Newmarket, Parnell and Britomart.

○ Outer Link (maximum $3.40, every 15 minutes) – Art Gallery, Ponsonby, Herne Bay, Westmere, MOTAT 2, Pt Chevalier, Mt Albert, St Lukes Mall, Mt Eden, Newmarket, Museum, Parnell, University.

Ferry Auckland's Edwardian baroque Ferry Building (Quay St) sits grandly at the end of Queen St. Fullers (p84) ferries (to Bayswater, Birkenhead, Devonport, Great Barrier Island, Half Moon Bay, Northcote, Motutapu, Rangitoto and Waiheke) leave direcly behind the building, while 360 Discovery (☎0800 360 3472; www.360discovery.co.nz) ferries (to Coromandel, Gulf Harbour, Motuihe, Rotoroa and Tiritiri Matangi) leave from adjacent piers.

Train There are just four train routes: one runs west to Waitakere, one runs south to Onehunga, and two run south to Pukekohe. Services are at least hourly from around 6am to 8pm (later on the weekends). Pay the conductor on the train (one stage $1.70); they'll come to you.

Taxi

Auckland Co-op Taxis (☎09-300 3000; www.3003000.co.nz) is one of the biggest companies. There's a surcharge for transport to and from the airport and cruise ships, and for phone orders.

HAURAKI GULF ISLANDS

The Hauraki Gulf, stretching between Auckland and the Coromandel Peninsula, is dotted with *motu* (islands) and gives the Bay of Islands stiff competition in the beauty stakes. Some islands are only minutes from the city and make excellent day trips: wine-soaked Waiheke and volcanic Rangitoto really shouldn't be missed.

Oneroa Bay, Waiheke Island
DAVID WALL / LONELY PLANET IMAGES ©

Rangitoto Island

Sloping elegantly from the waters of the gulf, 259m **Rangitoto** (www.rangitoto.org), the largest and youngest of Auckland's volcanic cones, provides a picturesque backdrop to all of the city's activities. As recently as 600 years ago it erupted from the sea and was probably active for several years before settling down.

The island makes for a great day trip. Its harsh scoria slopes hold a surprising amount of flora (including the world's largest pohutukawa forest) and there are excellent walks, but you'll need sturdy shoes and plenty of water. The walk to the summit only takes an hour and is rewarded with sublime views.

Fullers (☎09-367 9111; www.fullers.co.nz; adult/child return $27/14) has 20-minute ferry services to Rangitoto from Auckland's Ferry Building (Map p64; three daily on weekdays, four on weekends) and Devonport (two daily). It also offers the **Volcanic Explorer** (adult/child $59/30, incl ferry), a guided tour around the island in a canopied 'road train'.

Waiheke Island

Waiheke is 93 sq km of island bliss only a 35-minute ferry ride from the cenrtral business district. Once they could hardly give land away here; nowadays multimillionaires rub shoulders with the old-time hippies and bohemian artists who gave the island its green repute. While beaches are the big drawcard, wine is a close second.

 Sights & Activities

 Beaches

Waiheke's two best beaches are **Onetangi**, a long stretch of white sand at the centre of the island, and **Palm Beach**, a pretty little horseshoe bay between Oneroa and Onetangi. Both have nudist sections; head west just past some rocks in both cases. **Oneroa** and neighbouring **Little Oneroa** are also excellent, but you'll be sharing the waters with moored yachts in summer.

Wineries

Waiheke's hot, dry microclimate has proved excellent for Bordeaux reds, syrah and some superb rosés. We've also listed some of our favourite vineyards in the Eating section. Pick up the *Waiheke Island of Wine* map for a complete list of vinyards on the island.

GOLDIE VINEYARD   Winery
(www.goldieroom.co.nz; 18 Causeway Rd; tastings $5-10, refundable with purchase; ⏰noon-4pm Wed-Sun Mar-Nov, daily Dec-Feb) Founded as Goldwater Estate in 1978, this is Waiheke's pioneering vineyard. The tasting room sells well-stocked baskets for a picnic among the vines (for two people $55).

STONYRIDGE   Winery
(☎09-372 8822; www.stonyridge.com; 80 Onetangi Rd; tastings per wine $3-15; ⏰11.30am-5pm) Famous organic reds, an atmospheric cafe, tours ($10, 35 minutes, 11.30am Saturday and Sunday) and the occasional dance party.

Art & Culture

The *Waiheke Art Map* brochure, free from the i-SITE, lists 37 galleries and craft stores.

ARTWORKS COMPLEX   Arts Centre
(2 Korora Rd; @ 🛜) The Artworks complex houses a **community theatre** (☎09-372 2941; www.artworkstheatre.org.nz), an **art-house cinema** (☎09-372 4240; www.wicc.co.nz; adult/child $14/7), an attention-grabbing **art gallery** (☎09-372 9907; www.waihekeartgallery.org.nz; admission free; ⏰10am-4pm) and **Whittaker's Musical Museum** (☎09-372 5573; www.musical-museum.org; adult/child $5/free; ⏰1-4pm), a collection of antique concert instruments.

STONY BATTER HISTORIC RESERVE   Historic Site
(www.fortstonybatter.org.nz; Stony Batter Rd; adult/child $8/5; ⏰10am-3.30pm) At the bottom end of the island, Stony Batter has WWII tunnels and gun emplacements

that were built in 1941 to defend Auckland's harbour. Bring a torch and cash.

CONNELLS BAY
Sculpture Garden

(☎09-372 8957; www.connellsbay.co.nz; Cowes Bay Rd; adult/child $30/15; ⊗by appointment, late Oct to late Apr) A pricey but excellent private sculpture park featuring a stellar roster of NZ artists. Admission is by way of a two-hour guided tour; book ahead.

Walks

Ask at the i-SITE about the island's beautiful coastal walks (ranging from one to three hours) and the 3km Cross Island Walkway (from Onetangi to Rocky Bay).

Kayaking

ROSS ADVENTURES
Kayaking

(☎09-372 5550; www.kayakwaiheke.co.nz; Matiatia beach; half-/full-day trips $85/145, per hr hire from $25) It's the fervently held opinion of Ross that Waiheke offers kayaking every bit as good as the legendary Abel Tasman National Park.

Tours

ANANDA TOURS
Wine, Food

(☎09-372 7530; www.ananda.co.nz) Offers a gourmet wine and food tour ($110) and a wine connoisseur's tour ($210). Small-group, informal tours can be customised, including visits to artists' studios.

FULLERS
Wine, Food

(☎09-367 9111; www.fullers.co.nz) Runs a Wine On Waiheke Tour (adult $115, 4½ hours, departs Auckland 1pm) that visits three of the island's top wineries and includes a platter of nibbles. Taste Of Waiheke (adult $125, 5½ hours, departs Auckland 11am) also includes three wineries plus an olive grove and light lunch. There's also a 1½-hour Explorer Tour (adult/child $49/25, departs Auckland 10am, 11am and noon). All prices include the ferry and an all-day bus pass.

Eating

🍴 TE WHAU
Winery $$$

(☎09-372 7191; www.tewhau.com; 218 Te Whau Dr; mains $42-44; ⊗lunch Fri-Sun, dinner Sat, extended Dec-Feb) Perched on the end of Te Whau peninsula, this winery restaurant has exceptional views, food and service, and one of the finest wine lists you'll see in the country. Try its own impressive Bordeaux blends, merlot, chardonnay and rosé for $3 per taste (11am to 5pm).

DRAGONFIRED
Pizzeria $

(Little Oneroa Beach; mains $8-12; ⊗11am-8pm; 🍴) Specialising in what it describes as 'artisan woodfired food', this black caravan by the beach serves the three Ps: pizza, polenta plates and pocket bread. It's easily the best place for cheap eats on the island.

🍴 CABLE BAY
Winery $$$

(☎09-372 5889; www.cablebayvineyards. co.nz; 12 Nick Johnstone Dr; mains $42-45; ⊗lunch daily, dinner Thu-Sun, extended Dec-Feb) Impressive ubermodern architecture, sculpture and beautiful views set the scene for this acclaimed restaurant. The food is sublime but if the budget won't stretch to a meal, stop in for a wine tasting (from $8) or a snack on the terrace.

ℹ Information

Waiheke Island i-SITE (☎09-372 1234; www. waihekenz.com; 118 Ocean View Rd; ⊗9am-5pm) As well as the very helpful main office, there's a (usually unstaffed) counter in the ferry terminal at Matiatia Wharf.

ℹ Getting There & Away

360 Discovery (Map p64; ☎0800 360 3472; www.360discovery.co.nz) You can pick up the 360 Discovery tourist ferry at Orapiu on its journey between Auckland and Coromandel Town. However Orapiu is quite remote and not served by buses.

Fullers (☎09-367 9111; www.fullers.co.nz; return adult/child $35/18; ⊗5.20am-11.45pm Mon-Fri, 6.25am-11.45pm Sat, 7am-9.30pm Sun) Has

BLAINE HARRINGTON III / CORBIS ©

frequent passenger ferries from Auckland to Matiatia Wharf (on the hour from 9am to 5pm), some via Devonport.

ℹ Getting Around

Bike

Waiheke Bike Hire (☎ 09-372 7937; Matiatia Wharf) Hires mountain bikes (half/full day $25/35) from its base near the wharf and at the Oneroa i-SITE.

Bus

The island has regular bus services, starting from Matiatia Wharf and heading through Oneroa (adult/child $1.50/80c, five minutes) on their way to all the main settlements, as far west as Onetangi (adult/child $4.20/2.40, 30 minutes); see Maxx (☎ 09-366 6400; www.maxx.co.nz) for timetables. A day pass (adult/child $8.20/5) is available from the Fullers counter at Matiatia Wharf.

Car, Motorbike & Scooter

Waiheke Auto Rentals (☎ 09-372 8998; www.waihekerentals.co.nz; Matiatia Wharf; per calendar day car or scooter from $59, motorbike or 4WD from $79) Excess $1500, dropping to $1000 if you're over 25 years old. There's an additional charge of 65c per kilometre for cars or 4WDs.

Taxi

Waiheke Independent Taxis (☎ 0800 300 372)

WEST AUCKLAND

West Auckland epitomises rugged: wild black-sand beaches, bush-shrouded ranges, and mullet-haired, black-T-shirt-wearing 'Westies'. The latter is just one of several stereotypes of the area's denizens. Others include the back-to-nature hippie, the eccentric bohemian artist and the dope-smoking surfer dude, all attracted to a simple life at the edge of the bush.

Titirangi

This little village marks the end of Auckland's suburban sprawl and is a good place to spot all of the stereotypes mentioned above over a caffe latte, fine wine or cold beer. Once home to NZ's greatest modern painter, Colin McCahon, there remains an artsy feel to the place.

It's a mark of the esteem in which Colin McCahon is held that the house he lived and painted in during the 1950s, **McCahon House** (www.mccahonhouse.org.nz; 67 Otitori Bay Rd; admission $5; ⏱10am-2pm Wed, Sat & Sun), has been opened to the public as a minimuseum.

Piha

If you notice an Auckland surfer dude with a faraway look, chances are they're daydreaming about Piha... or just stoned. This beautifully rugged, iron-sand beach has long been a favourite for refugees from the city's stresses – whether for day trips, weekend teenage parties or family holidays.

Although Piha is popular, it's also incredibly dangerous, with wild surf and strong undercurrents; so much so that it's spawned its own popular reality TV show, *Piha Rescue*.

There's no public transport to Piha, but **NZ Surf'n'Snow Tours** (☎09-828 0426; www.newzealandsurftours.com; 1-way $25, return

trip incl surfing gear $99) provides shuttles when the surf's up.

COROMANDEL PENINSULA

ℹ Getting There & Around

AIR

Sunair (☎07-575 7799; www.sunair.co.nz) Twice-daily flights to Whitianga from Auckland and Great Barrier Island, and weekday flights to Whitianga from Hamilton, Rotorua and Tauranga.

BOAT

360 Discovery (☎0800 360 3472; www.360discovery.co.nz) Operates ferries to/from Auckland (one-way/return $55/88, two hours) via Orapiu on Waiheke Island (one-way/return $44/77, 70 minutes), five times per week (daily in summer). The boats dock at Hannafords Wharf, Te Kouma, where free buses shuttle passengers the 10km into Coromandel Town. It makes a great day trip from Auckland (same-day return $69), and there's a day-tour option that includes a hop-on, hop-off bus (adult/child $94/57).

BUS

Go Kiwi (☎07-866 0336; www.go-kiwi.co.nz) Has daily Auckland City–International Airport–Thames–Tairua–Whitianga shuttles year-round, with a connection to Opoutere and Whangamata.

InterCity (www.intercity.co.nz) Has two routes to/from the peninsula: Auckland–Thames–Paeroa–Waihi–Tauranga and Hamilton–Te Aroha–Paeroa–Thames–Coromandel Town. Local routes include Thames–Coromandel Town–Whitianga and Whitianga–Tairua–Thames.

Piha Beach
OLIVER STREWE / LONELY PLANET IMAGES ©

Detour:
Karekare

Few stretches of sand have more personality than Karekare. Wild and gorgeously undeveloped, this famous beach has been the setting for onscreen moments both high- and lowbrow, from Oscar-winner *The Piano* to *Xena, Warrior Princess*.

Karekare rates as one of the most dangerous beaches in the country, with strong surf and ever-present rips, so don't even think about swimming unless the beach is being patrolled by lifeguards (usually only in summer). Pearl Jam singer Eddie Vedder nearly drowned here while visiting Neil Finn's Karekare pad.

To get here take Scenic Dr and Piha Rd until you reach the well-signposted turn-off to Karekare Rd.

Naked Bus (www.nakedbus.com) Buses on the Auckland–Tauranga–Mt Maunganui–Rotorua–Gisborne route stop at Ngatea, where local associate Tairua Bus Company continues on to Whitianga.

Tairua Bus Company (07-864 7194; www.tairuabus.co.nz) As well as local buses on the Thames–Tairua–Hahei–Whitianga–Coromandel Town route, TBC has a Hamilton–Cambridge–Te Aroha–Thames–Tairua service.

CAR

Car is the only option for accessing some of the more remote areas, but be careful to check hire agreements as there are plenty of gravel roads and a few streams to ford.

Thames

Dinky wooden buildings from the 19th-century gold rush still dominate Thames, but grizzly prospectors have long been replaced by alternative lifestylers. If you're a vegetarian ecowarrior you'll feel right at home.

 Sights & Activities

GOLDMINE EXPERIENCE　　　　Mine
(www.goldmine-experience.co.nz; cnr Moanataiari Rd & Pollen St; adult/child $15/5; 10am-4pm daily Jan-Mar, 10am-1pm Apr & May, Sep-Dec) Walk through a mine tunnel, watch a stamper battery crush rock, learn about the history of the Cornish miners and try your hand at panning for gold ($2 extra).

EYEZ OPEN　　　　Cycling
(07-868 9018; www.eyezopen.co.nz; 1- to 4-day tours $150-770) Rents out bikes (per day $30) and organises small-group cycling tours of the peninsula.

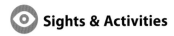 **Eating**

ROCCO　　　　Modern NZ $$
(07-868 8641; 109 Sealey St; mains $23-34; dinner Tue-Sun) Housed in one of Thames' gorgeous kauri villas, Rocco serves tapas and more substantial mains, making good use of local ingredients such as mussels and fish.

NAKONTONG　　　　Thai $$
(07-868 6821; 728 Pollen St; mains $16-20; lunch Mon-Fri, dinner daily;) The most popular restaurant in town by a country mile. Although the bright lighting may not induce romance, the tangy Thai dishes will provide a warm glow.

Information

Thames i-SITE (07-868 7284; www.thamesinfo.co.nz; 206 Pollen St; 9am-5pm)

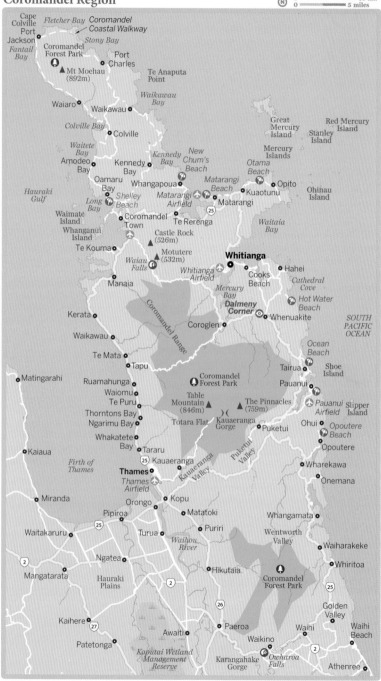

Coromandel Town

Even more crammed with heritage buildings than Thames, Coromandel Town is a thoroughly quaint little place. Its natty cafes, interesting art stores, excellent sleeping options and delicious smoked mussels could keep you here longer than you expected.

Sights & Activities

COROMANDEL GOLDFIELD CENTRE & STAMPER BATTERY   Historic Building
(07-866 8758; 360 Buffalo Rd; adult/child $10/5) The rock-crushing machine clatters into life during the informative one-hour tours of this 1899 plant; call ahead for times. You can also try panning for gold ($5). Outside of the tours it's worth stopping for a gander at NZ's largest working waterwheel.

DRIVING CREEK RAILWAY & POTTERIES   Narrow-Gauge Railway
(07-866 8703; www.drivingcreekrailway.co.nz; 380 Driving Creek Rd; adult/child $25/10; ⏱ departures 10.15am & 2pm) A lifelong labour of love for its conservationist owner, this unique train runs up steep grades, across four trestle bridges, along two spirals and a double switchback, and through two tunnels, finishing at the 'Eye-full Tower'.

COROMANDEL KAYAK ADVENTURES   Kayaking
(07-866 7466; www.kayakadventures.co.nz) Offers paddle-powered tours ranging from half-day ecotours (for one/two/three/four paddlers $200/220/270/360) to fishing trips (half/full day $200/385). It also rents kayaks (per hour/day from $25/65).

Sleeping

LITTLE FARM   Apartments $$
(07-866 8427; www.thelittlefarmcoromandel.co.nz; 750 Tiki Rd; r $115-130; 🔊) Overlooking a private wetland reserve at the rear of a fair-dinkum farm, these three comfortable units offer plenty of peace and quiet. The largest has a full kitchen and superb sunset views.

GREEN HOUSE   B&B $$
(07-866 7303; www.greenhousebandb.co.nz; 505 Tiki Rd; r $150-165; @🔊) Good old-fashioned hospitality and smartly furnished rooms are on offer here. The downstairs room opens onto the host's lounge, so it's worth paying $15 more for an upstairs room with a view.

JACARANDA LODGE   B&B $$
(07-866 8002; www.jacarandalodge.co.nz; 3195 Tiki Rd; s $80, d $135-165; 🔊) Located among 6 hectares of farmland and rose gardens, this two-storey cottage offers a bucolic retreat. Some rooms share bathrooms but expect fluffy towels and personalised soap in mini *kete* (woven flax bags).

Eating & Drinking

UMU   Cafe $
(22 Wharf Rd; breakfast $11-18, lunch $12-25, dinner $14-32; ⏱ breakfast, lunch & dinner; 🔊) Umu serves up classy cafe fare, including excellent pizza, mouth-watering counter food (tarts and quiches around $7), superb coffee and tummy-taming breakfasts.

PEPPER TREE   Modern NZ $$
(07-866 8211; www.peppertreerestaurant.co.nz; 31 Kapanga Rd; lunch $22-26, dinner $26-36; ⏱ lunch & dinner; 🔊) C-Town's most upmarket option dishes up generously proportioned meals with particular emphasis on local seafood. On a summer's evening, the courtyard tables under the shady tree are the place to be.

MUSSEL KITCHEN   Seafood $$
(www.musselkitchen.co.nz; cnr SH25 & 309 Rd; mains $15-20; ⏱ lunch daily year-round, dinner Dec-Mar) Designed to look like a historic store, this very cool cafe-bar sits among fields 3km south of town. Mussels are served in a multitude of ways alongside an eclectic globetrotting menu (laksa, barbecued pork ribs, pasta). In summer, the garden bar is irresistible.

Below: Driving Creek Railway (p89); **Right:** Cathedral Cove (p92)
(BELOW) DAVID WALL / LONELY PLANET IMAGES ©; (RIGHT) DAVID WALL / LONELY PLANET IMAGES ©

ⓘ Information

Coromandel Town i-SITE (📞 07-866 8598; www.coromandeltown.co.nz; 355 Kapanga Rd; 🕑 9am-5pm; @)

Whitianga

Whitianga's big attractions are the sandy beaches of Mercury Bay and the diving, boating and kayaking opportunities afforded by the craggy coast and nearby Te Whanganui-A-Hei Marine Reserve. The pretty harbour is a renowned base for game-fishing (especially marlin and tuna, particularly between January and March).

👁 Sights & Activities

BEACHES   Swimming, Walking
Buffalo Beach stretches along Mercury Bay, north of the Harbour. A five-minute passenger ferry ride will take you across the harbour to **Whitianga Rock Scenic & Historical Reserve**, **Flaxmill Bay**, **Shakespeare Cliff Lookout**, **Lonely Bay**, **Cooks Beach** and **Captain Cook's Memorial**, all within walking distance.

LOST SPRING   Spa
(www.thelostspring.co.nz; 121a Cook Dr; per hr/day $28/60; 🕑 11am-6pm Sun-Fri, 11am-8pm Sat) This expensive but intriguing Disney-meets-Rotorua thermal complex comprises a series of hot pools in a lush junglelike setting, complete with an erupting volcano. Yet this is an adult's indulgence (children under 14 not permitted), leaving the grown-ups to marinate themselves in tropical tranquillity, cocktail in hand.

👉 Tours

There are a baffling number of tours to **Te Whanganui-A-Hei Marine Reserve**, where

you'll see interesting rock formations and, if you're lucky, dolphins, fur seals, penguins and orcas.

BANANA BOAT Cruise
(☏07-866 5617; www.whitianga.co.nz/banana boat; rides $10-30; ☉Dec 26-Jan 31) Monkey around in the bay on the bright-yellow (naturally), motorised Banana Boat – or split to Cathedral Cove.

WINDBORNE Sailing
(☏027 475 2411; www.windborne.co.nz; day sail $95) Day sails in a 19m 1928 schooner.

 Eating

CAFE NINA Cafe $
(20 Victoria St; mains $9-19; ☉8am-3pm) Barbecue for breakfast? Why the hell not? Too cool to be constricted to four walls, the kitchen grills bacon and eggs on an outdoor hotplate while the punters spill out onto tables in the park.

SQUIDS Seafood $$
(☏07-867 1710; www.squids.co.nz; 15/1 Black-smith Ln; mains $17-25; ☉lunch & dinner Mon-Sat) On a corner facing the harbour, this informal restaurant offers that rarest of conjunctions: good-value seafood meals in a prime location. If you don't fancy the steamed mussels, smoked seafood platter, chowder or catch of the day, steak's an option.

🛈 **Information**

Whitianga i-SITE (☏07-866 5555; www. whitianga.co.nz; 66 Albert St; internet per 15min $3; ☉9am-5pm Mon-Fri, 9am-4pm Sat & Sun, extended in summer) Information and internet access.

🛈 **Getting There & Around**

Sunair (www.sunair.co.nz) operates flights to Whitianga from Auckland, Great Barrier Island, Hamilton, Rotorua and Tauranga. Bus services are offered by InterCity, Tairua Bus Company and Go Kiwi.

DAVID WALL / LONELY PLANET IMAGES ©

Don't Miss Hot Water Beach

Justifiably famous, Hot Water Beach is quite extraordinary. For two hours either side of low tide, you can access an area of sand in front of a rocky outcrop at the middle of the beach where hot water oozes up from beneath the surface. Bring a spade, dig a hole and voila, you've got a personal spa pool. Surfers stop off before the main beach to access some decent breaks.

Spades ($5) can be hired from the **Hot Water Beach Store** (Pye Pl), which has a cafe attached, while surfboards (per hour $20) and body boards ($15) can be hired from the neighbouring surf shop.

Hahei

A legendary Kiwi beach town, little Hahei balloons to bursting in summer but is nearly abandoned otherwise – apart from the busloads of tourists doing the obligatory stop-off at Cathedral Cove.

 Sights & Activities

CATHEDRAL COVE　　　　Beach
Beautiful Cathedral Cove, with its famous gigantic stone arch and natural waterfall shower, is best enjoyed early or late in the day – avoiding the worst of the hordes.

At the time of research the arch was roped off due to rock falls, but it's still worth taking the coastal walk to the cove regardless.

At the car park, a kilometre north of Hahei, the signs suggest that the walk will take 45 minutes, but anyone who's not on a ventilator will do it in 30. The walk from Hahei Beach to Cathedral Cove takes about 70 minutes.

HAHEI BEACH　　　　Beach
Long, lovely Hahei Beach is made more magical by the view to the craggy islands in the distance.

CATHEDRAL COVE
SEA KAYAKING _Kayaking_

(☎ 07-866 3877; www.seakayaktours.co.nz; 88 Hahei Beach Rd; half/full day $95/150; ⏰ tours 9am & 2pm) Runs guided kayaking trips around the rock arches, caves and islands in the Cathedral Cove area. The Remote Coast Tour heads the other way when conditions permit, visiting caves, blowholes and a long tunnel.

HAHEI EXPLORER _Boat Tour_

(☎ 07-866 3910; www.haheiexplorer.co.nz; adult/child $70/40) Hour-long jetboat rides touring the coast.

 Sleeping & Eating

TATAHI LODGE _Hostel, Motel_ **$**

(☎ 07-866 3992; www.tatahilodge.co.nz; Grange Rd; dm $29, r $86-123, units $150-400; @ 🛜) A wonderful place where backpackers are treated with at least as much care and respect as the lush bromeliad-filled garden. The dorm rooms and excellent communal facilities are just as attractive as the pricier motel units.

 CHURCH _Cottages_ **$$**

(☎ 07-866 3533; www.thechurchhahei.co.nz; 87 Hahei Beach Rd; cottages $135-230; @ 🛜) Set within a subtropical garden, these beautifully kitted-out, rustic timber cottages have plenty of character. The ultracharming wooden church at the top of the drive is Hahei's swankiest eatery (mains $33 to $37), offering an ambitious (if overpriced) menu of adventurous country-style cooking.

❶ Getting There & Around

See p87 for bus connections. In the height of summer the council runs a bus service from the Cooks Beach side of the ferry landing to Hot Water Beach, stopping at Hahei (adult/child $3/2). Another option on the same route is the Cathedral Cove Shuttle.

Rotorua & the Centre

Volcanic activity defines this region, and nowhere is this subterranean sexiness more obvious than in Rotorua. Here the daily business of life goes on among steaming hot springs, explosive geysers, bubbling mud pools and the billows of sulphurous gas responsible for the town's 'unique' eggy smell.

Rotorua is also a stronghold of Maori tradition: check out a power-packed concert performance, chow down at a *hangi* (feast) or learn the techniques behind Maori arts and crafts.

To the south of Auckland, verdant fields fold down into New Zealand's mightiest river, the Waikato, which lends its name to the region. Adrenaline junkies are drawn to the wild surf of Raglan and rough-and-tumble underground pursuits in the extraordinary Waitomo Caves. And the thrills don't stop there. The area around Taupo and Tongariro National Park now rivals Rotorua for daredevil escapades: jetboating, bungy jumping, sky-diving, skiing or just soaking in a thermal pool.

Wai-o-Tapu Thermal Wonderland (p109)

95

Whakaari (White Island; p125)
RICHARD CUMMINS / LONELY PLANET IMAGES ©

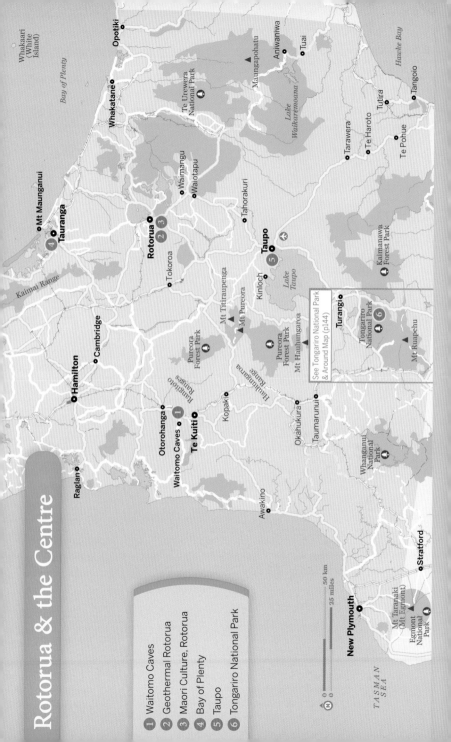

Rotorua & the Centre's Highlights

1

Waitomo Caves

Luring tourists for more than 100 years, Waitomo is an amazing place to explore, above ground or below. Hundreds of caves perforate the region's limestone landscape, and there are plenty of opportunities to delve underground, either on a dry walking tour or a wet, adrenaline-charged subterranean adventure.

Need to Know

BEST TIME TO VISIT Spring: cave water-levels are higher and visitor numbers not-so-high **SHORT ON TIME?** Take a 45-minute Glowworm Cave trip **For further coverage, see p133**

Waitomo Caves Don't Miss List

BY CELINA YAPP, WAITOMO I-SITE

1 GOING UNDERGROUND

There are five dry caving options here, including trips into the Waitomo Glowworm, Aranui and Ruakuri caves (p133). On the way out of the Glowworm Cave you take a boat ride under the glow-worms, which is a really magical experience; tours with Spellbound (p134) also involve a boat ride. The 1.6km-long Ruakuri Cave is the longest dry cave walk here, with some great cave formations. Then there are 10 different adventure caving options, five of which include black-water rafting. You don't have to be young to tackle these: we've booked a 70-year-old granny on one of the shorter trips!

2 LOCAL WALKS

The 5km Waitomo Walkway (p135) starts opposite the i-SITE, and winds through bush and farmland along the Waitomo Stream to the Ruakuri Scenic Reserve. Once you get there (you can also drive), the 1km Ruakuri Loop Walk is one of the best short walks in the country. It's steeped in history and has some amazing natural features: cliffs, outcrops, limestone arches...Take some time to absorb it all.

3 EATING & DRINKING

Waitomo General Store has basic provisions, and it does awesome breakfasts, sausages, pies, homemade burgers...all with organic meat. Huhu (p136) is superb in the evening, or Morepork Cafe (p136) does a mean pizza. Finish up with a beer at Curly's Bar (p136) and soak up some local atmosphere.

4 AROUND WAITOMO

About 25km from Waitomo along Te Anga Rd, follow a track to the 17m-high Mangapohue Natural Bridge (p135) – all that remains of an ancient cave. You can also see fossilised oysters here. A bit further on is the freely accessible Piripiri Cave: grab a torch and go down the steps. A further 2km walk brings you to Marokopa Falls – a magnificent 30m waterfall a short walk from the road.

Left: Mangapohue Natural Bridge

Go Geothermal!

It seems wherever you go in this region there's a bubbling pool of mud, a steaming hot spring, an erupting geyser or a plume of sulphurous gas egging its way into your nostrils. Much of it is stand-and-watch-type stuff (too hot to handle!), but don't miss the chance to immerse yourself in some hot springs: try Rotorua's Polynesian Spa (p111) for starters. Below: Geyser springs at Te Puia (p106)

Maori Rotorua

Rotorua is a great (and very organised) place to engage with Maori culture. Wander around a traditional Maori community at Whakarewarewa Thermal Village (p107; don't miss the geothermally cooked corn!) and catch a cultural performance while you're there. Other established concert-and-*hangi* faves include Tamaki Maori Village and Mitai Maori Village (both p115).

Bay of Plenty

Stretching north from Rotorua are the shimmering surf, sands and laid-back coastal towns of the Bay of Plenty. Swim with dolphins in Tauranga (p119), catch some waves and tramp up Mauao (aka Mt Maunganui, p121) or shake a leg east to sunny, chilled-out Whakatane (p123). And after all that action, there are some brilliant places to eat and drink here. Right: Mt Maunganui (p121)

Sporty Taupo

The main urban hub on the Central Plateau, Taupo (p137) is the North Island's version of Queenstown – a place to challenge your sense of self-preservation with skydiving, bungy jumping, white-water rafting, snow sports, mountain biking... It's a progressive, upbeat sort of town, the adrenaline generated by outdoor activities infusing both culture and commerce. Above: Bungy jumping over the Waikato River (p139)

Tongariro National Park

Want some alpine time? Make a beeline for Tongariro (p143), NZ's oldest national park. Crowned by three snowy volcanic peaks, the park is the North Island's best ski spot, and is also home to the country's best day walk, the Tongariro Alpine Crossing. If you have a bit more time up your sleeve (or in your boots), tackle the longer Tongariro Northern Circuit, which is dotted with volcanic craters and lakes. Above: Crater Lake (p146)

Rotorua & the Centre's Best...

Extreme Action

o **Black-water rafting** (p134) Fast, wet, dark, claustrophobic and subterranean: bring it on!

o **Skydiving** (p139) Cross it off your bucket list in Taupo

o **Zorbing** (p107) Rolling downhill inside a plastic bubble with a bucket of water thrown in...how fabulously illogical!

o **Snowboarding** (p145) Strap a plank to your ankles and career down Mt Ruapehu

Swim Spots

o **Ngarunui Beach** (p131) Lifesaver-patrolled kid-sized surf just south of Raglan

o **Waikite Valley Thermal Pools** (p109) Take a scenic drive south of Rotorua for a soothing geothermal soak

o **Whakaipo Bay** (p137) A 'refreshing' dip in chilly Lake Taupo will banish even the sternest of hangovers

o **Tauranga** (p119) Jump into the ocean and splash around with dolphins off Tauranga

Eat Streets

o **The Strand, Tauranga** (p120) Harbour-side eats, drinks and people-watching

o **Victoria St, Hamilton** (p126) Central Hamilton's hip foodie strip (with the Hood St bars around the corner)

o **Maunganui Rd, Mt Maunganui** (p122) While away a sunny afternoon in the Mount's cafes and bars

o **Tutanekai St, Rotorua** (p113) Cafes and multi-cultural eats down near Lake Rotorua

Need to Know

Small Towns

- **Raglan** (p129) Multicultural surfie nirvana on the wave-washed Waikato coast

- **Mt Maunganui** (p121) Solid surf and a cafe-strewn main street in the shadow of Mauao

- **Waitomo** (p133) It's not just about caves and glow-worms: Waitomo township is a wee winner!

- **Cambridge** (p132) Anglo eccentricities abound in this horse-happy town

ADVANCE PLANNING

- **One month before** Organise any internal flights, car hire, and seats on the *Overlander* train through the North Island's heartland

- **Two weeks before** Book accommodation across the region, a surf lesson in Raglan (if it's summer), and a ski lesson on Mt Ruapehu (if it's winter)

- **One week before** Book a Maori cultural performance in Rotorua, an underground adventure in Waitomo Caves and a skydive in Taupo

RESOURCES

- **Rotorua i-SITE** (www.rotoruanz.com) Info on accommodation, Maori culture, activities and family stuff

- **Tauranga i-SITE** (www.bayofplenty.co.nz) The Bay of Plenty's greatest hits

- **Hamilton i-SITE** (www.hamiltonwaikato.com) The low-down on NZ's fourth-biggest town

- **Great Lake Taupo** (www.greatlaketaupo.com) Deals and info on accommodation, events and things to do around the big lake

- **Visit Ruapehu** (www.visitruapehu.co.nz) Shine a light into NZ's moody, mountainous heart

GETTING AROUND

- **Hire a car** For the freedom to explore

- **Bus** Between the larger towns

- **Walk** Around the Mauao Base Track in Mt Maunganui

- **Cruise** Across Lake Rotorua and Lake Taupo

- **Train** The *Overlander* tracks between Auckland and Wellington via Hamilton, Waitomo Caves and Tongariro National Park

BE FOREWARNED

- **Surf Safety** The beaches around the Bay of Plenty and Raglan on the Waikato coast are fab for surfing, but go easy if you're not strapped to a board: rips and undertows take as much water away from the beach as the waves bring in

Left: Zorbing (p107); **Above:** Surfing at Ngarunui Beach (p131)

Rotorua & the Centre
Itineraries

Go for a roam around the middle of the North Island.
Between Auckland and Wellington you'll discover hip
cities, hippie surf towns, brilliant museums and an
overload of heart-starting activities.

HAMILTON TO TAURANGA

3 DAYS Waikato Wanderings

On the banks of the slow-rolling Waikato River, **(1) Hamilton** doesn't score heavily with scenery or big-ticket attractions, but it's a vibrant little city with great eateries, a beaut museum and an effervescent nocturnal scene. Trundle over the hills to **(2) Raglan**, NZ's quintessential surf town with a string of brilliant breaks south of town (great pub too!). Alternatively, over in **(3) Cambridge** you can express your equine enthusiasms on a horse-stud tour, or swan around the main street in your riding boots and jodhpurs.

Heading south, the amazing **(4) Waitomo Caves** are a must-see (or perhaps, a must-do). Here's your chance to don a wet suit and a helmet with a torch strapped to the top, and hurl yourself into an underground limestone chasm. Brilliant! Or, if adrenaline addiction is less of a motivator, take a tour of a dazzling glow-worm cave or just hang with the locals at the cafe and pub above ground.

To round out your tour, track north to the Bay of Plenty: **(5) Tauranga** is a sophisticated city and NZ's biggest port. And like any port town, the incoming tide keeps things worldly and progressive. Cool down with dinner and drinks on the Strand.

5 DAYS

TAURANGA TO TONGARIRO NATIONAL PARK
Sea to Summit

Seaside **(1) Tauranga** is lovely, but the locals insist **(2) Mt Maunganui** is lovelier (and we tend to agree). This sandy little town is home to a fab surf break, cool cafes and bars, and 'the Mount' itself. Walk around the base of this photogenic hill ('Mauao' in Maori), dappled with red pohutukawa blooms in summer, or hike up its steep slopes.

Track south to **(3) Rotorua**, a Kiwi highlight for any number of reasons: ogle the astonishing geothermal attractions (geysers, mud pools, mineral pools), catch an authentic Maori cultural performance and *hangi,* or blow away the cobwebs with some extreme sports (skydiving, zorbing,

jetboating, white-water rafting...). And don't miss the newly extended Rotorua Museum.

Further south, **(4) Taupo** sits on the shores of NZ's biggest lake. Drop a line in the water, or try kayaking, jetboating or skydiving (with 30,000-plus jumps a year, Taupo bills itself the 'Skydiving Capital of the World'). There are some hip places to eat and drink here, too.

Next stop is **(5) Tongariro National Park**, the oldest national park in NZ, and home to some awesome tramping tracks and winter skiing on Mt Ruapehu.

Mt Ruapehu (p143) erupting
RUTH EASTHAM & MAX PAOLI / LONELY PLANET IMAGES ©

Discover Rotorua & the Centre

Pier on Lake Rotorua
DAVID WALL / LONELY PLANET IMAGES ©

ROTORUA

Catch a whiff of Rotorua's sulphur-rich,
asthmatic airs and you've already got a
taste of NZ's most dynamic thermal area,
home to spurting geysers, steaming hot
springs and exploding mud pools. The
Maori revered this place, naming one of
the most spectacular springs Wai-O-
Tapu (Sacred Waters). Today 35% of the
population is Maori, with their cultural
performances and traditional *hangi*
as big an attraction as the landscape
itself.

 Sights

Rotorua's main drawcard is **Te
Whakarewarewa** (pronounced
'fa-ka-re-wa-re-wa'), a thermal
reserve 3km south of the city
centre. There are more than 500
springs here, including a couple
of famed geysers. The two
main tourist operations are
Te Puia and Whakarewarewa
Thermal Village.

TE PUIA   Geysers
(Map p118; ☎ 0800 837 842,
07-348 9047; www.tepuia.com;
Hemo Rd; tour & daytime cultural
performance adult/child $57.50/29,
tour, evening concert & hangi $110/55,
combination $145/72.50; ⏲8am-6pm
summer, to 5pm winter) The most
famous Te Whakarewarewa spring
is **Pohutu** ('Big Splash' or 'Explosion'),
a geyser which erupts up to 20 times a
day, spurting hot water up to 30m
skyward. You'll know when it's about
to blow because the **Prince of Wales'
Feathers** geyser will start up shortly
before. Both these geysers form part

of Te Puia, the most polished of New Zealand's Maori cultural attractions.

Tours take 90 minutes and depart hourly from 9am (the last tour departs at 4pm in winter, 5pm in summer).

Daytime 45-minute **cultural performances** commence at 10.15am, 12.15pm and 3.15pm; nightly three-hour **Te Po indigenous concerts** and *hangi* feasts start at 6pm.

WHAKAREWAREWA THERMAL VILLAGE   Springs, Village
(Map p118; ☑ 07-349 3463; www.whakarewarewa.com; 17 Tyron St; tour & cultural performance adult/child $30/13) Whakarewarewa Thermal Village, on the eastern side of Te Whakarewarewa, is a living village, where *tangata whenua* (the locals) still reside, as they and their ancestors have for centuries. It's these local villagers who show you around and tell you the stories of their way of life and the significance of the steamy bubbling pools, silica terraces and the geysers that, although inaccessible from the village, are easily viewed from vantage points (the view of Pohutu is just as good from here as it is from Te Puia, and considerably cheaper).

There are **cultural performances** at 11.15am and 2pm, and guided tours at 9am, 10am, 11am, noon, 1pm, 3pm and 4pm.

GOVERNMENT GARDENS   Gardens
The manicured English-style Government Gardens surrounding the Rotorua Museum are pretty-as-a-picture, with roses aplenty, steaming thermal pools dotted about and civilized amenities such as croquet lawns and bowling greens. Also here is the upmarket Polynesian Spa.

LAKE ROTORUA   Lake
Lake Rotorua is the largest of the district's 16 lakes and is – underneath all that water – a spent volcano. Sitting in the lake is Mokoia Island, which has for centuries been occupied by various subtribes of the area.

Activities

Extreme Sports

AGROVENTURES   Extreme Sports
(Map p118; ☑ 0800 949 888, 07-357 4747; www.agroventures.co.nz; Western Rd; ☺9am-5pm) Agroventures is a hive of action, 9km north of Rotorua on SH5 (shuttles available). Prices following are for single activities but combo deals abound.

Start off with the 43m **bungy** (adult/child $95/80) and the **Swoop** (adult/child $49/35), a 130km/h swing that can be enjoyed alone or with friends. If that's not enough, try **Freefall Xtreme** (three minutes, per adult/child $49/35), which simulates skydiving by blasting you 5m into the air on a column of wind.

Also here is the **Shweeb** (adult/child $39/29), a monorail velodrome from which you hang in a clear capsule and pedal yourself along recumbently at speeds of up to 60km/h. Alongside is the **Agrojet** (adult/child $49/35), allegedly NZ's fastest jetboat, splashing around a 1km manmade course.

ZORB   Extreme Sports
(Map p118; ☑0800 227 474, 07-357 5100; www.zorb.com; cnr Western Rd & SH5; rides from $30; ☺9am-5pm, to 7pm Dec-Mar) Across the road from Agroventures is the Zorb – look for the grassy hillside with large, clear, people-filled spheres rolling down it. Your eyes do not deceive you! There are three courses: 150m straight, 180m zigzag or 250m 'Drop'. Do your zorb strapped in and dry, or freestyle with water thrown in.

SKYLINE ROTORUA   Extreme Sports
(Map p118; ☑07-347 0027; www.skyline.co.nz; Fairy Springs Rd; adult/child gondola $25/12.50, luge 3 rides $41/31, sky swing $52/41; ☺9am-11pm) This gondola cruises up Mt Ngongotaha, about 3km north of town, from where you can take in panoramic lake views or ride a speedy luge back down on three different tracks. For even speedier antics, try the Sky Swing, a screaming swoosh through the air at speeds of up to 160km/h.

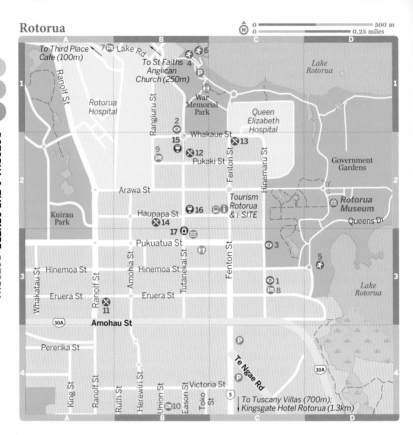

Rotorua

◎ Top Sights
Rotorua Museum.................................... D2

◎ Sights
1 Millennium Hotel Rotorua.................... C3
2 Novotel Rotorua.................................... B1
3 Tamaki Maori Village............................ C3

◎ Activities, Courses & Tours
4 Kawarau Jet... B1
Lakeland Queen.............................(see 6)
Mokoia Island Wai Ora
Experiences.................................(see 4)
5 Polynesian Spa...................................... D3
6 Volcanic Air Safaris............................. B1

◎ Sleeping
7 Jack & Di's Lake View Lodge.................. A1

8 Millennium Hotel C3
9 Regent of Rotorua.................................. B2
10 Six on Union... B4

◎ Eating
11 Bistro 1284.. A3
12 Indian Star... B2
13 Lime Caffeteria...................................... C2
14 Sabroso B2

◎ Drinking
15 Brew B2
16 Pig & Whistle... B2

◎ Shopping
17 Rotorua Night Market........................... B3

Mountain Biking

On the edge of town is the Redwoods Whakarewarewa Forest, home to some of the best **mountain-bike trails** in the country. There are close to 100km of tracks to keep bikers of all skill levels happy for days on end. Pick up a trail map at the forest visitor centre.

MOUNTAIN BIKE ROTORUA   Bicycle Rental
(Map p118; ☏0800 682 768; www.mt brotorua.co.nz; Waipa State Mill Rd; mountain bikes per 2hr/day from $30/45, guided half-/full-day rides $120/185; ◷9am-5pm) This outfit hires out bikes at the Waipa Mill car park entrance to the Redwoods Whakarewarewa Forest, the starting point for the bike trails. There's also a satellite bike depot across the forest at the visitor centre, so you can ride through the trees one-way then catch a shuttle back.

Whitewater Rafting & Sledging

There's plenty of white-water action around Rotorua with the chance to take on the Grade V **Kaituna River**, complete with a startling 7m drop at Okere Falls. Most of these trips take a day. Some companies head further out to the **Rangitaiki River** (Grade III–VI) and **Wairoa River** (Grade V), raftable only when the dam is opened every second Sunday.

RIVER RATS   Rafting, Kayaking
(☏0800 333 900; 07-345 6543; www.riverrats. co.nz) Takes on the Wairoa ($119), Kaituna ($99) and Rangitaiki ($129), and runs a scenic trip on the lower Rangitaiki (Grade II) that is good for youngsters (adult/child $129/100). Kayaking options include freedom hire (per half-/full-day hire from $30/40) and guided four-hour Lake Rotoiti trips ($95).

KAITUNA CASCADES   Rafting, Kayaking
(☏07-345 4199, 0800 524 8862; www.kaituna cascades.co.nz) Does rafting on the Kaituna ($82), Rangitaiki ($118) and Wairoa ($98), plus kayaking options.

♥ **If You Like...**
Geothermal Stuff

If you like Te Puia and Whakarewarewa Thermal Village, we think you'll like these other Rotorua hot spots.

1 HELL'S GATE & WAI ORA SPA
(Map p118; ☏07-345 3151; www.hellsgate.co.nz; SH30; admission adult/child/family $30/15/75, mud bath & spa $105, massage per 30min/1hr $85/135; ◷8.30am-8.30pm) A 10-hectare geothermal reserve with a huge thermal waterfall, Maori carvers and weavers, and the indulgent Wai Ora Spa.

2 WAIMANGU VOLCANIC VALLEY
(Map p118; ☏07-366 6137; www.waimangu.com; 587 Waimangu Rd; walking tour adult/child $34.50/11, boat cruise $42.50/11; ◷8.30am-5pm daily, to 6pm Jan, last admission 3.45pm, or 4.45pm in Jan) Spectacular geothermal features including the 80°C Inferno Crater Lake, and Frying Pan Lake, the largest hot spring in the world.

3 WAI-O-TAPU THERMAL WONDERLAND
(Map p118; ☏07-366 6333; www.waiotapu. co.nz; 201 Waiotapu Loop Rd; admission adult/child/family $32.50/11/80; ◷8.30am-5pm, last admission 3.45pm) The boiling, multihued Champagne Pool, bubbling mud pool, stunning mineral terraces and the Lady Knox Geyser... Amazing!

4 WAIKITE VALLEY THERMAL POOLS
(Map p118; ☏07-333 1861; www.hotpools.co.nz; 648 Waikite Valley Rd; public pools adult/child/family $14/7/35, private pools 40min $18; ◷10am-9pm) Excellent open-air thermal pools, formalised in the 1970s but utilised for centuries before then.

WET 'N' WILD   Rafting
(☏0800 462 7238, 07-348 3191; www.wetnwild rafting.co.nz) Runs trips on the Kaituna ($99), Wairoa ($110) and Mokau ($160), as well as easy-going Rangitaiki trips (adult/child $125/90) and longer trips to remote parts of the Motu and Mohaka (two to five days, $595 to $975).

PAUL KENNEDY / LONELY PLANET IMAGES ©

Don't Miss **Rotorua Museum**

This outstanding museum occupies a grand Tudor-style edifice. It was originally an elegant spa retreat called the Bath House (1908): displays in the former shower rooms give a fascinating insight into some of the eccentric therapies once practised here, including 'electric baths' and the Bergonie Chair.

A gripping 20-minute film on the history of Rotorua, including the Tarawera eruption, runs every 20 minutes from 9am (not for small kids – the seats vibrate and the eruption noises are authentic!). The fabulous new **Don Stafford Wing** houses eight object-rich galleries dedicated to Rotorua's Te Arawa people, featuring woodcarving, flax weaving, jade, interactive audiovisual displays and the stories of the revered WWII 28 Maori Battalion (a movie on the battalion runs every 30 minutes from 9.30am). Also here are two **art galleries** (with air swabbed clean of hydrogen sulphide), and a cool cafe with garden views (although the best view in town can be had from the viewing platform on the roof).

NEED TO KNOW

Map p108; www.rotoruamuseum.co.nz; Queens Dr; adult/child $18/7; ☉9am-5pm Apr-Sep, to 8pm Oct-Mar, tours hourly 10am-4pm plus 5pm Dec-Feb

Kayaking

GO WILD ADVENTURES Kayaking
(☎07-533 2926; www.adventurekayaking.co.nz; hire per day from $50, trips per 2hr/half day/full day from $80/95/140) Takes trips on Lakes Rotorua, Rotoiti, Tarawera and Okataina (from $80/95/140 for two hours/half day/full day); also offers freedom hire (from $50 per day).

KAITUNA KAYAKS Kayaking
(☎07-362 4486; www.kaitunakayaks.com; half-day trip $199, lessons half/full day $199/299) Guided tandem trips and kayaking lessons (cheaper for groups) on the Kaituna.

Thermal Pools & Massage

POLYNESIAN SPA Spa, Massage
(Map p108; ☎07-348 1328; www.polynesianspa.
co.nz; Government Gardens, off Hinemoa St;
adults-only pools $21.50, private pools per half-
hour adult/child from $18.50/6.50, family pool
adult/child/family $14.50/6.50/36, spa therapies
from $85; ◷8am-11pm, spa therapies 9am-8pm)
A bathhouse opened at these Government Gardens springs in 1882, and
people have been swearing by the waters
ever since. There is mineral bathing (36°C
to 42°C) in several picturesque pools at
the lake's edge, marble-lined terraced
pools and a larger, main pool. Also here
are luxury therapies (massage, mud and
beauty treatments) and a cafe.

Horse Trekking

**PARADISE VALLEY
VENTURES** Horse Riding
(☎07-348 3300; www.paradisetreks.co.nz; 679
Paradise Valley Rd; 60/90min $65/90) The
very safe and professional Paradise Valley Ventures takes treks for novices and
experienced riders through a 700-hectare
farm north of Rotorua. Pony rides for the
kids, too.

 # Tours

ELITE ADVENTURES Tour
(☎07-347 8282; www.eliteadventures.co.nz;
tours per half day adult/child from $85/55,
full day from $220/130) Small-group tours
covering a selection of Rotorua's major
cultural and natural highlights.

KAWARAU JET Jetboating
(Map p108; ☎0800 538 7746, 07-343 7600;
www.kjetrotorua.co.nz; lakefront; 30min adult/
child $74/54) Speed things up by jetboat-
ing with Kawarau Jet, which tears around
Lake Rotorua.

LAKELAND QUEEN Cruise
(Map p108; ☎0800 572 784, 07-348 0265; www.
lakelandqueen.com; lakefront) The *Lakeland
Queen* paddlesteamer offers one-hour
breakfast (adult/child $45/22.50),
and longer cruises (lunch $54/27.50;

Saturday-night summer dinner $70/35)
on Lake Rotorua.

**MOKOIA ISLAND WAI ORA
EXPERIENCES** Cruise, Cultural Tour
(Map p108; ☎07-349 0976; www.mokoia
island.co.nz; lakefront; tour adult/child $75/38;
◷9.30am & 2pm daily) This operator takes
visitors out to Mokoia Island, and offers a
2½-hour Ultimate Island Experience tour.
The tour includes wildlife-spotting and
hearing tales of the island, and lets you
dip your toes in the legendary hot pool of
Hinemoa.

ROTORUA DUCK TOURS Tour
(☎07-345 6522; www.rotoruaducktours.co.nz;
adult/child/family $68/38/155; ◷tours 11am,
1pm & 3.30pm Oct-Apr, 11am & 2.15pm May-Sep)
Ninety-minute trips in an amphibious
biofuelled vehicle taking in the major
sites around town and heading out
onto three lakes (Rotorua, Okareka and
Tikitapu). Longer Lake Tarawera trips
also available.

VOLCANIC AIR SAFARIS Scenic Flights
(Map p108; ☎0800 800 848, 07-348 9984;
www.volcanicair.co.nz; lakefront; 6min to 3¼hr
trips $70-862) A variety of floatplane and
helicopter flights taking in Mt Tarawera and surrounding geothermal sites
including Hell's Gate, the Buried Village
and Waimangu Volcanic Valley. A 3¼-
hour White Island/Mt Tarawera trip is
also available.

 # Sleeping

**REGENT
OF ROTORUA** Boutique Hotel $$$
(Map p108; ☎07-348 4079, 0508 734 368; www.
regentrotorua.co.nz; 1191 Pukaki St; d/1br/2br
from $169/239/359; ☎⊠) Wow! It's about
time Rotorua showed some slumbering
style, and the Regent (a renovated 1960s
motel) delivers. 'The '60s was a glamor-
ous time to travel,' say the owners: the de-
cor follows suit, with hip black-and-white
tones, funky mirrors, retro wallpaper and
colourful splashes. There's a pool and res-
taurant too, and the Tutanekai St eateries
are an amble away.

TUSCANY VILLAS
Motel $$

(Map p118; ☏0800 802 050, 07-348 3500; www.tuscanyvillasrotorua.co.nz; 280 Fenton St; d from $145; ☎) With its Italian-inspired architecture and pointy conifers, this family-owned eye-catcher is the pick of the Fenton St motels. It pitches itself perfectly at both the corporate and leisure traveller, who will appreciate the lavish furnishings, multiple TVs, DVD players and huge, deep spa baths.

JACK & DI'S LAKE VIEW LODGE
Lodge $$

(Map p108; ☏0800 522 526; www.jackanddis. co.nz; 21 Lake Rd; s/d/apt from $99/99/199; ☎) Lake views and a central but secluded location make this unique lodge a persuasive option. The upstairs penthouse is ideal for couples, while downstairs is better for families or groups (three bedrooms, three bathrooms). A spa pool, lazy lounge areas and full kitchens add to the appeal.

MILLENNIUM HOTEL
Hotel $$$

(Map p108; ☏07-347 1234; www.millennium rotorua.co.nz; cnr Eruera & Hinemaru Sts; d from $250; @☎☒) The slick Maori-inspired lobby sets the scene for this elegant five-storey motel. Lakefront rooms afford excellent views as does the club lounge, popular with the suits and internationalists swanning about. The poolside *hangi* (p115) is fab, as is the in-house restaurant Nikau.

SIX ON UNION
Motel $$

(Map p108; ☏0800 100 062, 07-347 8062; www. sixonunion.co.nz; 6 Union St; d/f from $105/145; ☎☒) Hanging baskets ahoy! This modest place is an affordable bonanza with pool, spa and small kitchenettes in all units. Rooms are functional, and the new owners (from Yorkshire) keep the swimming-pool area in good nick. It's away from traffic noise, but still an easy walk into town.

Left: Polynesian Spa (p111), overlooking Lake Rotorua; **Below:** Rafting over Okere Falls (p109)

(LEFT) CHRISTIAN KOBER /GETTY IMAGES ©; (BELOW) PAUL KENNEDY / LONELY PLANET IMAGES ©

Eating

THIRD PLACE CAFE
Cafe $$

(off Map p108; ☎07-349 4852; www.thirdplace cafe.co.nz; 36 Lake Rd; mains $15-18; ⏱8am-4pm Mon-Fri, 8am-3pm Sat) A really interesting cafe away from the hubbub, Third Place has leapfrogged into first by our reckoning. All-day breakfast/brunch sidesteps neatly between chicken jambalaya, fish and chips, and an awesome 'mumble jumble' of crushed kumara, green tomatoes and spicy chorizo topped with bacon, poached egg and hollandaise. Hangover? What hangover? Slide into a red-leather couch or score a window seat overlooking Ohinemutu.

LIME CAFFETERIA
Cafe $$

(Map p108; ☎07-350 2033; cnr Fenton & Whakaue Sts; mains $13-24; ⏱7.30am-4.30pm; 🖋) Occupying a quiet corner near the lake, this refreshing cafe is especially good for alfresco breakfasts and dishes with a welcome twist: try the chicken-and-chorizo salad or prawn-and-salmon risotto in lime sauce. It also offers classy counter snacks, excellent coffee and outdoor tables. 'This is the best lunch I've had in ages', says one happy punter.

INDIAN STAR
Indian $$

(Map p108; ☎07-343 6222; www.indianstar. co.nz; 1118 Tutanekai St; mains $14-22; ⏱lunch & dinner; 🖋) This is one of several Indian eateries around town, elevating itself above the competition with immaculate service and marvellous renditions of subcontinental classics. Sizeable portions and good vegetarian selections (try the chickpea masala).

SABROSO
Latin American $$

(Map p108; ☎07-349 0591; www.sabroso.co.nz; 1184 Haupapa St; mains $18-45; ⏱5-10pm Thu-Tue) What a surprise! This modest Latin American cantina – adorned with sombreros, guitars, hessian tablecloths and salt-and-pepper shakers made from

113

Corona bottles – serves adventurous south-of-the-border fare to spice up bland Kiwi palates. The black-bean chilli is a knock-out (as are the margaritas).

BISTRO 1284　　　　Modern NZ $$$
(Map p108; ☎07-346 1284; www.bistro1284. co.nz; 1284 Eruera St; mains $34-39; ☺6pm-late) Definitely one of RotoVegas' fine-dining hot spots, this intimate place (all chocolate and mushroom colours) serves stylish NZ cuisine with an Asian influence. It's an excellent place to sample great local ingredients (the lamb is always good); be sure to leave room for some delectable desserts.

 ## Drinking

BREW　　　　Bar, Craft Beer
(Map p108; ☎07-346 0976; www.brewpub.co.nz; 1103 Tutanekai St; ☺11am-late) Run by the lads from Croucher Brewing Co, Rotorua's best microbrewers, Brew sits in a sunny spot on Rotorua's main eat-street. Sip down a pint of fruity Pale Ale, aromatic

Drunken Hop Bitter or malty Pilsener and wonder how you'll manage a sleep-in tomorrow morning. Good coffee, too.

PIG & WHISTLE　　　Pub, Brewery
(Map p108; ☎07-347 3025; www.pigandwhistle. co.nz; cnr Haupapa & Tutanekai St; ☺11.30am-late) Inside a former police station, this busy microbrewery-pub serves up Swine lager, big-screen TVs, a beer garden and live music Thursday to Saturday, plus simple grub (mains $15 to $30). The menu runs the gamut from crispy pork-belly salad to burgers and vegetarian nachos.

 ## Shopping

ROTORUA NIGHT MARKET　　　Market
(Map p108; ☎07-350 0209; www.rotoruanight market.co.nz; Tutanekai St; ☺4.30pm-late Thu) Tutanekai St is closed off on Thursday nights to allow the Rotorua Night Market to spread its wings. Expect local arts and crafts, souvenirs, cheesy buskers, coffee, wine and plenty of deli-style food stalls for dinner.

 ## Information

Lakes Prime Care (☎07-348 1000; 1165 Tutanekai St; ☺8am-10pm) Urgent medical care.

Rotorua Hospital (☎07-348 1199; www.lakesdhb.govt.nz; Arawa St; ☺24hr) Round-the-clock medical care.

Tourism Rotorua & i-SITE (☎0800 768 678; 07-348 5179; www.rotoruanz.com; 1167 Fenton St; ☺8am-6pm Sep-May, to 5.30pm Jun-Aug) The hub for travel information and bookings, including Department of Conservation (DOC) walks.

Cooking corn in hot springs, Whakare-warewa Thermal Village (p107)

JOHN SONES / LONELY PLANET IMAGES ©

Don't Miss **Maori Concerts & Hangi**

Maori culture is a big-ticket item in Rotorua and, although it is commercialised, it's a great opportunity to learn about the indigenous culture of NZ. The two big activities are concerts and *hangi* feasts, often packaged together in an evening's entertainment featuring the famous *hongi, haka,* and *poi* dances.

An established favourite, **Tamaki Maori Village** does an excellent twilight tour to a *marae* (meeting house) and Maori village 15km south of Rotorua. The experience is hands-on, taking you on an interactive journey through Maori history, arts and customs from pre-European times to the present day. The concert is followed by an impressive *hangi*.

The family-run **Mitai Maori Village** offers a three-hour evening event with a concert, *hangi* and glowworm bushwalk. This can be combined with a tour of Rainbow Springs Kiwi Wildlife Park next door, with coloured nightlights and a walk through the Kiwi enclosure (four hours total, adult/child under nine/child $125/35/65). Pick-ups available.

Aside from these, Te Puia and Whakarewarewa Thermal Village also put on shows. Many of the big hotels, including **Kingsgate Hotel Rotorua**, **Millennium Hotel Rotorua** and **Novotel Rotorua**, also offer Maori concerts and *hangi,* making up for what they lack in ambience with convenience.

NEED TO KNOW

Tamaki Maori Village (Map p108; ☏07-349 2999; www.maoriculture.co.nz; booking office 1220 Hinemaru St; adult/child/family $105/60/250; ⊙tours depart 5pm, 6pm & 7.30pm summer, 6.30pm winter); **Mitai Maori Village** (Map p118; ☏07-343 9132; www.mitai.co.nz; 196 Fairy Springs Rd; adult/child 5-9yr/child 10-15yr/family $107/21/53/279; ⊙6.30pm); **Kingsgate Hotel Rotorua** (Map p118; ☏07-348 0199; www.millenniumhotels.co.nz; 328 Fenton St; concert adult/child $30/15, incl hangi $45/22.50); **Millennium Hotel Rotorua** (Map p108; ☏07-347 1234; www.millenniumrotorua.co.nz; cnr Eruera & Hinemaru Sts; concert adult/child $30/15, incl hangi $70/35); **Novotel Rotorua** (Map p108; ☏07-346 3888; www.novotelrotorua.co.nz; 11 Tutanekai St; concerts adult/child $39/18, incl hangi $59/28)

Also has an exchange bureau, cafe, showers and lockers.

Getting There & Away

Air

Air New Zealand (☎07-343 1100; www.airnewzealand.co.nz; 1267 Tutanekai St; ⊙9am-5pm Mon-Fri) Has direct flights between Rotorua and Auckland, Wellington and Christchurch, plus Sydney (every Tuesday and Saturday).

Qantas also links Auckland with Rotorua.

Bus

All the major bus companies stop outside i-SITE, from where you can arrange bookings.

InterCity (☎09-583 5780; www.intercity.co.nz) destinations include Auckland ($50, 3½ hours, seven daily), Gisborne ($61, 4½ hours, one daily), Hamilton ($32, 1½ hours, five daily), Napier ($53, three hours, three daily), Taupo ($32, one hour, four daily), Tauranga ($30, 1½ hours, three daily), Wellington ($65, eight hours, five daily) and Whakatane ($34, 1½ hours, one daily).

Naked Bus (☎0900 625 33; www.nakedbus.com) services run to the same destinations: Auckland ($19, four hours, six daily), Gisborne ($27, 4¾ hours, one daily), Hamilton ($16, 1½ hours, five daily), Napier ($29, three hours, three daily), Taupo ($15, one hour, two daily), Tauranga ($12, 1½ hours, five daily), Wellington ($36, eight hours, two daily) and Whakatane ($18, 1½ hours, one daily).

Twin City Express (☎0800 422 928; www.baybus.co.nz) buses run twice daily Monday to Friday between Rotorua and Tauranga/Mt Maunganui via Te Puke ($11.60, 1½ hours).

Getting Around

To/From the Airport

Rotorua Airport (☎07-345 8800; www.rotorua-airport.co.nz; SH30) is 10km northeast of town. **Super Shuttle** (☎09-522 5100, 0800 748 885; www.supershuttle.co.nz) offers a door-to-door airport service for $22 for the first person then $6 per additional passenger. A taxi to/from the city centre costs about $25.

Cityride runs a daily airport service ($2.30).

Taxi

Fast Taxis (☎07-348 2444)
Rotorua Taxis (☎07-348 1111)

Redwoods Whakarewarewa Forest

AROUND ROTORUA
Rainbow Springs Kiwi Wildlife Park

About 3km north of central Rotorua, **Rainbow Springs** (Map p118; 0800 724 626; www.rainbowsprings.co.nz; Fairy Springs Rd; 24hr pass adult/child/family $35/22.50/103; 8am-late) is a family-friendly winner. The natural springs here are home to wild trout and eels, which you can peer at through an underwater viewer. There are interpretive walkways, a new 'Big Splash' water ride, and plenty of animals, including tuatara, introduced species (wallabies, rainbow lorikeets) and native birds (kea, kaka and pukeko).

A highlight is the **Kiwi Encounter**, offering a rare peek into the lives of these endangered birds: excellent 30-minute tours have you tiptoeing through incubator and hatchery areas. Also available are joint four-hour **evening tours** (adult/child $125/65) with neighbouring Mitai Maori Village (p115).

Redwoods Whakarewarewa Forest

This magical **forest park** (Map p118; 07-350 0110; www.redwoods.co.nz; Long Mile Rd; gates 5.30am-8.30pm, visitor centre 8.30am-5.30pm) is 3km southeast of town on the Tarawera Rd. It was originally home to more than 170 tree species (a few less now) planted from 1899, to see which could be grown successfully for timber. Radiata pine proved a hit (as evident throughout New Zealand), but it's the mighty Californian redwoods that give the park its grandeur today.

Clearly signposted walking tracks range from a half-hour wander through the Redwood Grove to an enjoyable whole-day route to the Blue and Green Lakes. Most walks start from the **visitor centre** where you can get maps and view displays about the forest. Aside from walking, the park is great for picnics, and is acclaimed for its accessible **mountain biking**. Mountain Bike Rotorua (p109)

If You Like...
Wildlife Parks

If you like Rainbow Springs Kiwi Wildlife Park, we think you'll like these other wildlife encounters.

1 **WINGSPAN BIRDS OF PREY TRUST**
(07-357 4469; www.wingspan.co.nz; 1164 Paradise Valley Rd, Rotorua; adult/child $25/8; 9am-3pm) This organisation is dedicated to conserving three threatened NZ birds: the falcon, hawk and owl. Go in time to see the 2pm flying display.

2 **PARADISE VALLEY SPRINGS**
(07-348 9667; 467 Paradise Valley Rd, Rotorua; www.paradisevalleysprings.co.nz; adult/child $30/15; 8am-5pm) A 6-hectare park with trout, big slippery eels, deer, alpaca, possums and lions.

3 **ALTURA GARDENS & WILDLIFE PARK**
(07-878 5278; www.alturapark.co.nz; 477 Fullerton Rd, Waitomo Caves; adult/child $12/5, horse treks 60/90min $65/80; 9.30am-5pm) At this 2-hectare park you can chat with a cockatoo, outstare a morepork or pat a blue-tongue lizard. Horse treks available.

offers bike hire, across the park off Waipa State Mill Rd.

Te Wairoa

Fifteen kilometres from Rotorua on Tarawera Rd, beyond the pretty Blue and Green Lakes, is the buried village of **Te Wairoa** (Map p118; 07-362 8287; www.buriedvillage.co.nz; 1180 Tarawera Rd; adult/child/family $31/8/62; 9am-5pm Nov-Mar, to 4.30pm Apr-Oct), interred by the eruption of Mt Tarawera in 1886. Te Wairoa was the staging post for travellers coming to see the Pink and White Terraces. Today a museum houses objects dug from the ruins, and guides in period costume escort groups through the excavated sites. There's also a walk to the 30m **Te Wairoa Falls** (not suitable for kids or oldies), and a teahouse if you're feeling more sedate.

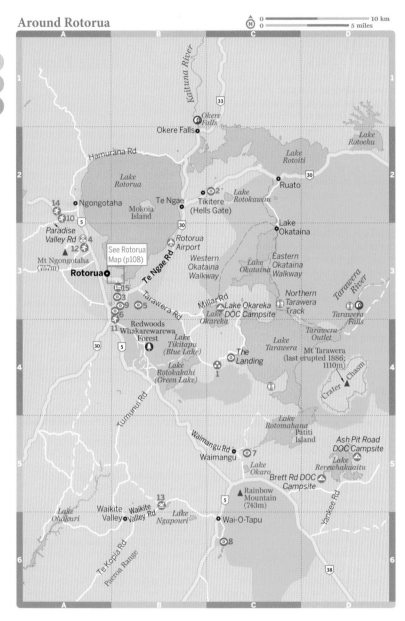

BAY OF PLENTY

The Bay of Plenty stretches along the pohutukawa-studded coast from Waihi Beach to Opotiki and inland as far as the Kaimai Range. This is where New Zealanders have come on holiday for generations, lapping up salt-licked activities and lashings of sunshine.

Around Rotorua

Tauranga

Tauranga (pronounced 'tao-wronger') has been booming since the 1990s and remains one of NZ's fastest-growing cities. It's also NZ's busiest port – with petrol refineries and mountains of coal and lumber – but it's beach-seeking holiday-makers who have seen the old workhorse reborn as a show pony.

 **Sights & Activities**

FREE **TAURANGA ART GALLERY** Gallery
(☎ 07-578 7933; www.artgallery.org.nz; cnr Wharf & Willow Sts; ⊙10am-4.30pm) The Tauranga Art Gallery presents historic and contemporary art, and houses a permanent collection along with frequently changing local and visiting exhibitions. Touring the ground and mezzanine galleries, with a stop to poke your nose into the video cube, will take an hour or so.

ELMS MISSION HOUSE Historic Building
(www.theelms.org.nz; 15 Mission St; house adult/child $5/50c, gardens free; ⊙house 2-4pm Wed, Sat & Sun, gardens 9am-5pm daily) Built in 1847, Elms Mission House is the oldest building in the Bay of Plenty. Furnished in period style, it sits among other well-preserved mission buildings in leafy gardens.

BUTLER'S SWIM WITH DOLPHINS Wildlife Tour
(☎ 0508 288 537, 07-578 3197; www.swimwithdolphins.co.nz; full-day trips adult/child $135/110; ⊙departs Tauranga 9am, Mt Maunganui 9.30am) Even without dolphins (and you're guaranteed of seeing them), these trips are always entertaining, particularly with Cap'n Butler, a real old salt who protested against nuclear testing at Mururoa Atoll.

WAIMARINO ADVENTURE PARK Kayaking, Water Sports
(☎ 07-576 4233, 0800 456 996; www.waimarino.com; 36 Taniwha Pl; kayak tours from $65, kayak hire per hr/day $26/55, park day-pass adult/child $40/32; ⊙10am-6pm Aug-Apr, reduced hours May-Jul) On the banks of the **Wairoa River** 8km west of town, Waimarino offers freedom kayak hire for leisurely paddles along 12km of flat water, and runs self-guided tours further up the river as well as sea kayaking trips. Waimarino also has an adventure park with all kinds of watery distractions: a kayak slide, diving board, rope course, water-walking zorbs, warm pools, and a terrifying human catapult called 'The Blob' – intense!

TAURANGA TANDEM SKYDIVING Skydiving
(☎ 07-576 7990, 0274 968 408; www.tandemskydive.co.nz; 2 Kittyhawk Way; jumps 8000/10,000/12,000ft $269/299/349) Tauranga Tandem Skydiving offers jumps from three different heights, with views of White Island, Mount Ruapehu and the East Cape on the way down.

😴 Sleeping

ROSELANDS MOTEL
Motel $$

(📞0800 363 093, 07-578 2294; www.roselands. co.nz; 21 Brown St; d/ste from $110/135; 📶) Tarted up with splashes of orange paint and new linen, this sweet, old-style motel is in a quiet but central location. Expect roomy units (all with kitchens), friendly first-name-basis hosts and new TVs. Nice one.

HARBOUR CITY MOTOR INN
Motel $$

(📞0800 253 525, 07-571 1435; www.tauranga harbourcity.co.nz; 50 Wharf St; d from $150; 📶) With a winning location right in the middle of town (and with plenty of parking), this newish, lemon-yellow motor inn has all the mod cons. There are spa baths in each room, and friendly staff who can of-fer sound advice on your itinerary.

HOTEL ON DEVONPORT
Hotel $$

(📞07-578 2668; www.hotelondevonport.net. nz; 72 Devonport Rd; d/ste $165/195; @) City-centre Devonport is top of the town, with bay-view rooms, noise-reducing glass, slick interiors and sassy staff, all of which appeal to business travellers and upmarket weekenders. No in-room wi-fi is a surprising downer.

🍴 Eating & Drinking

NAKED GRAPE
Modern NZ, Wine Bar $$

(📞07-579 5555; www.nakedgrape.co.nz; 97 The Strand; breakfast & lunch $9-19, dinner mains $21-32; ⏰breakfast & lunch daily, dinner Mon-Sat) With cheery staff, wine-coloured rugs and lilting jazz, this hip Strand wine bar draws the daytime crowds with pastas, pizzas, salads, good coffee and beaut breakfasts. At night it's moodier, with mains like spice-rubbed salmon with citrus salsa and eggplant parmesan with toasted pinenuts.

MEDITERRANEO CAFÉ
Cafe, Mediterranean $$

(The Med; 📞07-577 0487; www.mediterraneo cafe.co.nz; 62 Devonport Rd; mains $12-19; ⏰7am-4pm Mon-Fri, 7.30am-4pm Sat, 8am-4pm Sun; 📶) A hot spot reeling with regulars enjoying terrific coffee and scrump-tious all-day breakfasts. Order from the blackboard or from the cabinet crammed with sandwiches, salads, flans and cakes. Lunchtime crowds can be frantic (but the chicken salad is worth it). Plenty of gluten-free and vegetarian options.

SOMERSET COTTAGE
Modern NZ $$$

(📞07-576 6889; www.somersetcottage.co.nz; 30 Bethlehem Rd; mains $38-40; ⏰lunch Wed-Fri, dinner Tue-Sun) The most awarded restau-rant in the bay, Somerset Cottage is a simple-but-elegant venue for that special treat. The food is highly seasonal, made from the best NZ ingredients, impres-sively executed without being too fussy. Standout dishes include blue cheese soufflé, duck with coconut kumara and the famous liquorice ice cream.

ℹ️ Information

Tauranga i-SITE (📞07-578 8103; www. bayofplentynz.com; 95 Willow St; ⏰8.30am-5.30pm Mon-Fri, 9am-5pm Sat & Sun, reduced winter hours; 📶) Local tourist information, bookings, InterCity bus tickets and DOC maps.

ℹ️ Getting There & Away

Air

Air New Zealand (📞07-577 7300; www. airnewzealand.co.nz; cnr Devonport Rd & Elizabeth St; ⏰9am-5pm Mon-Fri) Has daily direct flights to Auckland, Wellington and Christchurch, with connections to other centres.

Bus

Twin City Express (📞0800 422 928; www. baybus.co.nz) buses run twice daily Monday to Friday between Tauranga/Mt Maunganui and Rotorua via Te Puke ($11.60, 1½ hours).

InterCity (📞09-583 5780; www.intercity. co.nz) tickets and timetables are available at the i-SITE. Destinations include Auckland ($46, four hours, seven daily), Hamilton ($33, two hours, two daily), Rotorua ($30, 1½ hours, two daily), Taupo ($50, three hours, three daily) and Wellington ($59, nine hours, four daily).

Naked Bus (📞0900 625 33; www.nakedbus.com) offers substantial fare savings when you book in advance. Destinations include Auckland ($15, 4¼ hours, three daily), Hamilton ($20, two hours, three daily), Napier ($50, 4½ hours, two daily), Rotorua ($9, 1½ hours, three to five daily), Taupo ($25, 2½ hours, two daily), Wellington ($27, nine hours, one daily) and Whakatane ($19, 6¼ hours, one daily).

SHUTTLE BUSES

A couple of companies can pick you up at Auckland or Rotorua airports and bus you to Tauranga (though you'll pay upwards of $100 for the privilege):

Apollo Connect Shuttles (📞07-218 0791; www.taurangashuttles.co.nz)

Luxury Airport Shuttles (📞07-547 4444, 0800 454 678; www.luxuryairportshuttles.co.nz)

Mt Maunganui

Named after the hulking 232m hill that punctuates the sandy peninsula occupied by the township, up-tempo Mt Maunganui is often just called 'the Mount', or Mauao, which translates as 'caught by the light of day'. Sun-seekers flock to the Mount in summer, supplied by an increasing number of 10-storey apartment towers studding the spit.

◎ Sights & Activities

The Mount lays claim to being NZ's premier **surfing** city (they teach surfing at high school!). You can carve up the waves at **Mount Beach**, which has lovely beach breaks and a 100m artificial surf reef not far offshore. Learn-to-surf operators include **Hibiscus** (📞07-575 3792, 027 279 9687; www.surfschool.co.nz; 2hr/2-day lesson $80/150)

and **Mount Surf Shop** (📞07-575 9133; www.mountsurfshop.co.nz; 96 Maunganui Rd; rental per day wet suit/body board/surf board $15/20/30, 2hr lesson $80).

MAUAO   Mountain, Lookout
Mauao (Mt Maunganui) itself can be explored via walking trails that wind around it and leading up to the summit. The **summit walk** takes about 40 minutes and gets steep near the top. You can also climb around the rocks on **Moturiki Island**, which adjoins the peninsula. The island and the base of Mauao also make up the **Mauao base track** (3½km, 45 minutes), wandering through magical groves of pohutukawa trees that bloom between November and January. Pick up a map at the i-SITE.

MOUNT MAUNGANUI HOT SALTWATER POOLS   Swimming
(📞08 575 0868; www.tcal.co.nz; 9 Adams Ave; adult/child/family $11/8/30; ⏰6am-10pm Mon-Sat, 8am-10pm Sun) If you've worked up a sweat walking up and down Mauao, take a long relaxing soak at these hot water pools at the foot of the hill.

Mt Maunganui
RICHARD CUMMINS / LONELY PLANET IMAGES ©

The Wreck of the Rena

On 5 October 2011, the 47,000 tonne cargo ship MV *Rena*, loaded with 1368 containers and 1900 tonnes of fuel oil, ran aground on Astrolabe Reef 22km off the coast of Mt Maunganui. Pitched acutely on the reef with a rupturing hull, the *Rena* stared spilling oil into the sea and shedding containers from its deck.

Salvors eventually managed to remove most of the oil, but on 7 January 2012 the *Rena* finally broke in two, spilling remnant oil and dozens more containers into the sea. With refloating the ship no longer an option, will the two halves be dragged off the rocks and scuttled? A future dive site for the Bay of Plenty? Whatever happens, the grounding has been an environmental and economic disaster, with beaches soiled, fisheries ravaged and countless local businesses suffering. Time will tell how far reparations – both environmental and fiscal – will go towards improving the situation.

Sleeping

MISSION BELLE MOTEL Motel $$
(☎ 0800 202 434, 07-575 2578; www.missionbelle motel.co.nz; cnr Victoria Rd & Pacific Ave; d/f from $125/185; ☎) With a distinctly Tex-Mex exterior (like something out of an old Clint Eastwood movie), this family-run motel goes all modern inside, with especially good two-storey family rooms with large bathtubs, plus sheltered barbecue and courtyard areas.

BELLE MER Hotel, Apartments $$$
(☎ 0800 100 235, 07-575 0011; www.bellemer. co.nz; 53 Marine Pde; apt $190-450; ☎ ☎) A classy beachside complex of one-, two- and three-bedroom apartments, some with sea-view balconies and others opening onto private courtyards (though you'll more likely head for the resort-style pool terrace). Rooms are tastefully decorated in warm tones with soft edges, and have everything you need for longer stays, with proper working kitchens and laundries.

Eating & Drinking

SLOWFISH Cafe $
(☎ 07-574 2949; www.slowfish.co.nz; shop 5, Twin Towers, Marine Pde; meals $7-20; ⏰ 6.30am-4.30pm; ☎) There's no slacking-off in the kitchen of this award-winning, eco-aware cafe, which promotes the art of savouring fine, locally sourced food. It's a hit with the crowds: you'll have to crowbar yourself in the door or pounce on any available alfresco seat, but it's worth it for its free-range eggs and ham, Greek salads and divine counter selection, all made on-site.

MAJOR TOM'S Bar, Live Music
(☎ 07-574 5880; www.majortomsbar.com; 297 Maunganui Rd; ⏰ 4pm-late Tue-Sat; ☎) A funky little bar set back from the main drag in what looks like Major Tom's spaceship. Inside it's all kooky antiques, vintage couches, dangling inverted desk lamps and prints of Elvis, the *Mona Lisa* and (of course) David Bowie. Fabulous streetside terrace, cool tunes, free wi-fi and occasional live acts. Everybody sing: 'Planet Earth is blue, and there's nothing I can do...'

ℹ Information

Mt Maunganui i-SITE (☎ 07-575 5099; www.bayofplentynz.com; Salisbury Ave; ⏰ 9am-5pm) The friendly Mt Maunganui i-SITE can assist with information and bookings (transport, accommodation and activities).

Getting There & Away

Bus

InterCity (☎09-583 5780, www.intercity.co.nz) and Naked Bus (☎0900 625 33; www.nakedbus. com) services visiting Tauranga also stop at Mt Maunganui, with fares similar to those to/from Tauranga. All buses depart from the i-SITE.

Whakatane

A true pohutukawa paradise, Whakatane (pronounced Fokka-*tar*-nay) sits on a natural harbour at the mouth of the river of the same name. It's the hub of the Rangitaiki agricultural district, but there's much more to Whakatane than farming – blissful beaches, a sunny main-street vibe and volcanic Whakaari (White Island) for starters.

Sights & Activities

FREE TE MANUKA TUTAHI
MARAE   Marae
(☎0800 464 284, 07- 307 0760; www.mataatua. com; Muriwai Dr) The centrepiece of this brand-new Ngati Awa *marae* isn't new: **Mataatua Wharenui** (The House That Came Home) is a fantastically carved 1875 meeting house. In 1879 it was dismantled and shipped to Sydney, before spending 71 years in the Otago Museum from 1925. It was returned to the Ngati Awa in 1996. Still a work-in-progress when we visited, a cultural experience for visitors is planned: until its completion you can enter the *marae* and check out Mataatua Wharenui from the outside (behave respectfully).

FREE WHAKATANE MUSEUM
& GALLERY   Museum, Gallery
(☎07-306 0505; www.whakatanemuseum. org.nz; 51-55 Boon St; ⏰10am-4.30pm Mon-Fri, 11am-3pm Sat & Sun) This impressive regional museum has artfully presented displays on early Maori and European settlement in the area: *taonga* (treasures) of local Maori trace their lineage back to the Mataatua waka. The art gallery presents a varied program of NZ and international exhibitions. Rumoured to be relocating: call the number if it's not where it's supposed to be.

Dolphin spotting (p124), near Whakatane

DOLPHIN & WHALE
NATURE RUSH
Wildlife Tour

(07-308 9588, 0800 733 529; www.dolphin andwhale.co.nz; 15 The Strand; trips adult/ child $80/50; ⏰10am daily Jan-Mar) Run by White Island Tours, Dolphin & Whale Nature Rush offers a two-hour trip out to Motuhora (Whale Island), with plenty of critter-spotting in the sea and sky.

🛏 Sleeping

CAPTAIN'S CABIN
Apartment $$

(☎07-308 5719; www.captainscabin.co.nz; 23 Muriwai Dr; r $125, 2 nights or more per night $115) In a serene part of town with sparkling harbour views, this homely self-contained unit is the perfect spot if you're hanging round for a few days. A cosy living area cleverly combines bedroom, lounge, kitchen and dining, with a second smaller room and bijou bathroom – all sweetly decorated along nautical lines. Sleeps three (extra person $25).

WHITE ISLAND
RENDEZVOUS
Hotel, B&B $$

(☎0800 242 299, 07-308 9588; www.white island.co.nz; The Strand; d from $140, 2br apt per 4 people $260, B&B $190; 🛜) An immaculate 26-room complex run by the on-the-ball White Island Tour people. Lots of balcony and deck space for inhaling the sea air, while interiors are decked out with timber floors for a nautical vibe. Deluxe rooms come with spas; disabled-access facilities available. The B&B next door includes cooked breakfast.

🍴 Eating

WHARF SHED
International $$

(0800 863 463, 07-308 5698; www.wharfshed. com; The Wharf, The Strand; mains $18-32; ⏰lunch & dinner) An award winner for beef and lamb but famous for fish (this is Whakatane, after all), which includes locally bagged crayfish, corpulent mussels and fresh Pacific oysters. Right on the waterside with alfresco dining on balmy evenings.

ROQUETTE
Modern NZ $$

(☎07-307 0722; www.roquette-restaurant. co.nz; 23 Quay St; mains $20-35; ⏰10am-late Mon-Sat) A modern waterside restaurant on the ground floor of one of the town's big new apartment buildings,

Whakaari (White Island)

Detour:
Whakaari (White Island)

New Zealand's most active volcano (it last erupted in 2000) lies 49km off the Whakatane coast. The island is dramatic, with hot water hissing and steaming from vents over most of the crater floor. Temperatures of 600°C to 800°C have been recorded.

Fixed-wing air operators run flyover tours only, while boat and helicopter tours will usually include a walking tour around the island including a visit to the ruins of the sulphur-mining factory – an interesting story in itself.

The only official boat trip to Whakaari (on board the good ship *Pee Jay*) is offered by **White Island Tours** (☏0800 733 529, 07-308 9588; www.whiteisland.co.nz; 15 The Strand; 6hr tours adult/child $185/120, per person 20 Dec-20 Jan $185; ⌚departures btwn 7-9.15am, plus 12.30pm Dec-Feb), with dolphin-spotting en route and a 90-minute tour of the island.

Vulcan Helicopters (☏0800 804 354, 07-308 4188; www.vulcanheli.co.nz; flights per person from $550) can take you on a two-hour scenic flight to Whakaari that includes a one-hour guided walk on the volcano.

For fixed-wing scenic flights over Whakaari, with lots of photo opportunities, try **White Island Flights** (☏0800 944 834; www.whiteislandflights. co.nz; flights per person $220).

sunny Roquette serves up refreshing Mediterranean-influenced fare with lots of summery salads, risotto and fish dishes. Laid-back tunes, lots of glass and mosaics, good coffee and sexy staff to boot. Try the haloumi salad niçoise.

ℹ Information

Whakatane i-SITE (☏0800 924 528, 07-306 2030; www.whakatane.com; cnr Quay St & Kakahoroa Dr; ⌚8am-5pm Mon-Fri, 10am-4pm Sat & Sun; @ 🛜) Free internet access (including 24-hour wi-fi on the terrace outside the building), tour bookings, accommodation and general enquiries for DOC.

ℹ Getting There & Around

Air

Air New Zealand (☏07-308 8397, 0800 737 000; www.airnewzealand.com) has daily flights linking Whakatane to Auckland, with connections to other centres.

Bus

InterCity buses stop outside the i-SITE and connect Whakatane with Rotorua ($34, 1½ hours, one daily), Tauranga ($27, three hours, one daily) and Gisborne ($45, three hours, one daily), with onward connections. Tauranga services run via Rotorua; Gisborne buses travel via Opotiki.

Naked Bus services run to Auckland ($33, 5½ hours, one daily), Gisborne ($20, 3¼ hours, one daily), Hamilton ($20, 1½ hours, one daily), Rotorua ($15, 1½ hours, one daily), Tauranga ($18, 5½ hours, one daily) and Wellington ($70, 10½ hours, one daily). Book in advance for big savings.

WAIKATO
Hamilton

Landlocked cities in an island nation are never going to have the glamorous appeal of their coastal cousins. However, something strange has happened in Hamilton recently. The city's main street has sprouted a sophisticated and vibrant stretch of bars and eateries around Hood and Victoria Sts that – on the weekend at least – leave Auckland's Viaduct Harbour for dead in the boozy fun stakes.

 Sights

WAIKATO MUSEUM — Museum
(☑07-838 6606; www.waikatomuseum.co.nz; 1 Grantham St; free-$6.50; ☺10am-4.30pm) The excellent Waikato Museum has five main areas: an art gallery; interactive science galleries; Tainui galleries housing Maori treasures, including the magnificently carved *waka taua* (war canoe), *Te Winika*; a Hamilton history exhibition entitled 'Never a Dull Moment'; and a Waikato River exhibition.

FREE HAMILTON GARDENS — Gardens
(☑07-838 6782; www.hamiltongardens.co.nz; Cobham Dr; ☺enclosed sector 7am-6pm, info centre 9am-5pm) More than 50 hectares southeast of the centre, Hamilton Gardens incorporates a large park, cafe, restaurant and extravagant **themed enclosed gardens**.

RIFF RAFF — Monument
(www.riffraffstatue.org; Victoria St; ☺) One of Hamilton's more unusual public artworks is a life-size **statue** of *Rocky Horror Picture Show* writer Richard O'Brien aka Riff Raff, the time-warping alien from the planet Transsexual. It looks over a small park on the site of the former Embassy Theatre where O'Brien worked as a hairdresser, though it's hard to imagine 1960s Hamilton inspired the tale of bisexual alien decadence.

 **Activities**

CITY BRIDGES RIVER TOUR — Kayaking
(☑07-847 5565; www.canoeandkayak.co.nz; ☺2hr trip adult/child $60/35) An interesting way to check out the Waikato River is on a City Bridges River Tour, a guided kayak tour through the city. No experience necessary; group of three people minimum.

CRUISE WAIKATO — Boat Tour
(☑0508 426 458; www.cruise-waikato.co.nz; Memorial Park Jetty, Memorial Dr; cruises from adult/child $25/10) Runs a range of river cruises, focussed variously on sightseeing, history or your belly (coffee and muffins, *hangis* or picnics).

KIWI BALLOON COMPANY — Ballooning
(☑021 912 679, 07-843 8538; www.kiwiballoon company.co.nz; flights per person $320) A hotair ballon flight is a lovely (and surprisingly un-scary) option for gazing down on the lush Waikato countryside. The whole experience takes about four hours and includes a champagne breakfast and an hour's flying time.

 Sleeping

ANGLESEA MOTEL — Motel $$
(☑0800 426 453, 07-834 0010; www.anglesea motel.co.nz; 36 Liverpool St; d/2-/3-br units from $138/265/310; @☺☺) Getting great feedback from travellers and a far preferable option to anything on Ulster St's 'motel row', the Anglesea has plenty of space, friendly managers, free wi-fi, pool and squash and tennis courts, and not un-stylish decor.

CITY CENTRE B&B — B&B $$
(☑07-838 1671; www.citycentrebnb.co.nz; 3 Anglesea St; s & d $90-150, extra person $30; @☺☺) At the quiet riverside end of a central city street (five-minutes' walk to the Victoria/Hood St action), this sparkling self-contained apartment opens on to a swimming pool. There's also a bedroom available in a wing of the main house. Self-catering breakfast provided.

 Eating

RIVER KITCHEN — Cafe $
(☑07-839 2906; www.theriverkitchen.co.nz; 237 Victoria St; mains $7-16; ☺7am-4pm Mon-Fri, 8am-4pm Sat & Sun; ☺) Hip River Kitchen does things with simple style: cakes, gourmet breakfasts and fresh seasonal lunches (angle for the salmon hash),

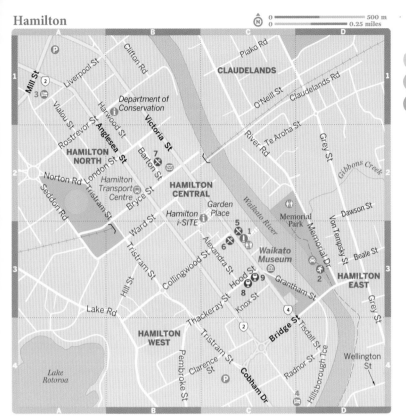

and a barista who knows his beans. It's the kind of place you visit for breakfast, come back to for lunch, then consider for breakfast the next day.

CHIM-CHOO-REE Modern NZ $$$
(📞07-839 4329; www.chimchooree.co.nz; 244 Victoria St; 🕓4.30pm-late Tue-Sat) Hip little Chim-Choo-Ree, with its clackety bent-wood chairs, concrete floor and kitsch art, is a casual fine-dining option that's been wowing the critics. Launch into the five-course tasting menu ($125/85 with/without wine), or mains like manuka-smoked eel and Canadian scallops with apple-and-radish salad.

ROCKET COFFEE Cafe $
(📞07-839 6422; www.rocketcoffee.co.nz; 302 Barton St; coffees from $4; 🕓8am-4pm Mon-Fri) Duck down Barton St for what some

Hamilton

Below: Hamilton Gardens (p126); **Right:** Raglan
(BELOW) DANITA DELIMONT / GETTY IMAGES ©; (RIGHT) MICAH WRIGHT /LONELY PLANET IMAGES ©

locals say is the coolest thing about Hamilton (other than perhaps the Riff Raff statue). Rocket Coffee is a warehouse-like bean barn, roasting on-site and enticing caffeine fiends to its communal table strewn with newspapers.

 **Drinking**

HOUSE ON HOOD Bar, Craft Beer
(☑07-839 2727; www.houseonhood.co.nz; 27 Hood St) A crafty place for a craft beer or four, House on Hood is a boozy 1915 barn with lots of drops to slake your thirst. Beer specials, tasting sessions and meal deals abound, plus Saturday night bands and Sunday afternoon DJs. Beer nirvana.

LIMESTONE Bar
(☑07-981 1363; 15 Hood St; ⊘8pm-late Wed, 7pm-late Thu & Sat, 4pm-late Fri)

Inside Hamilton's oldest stone buliding – a former haberdashery – moody Limestone offers respite from Hood St's otherwise raucous boozy nocturnal parade. An excellent range of bottled beers, a dazzling selection of spirits, and cigars to puff street-side.

ℹ️ **Information**

Hamilton i-SITE (☑07-958 5960; www. visithamilton.co.nz; 5 Garden Pl; ⊘9am-5pm Mon-Fri, 9.30am-3.30pm Sat & Sun; 📶) Accommodation, activities and transport bookings, plus free wi-fi right across Garden Pl.

ℹ️ **Getting There & Away**

Air

Air New Zealand (☑0800 737 000; www. airnewzealand.co.nz) Regular direct flights from Hamilton to Auckland, Christchurch, Palmerston North and Wellington.

Bus

All buses arrive and depart from the Hamilton Transport Centre (✆07-834 3457; www. hamilton.co.nz; cnr Anglesea & Bryce Sts).

InterCity (✆09-583 5780; www.intercity. co.nz) services numerous destinations: Auckland ($30, two hours, 11 daily), Cambridge ($23, 25 minutes, nine daily), Rotorua ($35, 1½ hours, five daily), and Wellington ($55, five hours, three daily).

Naked Bus (✆0900 625 33; www.nakedbus. com) services run to the following destinations (among many others): Auckland ($15, two hours, five daily), Cambridge ($20, 30 minutes, five to seven daily), Rotorua ($15, 1½ hours, four to five daily), and Wellington ($40, 9½ hours, one to two daily).

Train

Hamilton is on the Overlander (✆0800 872 467; www.tranzscenic.co.nz; ☺daily Oct-Apr, Fri-Sun May-Sep) route between Auckland ($68, 2½ hours) and Wellington ($129, 9½ hours) via Otorohanga ($68, 45 minutes).

Getting Around

To & From Airport

Hamilton International Airport (HIA; ✆07-848 9027; www.hamiltonairport.co.nz; Airport Rd) is 12km south of the city. The Super Shuttle (✆07-843 7778, 0800 748 885; www.supershuttle. co.nz; 1-way $23) offers a door-to-door service into the city. A taxi costs around $40.

Bus

Hamilton's Busit! (✆0800 4287 5463; www. busit.co.nz) network services the city-centre and suburbs daily from around 7am to 7.30pm (later on Friday). Busit! also runs a free bus 51 CBD shuttle looping around Victoria, Liverpool, Anglesea and Bridge Sts every 10 minutes (7am to 6pm weekdays, 9am to 1pm Saturday).

Raglan

Laid-back Raglan may well be NZ's perfect **surfing** town. It's small enough to have escaped mass development, but it's big enough to exhibit signs of life (good

129

eateries and a bar that attracts big-name bands in summer).

The nearby surf spots – Indicators, Whale Bay and Manu Bay – are internationally famous for their point breaks.

Sights & Activities

RAGLAN SURF SCHOOL   Surfing
(☎07-825 7873; www.raglansurfingschool. co.nz; 5b Whaanga Rd, Whale Bay; 3hr lesson incl transport $89) The instructors at Raglan Surf School pride themselves on getting 95% of first-timers standing during their first lesson. Experienced wave hounds can rent surfboards (from $20 per hour), body boards ($5 per hour) and wet suits ($5 per hour).

RAGLAN KAYAK   Kayaking
(☎07-825 8862; www.raglaneco.co.nz; Wallis St Wharf) Raglan Harbour is great for kayaking. This outfit runs three-hour guided harbour paddles (per person $70) and rents out single/double kayaks (per half day $40/60).

RAGLAN BONE CARVING STUDIO   Bone Carving
(☎07-825 7147, 021 0223 7233; www.maori bonecarving.com; 6 Snowden Pl; workshops $69, private lessons per hour $25) Carve your own bone pendant (now *that's* a souvenir!) with Rangi Wills, a reformed 'troubled teenager' who found out he was actually really good at carving things.

Sleeping

RAGLAN BACKPACKERS   Hostel $
(☎07-825 0515; www.raglanbackpackers.co.nz; 6 Wi Neera St; dm $28, s $57, tw & d $72-82; @) This chipper, purpose-built hostel has a laid-back holiday-house mood. It's right on the water, with sea views from some rooms, and the rest arranged around a garden courtyard. There's also a separate self-contained wing sleeping eight.

JOURNEY'S END B&B   B&B, Apartment $$
(☎07-825 6727; www.raglanaccommodation. co.nz; 49 Lily St; s/d $100/140, exclusive use $200; ☎) These two attractive en-suite rooms share a central modern lounge

Learning to surf at Raglan

with a kitchenette and a lovely deck overlooking the wharf and harbour. You can book out the whole place, or just one of the rooms and risk/enjoy the (potential) company of others.

RAGLAN SUNSET MOTEL Motel $$
(☎07-825 0050; www.raglansunsetmotel.co.nz; 7 Bankart St; d $140; 🛜) A block back from the action, this two-storey motel with faux shutters randomly adhered to the facade isn't quite a decade old. The owners also have self-contained apartments (doubles from $150) and beach houses (four people from $250) available around town.

 Eating

THE SHACK Cafe, International $
(☎07-825 0027; 19 Bow St; mains $9-18; ⏲8.30am-5pm Sat-Thu, 8.30am-late Fri; 🍴) Burgers, wraps, veggie fry-ups, curries, Middle Eastern plates, tapas... This shack ain't no hack when it comes to cafe fare. A longboard strapped to the wall, wobbly old floorboards, up-tempo tunes and international staff complete a very pretty picture.

ORCA Cafe, Modern NZ $$
(☎07-825 6543; www.orcarestaurant.co.nz; 2 Wallis St; breakfast $11-18, mains $19-33; ⏲9am-late Mon-Fri, 8am-late Sat & Sun) A day started at an Orca window seat, looking over the water, with some eggs Benedict and a superb coffee is a day well launched. Come back in the evening for rabbit pie, wine-appreciation nights and live music.

ℹ **Information**

Raglan Information Centre (☎07-825 0556; www.raglan.org.nz; 13 Wainui Rd; ⏲9.30am-5pm Mon-Fri, 10am-5pm Sat, 10am-4pm Sun) DOC brochures plus information about local accommodation and activities. Reduced winter hours.

ℹ **Getting There & Around**

Waikato District Council's **Busit!** (☎0800 4287 5463; www.busit.co.nz; adult/child $7.50/3.80) heads between Hamilton and Raglan (one hour)

three times daily on weekdays and twice daily on weekends.

Raglan Scenic Tours (☎07-825 0507; www.raglanscenictours.co.nz) runs a Raglan–Hamilton shuttle bus (one-way $30). **Raglan Shuttle Co** (☎0800 8873 2 7873; www.raglanshuttle.co.nz) offers a parallel service.

South of Raglan
Ngarunui Beach

About 5km south of town Ngarunui Beach is a great for grommets learning to surf. On the clifftop is the club for the volunteer lifeguards who patrol part of the black-sand beach from late October until April.

Manu Bay

Another 2.5km journey will bring you to Manu Bay, a legendary **surf spot** said to have the longest left-hand break in the world. The elongated uniform waves are created by the angle at which the Tasman Sea swell meets the coastline (it works best in a southwesterly swell).

The hippie hilltop hostel **Solscape** (☎07-825 8268; www.solscape.co.nz; 611 Wainui Rd, Manu Bay; sites from $16, caboose dm/d $26/68, tepees per person $34, cottages d $115-180; @🛜) has dorms in old train carriages. The ultimate greenie experience: chilling in a tepee (surprisingly comfortable, available December to April), surrounded by native bush, knowing that you're completely 'off grid' – while not sacrificing hot showers (solar) and decent toilets (composting). Self-contained sea-view cottages (try for the 'Ivy'), surf lessons and massage ($65 per hour) complete a bewildering array of services.

Whale Bay

Whale Bay is a renowned **surf spot** 1km west of Manu Bay and is usually less crowded. But from the bottom of Calvert Rd you have to clamber 600m over the rocks to get to the break.

Deep in native bush **Karioi Lodge** (☎07-825 7873; www.karioilodge.co.nz; 5b Whaanga Rd, Whale Bay; dm/d $30/75; @🛜) offers a sauna, a flying fox, mountain

Ngarunui Beach (p131)

OLIVER STREWE / LONELY PLANET IMAGES ©

bikes, bush and beach walks, sustainable gardening, tree planting and the Raglan Surf School. There are no en suites but the rooms are clean and cosy. These friendly folks also run **Sleeping Lady Lodging** (📞07-825 7873; www.sleepinglady. co.nz; 5b Whaanga Rd, Whale Bay; lodges $165-570), a collection of seven luxury self-contained houses nearby, all with ocean views.

Cambridge

The name says it all. Despite the rambunctious Waikato River looking nothing like the Cam, the good people of Cambridge have done all they can to assume an air of English gentility: village greens, avenues of deciduous trees, faux-Tudor houses.

Famous for breeding and training thoroughbred horses, you can almost smell the wealth along the main street.

 **Sights & Activities**

FREE **CAMBRIDGE MUSEUM**   Museum
(📞07-827 3319; www.cambridgemuseum. org.nz; 24 Victoria St; ⏰10am-4pm) In the former courthouse, quirky old Cambridge Museum has plenty of pioneer relics, a military history room and small display on the local Te Totara Pa before it was wiped out. Oh, and there's a stuffed kiwi if you haven't managed to see a real one.

CAMBRIDGE THOROUGHBRED LODGE   Guided Tour
(📞07-827 8118; www.cambridgethoroughbred lodge.co.nz; tours adult/child $12/5, show $12/5; ⏰tours 10am-2pm by arrangement) Cambridge Thoroughbred Lodge, 6km south of town on SH1, is a top-notch horse stud. Book ahead for 90-minute tours, or 'NZ Horse Magic' shows which get galloping several times a week.

 Sleeping & Eating

CAMBRIDGE COACH HOUSE   B&B, Cabin $$
(📞07-823 7922; www.cambridgecoachhouse. co.nz; 3796 Cambridge Rd, Leamington; d from $150, cottage $195) This farmhouse accommodation is a wee bit chintzy, but if you can forgive a chandelier or two it's a beaut spot to chill-out, in the thick of Waikato's bucolic splendour. There's a double in the

main building, two separate doubles and a self-contained cottage.

CAMBRIDGE MEWS Motel **$$**
(07-827 7166; www.cambridgemews.co.nz; 20 Hamilton Rd; 1/2br from $155/190;) All the spacious units in this chalet-style motel have double spa baths, decent kitchens and are immaculately maintained. The architect did a great job...the interior decorator less so.

RED CHERRY Cafe **$$**
(07-823 1515; www.redcherrycoffee.co.nz; cnr SH1 & Forrest Rd; meals $7-21; breakfast & lunch daily, dinner Fri & Sat;) With happy staff and a cherry-red espresso machine working overtime, barn-like Red Cherry offers coffee roasted on-site, delicious counter food and impressive cooked breakfasts (oh those corn-and-pumpkin fritters). It's Cambridge's best cafe by a country mile (it's actually a country 4km out of Cambridge on the way to Hamilton).

NASH Modern NZ **$$$**
(07-827 5596; www.thenash.net.nz; 47 Alpha St; mains $28-34; lunch & dinner) All white/grey/black paint and dapper, quick-moving staff, sexy Nash has transformed the old National Hotel, sinking the boot firmly into Ye Olde Cambridge. We hope it lasts: the braised lamb shoulder with roast-garlic mash and pea puree is sublime, and the streetside terrace is just made for quaffing Kiwi wine.

❶ Information

Cambridge i-SITE (07-823 3456; www.cambridge.co.nz; cnr Victoria & Queen Sts; 9am-5pm Mon-Fri, 10am-4pm Sat & Sun;) Free *Heritage & Tree Trail* and town maps, and internet access.

❶ Getting There & Away

Being on SH1, 22km southeast of Hamilton, Cambridge is well connected by bus. Environment Waikato's Busit! (0800 4287 5463; www.busit.co.nz) heads to Hamilton ($6.40, 40 minutes, seven/three daily weekdays/weekends).

InterCity (09-583 5780; www.intercity.co.nz) services numerous destinations including Auckland ($40, 2½ hours, 12 daily), Hamilton ($24, 30 minutes, eight daily), Rotorua ($33, 1¼ hours, five daily) and Wellington ($75, 8½ hours, three daily).

Naked Bus (0900 625 33; www.nakedbus.com) services the same destinations: Auckland ($13, 2½ hours, six daily), Hamilton ($20, 30 minutes, five daily), Rotorua ($15, 1¼ hours, four daily) and Wellington ($33, 9½ hours, one daily).

THE KING COUNTRY
Waitomo Caves

Even if damp, dark tunnels sound like your idea of hell, take a chill pill and head to Waitomo anyway. The limestone caves and glowing bugs here are one of the North Island's premier attractions.

 Sights

WAITOMO CAVES Caves
(07-878 8228, 0800 456 922; www.waitomo.com; visitor centre 39 Waitomo Caves Rd; Triple Cave Combo adult/child $89/39; visitor centre 9am-5pm) The big three caves are all operated by the same company, based at the snazzy new **Waitomo Glowworm Caves Visitor Centre** which incorporates a cafe and theatre.

The guided tour of the **Glowworm Cave** (39 Waitomo Caves Rd; tours adult/child $48/21; 45min tours every 30min 9am-5pm) which is behind the visitor centre, leads past impressive stalactites and stalagmites into a large cavern known as the Cathedral. The highlight comes at the tour's end when you board a boat and swing off onto the river. As your eyes grow accustomed to the dark you'll see a Milky Way of little lights surrounding you – these are the glowworms.

Three kilometres west from the Glowworm Cave is **Aranui Cave** (07-878 8228, 0800 456 922; 39 Waitomo Caves Rd; tours adult/child $46/21; 45min tours 10am, 11am, 1pm, 2pm, 3pm). This cave is dry (hence no glowworms) but compensates with an incredible array of limestone formations.

Thousands of tiny 'straw' stalactites hang from the ceiling.

Culturally significant **Ruakuri Cave** (📞0800 782 587, 07-878 6219; 585 Waitomo Caves Rd; tours adult/child $67/26; ⏰2hr tours 9am, 10am, 11.30am, 12.30pm, 1.30pm, 2.30pm & 3pm) has an impressive 15m-high spiral staircase, removing the need to trample through the Maori burial site at the cave entrance (as tourists did for 84 years). Tours lead through 1.6km of the 7.5km system, taking in vast caverns with glowworms, subterranean streams and waterfalls, and intricate limestone structures.

 Activities

Underground

LEGENDARY BLACK WATER RAFTING COMPANY   Adventure Tour
(📞0800 782 5874; www.waitomo.com; 585 Waitomo Caves Rd; ⏰Black Labyrinth tour 9am, 10.30am, noon, 1.30pm & 3pm, Black Abyss tour 9am & 2pm) These guys run a Black Labyrinth tour (three hours, $119), which involves floating in a wet suit on an inner

tube down a river that flows through Ruakuri Cave. The highlight is leaping off a small waterfall and then floating through a long, glowworm-covered passage. The Black Abyss tour (five hours, $220) is more adventurous and includes a 35m abseil into Ruakuri Cave, a flying fox and more glowworms and tubing. Minimum ages apply.

SPELLBOUND   Caving, Guided Tour
(📞0800 773 552, 07-878 7622; www.glowworm.co.nz; 10 Waitomo Caves Rd; tours adult/child $70/25; ⏰3hr tours 10am, 11am, 2pm & 3pm) Spellbound is a good option if you don't want to get wet, are more interested in glowworms than an 'action' experience, and want to avoid the big groups in the main caves. Small-group tours access parts of the heavily glowworm-dappled Mangawhitiakau cave system, 12km south of Waitomo (...and you still get to ride in a raft!).

WAITOMO ADVENTURES   Caving, Adventure Tour
(📞07-878 7788, 0800 924 866; www.waitomo.co.nz; 654 Waitomo Caves Rd) Waitomo Adventures offers five different cave adventures, with discounts for various combos and for

Descending for a Black Abyss tour, Waitomo Caves

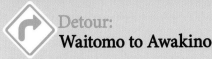

Detour:
Waitomo to Awakino

This obscure route, heading west of Waitomo on Te Anga Rd, is the definition of off-the-beaten-track.

The **Mangapohue Natural Bridge Scenic Reserve**, 26km west of Waitomo, is a 5.5-hectare reserve with a giant natural limestone arch. It's a five-minute walk to the arch on a wheelchair-accessible pathway.

About 4km further west is **Piripiri Caves Scenic Reserve**, where a five-minute walk leads to a large cave containing fossils of giant oysters. Steps wind down into the gloom...

The impressively tiered, 30m **Marokopa Falls** are 32km west of Waitomo. A short track (15 minutes return) from the road leads to the bottom of the falls.

advance bookings. The Lost World (four/seven hours $310/445) trip starts with a 100m abseil down into the cave, then – by a combination of walking, rock climbing, wading and swimming – you journey through a 30m-high cave to get back out, passing glowworms, amazing rock formations, waterfalls and more. The price includes lunch (underground) and dinner. The shorter version skips the wet stuff and the meals.

Haggas Honking Holes (four hours, $240) includes professional abseiling instruction followed by three waterfall abseils, rock climbing and travelling along a subterranean river, traversing narrow passageways and huge caverns.

TumuTumu Toobing (four hours, $165) is a walking, climbing, swimming and tubing trip. St Benedict's Cavern (three hours, $165) includes abseiling and a subterranean flying fox in a cave with amazing straw stalagmites.

Tramping

The i-SITE has free pamphlets on walks in the area. The walk from **Aranui Cave** to **Ruakuri Cave** is an excellent short path. From the Waitomo Glowworm Caves Visitor Centre, the 5km, three-hour-return **Waitomo Walkway** takes off through farmland, following Waitomo Stream to the **Ruakuri Scenic Reserve**, where a 30-minute return walk passes by a natural limestone tunnel.

 **Sleeping**

ABSEIL INN B&B $$
(☎ 07-878 7815; www.abseilinn.co.nz; 709 Waitomo Caves Rd; d inc breakfast from $150; 🖤) A *veeery* steep driveway (abseiling in from a helicopter might be an easier approach) takes you to this delightful B&B with four themed rooms, great breakfasts and witty hosts. The biggest room has a double bath and valley views.

WAITOMO CAVES GUEST LODGE B&B $$
(☎ 0800 465 762, 07-878 7641; www.waitomo cavesguestlodge.co.nz; 7 Te Anga Rd; s $80, d $105-130, extra person $25, all incl breakfast; 🖤) Bag your own cosy little hillside en-suite cabin at this central operation with a sweet garden setting. The top cabins have valley views. Large continental breakfast and resident dog included. Simple and unfussy.

WOODLYN PARK Motel $$$
(☎ 07-878 6666; www.woodlynpark.co.nz; 1177 Waitomo Valley Rd; d $170-245, extra person $15) Boasting the world's only hobbit motel (set into the ground with round windows and doors), Woodlyn Park's other sleeping options include the cockpit of a combat plane, train carriages and the *Waitanic* – a converted WWII patrol boat fitted with chandeliers, moulded ceilings and shiny brass portholes. It's extremely well done and the kids will love you for it.

Eating & Drinking

HUHU Cafe, Modern NZ **$$**
(☏07-878 6674; www.huhustore.co.nz/cafe; 10 Waitomo Caves Rd; lunch $11-19, dinner $25-30; ⏱10.30am-9pm; ☎) Come to Huhu twice a day – you won't be disappointed. Slick and modern with charming service, it has great views from the terrace and sublime contemporary NZ food. Sip a strong coffee, or graze through a seasonal tapas-style menu (large or small plates) of Kiwi delights like rabbit hotpot or organic braised beef, all locally sourced (right down to the specific cow). Wonderful!

MOREPORK CAFE Cafe, Pizzeria **$$**
(☏07-878 3395; waitomobackpackers@xtra.co.nz; Kiwi Paka, Hotel Access Rd; breakfast & lunch $7-15, dinner $14-27; ⏱8am-8pm) At the Kiwi Paka backpackers is this cheery joint, a jack-of-all-trades eatery serving breakfast, lunch and dinner either inside or out on the deck. The 'Caveman' pizza is a winner (the first person to ask for more pork will be shown the door).

CURLY'S BAR Pub
(☏07-878 8448; www.curlysbar.co.nz; Hotel Access Rd; ⏱11am-2am) An easy-going tavern with lots of beers on tap, good-value pub grub (steaks, lamb shanks, nachos...lunch and dinner mains $10 to $25), chunky wooden tables and occasional quiz nights and live music.

ℹ Information

Waitomo i-SITE (☏0800 474 839, 07-878 7640; www.waitomodiscovery.org; 21 Waitomo Caves Rd; ⏱8.15am-7pm Jan & Feb, 8.45am-5.30pm Nov, Dec, Mar & Apr, 8.45am-5pm Apr-Oct; @) Internet access, post office and booking agent.

ℹ Getting There & Away

Naked Bus (☏0900 625 33; www.nakedbus.com) runs once daily to Otorohanga ($20, 20 minutes), Hamilton ($20, 1¼ hours) and New Plymouth ($30, three hours).

Waitomo Shuttle (☏07-873 8279, 0800 808 279; waikiwi@ihug.co.nz; 1-way adult/child $12/7) heads to the caves five times daily from Otorohanga (15 minutes away), coordinating with bus and train arrivals. One-way adult/child $12/7.

Waitomo Wanderer (☏0800 000 4321, 03-477 9083; www.travelheadfirst.com) operates a daily return services from Rotorua or Taupo, with optional caving, glowworm and tubing add-ons (packages from $133). Shuttle-only services $99 return.

LAKE TAUPO REGION

NZ's largest lake, Lake Taupo, sits in the caldera of a volcano that began erupting about 300,000 years ago.

Today the 606-sq-km lake and its surrounding waterways are serene enough to attract fishing enthusiasts from all around the world. Well positioned by the

Lake Taupo
DAVID WALL / LONELY PLANET IMAGES ©

Taupo

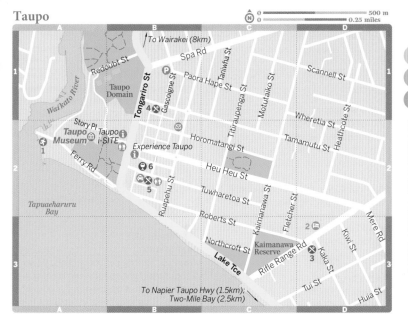

lake, both Taupo and Turangi are popular tourist centres.

Taupo

With a postcard-perfect setting on the northeastern shores of the lake, the increasingly exciting town of Taupo now rivals Rotorua as the North Island's adrenaline capital. There's an abundance of blood-pumping activities on offer but for those undesirous of white knuckles and churned stomachs, there's plenty of enjoyment to be had simply strolling by the lake and enjoying the views, which on clear days reveal the snowy peaks of Tongariro National Park.

👁 Sights

Lakeside

Taupo's main attraction is the lake and all the things you can do in, on and around it. The water is famously chilly, but in several places (such as **Hot Water Beach**, immediately south of the centre) there are thermal springs just below the

surface. You can swim right in front of the township, but **Acacia Bay**, 5km west, is a particularly pleasant spot. Even better and quieter is **Whakaipo Bay**, another 7km further on.

MAORI CARVINGS   Carvings
Accessible only by boat, these 10m-high carvings were etched into the cliffs near Mine Bay by master carver Matahi Whakataka-Brightwell in the late 1970s.

They depict Ngatoro-i-rangi, the visionary Maori navigator who guided the Tuwharetoa and Te Arawa tribes to the Taupo area a thousand years ago. There are also two smaller Matahi figures here, both of Celtic design, which depict the south wind and a mermaid.

TAUPO MUSEUM — Museum
(☎ 07-376 0414; www.taupomuseum.co.nz; Story Pl; adult/child $5/free; ⊙10am-4.30pm) With an excellent Maori gallery and quirky displays, which include a 1960s caravan set up as if the occupants have just popped down to the lake, this little museum makes an interesting rainy-day diversion. The centrepiece is an elaborately carved Maori meeting house, Te Aroha o Rongoheikume.

Wairakei Park

HUKA FALLS — Waterfall
(Huka Falls Rd) Clearly signposted and with a car park and kiosk alongside, these falls mark the spot where NZ's longest river, the Waikato is slammed into a narrow chasm, making a dramatic 10m drop into a surging pool. You can also take a few short walks around the area or pick up the Huka Falls Walkway back to town, or the Aratiatia Rapids Walking Track to the rapids.

WAIRAKEI TERRACES & THERMAL HEALTH SPA — Thermal Area
(☎ 07-378 0913; www.wairakeiterraces.co.nz; Wairakei Rd; thermal walk adult/child $18/9, pools $25; ⊙8.30am-5pm) Known to Maori as Waiora and latterly as Geyser Valley, this was one of the most active thermal areas in the world (with 22 geysers and 240 mud pools and springs) until 1958, when it was significantly affected by the opening of the geothermal power station. Today it's the site of a re-created Maori village, a small meeting house, a carving centre, massage rooms and a set of healing thermal pools.

The night-time **Maori Cultural Experience** – which includes a traditional challenge, welcome, concert and *hangi* meal – gives an insight into Maori life in the geothermal areas (adult/child $95/48).

VOLCANIC ACTIVITY CENTRE — Museum
(www.volcanoes.co.nz; Karetoto Rd; adult/child $10/6; ⊙9am-5pm Mon-Fri, 10am-4pm Sat & Sun) What's with all the geothermal activity around Taupo? This centre has the answers, with excellent, if text-heavy, displays on the region's geothermal and volcanic activity, including a live seismograph keeping a watch on what's currently going on.

Activities

Water Based

FREE SPA PARK HOT SPRING — Swimming
(Spa Park) The hot thermal waters of the Otumuheke Stream meet the bracing Waikato River at this pleasant and well-worn spot under a bridge, creating a free natural spa bath. It's near the beginning of the Huka Falls Walkway, about 20 minutes from the centre of town.

HUKAFALLS JET — Jetboating
(☎ 07-374 8572; www.hukafallsjet.com; 200 Karetoto Rd; trips adult/child $105/59) This 30-minute thrill ride takes you up the river to the spray-filled foot of the Huka Falls and down to the Aratiatia Dam, all the while dodging daringly and doing acrobatic 360-degree turns.

TAUPO DEBRETTS SPA RESORT — Swimming
(☎ 07-377 6502; www.taupodebretts.co.nz; 76 Napier Taupo Hwy; adult/child $20/12; ⊙7.30am-9.30pm) A variety of mineral-rich indoor and outdoor thermal pools are on offer. The kids will love the giant dragon waterslide, while the adults can enjoy a wide choice of treatments, such as massage and body scrubs.

CHRIS JOLLY OUTDOORS — Cruise, Kayaking
(☎ 07-378 0623; www.chrisjolly.co.nz; Marina; ⊙9am-5.30pm) Operates the Cruise Cat, a large, modern launch that offers fishing trips and daily cruises to the Maori

carvings (adult/child $44/16, 10.30am and 1.30pm). Sunday brunch trips (adult/child $62/34) are especially worthwhile. It also hires kayaks (single/double per hour $20/30) and self-drive boats ($70 to $85 per hour), and offers guided mountain-biking trips.

RAPID SENSATIONS & KAYAKING KIWI   Kayaking, Rafting
(☏ 0800 35 34 35; www.rapids.co.nz; 413 Huka Falls Rd) Offers kayak trips to the Maori carvings ($98, four hours), a gentle paddle along the Waikato ($48, two hours), white-water rafting on the Tongariro River ($88 to $145) and mountain-bike rides ($75).

Skydiving

SKYDIVE TAUPO   Skydiving
(☏ 0800 586 766; www.skydivetaupo.co.nz; 12,000ft/15,000ft $250/340) Packages are available, which include town pick-ups in a white limousine, DVDs, photos and T-shirts (from $439).

🖉 TAUPO TANDEM SKYDIVING   Skydiving
(☏ 0800 826 336; www.taupotandemskydiving. com; 12,000ft/15,000ft $249/339) Various

packages are available which include DVDs, photos, T-shirts etc ($388 to $679).

Other Activities

HUKA FALLS WALKWAY   Walking
Starting from the Spa Park car park at the end of County Ave (off Spa Rd), this scenic, easy walk takes just over an hour to reach the falls, following the east bank of the Waikato River. Continuing on from the falls is the 7km Huka Falls to Aratiatia Rapids walking track (another two-plus hours).

TAUPO BUNGY   Bungy
(☏ 07-377 1135; www.taupobungy.co.nz; 202 Spa Rd; solo/tandem $149/298; ⏱8.30am-5pm, extended in summer) Sitting on a cliff edge over the mighty Waikato River, this pictur-esque bungy site is the most popular on the North Island, with plenty of vantage points if you're too chicken to jump. Nonchickens will be led onto a platform jutting 20m out over the cliff (the world's first cantilever jump, for engineering bof-fins) and convinced, with masterly skill, to throw themselves off the edge. Alterna-tively, try the giant swing (solo/tandem $99/180).

Huka Falls

KAIMANAWA
HELI-BIKING   Mountain Biking

(07-384 2816; www.kaimanawahelibiking. co.nz; 4hr ride $395) For luxury rough riding, Heli-Biking will pick you up in a helicopter and drop you on top of the highest point in the Kaimanawa range, allowing you to ride all the way down.

 ## Tours

HELIPRO   Scenic Flights
(Map p118; 07-377 8805; www.helipro.co.nz; flights $99-1150) Specialises in heli-tours, which include alpine and White Island landings, as well as shorter scenic flights over the town, lake and volcanoes.

IZARDAIR   Scenic Flights
(07-378 7835; www.izardair.com; flights $100-310) Luxury light aircraft flights over Taupo, Orakei Korako or the volcanoes.

PARADISE TOURS   Bus Tour
(07-378 9955; www.paradisetours.co.nz; adult/child $99/45) Three-hour tours to the Aratiatia Rapids, Craters of the Moon and Huka Falls. Also offers day tours to Tongariro National Park, Orakei Korako, Rotorua, Hawke's Bay and Waitomo Caves.

 ## Sleeping

LAKE   Motel $$
(07-378 4222; www.thelakeonline.co.nz; 63 Mere Rd; apt $155-220) A reminder that 1960s and '70s design wasn't all Austin Powers–style groovaliciousness, this unusual boutique motel is crammed with furniture from the era's signature designers. The studio is a tight fit, but the four one-bedroom units all have kitchenettes and dining/living areas.

BEECHTREE   Motel $$
(07-377 0181; www.beechtreemotel.co.nz; 56 Rifle Range Rd; apt $140-390; @) The Beechtree, and its sister motel Miro next door, offer classy rooms at reasonable rates. The design is fresh and modern, with neutral-toned decor, large windows, ground-floor patios and upstairs balconies.

SACRED WATERS   Apartments $$$
(07-376 1400; www.sacredwaters.co.nz; 221-225 Lake Tce; apt $360-670;) Apart from some awful mass-produced 'art', these large apartments are stylish and well-designed. Each has a contemporary kitchen and its own private thermal plunge pool, and most have wonderful lake views.

ACACIA CLIFFS LODGE   B&B $$$
(07-378 1551; www.acaciacliffslodge.co.nz; 133 Mapara Rd, Acacia Bay; r $700; @) Pushing the romance switch way past 'rekindle', this luxurious B&B, high in the hills above Acacia Bay, offers four modern suites – three with sumptuous lake views and one that compensates for the lack of them with a curvy bath and a private garden.

 ### HILTON LAKE TAUPO   Hotel $$$
(07-378 7080; www.hilton.com/laketaupo; 80-100 Napier Taupo Hwy; from $230; @) Occupying the historic Terraces Hotel (1889) and a recent extension, this large complex offers the expected Hilton standard of luxury in nonthreatening shades of grey. It's a little out of town but is handy for the DeBretts thermal complex.

Eating & Drinking

BISTRO LAGO   Italian $$$
(07-377 1400; www.bistrolago.co.nz; 80-100 Napier Taupo Hwy; breakfast $25-35, pizza $22-23, mains $37-42; breakfast, lunch & dinner) Under the long-distance tutelage of Auckland-based celebrity chef Simon Gault, the Hilton's inhouse restaurant delivers inventive Italian-influenced dishes using quality regional ingredients. The view, stretching over the lake to the distant mountains, only adds to the magic.

VINE EATERY   Tapas $$
(www.sceniccellars.co.nz; 37 Tuwharetoa St; tapas $9-20; 9am-late) Sharing the Scenic Cellars wine store, this chic eatery continues the communal ethos with a 'shared plates' menu – offering traditional tapas alongside heftier divisible dishes. Of course, the wine list is excellent.

Boats moored on the lake at Taupo

OLIVER STREWE / LONELY PLANET IMAGES ©

BRANTRY   Modern NZ $$$
(☎ 07-378 0484; www.thebrantry.co.nz; 45 Rifle
Range Rd; mains $38-42, 2-/3-course set menu
$45/60; ✿dinner) It's an unusual set-up,
operating out of an unobtrusive 1950s
house, but the Campbell sisters have
turned Brantry into one of the most well-
regarded restaurants in the region. The
menu makes use of top-quality cuts of
beef and lamb.

PIMENTOS   International $$
(☎ 07-377 4549; 17 Tamamutu St; mains $28-30;
✿dinner Wed-Mon) Pimentos is such a local
favourite that you'd be wise to book ahead.
The lamb shanks and mash are legendary,
but the relatively short menu offers plenty
of well-considered experimentation.

SHED   Pub
(www.theshedbar.co.nz; 18 Tuwharetoa St;
✿3pm-late Mon & Tue, noon-late Wed-Sun) A
lively place to sup a beer and catch the
big game, sit outside and watch the world
go by, or strut your stuff to DJs on the
weekends. Food is punter-pleasing pub
fare in man-sized portions.

ⓘ Information

Taupo i-SITE (☎07-376 0027; www.
greatlaketaupo.com; Tongariro St; ✿8.30am-
5pm) Handles bookings for accommodation,
transport and activities; dispenses cheerful
advice; and stocks Department of Conservation
(DOC) maps and town maps.

ⓘ Getting There & Away

Taupo Airport (☎07-378 7771; www.
taupoairport.co.nz; 33 Anzac Memorial Dr) is 8km
south of town. InterCity buses stop at the **Taupo
Travel Centre** (☎07-378 9005; 16 Gascoigne St),
which operates as a booking office. **Naked Bus**
(☎0900 625 33; www.nakedbus.com) services
stop outside the i-SITE.

Shuttle services operate year-round between
Taupo, Turangi and Tongariro National Park; see
p147 for operators. In winter, services run to
Whakapapa Ski Area (1½ hours) and can include
package deals for lift tickets and ski hire.

ⓘ Getting Around

Shuttle 2U (☎07-376 7638; www.shuttle2u.
co.nz; per stop $4-10, day pass $15) operates
an on-demand shuttle service, picking up from

local accommodation and stopping at all major attractions in and around Taupo.

Hotbus (☏ 0508 468 287; www.alpinehotbus. co.nz; 1st stop $15, then per stop $5) is a hop-on, hop-off minibus that covers similar sights, departing from the i-SITE.

Turangi & Around

Sleepy Turangi's claim to fame is as the 'Trout Fishing Capital of the World' and as one of the country's premier white-water-rafting destinations. Set on the Tongariro River, the town is a shortish hop for snow-bunnies from the ski fields and walking tracks of Tongariro National Park.

◉ Sights & Activities

TONGARIRO NATIONAL TROUT CENTRE   Aquarium
(Map p144; www.troutcentre.com; SH1; adult/child $10/free; ⏲ 10am-3pm) The DOC-managed trout hatchery has polished educational displays, a collection of rods and reels dating back to the 1880s and freshwater aquariums displaying river life, both nasty and nice. A gentle stroll along the landscaped walkway leads to the hatchery, keeping ponds, an underwater viewing chamber and a picnic area.

TOKAANU THERMAL POOLS   Swimming
(Map p144; Mangaroa St, Tokaanu; adult/child $6/4, private pools per 20min $10/6; ⏲ 10am-9pm) Soak in thermally heated water at this unpretentious, family-orientated facility, 5km northwest of Turangi. A 20-minute stroll along the boardwalk (wheelchair accessible) showcases boiling mud pools, thermal springs and a trout-filled stream.

RAFTING NZ   Rafting
(☏ 0800 865 226; www.raftingnewzealand.com; 41 Ngawaka Pl) Offering a warm welcome, hot showers and a taste of Maori culture, this operator is a popular choice. The main trips offered are Tongariro Whitewater with an optional waterfall jump (Grade III, adult/child $119/109, four hours) and the Family Fun raft over more relaxed rapids (Grade II, adult/child $75/65, three hours).

WAI MAORI   Kayaking
(☏ 07-386 0315; www.waimaori.com; Tokaanu) Offers guided white-water kayaking (November to April, per person $159) or trips accompanied only by trout down the gentle Tokaanu Stream to Lake Taupo, passing boiling mud, hot pools and wetlands on the way (90 minutes/half day/full day $30/40/65).

FLYFISH TAUPO.COM   Fishing
(☏ 07-377 8054; www. flyfishtaupo.com; prices on application) Guide Brett Pirie offers a range of fishing excursions, including seniors-focussed 'Old Farts & Tarts' trips.

Mt Ruapehu
JOHN BANAGAN / LONELY PLANET IMAGES ©

 **Sleeping**

CREEL LODGE   Lodge $$
(☏07-386 8081; www.creel.co.nz; 183 Taupahi
Rd; s $110-130, d $125-145; 🛜) Set in green
and peaceful grounds, this heavenly
hideaway backs onto a fine stretch of the
Tongariro River. It's worth upgrading to an
executive garden suite for a smarter unit
in an attractive punga-fenced garden.

ORETI VILLAGE   Apartments $$$
(Map p144; ☏07-386 7070; www.oretivillage.
com; Mission House Dr, Pukawa; apt $220-280;
🛜) This enclave of luxury self-contained
apartments might give you a hankering
for 'village' life – which in Oreti's case en-
tails gazing at blissful lake views from the
comfort of a rolled-arm leather couch.
Take SH41 for 15km, heading northwest
of Turangi, and turn right into Pukawa Rd.

SPORTMANS LODGE   Guesthouse $$
(☏07-386 8150; www.sportmanslodge.co.nz;
15 Taupahi Rd; r $72, cottage $105-130; 🛜)
Backing on to the river, this lodge is a
hidden bargain for trout-fishing folk un-
bothered by punctuation. All the rooms
share the lounge and well-equipped
kitchen. The self-contained cottage
sleeps four.

ANGLERS PARADISE MOTEL   Motel $$
(☏07-386 8980; www.anglersparadise.co.nz;
cnr Ohuanga Rd & Raukura St; units $119-160;
@🏊) Looking like something out of *Twin
Peaks*, this very old-fashioned motel sits
in a 1-hectare leafy pocket where privacy
prevails. It's geared up for anglers, with
guides happily arranged and a smoke-
house on-site.

 Eating

TONGARIRO LODGE   Modern NZ $$$
(Map p144; ☏07-386 7946; www.tongarirolodge.
co.nz; 83 Grace Rd; mains $30-42; ⊙dinner)
Some of the world's most famous blokes
(Robert Mitchum, Liam Neeson, Larry
Hagman, Jimmy Carter, Timothy Dalton)
have come to this luxury riverside fishing

lodge, set in 9 hectares of parkland, to
relax in wood-panelled anonymity. Not
surprisingly, the menu is orientated
around man-sized slabs of meat but the
real squeals of delight come when lucky
lodgers are presented with their day's
catch, smoked and served to perfection.

ORETI VILLAGE   French $$$
(Map p144; ☏07-386 7070; Mission House Dr,
Pukawa; mains $30-38; ⊙lunch Sat & Sun,
dinner Tue-Sun) It's hard to imagine a more
romantic spot to while away a balmy
summer's evening than looking over the
lake from Oreti's terrace.

ℹ **Information**

Turangi i-SITE (☏07-386 8999; www.
greatlaketauponz.com; Ngawaka Pl; ⊙8.30am-
5pm; @🛜) A good stop for information on
Tongariro National Park, Kaimanawa Forest Park,
trout fishing, and snow and road conditions.

ℹ **Getting There & Away**

Both InterCity and Naked Bus coaches stop
outside the i-SITE.

THE CENTRAL PLATEAU

Tongariro National Park

Established in 1887, Tongariro was NZ's
first and the world's fourth national
park, and is one of NZ's three World
Heritage Sites. Its three towering, active
volcanoes – Ruapehu, Ngauruhoe and
Tongariro – rise from a vast, scrub-
covered alpine plateau, making this
one of the nation's most spectacular
locations. In winter it's a busy ski area.

◉ **Sights**

MT RUAPEHU   Volcano
(www.mtruapehu.com) The multipeaked summit of Ruapehu (2797m) is the highest
and most active of the park's volcanoes,
and the centrepiece of the national park,
with Whakapapa Village (pronounced

Tongariro National Park & Around

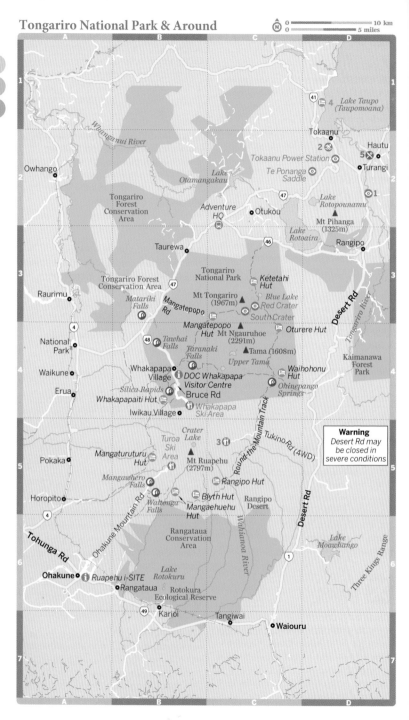

Warning
*Desert Rd may
be closed in
severe conditions*

Tongariro National Park & Around

'fa-ka-pa-pa'), numerous walking tracks and three ski fields on its slopes.

The name means 'pit of sound', a reference to its regular eruptions.

MT NGAURUHOE   Volcano

Much younger than the other two volcanoes, it is estimated that Ngauruhoe (2287m) formed in the last 2500 years. In contrast to the others, which have multiple vents, Ngauruhoe is a conical, single-vent volcano with perfectly symmetrical slopes – which is the reason that it was chosen to star as Mt Doom in Peter Jackson's *Lord of the Rings*. It can be climbed in summer, but in winter (under snow) this steep climb is only for experienced mountaineers.

MT TONGARIRO   Volcano

The Red Crater of Mt Tongariro (1968m) last erupted in 1926. This ancient but still active volcano has coloured lakes dotting its uneven summit. The Tongariro Alpine Crossing, a magnificent walk, passes beside the lakes, right through several craters, and down through lush native forest.

Activities

WHAKAPAPA & TUROA SKI AREAS   Skiing, Snowboarding

(☎ Turoa 06-385 8456, Whakapapa 07-892 4000; www.mtruapehu.com; daily lift pass adult/child $95/57, valid at both resorts) These linked resorts straddle either side of Mt Ruapehu and are NZ's two largest ski areas. Each offers similar skiing at an analogous altitude (around 2300m), with areas to suit each level of experience – from beginners' slopes to black diamond runs

for the pros. The same lift passes cover both ski areas.

The only accommodation at the ski fields is in private lodges (mainly owned by ski clubs), so most Whakapaka visitors stay at Whakapaka or National Park Village.

TUKINO SKI AREA   Skiing, Snowboarding

(☎ 0800 885 466, 06-387 6294; www.tukino. co.nz; daily lift pass adult/child $50/30) Club-operated Tukino is on Mt Ruapehu's east, 46km from Turangi. It's quite remote, 14km down a gravel road from the sealed Desert Rd (SH1), and you need a 4WD vehicle to get in. Uncrowded, with mostly beginner and intermediate runs.

42 TRAVERSE   Mountain Biking

This four- to six-hour, 46km mountain-bike trail through the Tongariro Forest is one of the most popular one-dayers on the North Island. The Traverse follows old logging tracks, making for relatively dependable going, although there are plenty of ups and downs – more downs as long as you start from Kapoors Rd (off SH47) and head down to Owhango.

TONGARIRO NORTHERN CIRCUIT   Tramping

Classed as one of NZ's Great Walks, the Northern Circuit circumnavigates Ngauruhoe and affords spectacular views all around, particularly of Mt Tongariro. The walk covers the famous Tongariro Alpine Crossing.

Highlights of the circuit include tramping through or past several volcanic craters, including the South Crater, Central Crater and Red Crater; brilliantly colourful volcanic lakes, including the Emerald Lakes, Blue Lake and the Upper and Lower Tama Lakes; the cold Soda

JOHN ELK III / LONELY PLANET IMAGES ©

Don't Miss **Tongariro Alpine Crossing**

Reputedly the best one-day walk in NZ, the Tongariro Alpine Crossing traverses spectacular volcanic geography, from an active crater to steaming vents and beautiful coloured lakes. And the views aren't bad either.

Although achievable in one day, the Crossing is exhausting and shouldn't be taken lightly. Weather can change without warning, so make sure you are adequately equipped. If you're not in top walking condition you may prefer to take two days, spending a night at Ketatahi Hut.

The Tongariro Alpine Crossing can be reached from Mangatepopo Rd, off SH47, and from Ketetahi Rd, off SH46.

Because of its popularity, there are plenty of shuttle services to both ends of the track. The shuttles need to be booked and you'll be expected to complete the track in a reasonable time.

Springs; and various other volcanic formations, including cones, lava flows and glacial valleys.

The safest and most popular time to walk the track is from December to March. The track is served by four well-maintained huts: Mangatepopo, Ketetahi, Oturere and Waihohonu.

CRATER LAKE   Tramping
The unmarked rugged route up to Ruapehu's Crater Lake (seven hours return) is a good one, allowing you to see the acidic lake up close, but this walk is strictly off limits when there's volcanic activity. You can cut three hours off it by catching the **chairlift** (adult/child $26/16; ⊙9am-3.30pm mid-Dec–Apr) from Whaka-papa Ski Area. **Guided walks** (☑0508 782 734; www.mtruapehu.com; adult/child incl lift pass $145/95) to Crater Lake run from mid-December to mid-April, weather dependent.

RIDGE TRACK   Walking

A 30-minute return walk that climbs through beech forest to alpine-shrub areas for views of all three peaks.

WHAKAPAPA NATURE WALK   Walking

Suitable for wheelchairs, this 15-minute loop track begins about 200m above the visitor centre, passing through beech forest and gardens typical of the park's vegetation zones.

Sleeping & Eating

Whakapapa Village has limited accommodation and prices quoted here are for summer; rates are generally much higher during the ski season. National Park village and Ohakune offer a greater range of options.

BAYVIEW CHATEAU TONGARIRO   Hotel $$

(07-892 3809; www.chateau.co.nz; Whakapapa Village; r from $155; @) NZ's great missed tourism opportunity promises much, with its sublime setting and manor house grandeur, but the old-world charm is fading fast. Which is a shame, as a cashed-up interior designer could swiftly transform the Chateau back into the iconic hotel it was when it first opened its doors in 1929. Within the hulking complex are a cinema, the elegant **Ruapehu Room** (mains $36-38; dinner), **Pihanga Cafe** (mains $20-27; lunch & dinner) and the T-bar, a cosy spot for a warming winter tipple. The operators also manage the neighbouring nine-hole public golf course, **Fergusson's**

Cafe (mains $5-10; breakfast & lunch; @) and Fergusson Motel, which has self-contained family chalets (from $155).

Information

Further national park information is available from the Ohakune and Turangi i-SITEs.

DOC Visitor Centre (Department of Conservation; 07-892 3729; www.doc.govt.nz; Whakapapa Village; 8am-5pm) Has maps and info on all corners of the park, including walks, huts and current skiing, track and weather conditions.

Getting There & Around

Bus

There are numerous shuttle services to Whakapapa Village, the Tongariro Alpine Crossing and other key destinations from Taupo, Turangi, National Park village and Ohakune. Book your bus in advance to avoid unexpected strandings.

Alpine Hotbus (0508 468 287; www.alpinehotbus.co.nz) Provides shuttles to the Crossing from Rotorua ($99), Taupo ($55) and Turangi ($40), and from Taupo to Whakapapa and National Park village ($60).

Mountain Shuttle (0800 117 686; www.tongarirocrossing.com) Runs shuttles from Turangi to Whakapapa and the Tongariro Alpine Crossing ($40), and one-way hike-to-your-car Crossing shuttles ($25).

Tongariro Expeditions (0800 828 763; www.tongariroexpeditions.com) Runs shuttles from Taupo ($59, 1½ hours), Turangi ($40, 45 minutes) and Whakapapa ($35, 15 minutes) for the Crossing and the Northern Circuit.

Wellington & Lower North Island

Rock into Wellington for a big-city hit: art-house cinema, designer boutiques, hip bars, live-music venues and late-night coffee shops – it's all in 'Windy Welly'.

Wellington is New Zealand's capital city, but Wellingtonians also lay passionate claim to the crown of 'cultural capital'. Suited-up civil servants abound, but the city also supports a significant population of creative types who foster an admirably active and accessible arts scene.

Less than an hour away to the north, the Kapiti Coast offers more settled weather and a beachy vibe, with the Kapiti Island nature reserve a highlight. An hour from Wellington to the northeast is the Wairarapa, a burgeoning weekend-away wine region where the pinot noir grapes hang heavy on the vine. Keep trucking north and you'll bump into the glorious beaches and prosperous wine towns of the East Coast.

Wellington Cable Car (p163)
OLIVER STREWE/LONELY PLANET IMAGES ©

Cape Palliser Lighthouse (p178)

Wellington & Lower North Island

1 Te Papa, Wellington
2 Napier Art Deco
3 Nocturnal Wellington
4 Museum of Wellington City & Sea
5 Kapiti Coast
6 Zealandia, Wellington
7 The Wairarapa

100 km
50 miles

Gisborne

Morere
Mahia
Mahia Peninsula

SOUTH PACIFIC OCEAN

Wairoa

Hawke Bay

See Hawke's Bay Map (p179)

Cape Kidnappers

Te Haroto
Tutira
Tangoio

Napier 7 2
Hastings
Havelock North

Waipukurau

Te Pōhue
Te Pōnui

Kaimanawa Mountains

Ruahine Forest Park

Dannevirke

Norsewood

Kaimanawa Forest Park

Tongariro National Park
Mt Ruapehu

Tohunga Junction

Taihape

Utiku

Mangaweka

Fielding

Taumatawhakatangihangakoauauotamateaturipukakapikimaungahoronukupokaiwhenuakitanatahu (305m)

Castlepoint

Whanganui National Park

Whanganui National Park

Waverley

Whanganui

Bulls

Palmerston North

Foxton
Shannon
Levin
Ohau

Otaki

Tararua Forest Park
Mt Hector
Alpha

Mt Holdsworth

Masterton
Carterton
Greytown
Featherston

The Wairarapa

New Plymouth

Mt Taranaki (Mt Egmont)

Egmont National Park

Stratford

Hawera

Opunake

South Taranaki Bight

Kapiti Island
Paraparaumu
Kapiti Coast
Paekakariki

Upper Hutt
Lower Hutt

Porirua
Petone
WELLINGTON

Rimutaka Forest Park

Tararua Range

Mitre

Martinborough

Rimutaka Range

Cape Palliser
Cape Palliser Lighthouse

Cook Strait

TASMAN SEA

D'Urville Island

Marlborough Sounds

Picton

Nelson
Richmond

Motueka

Tasman Bay

Golden Bay
Collingwood
Takaka

Kahurangi National Park

Blenheim

Wellington & Lower North Island's Highlights

① Te Papa

Occupying an unmissable building on the Wellington waterfront, Te Papa is New Zealand's national museum. 'Te Papa' translates into 'container of treasures'. And that's exactly what is: a giant six-storey treasure box with an intense, interactive NZ focus. Maori culture is a real highlight. Above: Mountains to Sea exhibit

Need to Know

WHEN TO VISIT Beat the crowds with a Thursday evening visit (until 9pm)
BEST PHOTO OP Views from level 6 **ADMISSION** Free!
For further coverage, see p167 and Map p164

Te Papa Don't Miss List

BY BRIDGET MACDONALD, TE PAPA

1 MAORI GALLERIES & TOURS

On level 4 you can see a beautiful example of a traditionally carved *marae* (meeting house), contrasting with a big contemporary *marae*. The museum also has many Maori guides, and dedicated Maori tours as well. The Bush City exhibit covers everything from wetlands to volcanic regions, forests and caves: you can learn about how Maori used to live and see how plants are used in modern-day life. Top left: Te Hono ki Hawaiki *marae*

2 NATIONAL ART COLLECTION, LEVEL 5

On upper level 5 we have an exhibition called Toi Te Papa: Art of the Nation: a chronological story of NZ's art history. It takes you right through from traditional woodcarving to big contemporary works that change regularly – there's always something new.

3 GOLDEN DAYS, LEVEL 4

The *Golden Days* film features nostalgic footage covering 80 years of iconic moments in NZ history. It's the good and bad of our national history: people from all over the world find a connection with it. It runs every 20 minutes.

4 OUR SPACE, LEVEL 2

Our Space (www.ourspace.tepapa.com) has a 14m satellite map of NZ. When you stand on it, imagery and video clips from that region light up on the wall beside you. People can look and see where they've been and where they're going. The Wall is where people can upload their own images to our database before they arrive. Using interactive wand technology, you can look for your images and manipulate them on giant screens. Bottom left: The Map, Our Space

5 AWESOME FORCES, LEVEL 2

The Awesome Forces earthquake house here gives visitors an insight into New Zealand's geology, so that when they're travelling across the country they can understand how tectonic forces have shaped our landscapes.

Napier Art Deco

Napier's 1931 earthquake (7.8 on the Richter scale) caused 261 casualties regionally – 157 in Napier. The town was subsequently rebuilt in architectural styles fashionable at the time: art deco, Spanish Mission, Prairie... Much of this cache is beautifully preserved, and art deco has become the town's pride and joy.

Below: Masonic Hotel (p181)

Need to Know

BEST TIME TO VISIT
Festivals in summer, fewer crowds in spring/autumn
BEST ARCHITECTURE
National Tobacco Company and AMP buildings **For further coverage, see p179**

Napier Art Deco Don't Miss List

BY ROBERT MCGREGOR, NAPIER ART DECO TRUST

1 ART-DECO HIGHLIGHTS

My favourite individual buildings are the National Tobacco Company, the Daily Telegraph and the Municipal Theatre. Also the landscaped gardens and architectural features along the waterfront – these were the final touches when they finished rebuilding the city. The plaza here provides a setting for civic events, which most towns don't have.

2 HOUSES IN MAREWA

Marewa, Napier's art-deco suburb, has a real concentration of art-deco houses. Most of them are well preserved – some have had pitched roofs put on them, but many of them look as they always did. The council now enforces regulations to preserve the architectural qualities here.

3 TAKE A GUIDED TOUR

You can do a self-guided tour around the main buildings (you could easily spend a couple of hours), or take a guided tour (p179). There's a one-hour morning walk, which is good for people who don't have much time or who are leaving town that day; and a two-hour afternoon walk.

4 ART DECO WEEKEND

Ticket sales for the annual **Art Deco Weekend** (www.artdeconapier.com) are always good! New Zealanders aren't traditionally into dressing up, but we see a lot of period costumes and vintage Packard cars driving around this weekend. There's lots of great Hawke's Bay wine and food, and jazz and dancing in the street. It's great fun.

5 A VISIT TO HASTINGS

Hastings (p183) is about 20km down the road. It was less damaged than Napier in the earthquake, but there are some lovely art-deco buildings there, too. There's always been a rivalry between the two cities – it's unusual to have two such towns in close proximity.

Nocturnal Wellington

Everyone in Wellington (p169) seems to be in a band and looks a tad depleted, as if they party too hard and spend their time daubing canvasses and scribbling poetry. It follows that there's a lot going on here at night! Wellington's pubs, live-music rooms and coffee shops are kickin' after dark. Go bar-hopping around Cuba St and Courtenay Pl and see what kind of fun comes your way. Below: Mighty Mighty bar

Museum of Wellington City & Sea
open every day 10 to 5

Back & Beyond & Here

Museum of Wellington City & Sea

Te Papa may have the national interests all sewn up, but the Museum of Wellington City & Sea (p162), inside a beautiful 1892 warehouse, puts a local spin on things. Wellington is a great seagoing city, and like any port there are plenty of influences flowing in and out on the tide. Learn how the ocean has shaped contemporary Wellington, and how local Maori connected with sea and land for centuries prior.

Kapiti Coast

When you're travelling around from A to B, it's easy to overlook the little (and often brilliant) places in between. The Kapiti Coast (p174) falls into this category: just an hour from Wellington and strewn with empty beaches and endearing coastal towns, and with Kapiti Island offshore, the area makes a great pit stop, detour or destination in its own right.

5

6

Zealandia

Up in the hills west of Wellington, Zealandia (p163) is a brilliant ecosanctuary – a leafy, fenced valley that's home to 30-plus species of native bird, including a free-ranging population of little spotted kiwi. Or, if you're more of a cold-blooded operator, this is your chance to see a tuatara, NZ's iconic native lizard. There's plenty of natural-history info to soak up, plus dozens of kilometres of walking tracks and daytime and nocturnal tours.

7

The Wairarapa

Over the hills (and not so far away) from Wellington is the Wairarapa (p176) district. Once a sleepy enclave of farms, farmers and farmers' families, it's now a booming wine region with a boutique bent. Pinot noir is the stuff that's doing the bending: sample plenty, then bed down for the night in an upmarket B&B and swan between cafes and restaurants the next day.

Wellington & Lower North Island's Best...

Cafes & Restaurants

○ **Ortega Fish Shack** (p166) The best of local submarine offerings (no, not big sandwiches)

○ **Scopa** (p167) Authentic Italian on Cuba St

○ **Fidel's** (p167) This longstanding, left-leaning boho cafe is still Wellington's best

○ **Logan Brown** (p168) Classy but unpretentious eats in a converted city-centre bank

○ **Trio Café at Coney Winery** (p178) The pick of the Wairarapa's wine-and-dine options

Places to Stretch Your Legs

○ **Mt Victoria Lookout** (p163) As AC/DC profess, it's a long way to the top, but the views are awesome

○ **Wellington Botanic Gardens** (p163) Catch the cable-car up the slope, then wander back down through the greenery

○ **Queen Elizabeth Park** (p174) Head for the dunes in this Kapiti Coast seaside park

○ **Napier art-deco walking tour** (p179) Check out Napier's architectural gems on foot

Places to Get Lost

○ **Kapiti Island** (p175) Talk with the animals (and birds) on this untrammelled offshore nature reserve

○ **Cape Palliser** (p178) Remote seal colonies and surf breaks

○ **Otari-Wilton's Bush** (p163) Native bushland enclave on Wellington's back doorstep

○ **Zealandia** (p163) Disappear along forested walking trails: it's hard to believe Wellington city is just 2km away!

Need to Know

Places to Get Boozy

○ **Cuba St** (p169) Bars, backpackers, buskers... The funky, artsy heart-and-soul of the capital

○ **Wairarapa Wine Country** (p177) Day-trip or overnight in the Wairarapa's wine-soaked valleys

○ **Hawke's Bay Wine Region** (p182) Sunny days and classy tastings around Napier

○ **Courtenay Pl** (p169) Get down-and-dirty with Wellington's thirsty throngs

ADVANCE PLANNING

○ **One month before** Organise domestic flights, car hire and tickets on the *Overlander* train between Wellington and Auckland

○ **Two weeks before** Book a South Island ferry crossing and accommodation across the region

○ **One week before** Book a seat on a Hawke's Bay winery tour, a tour to Kapiti Island and a table at one of Wellington's top restaurants

RESOURCES

○ **Wellington i-SITE** (www.wellingtonnz.com) The low-down on New Zealand's 'capital of cool'

○ **Dominion Post** (www.dompost.co.nz) News from the nation's political heartland

○ **Wairarapa NZ** (www.wairarapanz.com) Accommodation, wine, food and regional highlights

○ **Napier i-SITE** (www.napiercity.co.nz) Info on the art-deco city

○ **Hawke's Bay Tourism** (www.hawkesbaynz.com) Things to see, do, eat and drink around Hawke's Bay

GETTING AROUND

○ **Walk** Along Courtenay Pl and up and down Cuba St

○ **Bus** Across central Wellington

○ **Cable car** From Lambton Quay up the hill to the Wellington Botanic Gardens

○ **Hire a car** From Wellington through the Wairarapa and up the East Coast

○ **Minibus** Around the Hawke's Bay and Wairarapa wineries

○ **Ferry** From Wellington to Picton on the South Island, and out to Kapiti Island

○ **Train** Between Wellington and Auckland on the *Overlander*

BE FOREWARNED

○ **Windy Welly** The Crowded House song *Four Seasons In One Day* was written about Melbourne, but the same applies in Wellington: expect sun, rain and (most of all) wind at any moment

Left: Seals at Cape Palliser (p178);
Above: Wellington Botanic Gardens (p163)

Wellington & Lower North Island Itineraries

Rub shoulders with the elegantly wasted locals in Wellington's cafes, bars and pubs, then flush out your system with some fresh air and wilderness beyond the city's bohemian microcosm.

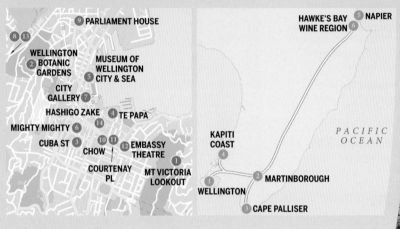

3 DAYS

WELLINGTON TO WELLINGTON

City Days, City Nights

Comprehend the hills, valleys and convolutions of this far-flung San Francisco of the South: drive (or walk) up to **(1) Mt Victoria Lookout**, or ride the cable car up to the **(2) Wellington Botanic Gardens**. After lunch on cool **(3) Cuba St**, immerse yourself in all things Kiwi at **(4) Te Papa** or the excellent, locally focused **(5) Museum of Wellington City & Sea**. Toast your efforts with a jug of beer at **(6) Mighty Mighty**.

The next day, fuel up with coffee and eggs at Nikau in the **(7) City Gallery**, then truck out to **(8) Zealandia** to meet the birds and learn about NZ conservation. Alternatively, encounter some other bird-brains on a tour

of **(9) Parliament House**. For dinner try **(10) Chow**, then spend your evening bar-hopping along **(11) Courtenay Pl.** Nocturnal entertainment could involve live music, a movie at the gloriously restored **(12) Embassy Theatre**, or a midnight snack at a late-closing cafe – or all three.

Get active on day three: storm the trails at **(13) Makara Peak Mountain Bike Park**, or go kayaking or paddle-boarding on the harbour. After all that activity, reward yourself with some NZ craft beer at **(14) Hashigo Zake**.

 5 DAYS

WELLINGTON TO HAWKE'S BAY WINE REGION
Wine & Wilderness

Done central **(1) Wellington** to death? Time to hightail it over the hills for some wine tasting around classy **(2) Martinborough** in the Wairarapa Wine Country: pinot noir is the name of the game here. A bike ride through the vines is a divine way to go, or book a seat on a minibus tour. Bunk down that night in a cosy country B&B.

Recharge in the local cafes and restaurants the next morning, then track south to explore the weird wilds of **(3) Cape Palliser**, which offers pungent seal colonies, a beach full of rusty tractors, a lonesome lighthouse and surreal, end-of-the-world vibes.

From here you can head west to the underrated **(4) Kapiti Coast** for a night (aim for beachy Paekakariki), or get your skates on a travel north to sunny **(5) Napier** in the Hawke's Bay region. The town is home to an improbably well-preserved collection of art-deco architecture, built in the 1930s after a devastating quake. There are some cool cafes and bars here too, and encircling Napier are the vineyards and wineries of the **(6) Hawke's Bay Wine Region** (brilliant chardonnay!).

Parliament House (p162), Wellington
DAVID WALL/LONELY PLANET IMAGES ©

Discover Wellington & Lower North Island

At a Glance

○ **Wellington** (p162) NZ's capital is flush with culture, coffee and crazy nightlife.

○ **The Wairarapa** (p176) Indulgent vales full of Wellington wine weekenders.

○ **Kapiti Coast** (p174) Holiday town and eerie Kapiti Island an hour north of Wellington.

○ **Hawke's Bay** (p178) Laid-back and sunny, with wine tasting, beach-bumming and art-deco architecture.

City Gallery, adorned with an exhibition by Yayoi Kusama
DAVID WALL/LONELY PLANET IMAGES ©

WELLINGTON

 Sights

Museums & Galleries

FREE **MUSEUM OF WELLINGTON CITY & SEA** Museum
(www.museumofwellington.co.nz; Queens Wharf; ☉10am-5pm) For an imaginative, interactive experience of Wellington's social and salty maritime history, swing into the Museum of Wellington. Highlights include a moving documentary about the tragedy of the *Wahine*, and ancient Maori legends dramatically told using tiny hologram actors and special effects. The building itself is an old Bond Store dating from 1892.

FREE **CITY GALLERY** Gallery
(www.citygallery.org.nz; Civic Sq, Wakefield St; charges may apply for major exhibits; ☉10am-5pm) Housed in the monumental old library in Civic Sq, Wellington's much-loved City Gallery does a cracking job of securing acclaimed contemporary international exhibitions, as well as unearthing and supporting those at the forefront of the NZ scene.

FREE **PARLIAMENT HOUSE** Cultural Building
(www.parliament.nz; Bowen St; ☉tours on the hour 10am-4pm Mon-Fri, 10am-3pm Sat, 11am-3pm Sun) The austere grey-and-cream Parliament House was completed in 1922. Free one-hour tours depart from the ground-floor foyer (arrive 15 minutes prior). Next door is the 1899 neo-Gothic

Parliamentary Library building, as well as the modernist **Beehive** designed by British architect Sir Basil Spence and built between 1969 and 1980.

Gardens & Lookouts

FREE **WELLINGTON BOTANIC GARDENS**   Gardens
The hilly, 25-hectare botanic gardens can be *almost* effortlessly visited via a cable-car ride (nice bit of planning, eh?). They boast a tract of original native forest along with varied collections including a beaut rose garden and international plant collections. The gardens are also accessible from the Centennial Entrance on Glenmore St (Karori bus 3).

CABLE CAR & MUSEUM   Tram
(www.wellingtoncablecar.co.nz; 1-way adult/child $3.50/1, return $6/2; ⊙departs every 10min, 7am-10pm Mon-Fri, 8.30am-10pm Sat, 9am-9pm Sun) One of Wellington's most famous attractions is the little red cable car that clanks up the steep slope from Lambton Quay to Kelburn. At the top is the Wellington Botanic Gardens, the Carter Observatory and the small-but-nifty **Cable Car Museum** (www.cablecarmuseum.co.nz; admission free), which tells the cable car's story since it was built in 1902 to open up hilly Kelburn for settlement. Take the cable car back down the hill, or ramble down through the gardens (a 30- to 60-minute walk, depending on your wend).

MT VICTORIA LOOKOUT   Lookout
For a readily accessible viewpoint of the city, harbour and surrounds, venture up to the lookout atop the 196m Mt Victoria, east of the city centre. You can take bus 2 some of the way up, but the rite of passage is to sweat it out on the walk (ask a local for directions or just follow your nose). If you've got your own wheels, take Oriental Pde along the waterfront and then scoot up Carlton Gore Rd.

FREE **OTARI-WILTON'S BUSH**   Park
(160 Wilton Rd; ⊙dawn-dusk) About 3km west of the city is Otari-Wilton's Bush, the only botanic gardens in NZ specialising in native flora. There are more than 1200 plant species here, including some of the city's oldest trees, as well as 11km of walking trails and delightful picnic areas. Bus 14 from the city passes the gates.

Wildlife

ZEALANDIA   Wildlife Reserve
(☏04-920 9200; www.visitzealandia.com; Waiapu Rd; adult/child/family exhibition only $18.50/9/46, exhibition & valley $28.80/14.50/71.50; ⊙10am-5pm, last entry 4pm) This groundbreaking ecosanctuary is tucked in the hills about 2km west of town (bus 3 passes nearby, or see the Zealandia website for the free shuttle). Living wild within the fenced valley are more than 30 native bird species including rare takahe, saddleback, hihi and kaka, as well as NZ's most accessible wild population of tuatara and little spotted kiwi. More than 30km of tracks can be explored and there's a daily tour (11.15am). The night tour provides an opportunity to spot nocturnal creatures including kiwi, frogs and glowworms (adult/child $76.50/36).

🤸 Activities

FERG'S KAYAKS   Kayaking
(www.fergskayaks.co.nz; Shed 6, Queens Wharf; ⊙10am-8pm Mon-Fri, 10am-6pm Sat & Sun) Punish your tendons with indoor rock climbing (adult/child $15/10), cruise the waterfront on a pair of in-line skates ($15 for two hours) or paddle around the harbour in a kayak or on a stand-up paddleboard (from $15 for one hour). There's also bike hire (one hour from $15) and guided kayaking trips.

MAKARA PEAK MOUNTAIN BIKE PARK   Mountain Biking
(www.makarapeak.org; South Karori Rd, Karori; admission by donation) In the hills of Karori, 4km west of the city centre (bus 3, 17 or 18), this excellent 200-hectare park is laced with 24km of single-track ranging from beginner to expert. The nearby **Mud Cycles** (☏04-476 4961; www.mudcycles.co.nz;

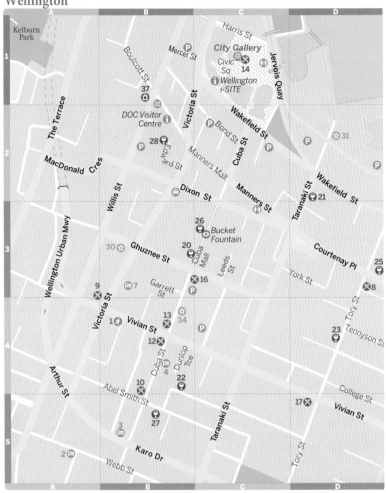

421 Karori Rd, Karori; half-/full-day/weekend bike hire from $30/45/75; ☺9.30am-6pm Mon-Fri) has mountain bikes for hire, and runs guided tours for riders of all abilities.

 Tours

WALK WELLINGTON Guided Tour
(✆04-802 4860; www.walkwellington.org.nz; adult/child $20/10; ☺tours 10am daily, plus 5.30pm Mon, Wed & Fri Nov-Mar) Informative and great-value two-hour walking tours

focussing on the city and waterfront, departing the i-SITE. Book online, phone or just turn up.

HAMMONDS SCENIC TOURS Guided Tour
(✆04-472 0869; www.wellingtonsightseeing tours.com; city tour adult/child $55/27.50, Kapiti Coast $100/50, Wairarapa $195/97.50) Runs a 2½-hour city highlights tour, four-hour tour of the Kapiti Coast, and a full-day Wairarapa experience including Cape Palliser.

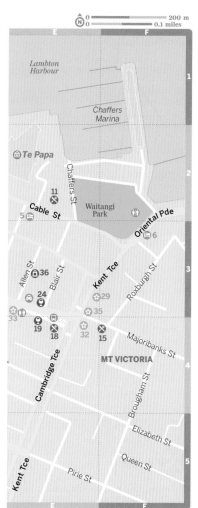

ZEST FOOD TOURS   Guided Tour
(☎04-801 9198; www.zestfoodtours.co.nz; tours from $128) Runs 2½- to 5½-hour small-group city sightseeing tours; longer tours include lunch with matched wines at Logan Brown (p168).

 Sleeping

OHTEL   Boutique Hotel $$$
(☎04-803 0600; www.ohtel.com; 66 Oriental Parade; d $265-395; ☎) Aesthetes check in and don't want to check out at this bijou hotel on Oriental Pde. Individually decorated rooms are beautified with stylish furniture and contemporary Kiwi artwork and ceramics, avidly collected by the architect-owner. The bathrooms in the deluxe rooms and suites, with their vista walls and deep tubs, are a designer's wet dream.

CAPITAL VIEW MOTOR INN   Motel $$
(☎0800 438 505, 04-385 0515; www.capitalview.co.nz; 12 Thompson St; d $125-160; ☎) Many of the rooms in this well-maintained, multistorey building close to Cuba St do indeed enjoy capital views – especially the large, good-value penthouse (sleeps five, $220). All are self-contained, and recent renovations have freshened things up.

BOOKLOVERS B&B   B&B $$
(☎04-384 2714; www.booklovers.co.nz; 123 Pirie St; s/d from $150/180; P @ ☎) This gracious, book-filled B&B run by award-winning author Jane Tolerton has four guest rooms with TV, CDs and CD/DVD player. Three have en suites, one has a private bathroom. Bus 2 runs from the front gate to Courtenay Pl and the train station, and the city's 'green belt' begins right next door. Free wi-fi and parking.

COMFORT & QUALITY HOTELS   Hotel $$
(☎04-385 2156, 0800 873 553; www.hotelwellington.co.nz; 223 Cuba St; d $104-200; @ ☎ ☱) Two hotels in one: the sympathetically renovated historic Trekkers building with its smaller, cheaper rooms (Comfort); and the snazzier high-rise Quality with modern styling and a swimming pool. Both share in-house bar and dining room (mains $22 to $30). Two solid options in the heart of Cuba.

CITY COTTAGES   Rental House $$
(☎0210 739 232; www.citybedandbreakfast.co.nz; Tonks Grove; d/q $170/200; ☎) Saved only after protracted public protest when the new bypass went through, these two tiny 1880 cottages sit among a precious precinct of historic Cuba St buildings. Clever conversion has transformed them

Wellington

into all-mod-con, self-contained one-bedroom pads, comfortable for two but sleeping up to four thanks to a sofa bed.

MUSEUM HOTEL   Hotel $$$
(✆0800 994 335, 04-802 8900; www.museum hotel.co.nz; 90 Cable St; r & apt Mon-Thu $205-399, Fri-Sun $199-349; @ ☎ ⊛) Formerly known as 'Museum Hotel de Wheels' (to make way for Te Papa, it was rolled here from its original location 120m away), this art-filled hotel keeps the quirk-factor high. Bright-eyed staff, a very good restaurant with outrageous decor, and groovy tunes piped into the lobby make a refreshing change from homogenised business hotels. Tasty weekend/weekly rates.

VICTORIA COURT   Motel $$
(✆04-385 7102; www.victoriacourt.co.nz; 201 Victoria St; r $149-205; P ☎) Our top motel choice in the city centre, with plenty of parking. The affable owners offer modern, spacious studios and apartments with spa baths, kitchenettes, slick blond-wood joinery and TVs. Two disabled-access units; larger units sleep six.

 Eating

Two excellent produce markets run from dawn till around 2pm on Sundays – the seriously fruit 'n' veg **Farmers Market** (cnr Victoria & Vivian Sts), and the more varied **Harbourside Market** (Wakefield St) next to Te Papa.

ORTEGA FISH SHACK   Seafood $$$
(✆04-382 9559; www.ortega.co.nz; 16 Marjoribanks St; mains $32-34) Fishing floats, salty portraits and Egyptian floor tiles set a colourful Mediterranean scene, a good hook on which to hang a seafood dinner. Fish comes many ways (with ratatouille and crayfish butter; on pork and prawn kedgeree with *nam prik* relish) while the afters head straight for France courtesy

Don't Miss **Te Papa**

Te Papa is the city's 'must-see' attraction, and for reasons well beyond the fact that it's NZ's national museum. It's highly interactive, fun, and full of surprises.

The riches inside include an amazing collection of Maori artefacts and the museum's own colourful *marae*; natural history and environment exhibitions; Pacific and NZ history galleries; national art collection; and themed hands-on 'discovery centres' for children. Exhibitions occupy impressive gallery spaces with a high-tech twist (eg motion-simulator rides and a house shaking through an earthquake).

You could spend a day exploring Te Papa's six floors but still not see it all. To cut to the chase, head to the information desk on level two. For exhibition highlights and to get your bearings, the one-hour 'Introducing Te Papa' tour ($14) is a good idea; tours leave from the info desk at 10.15am, 12pm and 2pm daily in winter, more frequently in summer.

NEED TO KNOW

Map p164; www.tepapa.govt.nz; 55 Cable St; admission free; ⊙10am-6pm Fri-Wed, to 9pm Thu

---

of orange crepes and one of Welly's best cheese boards. Excellent food in a relaxed yet upbeat environment.

SCOPA Italian $$
(cnr Cuba & Ghuznee Sts; mains $15-26; ⊙9am-late Mon-Sun; ✎) Perfect pizza, proper pasta and other authentic Italian treats make dining at this modern *cucina* a pleasure. The *bianche* (white) pizzas make a refreshing change as do the

pizzaiolo – pizzas of the week. Watch the groovy 'Cubans' from a seat in the window. Lunchtime specials; sexy evenings complete with cocktails.

FIDEL'S Cafe $
(234 Cuba St; meals $9-20; ⊙7.30am-late; ✎) A Cuba St institution for caffeine-craving, alternative types. Eggs any-which-way, pizza and splendid salads are cranked out of the itsy kitchen, along

167

with Welly's best milkshakes. Revolutionary memorabilia adorns the walls of the funky interior; decent outdoor areas too. A super-busy crew copes with the chaos admirably.

NIKAU GALLERY CAFE · Cafe $$
(City Gallery, Civic Sq; lunch $14-25; ⏱7am-4pm Mon-Fri, 8am-4pm Sat; 🛠) An airy affair at the sophisticated end of the cafe scene, Nikau consistently dishes up some of the simplest but most delightful fare in town. Refreshing aperitifs, legendary kedgeree and sage eggs, divine sweets, and a sunny courtyard.

LOGAN BROWN · Modern NZ $$$
(📞04-801 5114; www.loganbrown.co.nz; 192 Cuba St; mains $39-48; ⏱noon-2pm Mon-Sat, 5.30pm-late Mon-Sun) Located in a 1920s banking chamber, Logan Brown oozes class without being pretentious or overly formal. Believe the hype, sample the lamb two ways, snapper and paua, and peruse the epic wine list. The pretheatre menu ($39.50) is a fine way of indulging without cleaning out your account. Bookings recommended.

CHOW · Fusion $$
(45 Tory St; small plates $7-17, mains $15-24; ⏱noon-midnight; 📶🛠) Home of the legendary blue-cheese-and-peanut wonton, Chow is a stylish pan-Asian restaurant-cum-bar: a must-visit for people who love exciting food in sociable surroundings, accompanied by the odd cocktail. Daily deals, free wi-fi, and the fun Library bar through the back door.

MIDNIGHT ESPRESSO · Cafe $
(178 Cuba St; meals $8-17; ⏱7.30am-late Mon-Fri, 8am-late Sat & Sun; 🛠) The city's original hip cafe, with food that's hearty, tasty and inexpensive – heavy on the wholesome and vegetarian. Sitting in the window with Havana coffee and cake is the quintessential Wellington cafe experience.

Left: Museum Hotel (p166); **Below:** Waiter at Fidel's cafe (p167)
(LEFT) OLIVER STREWE/LONELY PLANET IMAGES ©; (BELOW) HAUKE DRESSLER/GETTY IMAGES ©

SWEET MOTHER'S KITCHEN
American $

(5 Courtenay Pl; mains $10-27; ⏰8am-late; 🖋) Perpetually full, predominantly with young cool cats, Sweet Mother's serves dubious takes on the Deep South, such as burritos, nachos, po' boys and jambalaya. Key lime pie is about as authentic as it gets. It's cheap, cute, has craft beer and good sun.

SHINOBI SUSHI LOUNGE
Sushi $$

(43 Vivian St; sushi plates $19-35, California rolls $7-19; ⏰noon-2pm Tue-Fri, 5.30-10pm Tue-Sun) Super-fresh fish, Japanese training and Kiwi flair combine to create the most exciting sushi joint in town, while seriously good cocktails and a quality drinks list keeps things lubricated.

🍷 Drinking

MIGHTY MIGHTY
Bar

(104 Cuba St; ⏰4pm-late Wed-Sat) This is the hippest of the capital's drinking and music venues. Inside-a-pinball-machine decor, pink velvet curtains, kitsch gewgaws and Wellington's best barmaid make this an essential port of call for those wanting to tilt or bang a bumper. A colourful slice of NZ bar life.

HASHIGO ZAKE
Craft Beer

(www.hashigozake.co.nz; 25 Taranaki St) The headquarters of the capital's underground beer movement, this brick-walled basement bar pours only quality craft brews to a wide range of hopheads. An oft-changing selection of a dozen beers on tap is reinforced by a united nations of around 140 beers by the bottle.

HAVANA
Bar

(www.havanabar.co.nz; 32 Wigan St; ⏰11am-late Mon-Fri, 3pm-late Sat) Much like the proverbial light under a bushel, one of Welly's most seductive bars is hidden away down a side street you'll never stumble across. You'll find it in two adjacent heritage

169

If You Like…
Drinking in Wellington

If you like Mighty Mighty, we think you'll appreciate the boozy offerings of these other Wellington bars.

1 VIVO
(www.vivowinebar.co.nz; 19 Edward St; ⏰3pm-late Mon-Fri, 5pm-late Sat) A tomelike list of approximately 600 wines plus excellent tapas-style food.

2 HUMMINGBIRD
(www.hummingbird.net.nz; 22 Courtenay Pl; ⏰3pm-late Mon-Fri, 10am-late Sat & Sun) Sophisticated Hummingbird is usually packed – both inside in the intimate, stylish dining room–bar, and outside on street-side tables. Croony music; regular live jazz.

3 GOOD LUCK
(basement, 126 Cuba St; ⏰5pm-late Tue-Sun) Cuba St's Chinese opium den, minus the opium. This is a slickly run, sultry basement bar playing fresh hip-hop and electronica.

4 LIBRARY
(53 Courtenay Pl; ⏰5pm-late Mon-Thu, 4pm-late Fri-Sun) Velveteen booths, books, booze and board games. A real page-turner, with cocktails you won't want to put down.

5 HAWTHORN LOUNGE
(82 Tory St; ⏰6pm-late Tue-Sat) Akin to a 1920s speakeasy, complete with waistcoats and wide-brimmed fedoras.

cottages, where you can eat tapas, drink your way along the top shelf, then chinwag, smoke, flirt and dance until very near dawn.

MALTHOUSE   Craft Beer
(www.themalthouse.co.nz; 48 Courtenay Pl; ⏰3pm-late Sun-Thu, noon-3am Fri & Sat) At last count there were 150 reasons to drink at this, the capital's original craft-beer bar.

Savvy staff will recommend brews from an epic list that showcases beers from NZ and around the globe. Enquire about new arrivals, and the aged selection of brews if you're a well-heeled beer geek.

SOUTHERN CROSS   Pub
(www.thecross.co.nz; 35 Abel Smith St; ⏰9am-late) Welly's most stylish crowd-pleasing pub combines a laid-back restaurant, lively bar, regular music, dance floor, pool table, the best garden bar in town and a welcoming attitude to children. Independent beer on tap and a good bowl of chips. Choice!

ANCESTRAL   Bar
(www.ancestral.co.nz; 31 Courtenay Pl; ⏰11am-late Tue-Fri, 3pm-late Mon & Sat) Asian-infused Ancestral has broken new ground in the Wellington bar scene. Designed by the architects responsible for the legendary Matterhorn, no effort has been spared to get every line and level right – lighting, music, shirt collars and cocktails. Whisky and cigars in the stripped and pimped garden bar are a highlight, but there's heaps to please here, including sake and the smoke, spark and crackle of the yakitori grill ($4 to $17).

MATTERHORN   Bar
(www.matterhorn.co.nz; 106 Cuba St; ⏰3pm-late Mon-Fri, 10am-late Sat & Sun) We're still gettin' the Horn, despite a change of ownership and some stiff competition. A perennially popular joint with three distinct but equally pleasing areas (long bar, dining room and garden bar), the Matterhorn still honours its patrons with reputable food (tapas from midafternoon, dinner daily, brunch weekends), solid service and regular live music.

 # Entertainment

Live Music & Clubs

SAN FRANCISCO BATH HOUSE   Live Music
(www.sfbh.co.nz; 171 Cuba St; ⏰4pm-late Tue-Sat) Wellington's best midsized live-music

venue, playing host to the cream of NZ artists, as well as quality acts from abroad. Somewhat debauched balcony action, five deep at the bar, but otherwise well run and lots of fun when the floor starts bouncing.

BODEGA — Live Music
(www.bodega.co.nz; 101 Ghuznee St; ☺4pm-late) A trailblazer of the city's modern live-music scene, and still considered an institution despite its move from a derelict heritage building to a concrete cavern. 'The Bodge' offers a full and varied program of gigs in a pleasant space with a respectable dance floor.

SANDWICHES — Club
(www.sandwiches.co.nz; 8 Kent Tce; ☺4pm-late Wed-Sat) Get yourself a slice of NZ's electronic artists and DJs, regular multi-flavoured international acts and a great sound system. Gritty club run by a dedicated team that isn't just in it for the bread.

Theatres

BATS — Theatre
(☎04-802 4175; www.bats.co.nz; 1 Kent Tce) Wildly alternative BATS presents cutting-edge and experimental NZ theatre – varied, cheap and intimate.

CIRCA — Theatre
(☎04-801 7992; www.circa.co.nz; 1 Taranaki St) Circa's main auditorium seats 240 people and its studio seats 100. Cheap tickets are available for preview shows, and there are also standby tickets available an hour before the show (which could be anything from pantomime to international comedy).

Cinemas

EMBASSY THEATRE — Cinema
(☎04-384 7657; www.deluxe.co.nz; 10 Kent Tce; from adult/child $15.50/12.50) Wellywood's cinema mothership, built in the 1920s. Screens mainstream films; bars and cafe on-site.

PARAMOUNT — Cinema
(☎04-384 4080; www.paramount.co.nz; 25 Courtenay Pl; from adult/child $13/9; ☺noon-midnight) A lovely old complex screening largely art-house, documentary and foreign flicks.

Drinks at Havana (p169)

OLIVER STREWE/LONELY PLANET IMAGES ©

🛍 Shopping

🌿 STARFISH — Clothing
(128 Willis St) Wellingtonian fashionistas' favourite treat. Beautiful clothing, sustainably made.

KURA — Arts & Crafts
(19 Allen St) Contemporary indigenous art: painting, ceramics, jewellery and sculpture.

KIRKCALDIE & STAINS — Department Store
(165-177 Lambton Quay) NZ's answer to Bloomingdale's or Harrods, established in 1863. Bring your travels documents with you for tax-free bargains.

ℹ Information

Medical Services

Wellington Accident & Urgent Medical Centre (📞04-384 4944; 17 Adelaide Rd, Newtown; ⏰8am-11pm) No appointment necessary; also home to the after-hours pharmacy.

Wellington Hospital (📞04-385 5999; www.ccdhb.org.nz; Riddiford St, Newtown; ⏰24hr) One kilometre south of the city centre.

Tourist Information

DOC Visitor Centre (Department of Conservation; 📞04-384 7770; www.doc.govt.nz; 18 Manners St; ⏰9am-5pm Mon-Fri, 10am-3.30pm Sat) Bookings, passes and information for national and local walks, parks, huts and camping, plus permits for Kapiti Island.

Wellington i-SITE (📞04-802 4860; www.wellingtonnz.com; Civic Sq, cnr Wakefield & Victoria Sts; ⏰8.30am-5pm) Staff book almost everything, and cheerfully distribute Wellington's *Official Visitor Guide,* other maps and walking guides. Internet access and cafe.

ℹ Getting There & Away

Air

Wellington Airport (WLG; 📞04-385 5100; www.wellington-airport.co.nz; Stewart Duff Dr, Rongotai; ⏰4am-1.30am) has touch-screen information kiosks in the luggage hall.

Air New Zealand (📞0800 737 000, 04-474 8950; www.airnewzealand.co.nz; cnr Lambton Quay & Grey St; ⏰9am-5pm Mon-Fri, 10am-1pm Sat) offers flights between Wellington and most domestic centres, including Auckland (from $69), Christchurch (from $59), Queenstown (from $89) and Nelson (from $79).

Jetstar (📞0800 800 995; www.jetstar.com) flies between Wellington and Auckland (tickets from $49), Christchurch (from $49) and Queenstown (from $59).

Soundsair (📞0800 505 005, 03-520 3080; www.soundsair.com) flies between Wellington and Picton up to eight times daily (from $90), as well as Nelson (from $107) and Blenheim (from $90).

Interislander ferry, Wellington

Air2there (☎0800 777 000, 04-904 5130; www.air2there.com) flies between Wellington and Blenheim ($99), and from Kapiti Coast Airport (www.kapitiairport.co.nz; Toru Rd, Paraparaumu Beach) to Blenheim ($125) and Nelson ($135).

Boat

There are two options for crossing the strait between Wellington and Picton: Bluebridge and the Interislander.

Bluebridge is based at Waterloo Quay, opposite the Wellington train station. The Interislander terminal is about 2km northeast of the city centre; a shuttle bus ($2) runs to the Interislander from platform 9 at Wellington train station (where long-distance buses also depart). It also meets arriving ferries, returning passengers to platform 9.

Bluebridge Ferries (☎04-471 6188, 0800 844 844; www.bluebridge.co.nz; 50 Waterloo Quay; adult/child from $51/26) Crossing takes three hours 20 minutes; up to four sailings in each direction daily. Cars and campervans up to 5.5m from $118; motorbikes $51; bicycles $10.

Interislander (☎04-498 3302, 0800 802 802; www.interislander.co.nz; Aotea Quay; adult/child from $55/28) Crossing takes three hours 10 minutes; up to five sailings in each direction daily. Cars are priced from $118; campervans (up to 5.5m) from $133; motorbikes from $56; bicycles $15.

Bus

InterCity (☎04-385 0520; www.intercity.co.nz) and Newmans (☎04-385 0521; www.newmanscoach.co.nz) buses depart from platform 9 at the train station.

Naked Bus (☎0900 625 33; www.nakedbus.com) runs north from Wellington to all major North Island destinations. Buses depart from opposite the Amora Hotel in Wakefield St and Bunny St opposite the train station.

Train

Wellington train station has six ticket windows (☎0800 801 700; ⊙6.30am-8pm Mon-Thu, to 1pm Fri & Sat, to 3pm Sun), two selling tickets for Tranz Scenic trains, Interislander ferries and InterCity and Newmans coaches; the other four ticketing local/regional Tranz Metro (☎0800 801 700; www.tranzmetro.co.nz) trains (Johnsonville, Melling, Hutt Valley, Paraparaumu and Wairarapa lines).

Long-haul Tranz Scenic (☎0800 872 467; www.tranzscenic.co.nz) routes include the daily *Overlander* between Wellington and Auckland (from $79, 12 hours, Thursday to Sunday May to September); and the *Capital Connection* between Wellington and Palmerston North (from $26, two hours, one daily Monday to Friday).

❶ Getting Around

Metlink (☎0800 801 700; www.metlink.org.nz) is the one-stop shop for Wellington's regional bus, train and harbour ferry networks all detailed below.

To & From Airport

Super Shuttle (☎0800 748 885; www.supershuttle.co.nz; 1/2 passengers $16/21; ⊙24hr) provides a door-to-door minibus service between the city and airport, 8km southeast of the city.

The Airport Flyer (☎0800 801 700; www.metlink.co.nz; airport–city per adult/child $8.50/5) bus runs between the airport, Wellington and the Hutt Valley. Buses run from around 6am to 9.30pm.

A taxi between the city centre and airport costs around $30.

Bus

Frequent and efficient bus services cover the whole Wellington region and run between approximately 6am and 11.30pm. Major bus terminals are at the Wellington train station, and on Courtenay Pl near the Cambridge Tce intersection. Fares are determined by zones: a trip across the city centre (Zone 1) costs $2, and all the way up the coast to Otaki (Zone 13) costs $16.50.

Metlink also runs the **After Midnight** bus service, departing from two convenient city stops (Courtenay Pl and Cuba St) between midnight and 4.30am Saturday and Sunday on a number of routes to the outer suburbs. Fares range from $6 to $12, depending on how far away your bed is.

Taxi

Green Cabs (☎0508 447 336)

Wellington Combined Taxis (☎04-384 444)

Train

Tranz Metro operates four train routes running through Wellington's suburbs to regional destinations. Trains run frequently from around 6am to 11pm, departing Wellington train station. The routes: Johnsonville via Ngaio and Khandallah; Waikanae via Porirua, Plimmerton and Paekakariki; Melling via Petone; the Hutt Valley via Waterloo to Upper Hutt. A train service also connects with the Wairarapa, calling at Featherston, Carterton and Masterton. Standard fares from Wellington to the ends of the five lines range from $4.50 to $17.50.

KAPITI COAST

With wide, crowd-free beaches, the Kapiti Coast acts as a summer playground and suburban extension for Wellingtonians. The region takes its moniker from Kapiti Island, a bird and marine sanctuary 5km offshore from Paraparaumu.

Comprehensive visitor information can be found at **Paraparaumu visitor information centre** (04-298 8195; www. naturecoast.co.nz; Coastlands, Rimu Rd; 9am-5pm Mon-Fri, 10am-3pm Sat & Sun).

Getting There & Around

Getting here from Wellington is a breeze: just track north on SH1. By car, it's about a 30-minute drive to Paekakariki, and around 45 minutes to Paraparaumui, much of it by motorway.

AIR

Kapiti Coast Airport in Paraparumu was expanded in 2011, and is a regular destination for **Air2there** (0800 777 000; www.air2there. com), with daily flights to Blenheim and Nelson, and **Air New Zealand** (0800 737 000; www. airnewzealand.co.nz), which flies direct to Auckland.

BUS

InterCity (www.intercity.co.nz) stops at major Kapiti Coast towns on its services between Wellington and the north.

The daily services into/out of Wellington run by **White Star Express** (04-478 4734, 0800 465 622; www.whitestarbus.co.nz) and **Naked Bus** (0900 625 33; www.nakedbus.com) also stop at major Kapiti Coast towns.

TRAIN

Tranz Metro (0800 801 700; www.tranzmetro. co.nz) commuter trains between Wellington and the coast are easier and more frequent than buses.

Tranz Scenic (0800 872 467; www. tranzscenic.co.nz) has long-distance *Overlander* trains connecting Wellington and Auckland stopping at Paraparaumu, while the weekday-only, peak-hour *Capital Connection,* travelling to Wellington in the morning and back to Palmerston North in the evening, stops at Paraparaumu, Waikanae and Otaki.

Paekakariki

Paekakariki is a little seaside village stretched along a black-sand beach, serviced by a train station and passed by the highway to Wellington, 41km to the south.

Sights & Activities

FREE **QUEEN ELIZABETH PARK**   Park (SH1; gates open 8am-8pm) This rambling but rather beautiful 650-hectare beachside park offers plenty of opportunities for swimming, walking, cycling and picnicking, as well as being the location of the Stables on the Park and Tramway Museum.

TRAMWAY MUSEUM   Museum (www.wellingtontrams.org.nz; MacKay's Crossing entrance, Queen Elizabeth Park; admission by donation, all-day tram rides adult/child/family $8/4/20; museum 10am-4.30pm daily, trams 11am-4.30pm Sat & Sun, daily 26 Dec-late Jan) A glimpse into historic Wellington by way of restored wooden trams and museum displays inside their big garage. A 2km track curls through Queen Elizabeth Park down to the beach. On-site ice-cream kiosk.

Sleeping & Eating

HILLTOP HIDEAWAY   Guesthouse $ (04-902 5967; www.wellingtonbeach backpackers.co.nz; 11 Wellington Rd; d $80; @) Formerly Paekakariki Backpackers, Peter and Denise now offer two double en-suite rooms in their hilltop home, one with sea and sunset views. The great-value rooms are homely but elegant, much like the hosts themselves.

FINN'S
Hotel $$

(☎04-292 8081; www.finnshotel.co.nz; 2 Beach Rd; mains$17-27; ⎙) Finn's is the flashy beige suit of the cutesy railway village, but redeems itself with spacious rooms (doubles $125 to $135), good-value meals and independent beer on tap. The hush glass keeps the highway at bay.

Paraparaumu

Low-key Paraparaumu is the principal town on the Kapiti Coast, and a suburban satellite of Wellington. The rough-and-tumble beach is the coast's most developed, sustaining cafes, motels and takeaway joints. Boat trips to Kapiti Island set sail from here.

 Sights & Activities

SOUTHWARD CAR MUSEUM
Museum

(www.southwardcarmuseum.co.nz; Otaihanga Rd; adult/child $12/3; ⎙9am-4.30pm) This museum has one of Australasia's largest collections of antique and unusual cars. Check out the DeLorean and the 1950 gangster Cadillac.

PARAPARAUMU BEACH GOLF CLUB
Golf

(☎04-902 8200; www.paraparaumubeachgolf club.co.nz; 376 Kapiti Rd; green fees $150; ⎙7.30am-dusk) This challenging and beautiful links course is ranked among NZ's best. It has hosted the NZ Open 12 times and tamed Tiger in 2002. Visitors are welcome: call for tee times, or book online.

 **Eating**

SOPRANO RISTORANTE
Italian $$

(☎04-298 8892; 7 Seaview Rd; mains $25-30; ⎙6pm-late Mon-Sat) A welcoming family-run joint with the liveliest evening atmosphere at the beach township. No-nonsense, affordable food and wine in a homely environment – *bella*!

Kapiti Island

Kapiti Island is the coastline's dominant feature, a 10km by 2km slice, which since 1897 has been a protected reserve. It's largely predator-free, allowing a remarkable range and number of birds – including many species that are now rare or

Kereru, New Zealand's native pigeon, Kapiti Island nature reserve

Detour:
New Zealand Rugby Museum

Fans of the oval ball holler about the **New Zealand Rugby Museum** (☏06-358 6947; www.rugbymuseum.co.nz; 326 Main St; adult/child/family $12.50/5/30; ☺10am-5pm) in otherwise missable Palmerston North, 90km north of Paraparaumu. The museum is an amazing new space overflowing with rugby paraphernalia, from a 1905 All Blacks jumper to a scrum machine and the actual whistle used to start the first game of every Rugby World Cup. Of course, NZ hosted the 2011 Rugby World Cup and beat France 7-8 in the final: don't expect anyone here to stop talking about it until 2015...

extinct on the mainland – to thrive on the island.

The island is open to visitors, limited to 86 people per day (or you can stay overnight with Kapiti Island Nature Tours), and it's essential that you book and obtain a permit (adult/child $11/5) online (www.doc.govt.nz), in person at Wellington's DOC visitor centre (p172), or via email (wellingtonvc@doc.govt.nz).

Transport is booked separately from the permit (arrange your permit before your boat trip). Two commercial operators are licensed to take visitors to the island, both running to/from Paraparaumu Beach (which can be reached by train).

Make all your bookings in advance; more information can be found in DOC's *Kapiti Island Nature Reserve* brochure.

The Barrett and Clark *whanau* (family), who have a long-standing connection to the island, run **Kapiti Island Nature Tours & Lodge**

(☏06-362 6606; www.kapitiislandnaturetours. co.nz; per person incl three meals $250-330), and offer very special nature tours that touch on the birds (in incredible range and number), seal colony, history and Maori traditions.

Both offering boat transport to the island a couple of times a day are **Kapiti Marine Charter** (☏04-297 2585, 0800 433 779; www.kapitimarinecharter.co.nz; adult/child $60/35) and **Kapiti Tours** (☏04-237 7965, 0800 527 484; www.kapititours.co.nz; adult/child $60/35).

THE WAIRARAPA

The Wairarapa is the large slab of land east and northeast of Wellington, beyond the craggy Tararua and Rimutaka Ranges. Named after Lake Wairarapa (Shimmering Waters), a shallow 8000-hectare lake, the region has traditionally been a frenzied hotbed of sheep farming. More recently, wineries have sprung up, accompanied by a vigorous foodie culture – around Martinborough, most famously – which has turned the region into a decadent weekend retreat.

❶ Getting There & Around

From Wellington, Tranz Metro (☏0800 801 700; www.tranzmetro.co.nz) commuter trains run to Masterton ($17.50, five or six daily on weekdays, two daily on weekends), calling at seven Wairarapa stations including Featherston and Carterton.

Martinborough

The sweetest visitor spot in the Wairarapa, Martinborough is a pretty town with a leafy town square and some charming old buildings, surrounded by a patchwork of pasture and a pinstripe of grapevines.

The town's cultural hub is arguably **Circus** (☏06-306 9442; www.circus.net. nz; 34 Jellicoe St; adult/child $15/10, mains $20-28; ☺4pm-late Wed-Mon), a stylish arthouse cinema (movieline ☏056-306 9434) where you can watch the cream of contemporary movies in a a modern, microsize complex. Reasonably priced

OLIVER STREWE/LONELY PLANET IMAGES ©

Don't Miss **Wairarapa Wine Country**

Wairarapa's wineries thrive on visitors; Martinborough's 20-odd are particularly welcoming with well-oiled cellar doors, and noteworthy food served in some gorgeous gardens and courtyards. The *Wairarapa Wine Trail Map* (available from the i-SITE and many other locations) will aid your navigations.

An excellent place to sample and purchase many wines, and for advice on local cellar doors, is the **Martinborough Wine Centre** (www.martinboroughwinecentre.co.nz; 6 Kitchener St; ⏰10am-5pm), which also sells olive oils, books, clothing and art.

RECOMMENDED WINERIES

Ata Rangi (www.atarangi.co.nz; 14 Puruatanga Rd; ⏰1-3pm Mon-Fri, noon-4pm Sat & Sun) One of the region's pioneering winemakers. Great drops across the board and cute cellar door.

Coney (www.coneywines.co.nz; Dry River Rd; ⏰11am-4pm Fri-Sun) Friendly, operatic tastings and lovely restaurant.

Margrain (www.margrainvineyard.co.nz; cnr Ponatahi & Huangarua Rds; ⏰11am-5pm Fri-Sun) Pretty winery and site of the Taste Vin Café, a good pit stop overlooking the vines.

Vynfields (www.vynfields.com; 22 Omarere Rd; ⏰11am-4pm) Five-star, savoury pinot noir and a lush lawn on which to enjoy a platter. Organic/biodynamic wines.

TOURS

Hammond's Scenic Tours (☎04-472 0869; www.wellingtonsightseeingtours.com; full-day tour adult/child $200/100) Full-day winery tours including gourmet lunch.

Tranzit Tours (☎0800 471 227, 06-370 6600; www.tranzittours.co.nz; from $142) Four vineyards and a platter lunch at Martinborough's Village Café.

Martinborough Wine Centre (☎06-306 9040; www.martinboroughwinecentre.co.nz; 6 Kitchener St; half-day $25, full day $35) Morning, afternoon or all-day bicycle rentals.

Detour:
Cape Palliser

The Wairarapa coast south of Martinborough around Palliser Bay and Cape Palliser is remote and sparsely populated. The bendy road to the Cape is stupendously scenic: a big ocean and black-sand beaches on one side; barren hills and sheer cliffs on the other.

Standing like giant organ pipes in the Putangirua Scenic Reserve are the **Putangirua Pinnacles**, formed by rain washing silt and sand away and exposing the underlying bedrock. Accessible by a track near the car park on Cape Palliser Rd, it's an easy three-hour return walk along a streambed to the pinnacles, or take the 3½-hour loop track past hills and coastal viewpoints.

Further south is the wind-worn fishing village Ngawi. The first things you'll notice here are the rusty bulldozers on the beach, used to drag fishing boats ashore. Next stop is the malodorous seal colony, the North Island's largest breeding area.

Get your thighs thumping on the steep, 250-step (or is it 249?) climb to **Cape Palliser Lighthouse**, from where there are yet more amazing coastal views.

---

food includes bar snacks, pizza, mains with plenty of seasonal veg, and gelato.

🛏 Sleeping & Eating

AYLSTONE RETREAT
Boutique Hotel $$$
(☏06-306 9505; www.aylstone.co.nz; 19 Huangarua Rd; d incl breakfast $230-260; 🛜) Set among the vines on the edge of the village, this elegant retreat is a winning spot for the romantically inclined. Six en-suite rooms exude a lightly floral, French-provincial charm, and share a pretty posh reading room. The on-site bistro does a magnificent croissant, and the whole shebang is surrounded by micromansion garden sporting lawns, boxed hedges and chichi furniture.

CLAREMONT
Motel $$
(☏06-306 9162, 0800 809 162; www.the claremont.co.nz; 38 Regent St; d $130-158, 4-person apt $280; @) A classy accommodation enclave off Jellicoe St, the Claremont has two-storey, self-contained units in great nick, modern studios with spa baths, and sparkling two-bedroom apartments, all at reasonable rates (even cheaper in winter and/or midweek).

TRIO CAFÉ AT CONEY WINERY
Modern NZ $$
(☏06-306 8345; www.coneywines.co.nz; Dry River Rd; snacks $12, mains $22-24; ⊙noon-3pm Sat & Sun; 🅿) Wine and dine in a courtyard of gorgeous white roses or in the light and airy dining room. The great-value food is sophisticated, fresh and delicious, and all made from scratch.

ℹ Information

The Martinborough i-SITE (☏06-306 5010; www.wairarapanz.com; 18 Kitchener St; ⊙9am-5pm Mon-Fri, 10am-4pm Sat & Sun) is small, helpful and cheery.

HAWKE'S BAY

Hawke Bay, the body of water that stretches from the Mahia Peninsula to Cape Kidnappers, looks like it's been bitten out of the North Island's eastern flank.

The southern edge of the bay is a travel-channel come to life – food, wine and architecture are the shared obsessions.

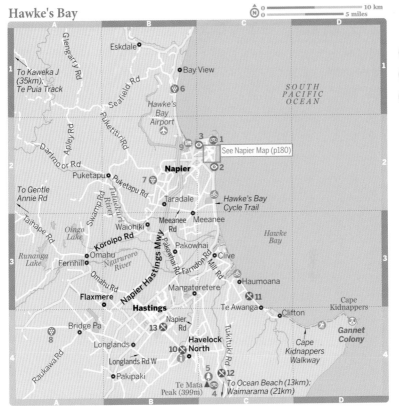

Napier

The Napier of today is the silver lining of the dark cloud that was one of NZ's worst natural disasters. Rebuilt after the deadly 1931 earthquake in the popular styles of the time, the city retains a unique concentration of art-deco buildings to which architecture obsessives flock from all over the world.

 Sights

Architecture

The 1931 quake demolished most of Napier's brick buildings. Frantic reconstruction between 1931 and 1933 caught architects in the throes of global art-deco mania.

Hawke's Bay

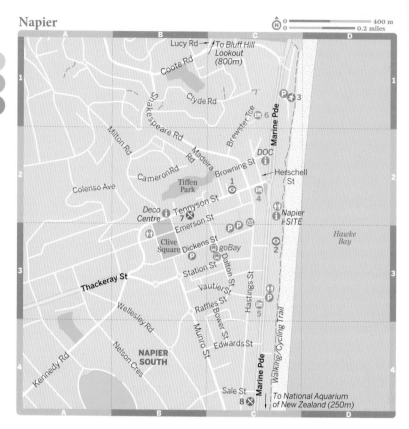

Napier

⊙ Sights
1 Daily Telegraph Building	C2
2 Sunken Gardens	C3

✛ Activities, Courses & Tours
3 Fishbike	C1

⌂ Sleeping
4 Masonic Hotel	C2
5 Sea Breeze	C3
6 Seaview Lodge B&B	C1

✕ Eating
7 Groove Kitchen Espresso	B2
8 Restaurant Indonesia	C4

The place to start your art-deco exploration is the home of the Art Deco Trust, the **Deco Centre** (www.artdeconapier.com; 163 Tennyson St; ☺9am-5pm) opposite colourful Clive Sq. Its one-hour guided deco walk ($16) departs the i-SITE daily at 10am; the two-hour version ($21) leaves the Centre at 2pm daily. The **Daily Telegraph Building** (49 Tennyson St) is one of the stars of the show, with superb zigzags, fountain shapes and ziggurat aesthetic.

Around the shore at Ahuriri, the **National Tobacco Company Building** (cnr Bridge & Ossian Sts) is arguably the region's deco masterpiece.

Other Sights

MARINE PARADE   Street
Napier's elegant avenue is lined with huge Norfolk pines, and dotted with motels and charming timber villas. Along its length are parks, **sunken gardens**, a minigolf course, a swimming complex and aquarium.

NATIONAL AQUARIUM OF
NEW ZEALAND   Aquarium
(www.nationalaquarium.co.nz; 546 Marine
Pde; adult/child/family $17.40/8.70/41.90;
⏱9am-5pm, feedings 10am & 2pm) Inside
this modern complex with its stingray-
inspired roof are piranhas, terrapins, eels,
kiwi, tuatara and a whole lotta fish.

 Tours

ABSOLUTE DE TOURS   Guided Tour
(☎06-844 8699; www.absolutedetours.co.nz)
Runs the 'Deco Tour' of the city, Marewa
and Bluff Hill ($38, 75 minutes) in con-
junction with the Deco Centre, as well
as half-day tours of Napier and Hastings
($60).

HAWKE'S BAY SCENIC
TOURS   Guided Tour
(☎06-844 5693; www.hbscenictours.co.nz;
tours $50-90) Five tour options including
the 'Napier Whirlwind' and wineries.

 Sleeping

SEAVIEW LODGE B&B   B&B $$
(☎06-835 0202; www.aseaviewlodge.co.nz;
5 Seaview Tce; s $130-140, d $170-180; 🛜)
This grand Victorian villa (1890) is
queen of all she surveys – which
is most of the town and a fair
bit of ocean. The elegant
rooms have tasteful period
elements and either bath-
room or en suite. It's
hard to resist a sunset
tipple on the veranda,
which opens off the
relaxing guest lounge.

MASONIC
HOTEL   Hotel $$
(☎06-835 8689; www.
masonic.co.nz; cnr Herschell
& Tennyson Sts; s $85-95,
d $95-130, tr $120-140;

🛜) The art-deco Masonic is arguably the
heart of town, its accommodation, restaurants and bars taking up most of a city
block. Lovers of heritage hotels will likely
fall in love with it, especially once they've
experienced the 1st-floor balcony.

ROCKS MOTORLODGE   Motel $$
(☎06-835 9626; www.therocksmotel.co.nz;
27 Meeanee Quay, Westshore; units $110-180;
@🛜) Located just 80m from the beach,
the Rocks has corrugated stylings and
woodcarving that have raised the bar on
Westshore's motel row. Interiors are plush
with a colour-splash, and some have a
spa bath, others a clawfoot.

SEA BREEZE   B&B $$
(☎06-835 8067; seabreeze.napier@xtra.co.nz;
281 Marine Pde; s $95, d $110-130; 🛜) Inside
this Victorian seafront villa are three
richly coloured themed rooms (Chinese,
Indian and Turkish), decorated with a
cornucopia of artefacts and exotic flair.

Marine Parade, Napier
DAVID WALL/LONELY PLANET IMAGES ©

Don't Miss **Hawke's Bay Wineries**

Once upon a time this district was most famous for its orchards. Today it's vines that have top billing, with Hawke's Bay now NZ's second-largest wine-producing region.

BEST WINING & DINING

Vidal (☏06-872 7440; www.vidal.co.nz; 913 St Aubyn St, Hastings; lunch mains $20-30, dinner mains $28-39; ⊙11.30am-late) The warm, wood-lined dining room is a worthy setting for the elegant food.

Elephant Hill (☏06-872 6060; www.elephanthill.co.nz; 86 Clifton Rd, Te Awanga; mains $32-38; ⊙11am-10pm) Ubermodern winery with edgy architecture, and food, wine and service to rival the stunning sea views; we went quackers over the duck tasting plate.

Terrôir at Craggy Range (☏06-873 0143; www.craggyrange.com; 253 Waimarama Rd, Havelock North; mains $37-40; ⊙lunch Mon-Sun, dinner Mon-Sat) Housed in a cathedral-like 'wine barrel', Terroir is one of the region's most consistent fine-dining experiences.

A TASTE OF THE TASTINGS

Pick up the *Hawke's Bay Winery Guide*, or download it from www.winehawkesbay.co.nz.

Crab Farm (☏06-836 6678; www.crabfarmwinery.co.nz; 511 Main North Rd, Bay View; ⊙10am-5pm Fri-Sun, 6pm-late Fri) Decent, reasonably priced wines and a great cafe.

Mission Estate (☏06-845 9354; www.missionestate.co.nz; 198 Church Rd, Napier) NZ's oldest winery with beautiful grounds, and a restaurant housed within a restored, historic seminary.

Sileni Estates (www.sileni.co.nz; 2016 Maraekakaho Rd, Bridge Pa) Wine, cheese, chocolate and charming cellar door experience.

Eating

GROOVE KITCHEN ESPRESSO   Cafe $

(www.groovekitchen.co.nz; 112 Tennyson St; ⏱breakfast & lunch; meals $9-19; 🖋) A sophisticated cafe squeezed into small, groovy space where the kitchen cranks out A1 brunch along with trendsetting wraps, baps and salads, plus ginger gems your granny would be proud of. Killer coffee. With luck you'll be around for one of the intermittent Thursday-night gigs.

RESTAURANT INDONESIA   Indonesian $$

(🖉06-835 8303; 409 Marine Pde; mains $20-27; ⏱dinner Tue-Sun; 🖋) Crammed with Indonesian curios, this intimate space oozes authenticity. Lip-smacking Indo-Dutch *rijsttafel* smorgasbords are the house speciality (14 dishes, $30 to $36). A romantic option for those inclined. Bookings advisable.

ℹ Information

Napier Health Centre (🖉06-878 8109; 76 Wellesley Rd; ⏱24hr)

Napier i-SITE (🖉06-834 1911; www.napiercity. co.nz; 100 Marine Pde; ⏱9am-5pm; @) Handy and helpful.

ℹ Getting There & Away

Air

Hawke's Bay Airport (🖉06-835 3427; www. hawkesbay-airport.co.nz) is 8km north of the city. **Air New Zealand** (🖉06-833 5400; www. airnewzealand.co.nz; cnr Hastings & Station Sts) offers daily direct flights to Auckland (from $89), Wellington (from $79) and Christchurch (from $129).

Bus

InterCity (www.intercity.co.nz) buses can be booked online or at the i-SITE, and depart from the **Dalton St Bus Stop**. If you're superorganised you can take advantage of $1 advance fares

♥ If You Like…
People-Free Detours

If you like Cape Palliser, we think you'll like these other windswept lost-worlds around the Lower North Island.

1 MAHIA PENINSULA
Northeast of Napier, the Mahia Peninsula's eroded hills, Dover-esque cliffs, black-sand beaches and vivid blue seas are the stuff of Van Gogh's dreams.

2 CASTLEPOINT
On the coast 68km east of Masterton in the Wairarapa is this awesome, end-of-the-world place, with a surf-battered reef, craggy 162m-high Castle Rock, fossil cliffs and rugged walking tracks.

3 CAPE KIDNAPPERS
Visit this far-flung neck of the woods east of Hastings between November and late February and check out the colony of gaggling gannets.

on **Naked Bus** (www.nakedbus.com) on the Auckland–Wellington route via Hastings and Taupo.

Hastings & Around

Positioned at the centre of the Hawke's Bay fruit bowl, bustling Hastings is the commercial hub of the region, 20km south of Napier. A few kilometres of orchards still separate it from Havelock North, with its prosperous village atmosphere and the towering backdrop of Te Mata Peak.

◎ Sights & Activities

As with Napier, Hastings was similarly devastated by the 1931 earthquake and also boasts some fine art-deco and Spanish Mission buildings, built in the aftermath. Main-street highlights include the **Westerman's Building** (cnr Russell & Heretaunga St E), arguably the Bay's best example of the Spanish Mission style, although there are many other architectural gems if you cast your eye around.

Don't Miss **Cycle the Bay**

The expanding network of **Hawke's Bay Cycle Trails** offers cycling opportunities from short, city scoots, to hilly, single-track shenanigans.

Napier is cycle-friendly, particularly along Marine Pde where you'll find Fishbike, renting comfortable bikes including tandems for those willing to risk divorce.

The *Hawke's Bay Cycle Map* can be picked up from the i-SITE or www.hawkesbaynz. com/visit/cyclinghawkesbay.

Given the conducive climate, terrain and multitudinous tracks, it's no surprise that numerous cycle companies pedal their fully geared-up tours around the Bay, including Bike About Tours, Bike D'Vine and On Yer Bike.

NEED TO KNOW

Fishbike (www.fishbike.co.nz; 26 Marine Pde; bike hire from $15; ⊙9am-5pm); **Bike About Tours** (☏06-845 4836; www.bikeabouttours.co.nz; ⊙half to full day $35-60); **Bike D'Vine** (☏06-833 6697; www.bikedevine.com; adult/child from $45/25); **On Yer Bike** (☏06-879 8735; www.onyerbikehb.co.nz; full day without/with lunch $50/60)

The i-SITE stocks the *Art Deco Hastings* brochure ($2), detailing two self-guided walks of the city centre.

TE MATA PEAK   Park

Rising melodramatically from the Heretaunga Plains, Te Mata Peak, 16km south of Havelock North, is part of the 98-hectare **Te Mata Trust Park**. The road to the 399m summit passes sheep trails, rickety fences and vertigo-inducing stone escarpments cowled in a bleak, lunar-meets-Scottish-Highland atmosphere.

The park's network of trails offers walks from 30 minutes to two hours. Our pick is the Peak Trail for views, but all are detailed in the *Te Mata Trust Park* brochure available from local visitor centres.

AIRPLAY PARAGLIDING

Paragliding

(☎ 06-845 1977; www.airplay.co.nz) Te Mata Peak is a paragliding hotspot, with voluminous updraughts offering exhilarating whooshes through the air. Airplay Paragliding has tandem paragliding ($140) and full-day beginners' courses (from $180).

Tours

LONG ISLAND GUIDES

Guided Tours

(☎ 06-874 7877; www.longislandtoursnz. com; half day from $180) Customised and personalised tours across a wide range of interests including Maori culture, bushwalks, kayaking, horse riding and, inevitably, food and wine.

EARLY MORNING BALLOONS

Ballooning

(☎ 06-879 4229; www.hotair.co.nz; per person $345) Provides inflated views over grapey Hawke's Bay.

Wine Tours

○ Bay Tours & Charters (☎ 06-845 2736; www.baytours.co.nz)

○ Grape Escape (☎ 0800 100 489; www. grapeescape.net.nz)

○ Odyssey NZ (☎ 0508 639 773; www. odysseynz.com)

Eating

DIVA

Modern NZ $$

(☎ 06-877 5149; 1/10 Napier Rd, Havelock North; meals $12-32; ⊙lunch Tue-Fri, dinner Tue-Sat) The most happening place in Havelock, Diva offers good-value lunch (from fish and chips to Caesar salad) and a bistro-style menu featuring fresh seafood and seasonal specialities. Eating is divided between flash dining room and groovy bar (snacks from $6), plus lively pavement tables.

ⓘ Information

Hastings i-SITE (☎ 06-873 0080; www. hastings.co.nz; cnr Russell St & Heretaunga St E; ⊙8.30am-5pm Mon-Fri, 9am-4pm Sat, to 3pm Sun; @) Internet access, free maps, trail brochures and bookings.

ⓘ Getting There & Away

Napier's Hawke's Bay Airport (☎ 06-835 3427; www.hawkesbay-airport.co.nz) is a 20-minute drive away.

The InterCity Bus Stop is on Russell St. Book InterCity (☎ 06-835 4326; www.intercity.co.nz) and Naked Bus (www.nakedbus.com) buses online or at the i-SITE.

Marlborough & Nelson

For many travellers, Marlborough and Nelson will be their introduction to what South Islanders refer to as the 'Mainland'. Having left windy Wellington, and made a white-knuckle crossing of Cook Strait, folk are often surprised to find the sun shining and temperatures up to 10 degrees warmer.

Good pals, these two neighbouring regions have much in common beyond an amenable climate: both boast renowned coastal holiday spots, particularly the Marlborough Sounds and Abel Tasman National Park.

And so it follows that these two regions have an abundance of luscious produce: summer cherries for a start, but most famously the grapes that work their way into the wine glasses of the world's finest restaurants.

In high season, these regions are popular and deservedly so. Plan ahead and be prepared to jostle for your gelato with Kiwi holidaymakers.

DAVID WALL / LONELY PLANET IMAGES ©

Ferry on Queen Charlotte Sound (p211)

Marlborough & Nelson

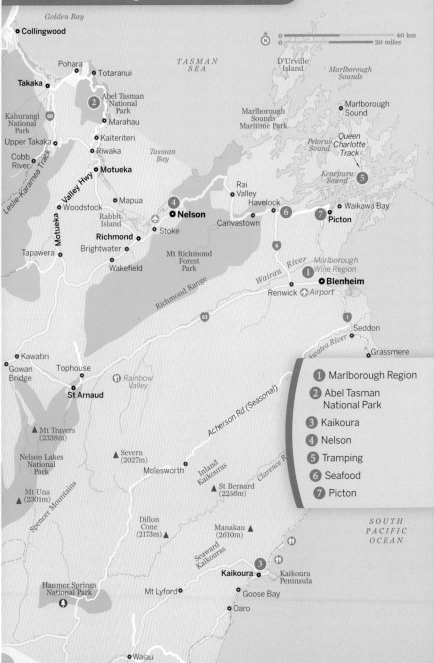

Golden Bay

Collingwood

TASMAN
SEA

D'Urville
Island

Marlborough
Sounds

N 0   40 km
   0   20 miles

Pohara

Totaranui

Takaka

Marlborough
Sound

Abel Tasman
National
Park

Marlborough
Sounds
Maritime Park

Kahurangi
National
Park

Marahau

60

Upper Takaka

Kaiteriteri

Pelorus
Sound

Queen
Charlotte
Track

Cobb
River

Riwaka

Tasman
Bay

Kenepuru
Sound

5

Leslie-Karamea Track

Motueka

Rai
Valley

Waikawa Bay

Woodstock

Valley Hwy

Mapua

Nelson

Havelock

4

6

7

Picton

Motueka

Rabbit
Island

Stoke

Canvastown

Richmond

Brightwater

Mt Richmond
Forest
Park

6

Tapawera

Wakefield

Wairau River

Marlborough
Wine Region

1

Richmond Range

Renwick Airport

Blenheim

63

1

Kawatiri

Seddon

Gowan
Bridge

Tophouse

Rainbow
Valley

Awatere River

Grassmere

St Arnaud

Mt Travers
(2338m)

Acherson Rd (Seasonal)

SOUTH
PACIFIC
OCEAN

Nelson Lakes
National
Park

Severn
(2027m)

Molesworth

Inland
Kaikouras

Clarence R

1 Marlborough Region

Mt Una
(2301m)

St Bernard
(2256m)

2 Abel Tasman
National Park

Spencer Mountains

3 Kaikoura

4 Nelson

Dillon
Cone
(2173m)

Manakau
(2610m)

5 Tramping

6 Seafood

7 Picton

Hanmer Springs
National Park

Seaward
Kaikouras

Kaikoura

Kaikoura
Peninsula

Mt Lyford

Goose Bay

Oaro

Waiau

Marlborough & Nelson's Highlights

① Marlborough Region

Marlborough is an incredibly diverse area. Most visitors spend a couple of days in the wine region, with a detour into the Marlborough Sounds... But there's plenty more to do here, especially if you feel like getting active: sea kayaking, mountain biking and hiking for starters. Above: Walking the Queen Charlotte Track (p202)

Need to Know

CELLAR DOOR TOUR OPTIONS Minibus, bicycle or self-drive BEST TIME TO VISIT March/April when the grapes are harvested and vines are in their autumn colours For further coverage, see p200

Marlborough Region Don't Miss List

BY SCOTT MACKENZIE, MARLBOROUGH TOUR GUIDE

1 MARLBOROUGH WINE

Lots of travellers want to check out Cloudy Bay (p207), but it's also worthwhile visiting a few little boutique wineries where you can taste wines with the owner and the winemaker (often it's the same person!). Sauvignon blanc is what Marlborough is famous for, but other wines to try here include pinot gris, gewürztraminer and chardonnay.

2 BEYOND THE VINES

The Marlborough region also grows superb hops: you can taste the final product at Blenheim's Moa Brewery and Renaissance Brewery (p204). Around the wine region there are also opportunities to try schnapps, handmade chocolates, olive oil and local cheeses.

3 MARLBOROUGH FARMERS' MARKET

Blenheim's **Marlborough Farmers' Market** (www .marketground.co.nz/fmnzmfm) is a great way to spend a Sunday morning. It's a top spot for brunch and coffee, or try some wine, beer or cheese tastings. There's usually live music, and you can chat with the people who actually grow and make the produce.

4 MARLBOROUGH SOUNDS

About 25 minutes' drive from the wine region are the Marlborough Sounds (p211). This is the place to visit a greenshell mussel farm: visitors can get an overview of Sounds history and an insight into why mussels grow so well here. Slurp down a few fresh ones with a glass of chilled sauvignon blanc.

5 QUEEN CHARLOTTE TRACK

The Queen Charlotte Track (p202) is the region's number-one walkway. Check-in with the Picton tour guides for guided- and independent-walk info, plus mountain biking, kayaking and transport options. Some guided walks offer local food and wine and excellent accommodation: visitors can tackle the track in real comfort.

191

Abel Tasman National Park

Of all New Zealand's national parks, Abel Tasman is the most accessible, offering bush-meets-sea landscapes, beautiful golden-sand beaches and amazingly clear water. The region also lays claim to NZ's highest sunshine hours, and has very settled weather, protected on all sides by mountains.

Need to Know

BEST PHOTO OP Early morning on the Marahau rocks **BEST TIME TO VISIT** March/April: the water is still warm and there are fewer holidaying New Zealanders **For further coverage, see p218**

Abel Tasman National Park Don't Miss List

BY STU HOUSTON, DEPARTMENT OF CONSERVATION

1 SEA KAYAKING

The best way to see the park is by water, kayaking up the coastline – you see the beaches, the forests, mountains and rocks. Most people do kayaking as a day trip, but a three-day trip will give you a real feel for the area. You can do a quarter-day or half-day, but it's hard to get a full sense of the landscape on such a short trip. Ask the local kayak operators (p220) about options: walk a few kilometres, paddle a few...

2 TRAMP THE COAST TRACK

The Abel Tasman is one of those parks where the further into it you go, the better it gets. There are four huts on the Abel Tasman Coast Track (p218) and 19 campsites – the camp spots are primo, with some on the beach, right beside the sea. Most people start at Marahau and head north, tramp for three days and then get a water taxi out at the end.

3 WILDLIFE

There's a huge seal population here and many little blue penguins within the park (if you don't see them, you'll hear them: they make a lot of noise at night!). We get quite a lot of dolphins travelling through and we see orcas two or three times a year. There are wood pigeons, tuis and bellbirds, too. A lot of the streams have native freshwater fish – kokopu, inanga – which trout and salmon have forced out in other areas.

4 TAKE A DIP

Swimming here is awesome! There's no glacial run-off and it's one of the few places in the country without any surf. In Marahau, where I live, the water temperature is around 21°C in summer (even down in Dunedin, which is not much further south, it's around 16°C).

Kaikoura Wildlife

Kaikoura (p206) is on the main migratory path for 14 different species of whale and dolphin: it's a kind of underwater highway where you can watch whales year-round. From June to August sperm whales come close to the land to feed; other regulars include humpback whales on their annual migration to Australia. Back on dry land there are seals and birds to ogle.

Below: Fur seals, Kaikoura

3

Nelson

4

Anyone here into the arts, good coffee, seafood restaurants, Victorian architecture and careening around the Great Outdoors? The good people of Nelson (p210) deliver it all, lashed with equal measures of eco-awareness and urban bohemia. This funky town offers 'liveability' to its residents and plenty of enticements to keep the itinerant population (you and me) here for a day or three. Left: Victorian-era workers' cottages, Nelso

Tramping

We hope you've packed your hiking boots! This region is the place to propel yourself onto a wonderfully wild walkway, whether it's a short stretch of the Abel Tasman Coast Track (p218) or a couple of days stamping along the Queen Charlotte Track (p202), here's your chance to get some sun on your skin and some miles into your calf muscles. Left: Abel Tasman Coast Track

Seafood

'I'm on a seafood diet... I see food, then I eat it!' But seriously, if you're partial to fish fillets and molluscs, then you're in the right culinary ocean here. Kaikoura (p210) is the place to try crayfish ('Kai' is Maori for food, and 'koura' means crayfish), while the Marlborough Sounds (p211) area is famous for greenshell mussels.

Above: Greenshell mussels

Picton

No doubt, Picton (p200) is underrated. Too many people just jump on/off the ferry here and continue on to wherever they're bound... But why not take a day to chill out? Picton is a photogenic wee town on one of the prettiest waterways you could imagine, with plenty of quality places to eat, sleep and drink. Above: Picton port

Marlborough & Nelson's Best…

NZ Wildlife, Up Close

○ **Kaikoura whales** (p206) Famous boat and aerial whale-watching tours off the Kaikoura coast

○ **Marlborough Sounds dolphins** See them chase the North Island ferry or get closer on a guided tour (p211)

○ **Abel Tasman National Park seals** (p220) A plethora of grunting mammals

○ **Albatross encounters** (p208) Check out the big birds on a tour from Kaikoura

Scenic Highways & Byways

○ **Picton–Havelock** Wiggly tarmac along the Marlborough Sounds' southern reaches

○ **Kaikoura–Blenheim** Route 1 passes surf beaches and lonesome coastlines

○ **Rapaura Road** The Marlborough wine region's vine-lined 'Golden Mile'

○ **Motueka–Takaka** Over the hills south of Abel Tasman National Park

Places to Get Wet

○ **Abel Tasman National Park** (p218) Kayak around this spectacular coastline

○ **Marahau** (p220) Clear, clean waters on the doorstep of Abel Tasman National Park

○ **Tahunanui Beach** People-filled sandy stretch 5km south of Nelson

○ **Queen Charlotte Track** (p202) Dunk a toe in the chilly, mirror-flat Marlborough Sounds

Need to Know

Excuses for a Drink

- **Marlborough Wine Region** (p207) We all know why you're here...now get sipping!

- **Blenheim Breweries** (p204) Sidestep the sav blanc with some microbrewed delights

- **Nocturnal Nelson** (p214) When the sun goes down Nelson's beery bars light up

- **Seafest Kaikoura** (p44) If you're here in October, don't miss this sensational seaside shindig

ADVANCE PLANNING

- **One month before** Is it summertime? Book your kayak/hike in Abel Tasman National Park pronto, plus tickets on the *Coastal Pacific* train between Picton and Christchurch via Kaikoura

- **Two weeks before** Book a ferry to/from Wellington on the North Island, and accommodation across the region

- **One week before** Book a Marlborough Wine Region winery tour and a whale-watching expedition in Kaikoura

RESOURCES

- Swing into the local i-SITE visitor centres for bookings and information on regional accommodation, transport, wine, food and activities, plus DOC info and contacts:

  - **Blenheim i-SITE** (www.lovemarlborough.co.nz)

  - **Kaikoura i-SITE** (www.kaikoura.co.nz)

  - **Nelson i-SITE** (www.nelsonnz.com)

  - **Picton i-SITE** (www.destinationmarlborough.com)

GETTING AROUND

- **Hike** Along the Queen Charlotte Track and Abel Tasman Coast Track

- **Kayak** Along the craggy, sandy coastline in Abel Tasman National Park

- **Minibus** Around the Marlborough Wine Region wineries

- **Mountain bike** Along the Queen Charlotte Track

- **Ferry** Between Picton (South Island) and Wellington (North Island)

- **Train** Between Picton and Christchurch (via Kaikoura) on the *Coastal Pacific*

BE FOREWARNED

- **Abel Tasman Coast Track** It's one of NZ's 'Great Walks', and it is indeed great: book your accommodation en route many moons in advance to ensure you'll have somewhere to rest your weary bones at night

- **Queen Charlotte Track** Unless you're camping, it pays to book your QCT accommodation *waaay* in advance, especially in summer

Left: Whitebait fritters; **Above:** Golden Bay, Abel Tasman National Park (p218)

Marlborough & Nelson Itineraries

If the name 'Marlborough' conjures images of chilled white wine and autumnal vine rows, the region won't disappoint. But explore further for outstanding tramping, mountain biking, sea kayaking and other activities.

3 DAYS

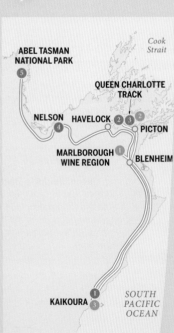

MARLBOROUGH WINE REGION TO KAIKOURA
Foodie Marlborough

With only three days to explore the top of the South Island, don't try to do too much. Change down a gear and focus on some of life's best things: food and wine done the Marlborough way.

First stop is the iconic **(1) Marlborough Wine Region** where you can spend a day visiting cellar doors, sampling gewürztraminer, pinot gris, chardonnay and, of course, the region's world-famous sauvignon blanc. If you're more of a beer boffin, there are some ace microbreweries, too.

Back in the calm, clean backwaters of the **(2) Marlborough Sounds**, greenshell mussels find it impossible not to breed, and grow in preposterous numbers. You'll find them on most menus in Picton – a generous bowl steamed with fennel, shallots, white wine and butter will cure whatever ails you.

Head southeast around the coast to **(3) Kaikoura** for a seafood frenzy. This is the town to try crayfish (aka lobster), paua (abalone), scallops and all manner of fresh ocean fish. Whip out one of those recently acquired bottles and crack into some crustaceans.

Top Left: Sunrise over a Marlborough vineyard (p207);
Top Right: Dolphins playing in Queen Charlotte Sound (p211)
(TOP LEFT) ROB BLAKERS /LONELY PLANET IMAGES ©; (TOP RIGHT) TIM CLAYTON / CORBIS ©

5
DAYS

KAIKOURA TO ABEL TASMAN NATIONAL PARK

Get Busy

Enough sitting around eating crayfish and swilling wine! Time to burn off some calories.

Around the **(1) Kaikoura** coast, sea kayaking is a great way to see dolphins and seals. To the northwest, another sea-kayaking hotspot is the **(2) Marlborough Sounds** (plenty of dolphins here too!).

Rather stay on dry land? Saddle-up on a mountain bike and career along the superbly scenic **(3) Queen Charlotte Track**. Traditionally a tramping route, water taxis now assist bikers to access remote sections of the track, and give hikers the chance to offload their packs and have them transported to the next campsite. Weightless walking! The hills around Nelson further west are also great for mountain biking.

While you're in the **(4) Nelson** area, defy gravity with a paragliding, kiteboarding or hang-gliding lesson, or succumb to its pull with some skydiving. Ask at the i-SITE about local rock-climbing, horse-riding and kayaking operators.

The main lure for trampers around here is the stellar **(5) Abel Tasman Coast Track** in Abel Tasman National Park. Tailor your adventure to include hiking along the track itself, and kayaking along sections of the spectacular coastline.

Discover Marlborough & Nelson

At a Glance

- **Marlborough Region** (p200)
Wine, whale-watching and wilderness from Kaikoura to Blenheim.

- **Marlborough Sounds** (p211)
Intricate landscape of bays, inlets, headlands and ridgelines.

- **Marlborough Wine Region** (p207) Superb sauvignon blanc vineyards and cellar doors behind Blenheim.

- **Nelson Region** (p210) National parks, groovy Nelson and boundless sunshine.

MARLBOROUGH REGION

Picton

Half asleep in winter, but hyperactive in summer (with up to eight fully laden ferry arrivals per day), boaty Picton clusters around a deep gulch at the head of Queen Charlotte Sound. It's the main traveller port for the South Island, and the best place from which to explore the Marlborough Sounds and tackle the Queen Charlotte Track.

👁 Sights & Activities

EDWIN FOX MARITIME MUSEUM — Museum
(www.edwinfoxsociety.co.nz; Dunbar Wharf; adult/child $10/4; ☉9am-5pm) Purportedly the world's third-oldest wooden ship, the *Edwin Fox* was built of teak in Calcutta and launched in 1853. During its chequered career it carried troops to the Crimean War, convicts to Australia and immigrants to NZ. This museum has maritime exhibits, including the venerable old dear, which is preserved under cover.

🌿 ECO WORLD AQUARIUM — Wildlife Centre
(www.ecoworldnz.co.nz; Dunbar Wharf; adult/child/family $20/10/55; ☉10am-8pm Dec-Feb, 10am-5.30pm Mar-Nov) The primary purpose of this centre is animal rehab; all sorts of critters come here for fix-ups and rest-ups, and the odd bit of how's-your-father goes on, too. Very special specimens in residence here include NZ's 'living dinosaur' – the tuatara – as well

Boats moored at Picton
SIMON GREENWOOD / LONELY PLANET IMAGES ©

as blue penguins, gecko and giant weta. Fish-feeding time (11am and 2pm) is a splashy spectacle.

 Sleeping

HARBOUR VIEW MOTEL
Motel **$$**

(☎ 0800 101 133, 03-573 6259; www.harbourviewpicton.co.nz; 30 Waikawa Rd; d $125-200; 🛜) The elevated position of this motel commands good views of Picton's mast-filled harbour from its tastefully decorated, self-contained studios with timber decks.

JASMINE COURT
Motel **$$**

(☎ 0800 421 999, 03-573 7110; www.jasminecourt.co.nz; 78 Wellington St; d $145-235, f $185-245; @ 🛜) Top-notch, spacious motel with plush interiors, kitchenette, DVD player, plunger coffee and locally milled soap. Some rooms have a spa, and the odd one has a decent harbour view. Flash new studio units exhibit further excellence.

GABLES B&B
B&B **$$**

(☎ 03-573 6772; www.thegables.co.nz; 20 Waikawa Rd; s $100, d $140-170, units $155-200, all incl breakfast; @ 🛜) This historic B&B (once home to Picton's mayor) has three spacious, themed en-suite rooms in the main house and two homely self-contained units out the back. Prices drop if you organise your own breakfast. Lovely hosts show good humour (ask about the Muffin Club).

 Eating

LE CAFÉ
Cafe **$$**

(London Quay; lunch $10-23, dinner $19-33; ⏰ 7.30am-10.30pm; 🥄) A perennially popular spot both for its quayside location, dependable food and Havana coffee. The likes of salami sandwiches and sweets are in the cabinet, while a good antipasto platter, generous pasta, local mussels, lamb loin and expertly cooked fresh fish feature a la carte. Laid-back atmosphere, craft beer and occasional live gigs make this a good evening hang-out.

GUSTO
Cafe **$**

(33 High St; meals $14-20; ⏰ 7.30am-2.30pm; 🥄) This workaday joint, with friendly staff and outdoor tables, does beaut breakfasts including first-class salmon-scrambled egg and a 'Morning Glory' fry-up worth the calories. Lunch options may include local mussels and a steak sandwich.

❶ Information

Picton i-SITE (☎ 03-520 3113; www.destinationmarlborough.com; Foreshore; ⏰ 9am-5pm Mon-Fri, to 4pm Sat & Sun) All vital tourist guff including maps, Queen Charlotte Track information, lockers and transport bookings. Department of Conservation (DOC) counter staffed during summer.

❶ Getting There & Away

Make bookings for ferries, buses and trains at Picton i-SITE.

Air

Soundsair (☎ 03-520 3080, 0800 505 005; www.soundsair.com) flies daily between Picton and Wellington (adult/child $100/88).

Boat

There are two operators crossing Cook Strait between Picton and Wellington, and although all ferries leave from more or less the same place, each has its own terminal.

Bluebridge Ferries (☎ 0800 844 844, in Wellington 04-471 6188; www.bluebridge.co.nz; adult/child from $51/26) crossings take three hours 20 minutes; up to four sailings in each direction daily. Cars and campervans up to 5.5m from $118, motorbikes $51, bicycles $10. Passenger fares from adult/child $51/26.

Interislander (☎ 0800 802 802, in Wellington 04-498 3302; www.interislander.co.nz; adult/child from $46/23) crossings take three hours 10 minutes; up to five sailings in each direction daily. Cars are priced from $118, campervans (up to 5.5m) from $133, motorbikes $56, bicycles $15. Passenger fares from adult/child $55/28.

Bus

Buses serving Picton depart from the Interislander terminal or nearby i-SITE.

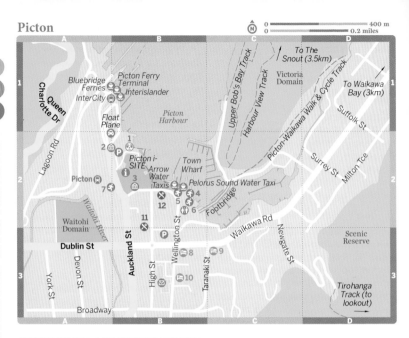

Picton

InterCity (☎03-365 1113; www.intercitycoach.
co.nz; Picton Ferry Terminal) runs services
south to Christchurch (from $26, 5½ hours) via
Kaikoura (from $17, 2½ hours), with connections
to Dunedin, Queenstown and Invercargill. Services
also run to/from Nelson (from $26, 2¼ hours),
with connections to Motueka and the West Coast;

and to/from Blenheim (from $10, 30 minutes).
At least one bus daily on each of these routes
connects with a Wellington ferry service.

Smaller shuttle buses running from Picton to
Christchurch include Atomic Shuttles (☎03-
349 0697; www.atomictravel.co.nz) and Naked
Bus (☎0900 625 33; www.nakedbus.com).

Ritchies Transport (☎03-578 5467; www.
ritchies.co.nz) buses traverse the Picton–
Blenheim line daily (from $12), departing from the
Interislander ferry terminal.

Train

Tranz Scenic (☎0800 872 467, 04-495 0775;
www.tranzscenic.co.nz) runs the Coastal Pacific
service daily each way between Picton and
Christchurch via Blenheim and Kaikoura (and 22
tunnels and 175 bridges!), departing Christchurch
at 7am, Picton at 1pm. Adult one-way Picton–
Christchurch fares range from $59 to $99. The
service connects with the Interislander ferry.

Queen Charlotte Track

The hugely popular, meandering 71km
Queen Charlotte Track offers gorgeous
coastal scenery on its way from historic
Ship Cove to Anakiwa, passing through a

Detour:
Kenepuru & Pelorus Sounds

To the west of Queen Charlotte, Kenepuru and Pelorus Sounds are less populous and therefore offer fewer traveller services, including transport. There's some cracking scenery, however, and those with time to spare will be well rewarded by their explorations.

Havelock is the hub of this area, the western bookend of the 35km-long Queen Charlotte Dr (Picton being the eastern) and the self-proclaimed 'Greenshell Mussel Capital of the World'. While hardly the most rock'n'roll of NZ towns, Havelock makes a practical base from which to set off, as you'll readily locate most necessaries, including fuel and food.

For finer detail, including a complete list of visitor services, visit www.pelorus. co.nz, which covers Havelock, Kenepuru and Pelorus Sounds, and the extreme extremeties of **French Pass** and **D'Urville Island**.

mixture of privately owned land and DOC reserves.

Queen Charlotte is a well-defined track, suitable for people of average fitness. You can do the walk in sections using local water-taxi transport, walk the whole three- to five-day journey, or embark on a combo of walking, kayaking or biking.

Numerous boat and tour operators service the track, allowing you to start and finish where you like, on foot or bike or by kayak (see p211).

Sleeping options are no more than a few hours' walk apart; boat operators will transport your pack along the track for you.

Your overnight stops will depend on how far you want to walk on any given day – do your research and book ahead.

Information

The Picton i-SITE books and stocks everything Queen Charlotte Track, and loads more besides. Check online details at www.qctrack.co.nz.

Blenheim

Blenheim (pronounced 'Blenum') is an agricultural town 29km south of Picton on the Wairau Plain between the Wither Hills and the Richmond Ranges. The town has yet to demonstrate any real power as

a visitor magnet; it is the neighbours over the back fence that pull in the punters.

 Sights & Activities

**OMAKA AVIATION
HERITAGE CENTRE**   Museum
(www.omaka.org.nz; 79 Aerodrome Rd; adult/child/family $25/10/55; ⊙10am-4pm) Blenheim's 'big attraction' has always been its wineries, but the Omaka Aviation Heritage Centre has blown the wine out of the water. Aided by Peter Jackson and his team of creative types, this captivating collection of original and replica Great War aircraft is brought to life with a series of dioramas depicting dramatic wartime scenes such as the death of Manfred von Richthofen, the Red Baron. The guided tour is an extra $5 extremely well spent. There's a cafe and shop on-site, and next door is **Omaka Classic Cars**: more than 100 vehicles from the '50s to the '80s (adult/child $12.50/5).

Sleeping

Blenheim Town
171 ON HIGH   Motel $$
(☎ 0800 587 856, 03-579 5098; www.171 onhighmotel.co.nz; 171 High St; d $140-180;

If you like rather amazing Omaka Aviation Heritage Centre in Blenheim, here are a few other small-town museums chock-full of local lore.

1 MARLBOROUGH MUSEUM

(www.marlboroughmuseum.org.nz; 26 Arthur Baker Pl off New Renwick Rd, Blenheim; adult/child $10/5; ⏲10am-4pm) Besides a replica township, vintage mechanicals, train rides (every first and third Sunday) and well-presented artefact displays, there's the *Wine Exhibition* for those looking to cap-off their vineyard experiences.

2 KAIKOURA DISTRICT MUSEUM

(14 Ludstone Rd, Kaikoura; adult/child $5/1; ⏲10am-4.30pm Mon-Fri, 2-4pm Sat & Sun) This provincial museum houses the old town jail, historical photos, Maori and colonial artefacts, a huge sperm-whale jaw and the fossilised remains of a plesiosaur.

3 PICTON MUSEUM

(London Quay, Picton; adult/child $5/1; ⏲10am-4pm) If you dig local history – whaling, sailing and the 1964 Roller Skating Champs – this place is good rainy-day diversion. The photo displays are well worth a look.

(@ 🛜) A welcoming option close to town, these tasteful, splash-o-purple studios and apartments are bright and breezy in the daytime, warm and shimmery in the evening. Expect a wide complement of facilities and 'extra mile' service.

Wine Region

WATSON'S WAY LODGE Lodge $

(📞03-572 8228; www.watsonswaybackpackers.co.nz; 56 High St, Renwick; dm $30, d $70-90; ⏲closed Aug-Sep; @ 🛜) This traveller-focused, purpose-built hostel has spick-and-span rooms, mainly twins and doubles, some with en suite. There are spacious leafy gardens dotted with fruit trees and hammocks, an outdoor claw-foot bath, bikes for hire (guest/public rate $15/25 per day) and local information aplenty.

OLDE MILL HOUSE B&B $$

(📞03-572 8458; www.oldemillhouse.co.nz; 9 Wilson St, Renwick; s/d $120/145; @ 🛜) On an elevated section in otherwise flat Renwick, this charming old house is a treat. Dyed-in-the-wool local hosts run a welcoming B&B, with stately decor, and home-grown fruit and homemade goodies for breakfast. Free bikes, an outdoor spa and gardens make this a tip-top choice in the heart of the wine country.

ST LEONARDS Cottages $$

(📞03-577 8328; www.stleonards.co.nz; 18 St Leonards Rd; d $115-310, extra adult $35; 🛜) Tucked into the grounds of an 1886 homestead, these four rustic cottages offer privacy and a reason to stay put. (Anyone for tennis?) Each has its own history, lay-out and individual outlook to the gardens and vines. Our pick is the Stables, with its lemon-grove view.

VINTNERS HOTEL Hotel $$$

(📞0800 684 190, 03-572 5094; www.mvh.co.nz; 190 Rapaura Rd; d $150-295; 🛜) Sixteen architecturally designed suites make the most of wine-valley views, while inside classy suites boast wet-room bathrooms and abstract art.

Eating & Drinking

Hospitality can be pretty hit and miss in Blenny, with some of the best food found yonder at the wineries. While you're at it, keep an eye out for the scrumptious craft beers made by local brewers, **Renaissance** (www.renaissancebrewing.co.nz), and its associate **8-Wired** (www.8wired.co.nz), 2011 Brewer's Guild champion. Winemaker's son, Josh Scott, also brews the good range of bottle-fermented beers and thirst-quenching ciders known as **Moa** (www.moabeer.co.nz).

Marlborough Wine Region

RAUPO   Modern NZ **$$**
(6 Symons St; breakfast $13-19, lunch & dinner $18-33; ⏰7.30am-late) Blenheim's best restaurant since the day it opened. It boasts stylish timber-and-stone architecture and a pleasant riverside location. This promise is backed up by consistent, modern cafe fare along the lines of macadamia muesli, aged feta and chorizo salad, local mussels and salmon, and superfine Euro-sweets: truffles, sorbet and pastries.

ℹ Information

Blenheim i-SITE (☎0800 777 181, 03-577 8080; www.destinationmarlborough.com; 8 Sinclair St; ⏰8.30am-5.30pm Mon-Fri, 9am-5pm Sat, 9am-4pm Sun) Information on Marlborough and beyond. Wine-trail maps and bookings for everything under the sun.

ℹ Getting There & Around

Air

Air New Zealand (☎03-577 2200, 0800 747 000; www.airnewzealand.co.nz; 29 Queen St; ⏰9am-5pm Mon-Fri) has direct flights to/from Wellington (from $99), Auckland (from $139) and Christchurch (from $99) with onward connections. **Soundsair** (☎0800 505 005; www.soundsair.com) and **Air2There** (☎0800 777 000; www.air2there.com) connect Blenheim with Wellington and Paraparaumu.

Marlborough Wine Region

Bus

InterCity (☎03-365 1113; www.intercitycoach.co.nz) buses run daily from the Blenheim i-SITE to Picton (from $11, 30 minutes) continuing through to Nelson (from $18, 1¾ hours). Buses also head down south to Christchurch (from $25, three daily) via Kaikoura (from $16).

Naked Bus (☎0900 625 33; www.nakedbus.com) runs from Blenheim to many South Island destinations, including Kaikoura ($18, two hours), Nelson ($23, 1¾ hours) and Motueka ($36, 3¾ hours).

Ritchies Transport (☎03-578 5467; www.ritchies.co.nz) buses traverse the Blenheim–Picton line daily (from $12), departing from Blenheim Railway Station.

Shuttles (and tours) around Picton and wider Marlborough are offered by **Marlborough Sounds Shuttles** (☑03-573 7122; www.marlboroughsoundssshuttles.co.nz).

Train

Tranz Scenic (☑0800 872 467, 04-495 0775; www.tranzscenic.co.nz) runs the daily *Coastal Pacific* service, stopping at Blenheim en route to Picton (from $29) heading north, and Christchurch (from $59) via Kaikoura (from $59) heading south.

Kaikoura

Until the 1980s Kaikoura was a sleepy crayfishing town ('Kai' meaning food, 'koura' meaning crayfish) with grim prospects. These days it has grown into a tourist mecca, with a range of quality accommodation and many other enticements including eye-popping wildlife tours.

Sights & Activities

POINT KEAN SEAL COLONY
Wildlife Reserve

At the end of the peninsula seals laze around in the grass and on the rocks, lapping up all the attention. Give them a wide berth (10m), and never get between them and the sea – they will attack if they feel cornered and can move surprisingly fast.

KAIKOURA PENINSULA WALKWAY
Walking

A foray along this walkway is a must-do if humanly possible. Starting from the town, this three- to four-hour loop heads out to Point Kean, along the cliffs to South Bay, then back to town over the isthmus (or in reverse, of course). En route you'll be able to see fur seals and red-billed seagull and shearwater (aka mutton bird) colonies. Lookouts and interesting interpretive panels abound along the way. Collect a map at the i-SITE or follow your nose.

Tours

Whale-Watching

Your choices are boat, plane or helicopter. Aerial options are shorter and pricier, but allow you to see the whole whale, as opposed to just a tail, flipper or spout.

WHALE WATCH KAIKOURA
Ecotour

(☑0800 655 121, 03-319 6767; www.whalewatch.co.nz; Railway Station; 3hr tour adult/child $145/60) With knowledgeable guides and fascinating 'world of whales' onboard animation, Kaikoura's biggest operator heads out on boat trips (with admirable frequency) to introduce you to some of the big fellers. It'll refund 80% of your fare if no whales are sighted (success rate: 98%). If this trip is a must for you, allow a few days flexibility in case the weather turns to custard.

KAIKOURA HELICOPTERS
Scenic Flights

(☑03-319 6609; www.worldofwhales.co.nz; Railway Station; 15-60min flight $100-490) Reliable whale-spotting flights (standard 30-minute tour $220 each for three or more people), plus jaunts around the peninsula, Mt Fyffe and peaks beyond.

Dolphin- & Seal-Spotting

DOLPHIN ENCOUNTER
Ecotour

(☑0800 733 365, 03-319 6777; www.dolphin.co.nz; 96 Esplanade; swim adult/child $175/160, observation $90/45; ⊙tours 8.30am & 12.30pm year-round, plus 5.30am Nov-Apr) Here's your chance to rub shoulders with pods of dusky dolphins on three-hour tours. Limited numbers, so book in advance.

KAIKOURA KAYAKS
Kayaking

(☑0800 452 456, 03-319 7118; www.kaikourakayaks.co.nz; 19 Killarney St; seal tours adult/child $95/70; ⊙tours 8.30am, 12.30pm & 4.30pm Nov-Apr, 9am & 1pm May-Oct) Guided sea-kayak tours to view fur seals and explore the peninsula's coastline. Kayaking lessons, freedom hire, family-friendly options and kayak fishing also available.

PAUL KENNEDY / LONELY PLANET IMAGES ©

Don't Miss **Marlborough Wineries**

Marlborough is NZ's vinous colossus producing around three quarters of the country's wine. Sunny days and cool nights create the perfect microclimate for cool-climate grapes: world-famous sauvignon blanc, top-notch pinot noir, and notable chardonnay, riesling, gewürztraminer, pinot gris and bubbly.

A TASTE OF THE TASTINGS

Clos Henri (www.closhenri.com; 639 SH63) French winemaking meets Marlborough terroir with *très bien* results.

Cloudy Bay (www.cloudybay.co.nz; Jacksons Rd) Understated exterior belies the classy interior of this blue-ribbon winery and cellar door.

Huia (www.huia.net.nz; 22 Boyces Rd) Sustainable, small-scale winegrowing and the cutest yellow tasting room in town.

Seresin Estate (www.seresin.co.nz; 85 Bedford Rd) Organic and biodynamic wines and olive oils from cinematographer Michael Seresin.

Spy Valley Wines (www.spyvalleywine.co.nz; 37 Lake Timara Rd, Waihopai Valley) Stylish, edgy architecture at this espionage-themed winery with great wines across the board.

WINE TOURS

Wine tours are generally conducted in a minibus, last between four and seven hours, take in four to seven wineries, and range in price from $55 to $90 (with a few grand tours up to around $200 for the day, including a winery lunch). **Bubbly Grape** (☏0800 228 2253, 027 672 2195; www.bubblygrape.co.nz) offers three different tours including a gourmet lunch option.

Take a self-guided, fully geared and supported tour with **Bike2Wine** (☏0800 653 262, 03-572 8458; www.bike2wine.co.nz; 9 Wilson St, Renwick; standard/tandem $30/60 per day, delivery/pick-up $5-10 per bike).

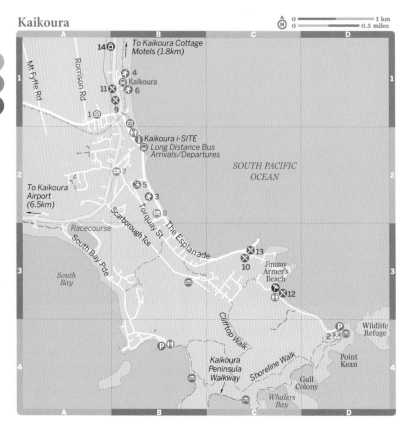

To Kaikoura Cottage Motels (1.8km)

14

4
Kaikoura
11
6
9
1

Kaikoura i-SITE
Long Distance Bus
Arrivals/Departures

SOUTH PACIFIC
OCEAN

To Kaikoura
Airport
(6.5km)

7

5
3

8

Torquay St
Scarborough Tce
The Esplanade
Racecourse
South Bay Pde

13
10

Jimmy
Armer's
Beach

12

South
Bay

Clifftop Walk

2

Wildlife
Refuge

Kaikoura
Peninsula
Walkway

Shoreline Walk

Point
Kean

Gull
Colony

Whalers
Bay

Birdwatching

**ALBATROSS
ENCOUNTER** Birdwatching

(☎ 0800 733 365, 03-319 6777; www.albatross
encounter.co.nz; 96 Esplanade; adult/child
$120/60; ☷ tours 9am & 1pm year-round,
plus 6am Nov-Apr) Kaikoura is heaven
for bird-nerds, who fly at the opportunity for a close encounter with pelagic
species such as shearwaters, shags,
mollymawks, petrels and the inimitable
albatross.

Sleeping

NIKAU LODGE B&B

(☎ 03-319 6973; www.nikaulodge.com; 53
Deal St; d $190-250; @ ☷) A waggly-tailed

welcome awaits at this beautiful B&B
high on the hill with grand-scale vistas.
Four en-suite rooms are plush and comfy,
with additional satisfaction arriving
in the form of cafe-quality breakfasts
accompanied by fresh local coffee. Good-
humour, home-baking, free wi-fi, hot-tub
and blooming gardens: you may want to
move in.

**KAIKOURA COTTAGE
MOTELS** Motel $$

(☎ 0800 526 882, 03-319 5599; www.kaikoura
cottagemotels.co.nz; cnr Old Beach & Mill Rds; d
$120-140; ☷) This enclave of eight modern
tourist flats is looking mighty fine, sur-
rounded by attractive native plantings
now in full flourish. Oriented for mountain
views, the self-contained units sleep four
between an open plan studio-style living
room and one private bedroom. Soothing

Kaikoura

sand-and-sky colour scheme and quality chattels.

SAILS MOTEL — Motel $$

(✆03-319 6145; www.sailsmotel.co.nz; 134 Esplanade; d $115; unit $140; 📶) There are no sea (or sails) views at this motel, so the cherubic owners have to impress with quality. Their four secluded, tastefully appointed self-contained units are down a driveway in a garden setting (private outdoor areas abound). The apartment sleeps four.

DYLAN'S COUNTRY COTTAGES — Cottages $$

(✆03-319 5473; www.lavenderfarm.co.nz; 268 Postmans Rd; d $175; ☺closed May-Aug; 📶) On the grounds of the delightful Kaikoura Lavender Farm, northwest of town, these two self-contained cottages make for an aromatic escape from the seaside fray. One has a private outdoor bath and a shower emerging from a tree; the other an indoor spa and handkerchief lawn. Homemade scones, preserves and free-range eggs for breakfast. Sweet, stylish and romantic.

Eating & Drinking

GREEN DOLPHIN — Seafood $$$

(✆03-319 6666; www.greendolphinkaikoura. com; 12 Avoca St; mains $25-46; ☺5pm-late) Quality Kaikoura fish multiple ways, and the omnipresent bovine, porcine and lobstery treats, all made with care and a fondness for good local produce. On busy nights, book ahead or nurse a cocktail or aperitif in the pleasant bar or garden. Those with foresight should plump for a table with a view by the floor-to-ceiling windows.

HISLOPS — Cafe $$

(33 Beach Rd; lunch $9-24, dinner $22-37; ☺9am-late, closed Tue & Wed May-Sep; ✒) This snappy, feel-good cafe maintains its reputation for fresh, wholesome food. Start the morning with a guilt-free fry-up, then come back at night for organic meats plus local seafood, veg and vegan choices. Notable salads, such as goat's feta and avocado.

CORIANDERS — Indian $$

(17 Beach Rd; mains $14-20; ✒) Spicing up Kaikoura life, this branch of the Corianders chain keeps the bar raised with dependable Indian food in a pleasant environment. The epic menu has all your favourites and some you've never heard of. Excellent pakora, good breads and extensive veggie options.

PIER HOTEL — Modern NZ $$

(www.thepierhotel.co.nz; 1 Avoca St; snacks $7-18, mains $24-34; ☺11am-late) Wide views of the bay and the mountains beyond make this the grandest dining room in town. A cheerful crew serves up generous portions of honest food, such as fresh local fish, baby back spare ribs and BBQ crayfish for those with fat wallets. The enticing public bar has reasonably priced beer and bar snacks, historical photos and a garden bar. Upstairs lodgings are worn and creaky, but good value (double room, including breakfast, from $115).

If You Like...
Kaikoura Seafood

If you like the seafood at Green Dolphin in Kaikoura, here are a few less-formal ways to get some koura (crayfish) on your plate. At most local restaurants you'll shell out (pardon the pun) around $55 for half a cray or over $100 for the whole beast, but the following options will save you a few dollars:

1 **ORIGINAL KAIKOURA SEAFOOD BBQ**
(Fyffe Quay; ⏱10.30am–early evening) Alfresco roadside stall near the seal colony – try a fish or scallop sandwich (white bread, of course) if crayfish doesn't float your boat.

2 **NINS BIN**
(SH1; ⏱8am-6pm) An iconic surf-side caravan 23km north of town. Upwards of $50 should get you a decent specimen.

3 **CODS & CRAYFISH**
(81 Beach Rd; ⏱8am-6pm) A no-frills shopfront selling fresh cooked or uncooked crays.

ℹ Information

Kaikoura i-SITE (☏03-319 5641; www.kaikoura.co.nz; West End; ⏱ 9am-5pm Mon-Fri, to 4pm Sat & Sun, extended hours in summer) Helpful staff make tour, accommodation and transport bookings, and help with DOC-related matters.

ℹ Getting There & Away

Bus

InterCity (☏03-365 1113; www.intercity.co.nz) buses run between Kaikoura and Nelson (from $49, 3½ hours), Picton (from $17, 2¼ hours) and Christchurch (from $15, 2¾ hours).

Naked Bus (☏0900 625 33; www.nakedbus.com) also runs to/from Kaikoura to most South Island destinations, departing from the i-SITE.

Train

Tranz Scenic (☏0800 872 467, 04-495 0775; www.tranzscenic.co.nz) runs the *Coastal Pacific*

service, stopping at Kaikoura on its daily run between Picton (from $59, 2¼ hours) and Christchurch (from $59, three hours).

NELSON REGION
Nelson

Dishing up a winning combination of great weather and beautiful surroundings, Nelson is hailed as one of New Zealand's most 'liveable' cities.

◎ Sights

THE WONDROUS WORLD OF WEARABLEART   Museum
Nelson exudes creativity, so it's hardly surprising that NZ's most inspiring fashion show was born here. The concept was to create a piece of art that could be worn and modelled.

The idea caught on, and the World of WearableArt Awards Show became an annual event.

The awards show has been transplanted to Wellington, but you can ogle entries at Nelson's **World of WearableArt & Classic Cars Museum** (WOW; ☏03-547 4573; www.wowcars.co.nz; 1 Cadillac Way; adult/child $22/8; ⏱10am-5pm). High-tech galleries include a carousel mimicking a catwalk, and glow-in-the-dark room.

More car than bra? Under the same roof are 50 mint-condition classic cars and motorbikes. Exhibits change, but may include a 1959 pink Cadillac, a yellow 1950 Bullet Nose Studebaker convertible and a BMW bubble car. You can view another 70 vehicles in the Classic Collection next door ($8 extra).

CHRIST CHURCH CATHEDRAL   Church
(www.nelsoncathedral.org; Trafalgar Sq; admission free; ⏱8am-7pm summer, to 5pm winter) The enduring symbol of Nelson, the art-deco Christ Church Cathedral lords over the city from the top of Trafalgar St. Work began in 1925, but this architectural hybrid wasn't completed until 1965.

Don't Miss **Exploring the Marlborough Sounds**

The Marlborough Sounds are a geographic maze of inlets, headlands, peaks, beaches and watery reaches, formed when the sea flooded into deep valleys after the last ice age.

Sounds travel is quicker by boat (for example, Punga Cove from Picton by car takes two to three hours, but just 45 minutes by boat). Numerous operators ply the waters; most can be found at the Picton Town Wharf. Bikes and kayaks can also be transported.

Cougar Line (03-573 7925, 0800 504 090; www.cougarlinecruises.co.nz; Town Wharf; track round-trip $103, full day tour from $75) QC Track transport, plus various half- and full-day cruise/walk trips including the rather special (and flexible) ecocruise trip to Motuara Island and a Ship Cove picnic.

Marlborough Sounds Adventure Company (03-573 6078, 0800 283 283; www.marlboroughsounds. co.nz; Town Wharf; half- to 3-day packages $85-545) Bike-walk-kayak trips, with options for everyone.

Wilderness Guides (03-573 5432, 0800 266 266; www.wildernessguidesnz.com; Picton Railway Station; 1-day trip from $125, kayak or bike hire per day $60) Host of the popular and flexible 'multisport' day trip (kayak/walk/cycle) plus many other guided and independent biking, hiking and kayking tours around the Queen Charlotte Sound.

Dolphin Watch Ecotours (03-573 8040, 0800 9453 5433; www.naturetours.co.nz; Town Wharf; dolphin swimming/viewing $165/100, other tours from $75) Half-day 'swim with dolphins' and wildlife tours including trips to Motuara Island.

Picton Water Taxis (027 227 0284, 03-573 7853; www.pictonwatertaxis.co.nz) Water taxi and sightseeing trips around Queen Charlotte, on demand.

Myths & Legends Eco-Tours (03-573 6901; www.eco-tours.co.nz; half-/full-day cruises $200/250) A chance to get out on the water with a local Maori family – longtime locals, storytellers and environmentalists.

Nelson

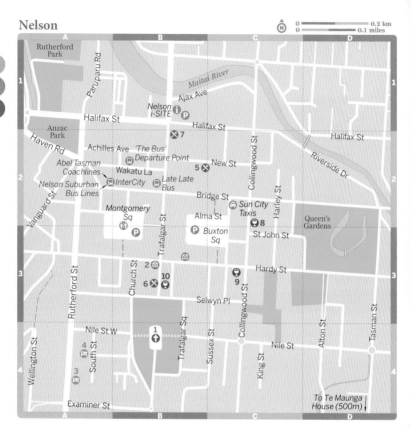

Nelson

⊙ Sights
1 Christ Church Cathedral B4
2 Nelson Provincial Museum B3

⊜ Sleeping
3 Palazzo Motor Lodge A4
4 South Street Cottages A4

⊗ Eating
5 DeVille B2
6 Hopgood's B3
7 Stefano's B2

⊖ Drinking
8 Free House C2
9 Sprig & Fern C3
10 Vic B3

**NELSON PROVINCIAL
MUSEUM** Museum
(www.nelsonmuseum.co.nz; cnr Hardy & Trafalgar
Sts; admission from adult/child $5/3; ⊙10am-
5pm Mon-Fri, 10am-4.30pm Sat & Sun) This
modern museum space is filled with
cultural heritage and natural history
exhibits with a regional bias, as well as
regular touring exhibitions (admission
price varies). It also features a great
rooftop garden.

 **Activities**

**TOP
CHOICE NELSON
BONECARVING** Carving
(☎03-546 4275; www.carvingbone.co.nz;
87 Green St, Tahunanui; full-day course $79)

Admirers of Maori design will love Stephan's acclaimed bone-carving course. He'll supply all materials, tools, instruction, encouragement and cups of tea (plus free pick-up/drop-off in town if needed); you supply inspiration and talent and you'll emerge with your very own bone carving.

BIKING NELSON Mountain Biking
(0800 224 532, 021 861 725; www.bikingnelson.co.nz; 3hr guided ride $115, bike hire half/full day $45/65) Hit the hillside mountain-bike trails with Dave and company, who run guided rides (all gear provided) and offer freedom rental and advice.

Paragliding, Hang Gliding & Kiteboarding

Tandem paragliding costs around $180, while introductory courses are around $250. Tandem hang gliding is around $185, and introductory kiteboarding starts at $150.

Nelson Paragliding (03-544 1182, 0508 359 669; www.nelsonparagliding.co.nz)

Cumulus Paragliding (03-929 5515; www.tandem-paragliding.co.nz)

Kite Surf Nelson (0800 548 363; www.kitesurfnelson.co.nz)

Nelson Hang Gliding Adventures (03-548 9151; www.flynelson.co.nz)

Tours

BAY TOURS Guided Tour
(0800 229 868, 03-548 6486; www.baytoursnelson.co.nz; half-/full-day tours from $89/144) Nelson city, region, wine, beer, food and art tours. The full-day scenic tour includes a visit to Kaiteriteri and a cruise in Abel Tasman National Park.

SIMPLY WILD Guided Tour
(03-548 8500; www.simplywild.co.nz) A swathe of half- to five-day active wilderness adventures: walking, mountain biking, sailing, caving, rafting and canoeing around Nelson's national parks. Prices on application.

 Sleeping

PALAZZO MOTOR LODGE Motel $$
(03-545 8171, 0800 472 5293; www.palazzomotorlodge.co.nz; 159 Rutherford St; studios $130-225, apt $225-390; @) Hosts with the most offer a cheerful welcome at this popular, modern, Italian-tinged motor lodge. The stylish studios and one- and two-room apartments feature enviable kitchens with decent cooking equipment, classy wineglasses and a dishwasher. The odd bit of dubious art is easily forgiven, particularly as Doris' sausage is available for breakfast.

TE MAUNGA HOUSE B&B $$
(03-548 8605; www.nelsoncityaccommodation.co.nz; 15 Dorothy Annie Way; s $90, d $100-135; @) Aptly named (Te Maunga means 'the mountain'), this is a grand old family home on a knoll with exceptional views. Two doubles and a single, with their own bathrooms, are filled with characterful furniture and made up with good linens. Your hearty breakfast can be walked off up and down *that* hill. It's only a 10-minute climb (15 minutes in all, from town), but only the leggy ones will revel in it. Closed from May to September.

SOUTH STREET COTTAGES Rental House $$$
(03-540 2769; www.cottageaccommodation.co.nz; South St; d from $225) Stay on NZ's oldest preserved street in one of several endearing, two-bedroom self-contained cottages built in the 1860s. Each has all the comforts of home, including kitchen, laundry and courtyard garden; breakfast provisions supplied. There is a two-night minimum stay.

Eating

DEVILLE Cafe $$
(22 New St; meals $13-20; 9am-4pm Mon-Sat;) Most of DeVille's tables lie in its sweet walled courtyard, a hidden boho oasis in the inner city and the perfect place for a meal or morning tea. The food's good,

Below: Racks of bottles in a winery tasting room;
Right: Trafalgar Street, Nelson
(BELOW) ML HARRIS / GETTY IMAGES © (RIGHT) DAVID WALL / LONELY PLANET IMAGES ©

from fresh baked goods to the eggy brunch, caesar salad and sticky pork sandwich. Open late for live music Friday and Saturday in summer.

STEFANO'S   Pizzeria **$**
(03-546 7530; 91 Trafalgar St; pizzas $6-29; lunch & dinner;) Located upstairs in the State Cinema complex, this Italian-run joint turns out some of NZ's best pizza. Thin, crispy and delicious, and some variations really very cheap. Wash it down with a beer or wine in the ambience-free interior or out on the tiny balcony.

HOPGOOD'S   Modern NZ **$$$**
(03-545 7191; 284 Trafalgar St; mains $34-37; 5.30pm-late Mon-Sat) Tongue-and-groove-lined Hopgood's is perfect for a romantic dinner or holiday treat. The food is decadent and skilfully prepared but unfussy, allowing quality local ingredients to shine. The Asian crispy duck followed by twice-cooked pork belly with butter beans, spinach and bacon are knockouts. Desirable, predominantly Kiwi wine list. Bookings advisable.

 **Drinking**

FREE HOUSE   Craft Beer
(www.freehouse.co.nz; 95 Collingwood St) Come rejoice at this church of ales. Tastefully converted from its original, more reverent purpose, it's now home to an excellent, oft-changing selection of NZ craft beers. You can imbibe inside or out. Hallelujah.

VIC   Pub
(www.vicbrewbar.co.nz; 281 Trafalgar St) A commendable example of a Mac's Brewbar, with trademark, quirky Kiwiana fit-out, including a striped, knitted stag's head. Quaff a few handles of ale, maybe grab a bite to eat (mains $10 to $30) and tap a toe to live music, including Tuesday-night jazz. Good afternoon sun and people-watching from streetside seating.

MARLBOROUGH & NELSON NELSON

ℹ Information

Nelson i-SITE (☎ 03-548 2304; www.nelsonnz.
com; cnr Trafalgar & Halifax Sts; ☺ 8.30am-5pm
Mon-Fri, 9am-5pm Sat & Sun; @) A slick centre
complete with DOC information desk for the
low-down on national parks and walks (including
Abel Tasman and Heaphy tracks). Pick up a copy
of the *Nelson Tasman Visitor Guide*.

ℹ Getting There & Away

Air

Air New Zealand (☎ 03-546 3100, 0800 737
000; www.airnewzealand.co.nz; cnr Trafalgar
& Bridge Sts; ☺ 9am-5pm Mon-Fri) has direct
flights to/from Wellington (from $79, up to 10
daily), Auckland (from $99, up to nine daily) and
Christchurch (from $79, up to seven daily).

Soundsair (☎ 03-520 3080, 0800 505 005;
www.soundsair.com) flies daily between Nelson
and Wellington (from $107, up to three daily).

Bus

Book Abel Tasman Coachlines, InterCity, Tranz
Scenic and Interisland ferries at the **Nelson
SBL Travel Centre** (☎ 03-548 1539; www.
nelsoncoaches.co.nz; 27 Bridge St).

Also based here are **Abel Tasman Coachlines**
(☎ 03-548 0285; www.abeltasmantravel.co.nz;
27 Bridge St), operating services to Motueka ($12,
one hour), Takaka ($35, two hours), Kaiteriteri and
Marahau (both $20, two hours).

Atomic Shuttles (☎ 03-349 0697; www.
atomictravel.co.nz) runs from Nelson to Picton
($25, 2¼ hours), and daily to West Coast centres
like Greymouth ($54, 5¾ hours) and Fox Glacier
($78, 9½ hours). Services can be booked at (and
depart from) Nelson i-SITE.

InterCity (☎ 03-548 1538; www.intercity.
co.nz; Bridge St) runs from Nelson to most
key South Island destinations including Picton
(from $18, two hours), Kaikoura (from $49, 3½
hours), Christchurch (from $54, seven hours) and
Greymouth (from $40, six hours).

Motueka

Motueka (pronounced Mott-oo-ecka, meaning 'Island of Wekas') is a bustling town, one which visitors will find handy for stocking up en route to Golden Bay and the Abel Tasman and Kahurangi National Parks.

Activities

SKYDIVE ABEL TASMAN Extreme Sports
(**☎0800 422 899, 03-528 4091; www.skydive.co.nz; Motueka Aerodrome, College St; jumps 13,000ft/16,500ft $299/399)** Move over Taupo tandems: we've jumped both and think Mot takes the cake (presumably so do the many sports jumpers who favour this drop zone, some of whom you may see rocketing in). DVDs and photos cost extra, but pick-up/drop-off from Motueka and Nelson are free.

TASMAN SKY ADVENTURES Scenic Flights
(**☎0800 114 386, 027 229 9693; www.skyadventures.co.nz; Motueka Aerodrome, College St; 30min flight $185)** A rare opportunity to fly in a microlight. Keep your eyes open and blow your mind on a scenic flight above Abel Tasman National Park. Wow. And there's tandem hang gliding for the eager (15/30 minutes, 2500ft/5280ft $185/275).

Sleeping

NAUTILUS LODGE Motels **$$**
(**☎0800 628 845, 03-528 4658; www.nautiluslodge.co.nz; 67 High St; d $160-220; @ 📶)** A top-notch motel complex with 12 units decorated in neutral tones with low-profile furniture including European slatted beds. There are kitchenettes in larger units, spa baths in some, full Sky TV and classy bathrooms in all, and balconies and patios collecting afternoon sun.

RESURGENCE Lodge, Chalets **$$$**
(**☎03-528 4664; www.resurgence.co.nz; Riwaka Valley Rd; lodge from $625, chalets from $525; @ 📶 🏊)** Choose a luxurious en-suite lodge room or self-contained chalet at this magical 20-hectare bushland retreat 15 minutes' drive north of Motueka, and half an hour's walk from the picturesque

Lake Rotoiti, Nelson Lakes National Park

PAUL KENNEDY / LONELY PLANET IMAGES ©

Detour:
Nelson Lakes National Park

Pristine Nelson Lakes National Park surrounds two lakes – Rotoiti and Rotoroa – fringed by sweet-smelling beech forest with a backdrop of greywacke mountains. At the northern end of the Southern Alps, with a dramatic glacier-carved landscape, it's an awe-inspiring place to get up on high. The park is flush with bird life, and is famous for brown-trout fishing.

Many spectacular walks allow you to appreciate this rugged landscape, but before you tackle them, stop by the Department of Conservation (DOC) Visitor Centre for maps, track/weather updates, to leave intentions and to pay your hut or camping fees.

The five-hour **Mt Robert Circuit Track** starts south of St Arnaud and circumnavigates the mountain, with options for a side trip along Robert Ridge. Alternatively, the **St Arnaud Range Track** (five hours return), on the east side of the lake, climbs steadily to the ridgeline via Parachute Rocks.

There are also plenty of shorter (and flatter) walks starting from Lake Rotoiti's Kerr Bay and the road end at Lake Rotoroa. These and the longer day tramps in the park are described in DOC's *Walks in Nelson Lakes National Park* pamphlet ($2).

The DOC Visitor Centre (☑03-521 1806; www.doc.govt.nz; View Rd; ⏲8am-4.30pm) offers park information (weather, activities), hut passes, plus displays on park ecology and history. See also www.starnaud.co.nz.

source of the Riwaka River. Lodge rates include cocktails and a four-course dinner as well as breakfast, or you can fire up the barbecue if you're staying in one of the chalets. Chalet rates are for B&B; lodge dinner extra ($90).

🍴 Eating & Drinking

UP THE GARDEN PATH   Cafe $$
(473 High St; meals $15-27; ⏲9am-5pm Mon-Sun; 🍴) Perfect for lunch or a peppy coffee, this licensed cafe-gallery kicks back in an 1890s house amid idyllic gardens. Unleash the kids in the playroom and linger over your *panini,* cheese platter, mushroom burger, seafood chowder, pasta or lemon tart. Vegetarian, gluten- and dairy-free options, too.

SPRIG AND FERN   Pub
(www.sprigandfern.co.nz; Wallace St; meals $14-19; ⏲2pm-late) Recently born of the expanding Sprig and Fern family, this branch has upped the ante among Motueka's drinking holes. Small but pleasant, with two courtyards, it offers 20 hand-pulled beers, simple food (burgers, pizza, platters) and occasional live music.

ℹ Information

Motueka i-SITE (☑03-528 6543; www.abeltasmanisite.co.nz; 20 Wallace St; ⏲8.30am-5pm Mon-Fri, 9am-4pm Sat & Sun) An excellent centre with helpful staff who will make bookings from Kaitaia to Bluff and provide local national-park expertise and necessaries.

ℹ Getting There & Away

Abel Tasman Coachlines (☑03-528 8850; www.abeltasmantravel.co.nz) runs two to four times daily from Motueka to Nelson ($12, one hour), Marahau ($10, 30 minutes), Kaiteriteri ($10, 25 minutes) and Takaka ($26, one hour).

Golden Bay Coachlines (☑03-525 8352; www.goldenbaycoachlines.co.nz) runs from Motueka to Takaka ($26, one hour) and Collingwood ($39, 1½ hours), as well as other

Golden Bay destinations in summer, including the Heaphy Track and Totaranui.

Naked Bus (📞0900 625 33; www.nakedbus.com) runs from Motueka to Nelson ($11, one hour).

Abel Tasman National Park

The accessible, coastal Abel Tasman National Park blankets the northern end of a range of marble and limestone hills extending from Kahurangi National Park. Various tracks in the park include an inland route, although the coast track is what everyone is here for – it sees more foot traffic than any other Great Walk in New Zealand.

 ## Activities

The 51km, three- to five-day **Abel Tasman Coast Track** is one of the most scenic in the country, passing through native bush overlooking golden beaches lapped by gleaming azure water. Numerous bays, small and large, are like a travel brochure come to life. Visitors can walk into the park, catch water taxis to beaches and resorts along the track, or kayak along the coast.

In summer hundreds of trampers tackle the track at the same time. Track accommodation works on a booking system: huts and campsites must be prebooked year-round. There's no charge for day walks – if you're after a taster, the two- to three-hour stretch from Tonga Bay to Bark Bay is as photogenic as any, or get dropped at a beach and just hang out.

For a full description of the route, see DOC's *Abel Tasman Coast Track* brochure.

 ## Tours

ABEL TASMAN SAILING ADVENTURES
Sailing

(📞03-527 8375, 0800 467 245; www.sailingadventures.co.nz; Kaiteriteri; half/full day $85/169) Offers the only scheduled sailing trips into the park on baord a catamaran. Sail/walk/kayak combos available; day-trip includes lunch.

ABEL TASMAN TOURS & GUIDED WALKS
Walking

(📞03-528 9602; www.abeltasmantours.co.nz; $220) Small-group, day-long walking tours (minimum two people) that include packed lunch and water taxis.

WILSONS ABEL TASMAN
Walking, Kayaking

(📞0800 221 888, 03-528 2027; www.abeltasman.co.nz; 265 High St, Motueka; half-day cruise $70, cruise & walk $55-70, kayak & walk $89-195) Impressive array of cruises, walks, kayak and combo tours, including $32 backpacker special and the barbecue cruise (great winter option). Luxurious beachfront lodges at Awaroa and Torrent Bay for guided-tour guests.

 ## Sleeping & Eating

At the southern edge of the park, Marahau is the main jumping-off point for the Abel Tasman National Park. From the northern end of the park, the nearest towns with accommodation are Pohara and Takaka. The whopping **Totaranui DOC Campsite** (📞03-528 8083; www.doc.govt.nz; unpowered sites adult/child $12.50/6.50) is also in the north, 32km from Takaka on a narrow, winding road (12km unsealed – check with DOC or the Golden Bay i-SITE for latest conditions). It's serviced by **Abel Tasman Coachlines** (www.abeltasmantravel.co.nz) from October to April. Sites at Totaranui from December to mid-February are now allocated via ballot; download a booking form from the DOC website.

Along the Coast Track there are four huts: **Anchorage** (24 bunks), Bark Bay (34 bunks), **Awaroa** (26 bunks) and **Whariwharangi** (20 bunks), plus 19 designated campsites. None of these have cooking facilities – BYO stove. Some of the campsites have fireplaces but, again, you must carry cooking equipment. Hut and camp passes should be purchased before

Abel Tasman National Park

N 0 —————— 4 km
0 —————— 2 miles

Abel Tasman National Park

🛏 Sleeping

1	Anchorage Hut	B5
	Aquapackers	(see 1)
2	Awaroa Hut	A3
3	Totaranui DOC Campsite	A2
4	Whariwharangi Hut	A1

www.aquapackers.co.nz; Anchorage; dm/d incl breakfast $70/195) is a rockin' option. This specially converted 13m *Catarac* catamaran provides unusual but buoyant backpacker accommodation for 22. Facilities are basic but decent; prices include bedding, dinner and breakfast. Bookings essential.

Further sleeping options in the park (accessible on foot, by kayak or water taxi, but not by road) are largely confined to holiday homes. Ask about these at the Nelson or Motueka i-SITEs or browse online.

ℹ Information

The track operates on DOC's Great Walks Pass (sites/huts per person $12.20/35.70). Children are free but booking is still required. Book online (www.doc.govt.nz), contact the Nelson Marlborough Bookings Helpdesk (📞03-546 8210; nmbookings@doc.govt.nz), or in person at the Nelson, Motueka and Takaka i-SITES or DOC offices, where staff can offer suggestions to tailor the track to your needs and organise transport at each end. Book your trip well ahead of time, especially the huts between December and March.

ℹ Getting Around

Common setting-out points for the Abel Tasman are Kaiteriteri and Marahau in the south, and Takaka in the north. All are serviced by Abel Tasman Coachlines (www.abeltasmantravel.co.nz), with connections to Nelson and Motueka.

Once you hit the park, it is easy to get to/from any point on the track by water taxi, either from Kaiteriteri or Marahau. Typical one-way prices from either Marahau or Kaiteriteri: Anchorage and Torrent Bay ($33), Bark Bay ($38), Tonga ($40), Awaroa ($43) and Totaranui ($45). Key operators include the following.

you enter the park. From Christmas Day to February, huts and campsites fill to the rafters (book with DOC).

Moored permanently in Anchorage Bay, the **Aquapackers** (📞0800 430 744;

DAVID WALL / LONELY PLANET IMAGES ©

Don't Miss **Paddling the Abel Tasman**

The Abel Tasman Coast Track has long been trampers' territory, but its coastal beauty makes it an equally seductive spot for sea kayaking, which can easily be combined with walking and camping.

You can kayak from half a day up to three days, camping ($12.20 per night) or staying in Department of Convservation (DOC) huts ($35.70 per night), baches, even a floating backpackers, either fully catered for or self-catering. You can kayak one day, camp overnight then walk back, or walk further into the park and catch a water taxi back.

Most operators offer similar trips at similar prices. Marahau is the main base, but trips also depart Kaiteriteri. A popular choice if time is tight is spend a few hours kayaking in the Tonga Island Marine Reserve, followed by a walk from Tonga Quarry to Bark Bay. This will cost around $160 including water taxis. Three-day trips usually drop you at the northern end of the park, then you paddle back (or vice versa) and cost around $600 including food. One-day guided trips are around $200.

November to Easter is the busiest time, with December to February the absolute peak. You can, however, paddle all year round, with winter offering its own rewards. The weather is surprisingly amenable, the seals are more playful, there's more bird life and less haze.

NEED TO KNOW

These are the main players in this competitive market. Shop around.

Abel Tasman Kayaks (📞03-527 8022, 0800 732 529; www.abeltasmankayaks.co.nz; Main Rd, Marahau); **Kahu Kayaks** (📞03-527 8300, 0800 300 101; www.kahukayaks.co.nz; cnr Marahau Valley Rd); **Kaiteriteri Kayaks** (📞03-527 8383, 0800 252 925; www.seakayak.co.nz; Kaiteriteri Beach & Marahau Beach Rd); **Marahau Sea Kayaks** (📞03-527 8176, 0800 529 257; www.msk.co.nz; Abel Tasman Centre, Franklin St); **Sea Kayak Company** (📞03-528 7251, 0508 252 925; www.seakayaknz. co.nz; 506 High St, Motueka); **Wilsons Abel Tasman** (📞0800 221 888, 03-528 2027; www. abeltasman.co.nz; 265 High St, Motueka)

Detour:
Farewell Spit

Bleak, exposed and slighly sci-fi, **Farewell Spit** is a wetland of international importance and a renowned bird sanctuary – the summer home of thousands of migratory waders, notably the godwit (which flies all the way from the Arctic tundra), Caspian terns and Australasian gannets. The 35km beach features colossal, crescent-shaped dunes, from where panoramic views extend across Golden Bay and a vast low-tide salt marsh. Walkers can explore the first 4km of the spit via a network of tracks, but beyond that point access is via tour only.

Farewell Spit Eco Tours (0800 808 257, 03-524 8257; www.farewellspit.com; Tasman St, Collingwood; tours $120-145) Operating for more than 65 years, this outfit runs a range of tours from three to 6½ hours, taking in the spit, lighthouse, gannets and godwits. Tours depart from Collingwood.

Farewell Spit Nature Experience (0800 250 500, 03-524 8992; www.farewellspittours. com; tours $120-135) Four-hour spit tours depart Farewell Spit Visitor Centre; six-hour tours depart the Old School Café, Pakawau.

Abel Tasman Aqua Taxi (0800 278 282, 03-527 8083 ; www.aquataxi.co.nz; Kaiteriteri & Marahau) Scheduled and on-demand services as well as boat/walk options.

Abel Tasman Sea Shuttle (0800 732 748, 03-527 8688; www.abeltasmanseashuttles.co.nz; Kaiteriteri) Scheduled services plus cruise/walk options. Also runs between Nelson and Kaiteriteri during peak season (adult/child $30/15).

Wilsons Abel Tasman (0800 223 582, 03-528 2027; www.abeltasman.co.nz; 265 High St, Motueka; pass adult/child $145/72.50) Offers an explorer pass for unlimited taxi travel on three days over a five-day period, plus backpacker specials and an array of tours.

Marahau Water Taxis (x0800 808 018, 03-528 2027; www.abeltasmancentre.co.nz; Abel Tasman Centre, Franklin St, Marahau) Scheduled services plus boat/walk options.

Christchurch & Central South

Nowhere in New Zealand is changing and developing as fast as post-earthquake Christchurch, and visiting the country's second-largest city as it's being rebuilt and reborn is both interesting and inspiring.

A short drive from Christchurch's dynamic re-emergence, Banks Peninsula conceals hidden bays and beaches – a backdrop for kayaking and wildlife cruises with a sunset return to the attractions of Akaroa. Throughout the seasons, Aoraki/Mt Cook, the country's tallest peak, stands sentinel over this diverse region.

Over the craggy Southern Alps, hemmed in by the wild Tasman Sea, the West Coast (aka Westland) is like nowhere else in New Zealand. During summer a phalanx of campervans and tourist buses tick off the must-see Punakaiki Rocks and Franz Josef and Fox Glaciers. Deviate from the trail even a short way, however, and you'll be awed by the spectacular sights that await you alone.

View of the Southern Alps across Canterbury countryside

RACHEL LEWIS / LONELY PLANET IMAGES ©

Punting on the Avon River (p239)

Christchurch & Central South

Lake
Rotoroa

St Arnaud

Mt Travers ▲
(2338m)

Mt Uriah ▲
(1525m)

Nelson Lakes
National
Park

Punakaiki ○ ⑤ ○ Paparoa
National
Park

Victoria
Forest
Park

Mt Una ▲
(2301m)

Faerie
Queen ▲
(2237m)

Hanmer
Springs
National
Park

Mt Ryall ▲
(1220m)

Mt Haast ▲
(1587m)

Lewis
Pass

St James
Walkway

Grey River

*TASMAN
SEA*

Greymouth

Kumara
Junction

Mt Ajax ▲
(1832m)

Lake
Sumner
Forest Park

Hanmer
Springs ⑥

Lake Brunner
*(Moana
Kotuku)*

Hokitika ③

*Lake
Mahinapua*

Arthur's Pass
National Park

Lake
Sumner ▲ Mt Longfellow
(1898m)

Hokitika
Gorge) (

Mt Rolleston ▲
(2272m)

Arthur's
Pass ▲
(924m)

Ross ○

*Lake
Kaniere*

Arthur's
Pass

Pukekura ○

Mt Murchison ▲
(2400m)

Lake
Pearson

Waipara ○

*Lake
Ianthe*

Mt Bryce ▲
(2188m)

*Lake
Wahapo*

Mt Whitcombe ▲
(2638m)

Porters
) (Pass
(945m)

Woodend ○

Westland
National
Park

Mt Arrowsmith ▲
(2795m)

*Lake
Coleridge*

*Pegasus
Bay*

Franz Josef ④

*Lake
Mapourika*

*Lake
Heron*

Mt Hutt ○

Christchurch ①
● Lyttelton

Fox
Glacier

④

Aoraki/Mt Cook
National Park

Rangitata River

Methven ○ ⑦

Aoraki/
Mt Cook ▲
③ (2754m)

Rakaia

Banks
Peninsula

Rakaia River

*Lake
Ellesmere*

② Akaroa

*Lake
Tekapo*

Lake
Tekapo ○

) (Burkes
Pass
(701m)

Fairlie ○

Geraldine ○

*Lake
Pukaki*

Twizel ○

Timaru ○

*Lake
Benmore*

*Lake
Aviemore*

*Canterbury
Bight*

Waitaki River

○ Oamaru

---

① Christchurch

② Akaroa & Banks
Peninsula

③ Aoraki/Mt Cook

④ Glaciers

⑤ Punakaiki Rocks

⑥ Hanmer Springs

⑦ Methven

Christchurch & Central South's Highlights

1

Post-Quake Christchurch

On 22 February 2011 Christchurch was wracked by a huge earthquake, killing 185 people and leaving hundreds of buildings requiring demolition. Reconstruction is a long-term prospect, but around town things are changing daily. There's a real vigour and creative energy in the way locals are redesigning their city and their lives.

Above: Re:START Mall (p244)

Need to Know

THE LATEST Check out www.christchurchnz.com ONLY A FEW HOURS? Visit Re:START shipping-container mall or explore the Botanic Gardens For further coverage, see p236

Christchurch Don't Miss List

BY JEFF PETERS, CENTREPOINT ON COLOMBO MOTEL

1 THE MAIN SIGHTS

Christchurch is still the South Island's main gateway and hub: most tourist things are up and running, including the International Antarctic Centre (p237), Canterbury Museum (p236), which escaped with very little damage, and the Botanic Gardens (p236). Sadly, we've lost the cathedral, and the tram and gondola will be closed for some time. The Art Gallery won't open till mid-2013 and the Arts Centre won't open for many years... But the city is still a great place to visit! Left: Little blue penguin, International Antarctic Centre (p237); Below left: Canterbury Museum (236)

2 CREATIVE REBUILDING

Rebuilding will be a long process – 10, 15, 20 years. So people are finding creative opportunities to get on with things. The quintessential Christchurch experience now is to open a cafe, bar or restaurant in a shipping container, semitrailer or caravan. The shipping-container mall Re:START (p244) really symbolises this kind of spirit.

3 EATING & DRINKING

We lost around half the pubs and restaurants around town, so the ones that are still operating are really busy! A certain amount of pride has kicked in: their tables are probably going to be full anyway, but the service and food are usually pretty great. Christchurch has stood up and said, 'No earthquake's gunna beat us!'

4 EMERGING AREAS

Addington is emerging as an events area – Dux Live (p241), a music venue, and the Court Theatre (p244) are there now, plus some great cafes. The city centre will come back, but satellite areas around Christchurch are really going to thrive in the meantime.

5 QUAKE TOURISM

Take some time to understand what's happened here; walk around the city centre, or take a ride out to Sumner where there are houses half-hanging over the edges of cliffs. Chat with the locals – your waiter or someone in the Botanic Gardens – and listen to their stories. 'Disaster tourism' is no problem, but it's probably best to stay away from residential areas.

Akaroa & Banks Peninsula

A haven for artists, gardeners and holiday-makers, Akaroa (population 550) on the Banks Peninsula offers an engaging mix of volcanic landscapes, a gorgeous harbour and French colonial heritage. And with its own microclimate (locals grow grapes, olives and citrus), Akaroa is always a few degrees warmer than nearby Christchurch.

Need to Know

BEST SEASON Spring or autumn **SHORT ON TIME?** Akaroa waterfront promenade **PHOTO OP** Summit Rd along the old volcano rim **For further coverage, see p246**

Akaroa & Banks Peninsula Don't Miss List

BY HOLLIE HOLLANDER, AKAROA DISTRICT PROMOTIONS

1 WATERFRONT AKAROA

Christchurch people used to call Akaroa the 'Riviera of Canterbury'. Along the waterfront are plenty of places to relax with a coffee or a glass of wine, and there's a lovely promenade right along the shore. Boats moor in the harbour, and a local fisherman sells his catch on the main wharf. There aren't many places left in NZ where you can buy fresh fish off the wharf!

2 FRENCH HISTORY

In the 1830s Akaroa was a whaling port. French whaler Captain Langlois saw a future here and purchased Banks Peninsula in a dodgy deal with local Maori. He returned to France to round up some colonists, but in the meantime Maori signed the Treaty of Waitangi with the British. So in the end it was the Union Jack flying here, not *Le Tricolore*. The French settlers stayed anyway, leaving a legacy of beautiful timber buildings, gardens and French street names. And now you can buy baguettes and croissants at the deli on the main street!

3 DOLPHINS & PENGUINS

Hector's Dolphins are a big drawcard here – they're the smallest dolphins in the world, like little torpedoes! You can swim with them out in the harbour, or take a cruise and see them from a boat. Sea-kayak operators run dolphin trips too, or you can hire a kayak from the Adventure Centre (p247). We've also got an amazing white-flippered penguin colony here – there's lots of conservation work happening.

4 PENINSULA WALKS

The walking tracks around the Peninsula are one of the things that make the region so special: you can be down by the water in Akaroa by the cafes, then half an hour later be walking in the hills with amazing views and bird life. There's also the two- or four-day Banks Peninsula Track (p247), a commercially operated coastal walk that's been getting some rave reviews.

Aoraki/Mt Cook

Standing proud at 3754m, Aoraki/Mt Cook (p251) is something to behold. It's quite cloud-covered, but on a clear day the jagged, heaven-high peak is inspiring and humbling. Even when it is cloudy, this mountain's magnitude is undeniable. Walking around the lake-strewn foothills in the crisp alpine air as avalanches rumble on distant slopes, you'll be forgiven for feeling a tad insignificant!

3

Glaciers

4

Quick, scoot over to the West Coast and see Franz Josef Glacier (p257) and Fox Glacier (p261) before global warming melts them. You probably don't have to be there in the next 10 minutes – there's a heckuva lot of ice here. Take a hike around the jagged glacial faces (but not too close – these things are moving!) or a scenic flight above or onto these massive rivers of ice.

Hikers on Franz Josef Glacier

Punakaiki Rocks

Weird! Piled up like giant-sized flap-jacks, the West Coast's Punakaiki Rocks (p255) are worth writing home about – these oddball geologic formations will make you wonder if someone/something really did design this lonely planet (and possibly make you hungry). The ocean booms through blowholes nearby, and there's an easy walking track from the parking area (have you ever seen so many campervans?).

5

6

7

Hanmer Springs

Forget your Blackberry, your briefcase, your business... You've come on holiday to *really* de-stress, haven't you? Take a trip 1½ hours north from Christchurch to hassle-free Hanmer Springs (p248), passing rivers, vineyards, mountains and country towns en route. Once you arrive you can take a dip in hot mineral springs or have a massage before hitting the restaurants and bars. There's skiing and snowboarding here in winter, too.

Methven Activities

The laid-back little Central Canterbury town of Methven (p250) is a real outdoorsy hub, functioning in winter as a base for skiing and snowboarding at nearby Mt Hutt (p349), and in summer as *the* place in NZ to try hot-air ballooning. You can also tackle horse riding, mountain biking, jetboating and (if the whole self-preservation instinct thing doesn't kick in) skydiving. Skiing on Mt Hutt

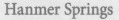

Christchurch & Central South's Best…

Natural Wonders

⊙ Franz Josef & Fox Glaciers (p257 and p261) There's only one word that fits – awesome!

⊙ Aoraki/Mt Cook (p251) Nobody bagged this lofty peak until 1894 – it's *really* big

⊙ Banks Peninsula (p246) Spaghetti-like volcanic coastlines

⊙ Punakaiki Rocks (p255) Stacks of giant dolomite pancakes… Pass the maple syrup

Short Strolls

⊙ Mt John (p251) A fab three-hour return hike to the summit above Lake Tekapo

⊙ Banks Peninsula Track (p247) Two- or four-day hop across farmland by the coast

⊙ Hooker Valley (p252) Glacial streams, swing bridges and Aoraki panoramas (hope for a sunny day)

⊙ Christchurch Botanic Gardens (p236) Work the plane-seat kinks out of your legs in these beautiful gardens

Places to Unwind

⊙ Banks of the Avon (p239) While away a few hours by the riverside in central Christchurch

⊙ Hanmer Springs (p248) Slip into a hot spa, get your spine massaged, or revel in après-ski good times

⊙ Akaroa waterfront (p248) Sip a strong coffee, munch a French pastry and assess the passers-by

⊙ Monteith's Brewing Co (p254) Big, beery and beautiful on the West Coast

Need to Know

Places to Get Giddy

○ **Aoraki/Mt Cook from Above** (p253) As high as Kiwis get without wings (take a scenic flight unless you're a hard-core mountaineer)

○ **Methven Hot-air Balloons** (p250) Everybody sing: 'Up, up and away, my beautiful, my beautiful balloon'

○ **TranzAlpine** (p256) Climb high over the Southern Alps on this epic train ride

○ **Franz Josef & Fox Glaciers Scenic Flights** (p257 and p261) See them from above via wings, rotor blades or a parachute

ADVANCE PLANNING

○ **One month before** Book a seat on the *TranzAlpine* train, and your beds from Akaroa to Fox Glacier

○ **Two weeks before** Organise a scenic flight above Aoraki/Mt Cook or the West Coast glaciers, or a balloon trip in Methven

○ **One week before** Book a table at a top Christchurch restaurant and a tour at Monteith's Brewing Co in Greymouth

RESOURCES

○ **Christchurch & Canterbury** (www.christchurchnz.com) For the latest post-quake updates. Also see www.popupcity.co.nz for an ongoing blog of new eating and drinking opportunities around town

○ **Christchurch City Council** (www.christchurch.org.nz)

○ **Akaroa Information Centre** (www.akaroa.com) Banks Peninsula and Akaroa info

○ **DOC Aoraki/Mt Cook Visitor Centre** (www.doc.govt.nz) Advises on weather conditions, guided tours and tramping

○ **Westland Tai Poutini National Park Visitor Centre & i-SITE** (www.glaciercountry.co.nz, www.doc.govt.nz) At Franz Josef; also the regional DOC office

GETTING AROUND

○ **Bus** From town to town across Canterbury

○ **Hire a car** To explore beyond the Christchurch city limits

○ **Campervan** Up and down the wild, driftwood-strewn shores of the West Coast

○ **Train** Across the snowy crags of the Southern Alps on the *TranzAlpine*

○ **Punt** Along the lazy, languid River Avon (bring some cucumber sandwiches, a boater hat and some champagne)

BE FOREWARNED

○ **Mt Cook Village Accommodation** Weary travellers without a reservation might find themselves without a bed at Mt Cook Village. Accommodation here is scant (especially midrange) and pricey: unless you want to backtrack to Twizel, book well in advance.

Christchurch & Central South Itineraries

Christchurch is the real deal: culture, class and southern spirit. Across Canterbury are incredible summits, peninsulas and lakes, while over the mountains are the West Coast's glaciers, rock formations and wilderness.

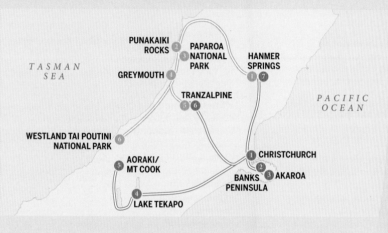

3 DAYS

CHRISTCHURCH TO HANMER SPRINGS
Christchurch & Canterbury

There's too much to see and too much to do in Canterbury: don't waste time! Hit **(1) Christchurch** running, with a kick-arse cafe coffee, a visit to the Canterbury Museum and a float through the Botanic Gardens on an Avon River punt. The city is rebuilding and reinventing itself: connect with the locals over a meal or a drink and discover a city getting back on its feet.

The next day cruise out to the formerly volcanic folds of **(2) Banks Peninsula**: explore the very Frenchy **(3) Akaroa**, with its wildlife-rich harbour, and the peninsula's photogenic outer bays. You can also swim with dolphins here, and kayak around the coast.

Day three already! Give your Canterbury compass a twirl: you could wander west to **(4) Lake Tekapo** and the snowy heights of **(5) Aoraki/Mt Cook**, where you can tramp, ski or take a scenic flight; or head over to the West Coast and back in a day on the **(6) TranzAlpine** train... But our vote is to point the needle north to **(7) Hanmer Springs**, a chilled-out hot-springs resort town from which you can launch a wintertime skiing sortie or spa yourself silly. And, if you have more time, the West Coast awaits beyond the mountains...

234

5 DAYS

HANMER SPRINGS TO WESTLAND TAI POUTINI NATIONAL PARK
Heading for the Coast

Shake yourself from your relaxed stupor in **(1) Hanmer Springs** and leap over the Alps to Westport and the **(2) Punakaiki Rocks** south of town. You can also tramp near here in **(3) Paparoa National Park**.

Next stop heading south is **(4) Greymouth**. The town itself might not hold your attentions: prosects improve with a tour of Monteith's Brewing Co, a West Coast brewery that started small but now has taps and barrels in pubs and bars across NZ (its Celtic Red ale is a knockout). Then, if you're still not wild about the West Coast, the **(5) TranzAlpine** train trundles back over the mountains from here to Christchurch.

The Big Daddies of West Coast tourism are, however, further south: the momentous Franz Josef Glacier and Fox Glacier in **(6) Westland Tai Poutini National Park**. If you've never seen a glacier before, these two will knock your socks off! Take a hike around or actually *on* one of them, or hop on a scenic flight to really grasp the enormity and power of these incredible ice rivers.

From the West Coast, you can save time with a short flight back to Christchurch from Hokitika.

Cruise boat near Akaroa (p247)
DAVID WALL / LONELY PLANET IMAGES ©

Discover Christchurch & the Central South

CHRISTCHURCH

Welcome to a vibrant city in transition, coping resiliently and creatively with the aftermath of NZ's second-biggest natural disaster (especially as tremors can still be felt regularly). Traditionally the most English of NZ cities, Christchurch is now adding a modern and innovative layer to its damaged heritage heart.

⊙ Sights & Activities

FREE BOTANIC GARDENS — Gardens
(Map p242; www.ccc.govt.nz; Rolleston Ave; admission free, guided walks $10, train tour adult/child $18/9; ☻grounds 7am-1hr before sunset, conservatories 10.15am-4pm, cafe 9am-4pm Mon-Fri, 10.15am-4pm Sat & Sun; **P**)
The Botanic Gardens comprise 30 riverside hectares planted with 10,000-plus specimens of indigenous and introduced plants. Guided walks depart daily at 1.30pm (September to April) from the Canterbury Museum, or you can ride around the gardens in the electric **'Caterpillar' train** (www.gardentour.co.nz). Hop-on/hop-off tickets are valid for two days (10am to 4pm) and include a commentary.

CANTERBURY MUSEUM — Museum
(Map p242; ☏03-366 5000; www.canterburymuseum.com; Rolleston Ave; admission by donation; ☻9am-5pm Apr-Sep, to 5.30pm Oct-Mar) The absorbing Canterbury Museum has a wonderful collection of items of significance to NZ. Highlights include the Maori gallery, with some stunning *pounamu* (greenstone) pieces on display; the coracle in the Antarctic Hall that was

Fountain in the Christchurch Botanic Gardens
DAVID WALL / LONELY PLANET IMAGES ©

used by a group shipwrecked on Disappointment Island in 1907; and a wide array of stuffed birds from the Pacific and beyond: don't miss the statuesque Emperor penguin. Guided tours (donations appreciated) run from 3.30pm to 4.30pm on Tuesday and Thursday.

INTERNATIONAL ANTARCTIC CENTRE
Wildlife

(☎03-353 7798, 0508 736 4846; www.iceberg.co.nz; 38 Orchard Rd; adult/child/family from $35/20/95; Penguin Backstage Pass adult/child/family $25/15/80; ⌚9am-5.30pm; P) The International Antarctic Centre is part of a huge complex built for the administration of the NZ, US and Italian Antarctic programs. See penguins and learn about the icy continent via historical, geological and zoological exhibits.

BONE DUDE
Art

(Map p238; ☎03-385 4509; www.thebonedude.co.nz; 153 Marshland Rd, Shirley; per person $60; ⌚1-4pm Mon-Fri, 10am-1pm Sat) Creative types should book a session with the Bone Dude, now relocated to the suburb of Shirley, where you can craft your own bone carving (allow three hours). Owner John Fraser, who's of Ngati Rangitihi ancestry, provides a range of traditional Maori templates, or you can work on your own design.

NATURAL HIGH
Bicycle Rental

(☎03-982 2966, 0800 444 144; www.naturalhigh.co.nz) Rents touring and mountain bikes (per day/week from $40/154), and can advise on guided and self-guided bicycle touring through Canterbury and the South Island.

Tours

CANTERBURY LEISURE TOURS
Guided Tour

(☎0800 484 485, 03-384 0999; www.leisuretours.co.nz; tours from $60) Touring options in and around Christchurch, with everything from three-hour city tours to full-day outings to Akaroa, Mt Cook, Arthur's Pass and Kaikoura.

CHRISTCHURCH BIKE TOURS
Guided Tour

(☎0800 733 257; www.chchbiketours.co.nz; tours from $40; ⌚departs 2pm daily) Informative, two-hour tours loop around the city along quiet cycleways and leafy park tracks. Also available is a gourmet food tour and a Saturday-morning foodie spin, taking in the Christchurch Farmers Market.

CHRISTCHURCH PERSONAL GUIDING SERVICE
Walking Tour

(☎03-379 9629; tours $15; ⌚11am & 1pm Oct-Apr, 1pm May-Sep) Nonprofit organisation offering informative two-hour city walks. Buy tickets and join tours at the i-SITE departure point.

Sleeping

ORARI B&B
B&B $$$

(Map p242; ☎03-365 6569; www.orari.net.nz; 42 Gloucester St; d $195-255; P ⟨⟩) Orari is a late-19th-century home that has been stylishly updated with light-filled, pastel-toned rooms and inviting guest areas, as well as a lovely front garden. Wine connoisseurs can look forward to complimentary wine after a busy day.

🏄 WISH
B&B $$

(Map p238; ☎03-356 2455; www.wishnzcom; 38 Edgeware Rd, St Albans; s/d incl breakfast from $125/150; P @ ⟨⟩) The rooms and beds at the stylish Wish are supercomfy, but it could be the locally sourced, sustainable and organic breakfasts that you recommend to other travellers. Contemporary NZ art dots the walls, and the huge native-timber kitchen table is just made for catching up with other guests over an end-of-day glass of wine.

CENTREPOINT ON COLOMBO
Motel $$

(Map p242; ☎0800 859 000, 03-377 0859; www.centrepointoncolombo.co.nz; 859 Colombo St; d $155-165, apt $180-260; P @ ⟨⟩) CentrePoint on Colombo has super-comfortable facilities and the bonus of a friendly Kiwi-Japanese management. The owners are a

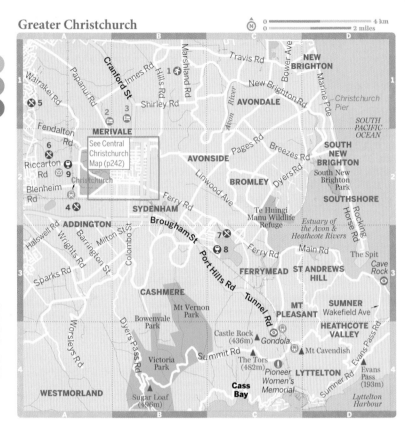

Greater Christchurch

mine of information on how Christchurch is bouncing back after the earthquakes, and happily provide guests with up-to-date information on the best places to eat around town.

GEORGE Boutique Hotel $$$
(Map p242; ☎ 0800 100 220, 03-379 4560; www.thegeorge.com; 50 Park Tce; d $506-886; 🅿 @ 🛜) The George has 53 handsomely decorated rooms and suites on the fringe of Christchurch's sweeping Hagley Park. Discreet staff attend to every whim; there are two excellent restaurants; and ritzy features including huge TVs, luxury toiletries and glossy magazines. Check online for good-value packages and discounts.

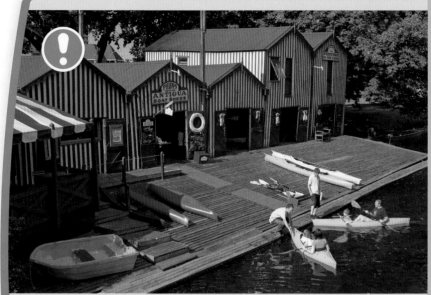

JOHN ELK III / LONELY PLANET IMAGE

Don't Miss **Antigua Boatsheds**

Dating from 1882, the photogenic green-and-white Antigua Boatsheds are the starting point for **Punting on the Avon**, where someone else does all the work during a half-hour return trip in a flat-bottomed boat. There's also an excellent cafe which is a great spot for brunch or lunch. Kayaks and rowboats can be rented for independent Avon River exploration.

NEED TO KNOW

Map p242; www.punting.co.nz; 2 Cambridge Tce; punting adult/child/family $25/12/65; ⊘9am-6pm, cafe 7am-5pm

---

CLASSIC VILLA   B&B $$$
(Map p242; ☑03-377 7905; www.theclassicvilla.
co.nz; 17 Worcester Ave; d $269-489; **P** 🛜)
Ideally located near the Botanic Gardens and Canterbury Museum, the Classic Villa is one of Christchurch's most elegant accommodation options. Rooms are trimmed with antiques and Turkish rugs for a classy ambience, and the expansive, Mediterranean-style breakfast is a shared social occasion around the dining room's big wooden table. No children under 12 years old allowed.

MERIVALE MANOR   Motel $$
(Map p238; ☑03-355 7731; www.merivalemanor.
com; 122 Papanui Rd; d $145-185; **P** 🛜) A gracious 19th-century Victorian residence is now the hub of an elegant motel. Accommodation ranges from studios (some with spa baths) to one- and two-bedroom apartments. In keeping with the property's history, decor is understated, and the classy shopping and good bars and restaurants of Merivale are just a few hundred metres away.

Eating

BODHI TREE
Burmese $$

(Map p238; ☎03-377 6808; www.bodhitree.
co.nz; 39 Ilam Rd; dishes $13-24; ⏱6-10pm
Tue-Sun; 🖉) Christchurch's only Burmese
restaurant is also one of the city's best
eateries. Standout dishes include the *le
pet thoke* (pickled tea-leaf salad) and the
ciandi thoke (grilled eggplant). Dishes
are starter-sized, so drum up a group and
sample lots of different flavours.

HOLY SMOKE
Steakhouse $$

(Map p238; www.holysmoke.co.nz; 650 Ferry Rd;
brunch & lunch mains $18-25, dinner mains $26-
36; ⏱9am-late Mon-Sat, to 4pm Sun) At Holy
Smoke, the native wood manuka (NZ tea
tree), is used to smoke everything from
pork ribs and chicken wings to bacon
and salmon. Other menu items include
robust slabs of venison, lamb and beef,
all teamed with Kiwi craft beers and Central Otago wines.

ADDINGTON COFFEE CO-OP
Cafe $

(Map p238; www.addingtoncoffee.org.nz; 297
Lincoln Rd; snacks & mains $6-20; 🛜🖉) One of
Christchurch's biggest and most bustling
cafes is also one of its best. Fair-trade
coffee and a compact stall selling organic
cotton T-shirts jostle for attention with
delicious cakes and slices, while a cross-
section of the city comes for the free
wi-fi, gourmet pies and wraps, and the
legendary big breakfasts.

BEAT STREET
Cafe $

(Map p242; 324 Barbadoes St; snacks & mains
$8-16; 🖉) Welcome to the grungy hub of
Christchurch cafe-cool. Free range this
and organic that combine with terrific
eggy breakfasts, gourmet pies (try the
feta and vegie one) and robust Havana
coffee. Beat Street hosts a bohemian

The Christchurch Earthquakes

Christchurch's seismic nightmare began at 4.35am on 4 September 2010.
Centered 40km west of the city, a 40-second, 7.1-magnitude earthquake jolted
Cantabrians from their sleep, and caused widespread damage to older buildings
in the central city.

Fast forward to 12.51pm on 22 February 2011, when central Christchurch
was busy with shoppers and office and retail workers enjoying their lunch
break. This time the 6.3-magnitude quake was much closer, centred just 10km
southeast of the city and only 5km deep.

When the dust settled after 24 traumatic seconds, NZ's second-largest city
had changed forever. The towering spire of the iconic Christ Church Cathedral
lay in ruins; walls and verandas had cascaded down on the city's central retail
hub; and two multistorey buildings had pancaked, causing scores of deaths.
Around half of the quake's total of 181 deaths (across 20 nationalities) occurred
in the Canterbury TV building, including many international students at a
language school.

Around a quarter of the buildings within the city's famed four avenues
need to be demolished. Entire streets and family neighbourhoods in the
eastern suburbs will be abandoned, and Christchurch's heritage architecture is
irrevocably damaged.

Draft plans for the city's rebuild over 20 years include a compact, low-rise city
centre, neighbourhood green spaces and parks and cycleways along the Avon
River. Coupled with the endurance and energy of the people of Christchurch,
the city's future promises to be both interesting and innovative.

open-mic night featuring music and poetry on the third Thursday of every month from 6pm.

SIMO'S DELI Moroccan **$**
(Map p238; www.simos.co.nz; 3/300 Lincoln Rd; wraps $6.50-$9.50, tapas & mains $7-17) Part cafe and part deli, Simo's in Addington is popular for its takeaway *bocadillos* (grilled wraps filled with a huge selection of Middle Eastern and African-inspired fillings, sauces and toppings). Other tasty offerings include small plates of grilled calamari or spicy *merguez* sausages, or more robust *tagines* (Moroccan casseroles) and beef kofta with pomegranate sauce.

 **Drinking**

POMEROY'S OLD BREWERY INN Craft Beer
(Map p242; www.pomeroysonkilmore.co.nz; 292 Kilmore St) The welcoming Pomeroy's is the city's hoppy hub for fans of NZ's rapidly expanding craft beer scene. A wide range of guest taps showcase brews from around the country, often including seasonal beers and limited releases. Check the website for what's coming up. There's occasional live music, and the attached Victoria's Kitchen does great pub food (mains $20 to $30).

VOLSTEAD TRADING COMPANY Bar
(Map p238; www.volstead.co.nz; 55 Riccarton Rd) Volstead is a great example of what Christchurch has always done better than the rest of NZ: shabbily chic bars with a real sense of individuality. Comfy old sofas from your last student flat combine with quirky artwork, interesting beers from the Moa Brewery, and funky cocktails.

THE BREWERY Craft Beer
(Map p238; www.casselsbrewery.co.nz; 3 Garlands Rd) Out in Woolston, it's a fair schlep from the city, but the Brewery is an essential destination for beer-loving travellers. Cassels & Sons crafts all its beer using a wood-fired brew kettle,

resulting in big, bold beers like its 1PA and Best Bitter. Tasting trays are available for the curious and the indecisive, and the food – including wood-fired pizzas – is top-notch, too.

 Entertainment

DUX LIVE Live Music
(Map p242; 363 Lincoln Rd) Dux de Lux was an excellent restaurant, microbrewery and live-music venue in Christchurch's Arts Centre, but it was forced to close after the February 2011 earthquake. The beer is still being brewed (try it here and at at Dux de Lux in Queenstown) and in late 2011 this Addington venue opened for live music.

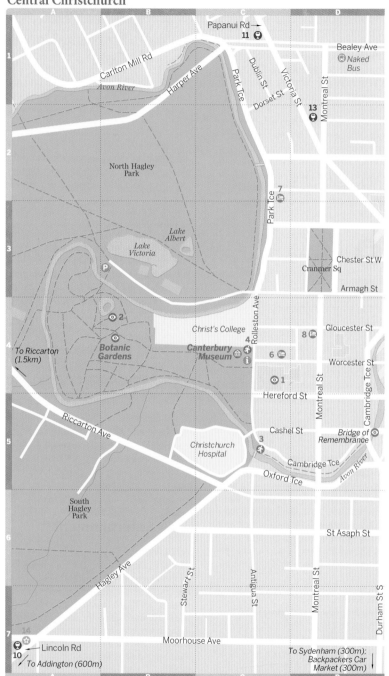

Carlton Mill Rd

Avon River

Harper Ave

Papanui Rd →
11

Park Tce

Dublin St

Dorset St

Victoria St

Montreal St

Bealey Ave
Naked Bus

13

North Hagley Park

Park Tce

7

Lake Albert

Lake Victoria

Chester St W

Cranmer Sq

Armagh St

P

Christ's College

Rolleston Ave

Gloucester St

8

2

Botanic Gardens

Canterbury Museum

4

6

1

Hereford St

Montreal St

Cambridge Tce

To Riccarton (1.5km)

Riccarton Ave

Christchurch Hospital

Cashel St

Bridge of Remembrance

3

Cambridge Tce

Oxford Tce

Avon River

South Hagley Park

St Asaph St

Hagley Ave

Stewart St

Antigua St

Montreal St

Durham St S

Moorhouse Ave

To Sydenham (300m);
Backpackers Car
Market (300m)

16

Lincoln Rd

10

To Addington (600m)

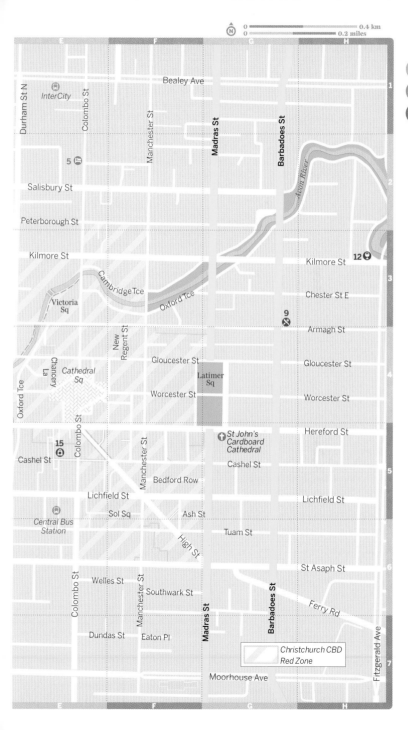

0.4 km
0.2 miles

Bealey Ave

Durham St N

InterCity

Colombo St

Manchester St

Madras St

Barbadoes St

Avon River

5

Salisbury St

Peterborough St

Kilmore St

Kilmore St

12

Cambridge Tce

Victoria Sq

Oxford Tce

Chester St E

9

New Regent St

Armagh St

Gloucester St

Gloucester St

Chancery La

Cathedral Sq

Latimer Sq

Oxford Tce

Worcester St

Worcester St

Hereford St

15

St John's Cardboard Cathedral

Cashel St

Colombo St

Cashel St

Manchester St

Bedford Row

Lichfield St

Lichfield St

Central Bus Station

Sol Sq

Ash St

Tuam St

High St

St Asaph St

Colombo St

Welles St

Manchester St

Southwark St

Barbadoes St

Ferry Rd

Fitzgerald Ave

Madras St

Dundas St

Eaton Pl

Christchurch CBD Red Zone

Moorhouse Ave

Central Christchurch

COURT THEATRE   Theatre
(Map p238; ☏0800 333 100, 03-963 0870;
www.courttheatre.org.nz; off Bernard St)
Christchurch's original Court Theatre was
an iconic part of the city's Arts Centre,
but it was forced to relocate after the
earthquakes. Its new premises in up-and-
coming Addington are more modern and
spacious, and it's a great venue to see
popular international plays and works by
NZ playwrights. Check the website for
what's playing.

 **Shopping**

RE:START MALL   Mall
(Map p242; www.restart.org.nz) Opened
in late October 2011, this colourful

labyrinth of shops based in shipping
containers was the first retail activity in
the Christchurch CBD after the February
2011 earthquake. With a couple of decent
cafes, and including two iconic Christchurch stores – Scorpio Books and John-
son's Grocers – it's a pleasant place to
stroll. Visit Hapa for a good selection of
design and crafts from local artists.

 Information

Medical Services

Bealey Avenue Medical Centre (☏03-365
7777; www.pegasus.org.nz; cnr Bealey Ave &
Colombo St; ⊙24hr) Located north of town,
with no appointment necessary.

Christchurch Hospital (☏03-364 0640,
emergency dept 03-364 0270; www.cdhb.govt.nz;
2 Riccarton Ave) Centrally located.

Tourist Information

Christchurch i-SITE (☏03-379 9629; www.
christchurchnz.com; Rolleston Ave, beside
the Canterbury Museum; ⊙8.30am-5pm,
later in summer) Transport, activities and
accommodation. Note that this location may
change during the life of this book. Check
online for the current location when you visit.

 Getting There & Away

Air

Christchurch Airport (CHC; ☏03-358 5029;
www.christchurchairport.co.nz) is the South
Island's main international gateway. **Air New
Zealand** (☏0800 737 000; www.airnewzealand.
co.nz) Direct flights to/from Auckland (from
$79), Blenheim (from $99), Dunedin (from $79),
Hamilton (from $109), Hokitika (from $109),
Invercargill (from $109), Napier (from $109),
Nelson (from $79), New Plymouth (from $109),
Palmerston North (from $119), Queenstown
(from $59), Rotorua (from $119), Tauranga (from
$109), Wanaka (from $99) and Wellington (from
$59).

Jetstar (☏0800 800 995; www.jetstar.
com) has direct flights to/from Auckland
($79), Queenstown ($59), and Wellington ($59).

Detour:
Lyttelton

Southeast of Christchurch are the prominent Port Hills, which slope down to the city's port at Lyttelton Harbour. Following the earthquakes, Lyttelton has re-emerged as one of Christchurch's most interesting and resilient communities. The town's artsy, independent and bohemian vibe is stronger than ever, and it's again becoming a hub for good bars, cafes and restaurants. It's well worth catching the bus from Christchurch and getting immersed in the local scene.

Lyttelton is linked to Christchurch via a road tunnel, but there's a more scenic (and 10km longer) route along the narrow Summit Rd, which has breathtaking city, hill and harbour views, as well as vistas of the Southern Alps. The **Lyttelton visitor information centre** (☏ 03-328 9093; www.lytteltonharbour.info; London St; ☉ 9am-5pm Sep-May, to 4pm Jun-Aug) has accommodation and transport information.

Bus

InterCity (☏ 03-365 1113; www.intercity.co.nz; 118 Bealey Ave) Northbound buses go to Kaikoura (2¾ hours), Blenheim (five hours) and Picton (5½ hours), with connections to Nelson (eight hours). One daily bus also goes southwest to Queenstown direct (eight hours). Heading south, two buses run daily along the coast via the towns along SH1 to Dunedin (six hours), with connections via Gore to Invercargill (9¾ hours) and Te Anau (10½ hours).

Naked Bus (www.nakedbus.com; 70 Bealey Ave) Heads north to Picton and Nelson, south to Dunedin and southwest to Queenstown.

Train

Christchurch railway station (☏ 0800 872 467, 03-341 2588; www.tranzscenic.co.nz; Troup Dr; ☉ ticket office 6.30am-3.30pm Mon-Fri, to 3pm Sat & Sun) is serviced by a free shuttle that picks up from various accommodation; ring the i-SITE to request pick-up. An alternative is Steve's Airport Shuttle (☏ 0800 101 021) for $5.

The *Coastal Pacific* runs daily each way between Christchurch and Picton via Kaikoura and Blenheim, departing from Christchurch at 7am and arriving at Picton at 12.13pm. The standard adult one-way fare to Picton is $99, but fares can be discounted to $59.

The *TranzAlpine* has a daily route between Christchurch and Greymouth via Arthur's Pass. The standard adult one-way fare is $129, but fares can be discounted to $89.

Contact **Kiwi Rail Scenic** (☏ 0800 872 467; www.tranzscenic.co.nz).

❶ Getting Around

To/From the Airport

The airport is 12km from the city centre.

Super Shuttle (☏ 0800 748 885; www.supershuttle.co.nz) operates 24 hours and charges $24 for one person between the city and the airport, plus $5 for each additional person. A cheaper alternative is **Steve's Airport Shuttle** (☏ 0800 101 021; 1/2/4 persons $15/20/20) offering a door-to-door service from 3am.

The airport is serviced by the **City Flyer bus** (☏ 0800 733 287; www.redbus.co.nz; adult/child $7.50/4.50), which runs to/from the Central Bus Station between 7.15am and 10.15pm Monday to Friday and 7.15am to 9.15pm Saturday and Sunday.

A taxi between the city centre and airport costs around $45 to $55.

Public Transport

The Christchurch **bus network** (Metro; ☏ 03-366 8855; www.metroinfo.org.nz; ☉ 7am-9pm Mon-Sat, 9am-7pm Sun) is inexpensive and efficient. Tickets (adult/child $3.20/1.60) include one free transfer within two hours. Metrocards allow unlimited two-hour/full-day travel for $2.30/4.60, but the cards must be loaded up with a minimum of $10.

Taxi

Blue Star (☏ 0800 379 979; www.bluestartaxis)

First Direct (☏ 0800 505 555; www.firstdirect.net.nz)

AROUND CHRISTCHURCH
Akaroa & Banks Peninsula

Banks Peninsula and its hills were formed by two giant volcanic eruptions about eight million years ago. The historic town of Akaroa is a highlight, as is the absurdly beautiful drive along Summit Rd around the edge of the original crater.

 Sights

GIANT'S HOUSE Garden
(www.thegiantshouse.co.nz; 68 Rue Balguerie; adult/child/family $20/10/45; ⏱ noon-5pm 26 Dec-22 April, 2-4pm in winter) An ongoing labour of love from local artist Josie Martin, this playful and whimsical combination of

sculpture and mosaics cascades down a hillside garden above Akaroa.

AKAROA MUSEUM Museum
(cnr Rues Lavaud & Balguerie; adult/child/family $4/1/8; ⏱ 10.30am-4.30pm Oct-Apr, to 4pm May-Sep) This interesting museum is spread over several historic buildings, including the old courthouse; the tiny Custom House by Daly's Wharf; and one of NZ's oldest houses, Langlois-Eteveneaux. It has modest displays on the peninsula's once-significant Maori population, a courtroom diorama, a 20-minute audiovisual on peninsular history, and Akaroa community archives.

 Activities

The *Akaroa – An Historic Walk* booklet ($9.50) details a walking tour starting at the 1876 **Waeckerle Cottage** (Rue Lavaud) and finishing at the old Taylor's Emporium premises near the main wharf. The route takes in the old wooden buildings and churches that give Akaroa its character. Audio guides for self-guided

Around Christchurch

Ⓝ 0 ▮▮▮▮▮▮▮▮ 10 km
   0 ▮▮▮▮▮▮▮▮ 5 miles

Halswell

See Greater Christchurch Map (p238)

Godley Head
Adderley Head
Governers
Ohinetahi Bay
Ripapa Island
Wakaroa Point
Menzies Bay
Otohuao Head
Diamond Harbour
Purau
Port Levy
Allandale
Decanter Bay
SOUTH PACIFIC OCEAN
Teddington
Port Levy
Pigeon Bay
Pa Rd
Pigeon Bay
Little Akaloa
Stony Bay
Gebbies Valley
Chorlton
West Head
Okains Bay
East Head
▲ Mt Herbert (920m)
View Hill ▲ (759m)
Motukarara
Western Valley
Okains Bay
Pukakoto Head
Kaituna Valley Rd
Montgomery Park
Robinson's Bay
Le Bons Bay
Kaituna
Hiltop
Cooptown
Barrys Bay
Coombe Farm
Le Bons Bay
Lake Ellesmere (Te Waihora)
Kaituna Lagoon
Little River
Okuti Valley
French Farm
Ellangowan
Saddle ▲ Hill (841m)
Tikao
Takamatua
Lake Forsyth
Wainui
Akaroa
Goughs Bay
Kaitorete Spit
Birdlings Flat
Flag ▲ Peak (809m)
Long Bay Rd
Goat Point
Onuku
Otanerito Bay
Te Oka Bay
Lucas Peak (381m) ▲
Stony Bay
Redcliffe Point
Peraki Bay
Flea Bay
Snuffle Nose
Whakamoa Reef
Timutimu Point
Dyke Head

walking tours ($10 per 90 minutes) are also available at the visitor information centre.

BANKS PENINSULA
TRACK
Tramping

(☎03-304 7612; www.bankstrack.co.nz; per person $220) This 35km four-day tramp traverses private farmland around the dramatic coastline of Banks Peninsula. Costs includes transport from Akaroa and hut accommodation. A two-day option ($145) covers the same ground at twice the speed.

AKAROA ADVENTURE
CENTRE
Adventure Sports

(☎03-304 8709; Rue Lavaud; ◷8.30am-5.30pm) The Akaroa Adventure Centre rents out sea kayaks, bikes, golf clubs, fishing rods and windsurfing gear.

CAPTAIN HECTOR'S
SEA KAYAKS
Kayaking

(☎03-304 7866; www.akaroaseakayaks.co.nz; Beach Rd; kayak hire per half/full day $35/60) Rental kayaks, canoes and rowboats for self-exploration.

BLACK CAT CRUISES
Wildlife Tours

(☎03-304 7641; www.blackcat.co.nz; Main Wharf; ◷5 tours daily 6am-3.30pm Oct-Apr, 1 tour daily 11.30am May-Sep) The waters around Akaroa are home to the world's smallest and rarest dolphin, the Hector's dolphin, found only in NZ waters. If viewing the dolphins on a harbour cruise isn't enough, Black Cat Cruises can also get you swimming alongside the dolphins (assuming it's not the calving season). Cost are $139/115 per adult/child for a cruise and swim and $72/35 for a cruise only.

🛏 Sleeping

OLD SHIPPING
OFFICE
Apartment $$$

(☎0800 695 2000; www.akaroavillageinn.co.nz; Church St; d $230) A self-contained apartment in a restored heritage building with

an interesting past. (No prizes for guessing the building's former incarnation.) Two bedrooms, a spacious shared lounge and an outdoor spa pool make the Old Shipping Office a good option for families or for two couples.

TRESORI MOTOR LODGE
Motel $$

(☎0800 273 747, 03-304 7500; www.tresori.co.nz; cnr Rue Jolie & Church St; d $155-205; @☎) For designer-conscious lodgings treat yourself to the Tresori; its rich, colourful decor is anything but bland. It's a short walk to Akaroa's waterfront cafe and restaurant strip.

COOMBE FARM
B&B $$

(03-304 7239; www.coombefarm.co.nz; 18 Old Le Bons Track; d incl breakfast $145-165) Choose between staying in the private and romantic Shepherd's Hut – complete with an outdoor bath – or in the historic farm house, now lovingly restored and dotted with interesting contemporary art and Asian antiques. After breakfast (including homemade jam and organic yoghurt), you can negotiate Coombe Farm's private forest and stream walkway.

 Eating & Drinking

LITTLE BISTRO
French $$

(03-304 7314; 33 Rue Lavaud; mains $27-35; 6pm-late Tue-Sun;) Très petite, très chic and very tasty. Look forward to classic bistro style given a proud Kiwi spin with local seafood, South Island wines and Canterbury craft beers. The menu changes seasonally, but usually includes favourites such as pistachio-encrusted lamb or Akaroa salmon terrine; vegetarians are not ignored. Booking ahead is definitely necessary. Sometimes open for lunch in summer – check the blackboard out the front.

TRUBY'S BAR ON THE BEACH
Bar

(Rue Jolie) A perfect waterfront location combines with rustic outdoor seating to produce Akaroa's best place for a sundowner drink. Truby's blue cod and chips for dinner are world-famous in Akaroa, and baked cheesecake and good coffee are other distractions earlier in the day.

Information

Akaroa Information Centre (03-304 8600; www.akaroa.com; 80 Rue Lavaud; 9am-5pm) Tours, activities and accommodation.

Getting There & Away

From November to April the Akaroa Shuttle (0800 500 929; www.akaroashuttle.co.nz; return $45) departs Christchurch daily at 8.30am and 2pm, returning from Akaroa at 10.30am,

3.35pm and 4.30pm. Bookings are recommended. From May to September, there's only a 10am departure from Christchurch. Check the website for Christchurch pick-up options. Scenic tours from Christchurch exploring Banks Peninsula are also available.

French Connection (0800 800 575; www.akaroabus.co.nz; return $45) has a year-round daily departure from Christchurch at 9.15am, returning from Akaroa at 4pm.

NORTH CANTERBURY
Hanmer Springs

Hanmer Springs, the main thermal resort on the South Island, is 10km off SH7. It's a pleasantly low-key spot to indulge in bathing in hot pools and being pampered in the spa complex. There are good restaurants and lots of family-friendly activities.

 Sights

HANMER SPRINGS THERMAL POOLS
Bathhouse

(03-315 0000; www.hanmersprings.co.nz; entry on Amuri Ave; adult/child $18/9; 10am-9pm) Visitors have been soaking in the waters of Hanmer Springs Thermal Pools for more than 100 years. In addition to mineral pools, there are landscaped rock pools, a freshwater 25m lap pool, private thermal pools ($25 per 30 minutes) and a restaurant. The adjacent **Hanmer Springs Spa** (03-315 0029, 0800 873 529; www.hanmerspa.co.nz; 10am-7pm) has massage and beauty treatments from $70.

 Activities

Other Hanmer Springs activities include kayaking, scenic flights, fishing trips and claybird shooting. Family-friendly activities include minigolf and tandem bicycles.

There are two skiing areas nearby. **Hanmer Springs Ski Field** is the closest, 17km (unsealed road) from town, and **Mt Lyford Ski Field** is 60km away.

HANMER SPRINGS ADVENTURE
CENTRE   Adventure Sports
(0800 368 7386, 03-315 7233; www.hanmer
adventure.co.nz; 20 Conical Hill Rd; 9am-5pm)
Books activities, and rents quad bikes
(from $129), mountain bikes (per hour/
day from $19/45), fishing rods (per day
$25) and ski and snowboard gear.

 Sleeping

CHELTENHAM HOUSE   B&B $$$
(03-315 7545; www.cheltenham.co.nz; 13
Cheltenham St; s $195-235, d $235-265; @)
Centrally located B&B with six snooze-
inducing suites, all with bathroom, and
including two in cosy garden cottages;
there's a billiard table, grand piano and
complimentary predinner wine. Cooked
gourmet breakfasts can be delivered to
your room. Avoid the crowds up the road
in the private hot tub.

TUSSOCK PEAK
MOTOR LODGE   Motel $$
(0800 8877 625, 03-315 5191; www.tussock
peak.co.nz; cnr Amuri Ave & Leamington St; d

$145-225;) Modern, spotless and central,
Tussock Peak has colourful decor and
friendly service that's an eclectic cut above
other motels on Hanmer's main drag. The
hardest part is choosing what kind of room
to get: studio, one- or two-bedroom units,
spas, courtyards or balconies.

 Eating & Drinking

CHANTELLINI'S   French $$
(03-315 7667; www.chantellinis.com; 11 Jol-
lies Pass Rd; mains $30-36; 10am-10.30pm)
Tucked away behind the main street, this
quiet oasis is a relaxed cafe with outdoor
garden seating by day, and an intimate
French bar and restaurant by night.
Chandeliers and black drapes create an
elegant ambience. Portions are generous,
and the daily two-/three-course lunch for
$25/30 is great value – try the leek tart
or onion soup. Bookings are recommend-
ed for dinner.

MONTEITH'S BREWERY BAR   Pub
(www.mbbh.co.nz; 47 Amuri Ave) The best
pub in town features lots of different

Boats on Akaroa Harbour (p246)

Monteiths beers and tasty tucker from bar snacks ($10 to $17) to full meals ($17 to $32). Platters ($27 to $54) are good value if you've just met some new friends in the hot pools across the road.

ℹ️ Information

Hanmer Springs i-SITE (☎️0800 733 426, 03-315 7128; www.visithanmersprings.co.nz; 42 Amuri Ave; ⏰10am-5pm) Books transport, accommodation and activities.

ℹ️ Getting There & Away

Hanmer Backpackers run daily shuttles between Hanmer and Christchurch (90 minutes) and also operates a convenient service to and from Kaikoura (two hours; Monday, Wednesday and Friday). **Hanmer Connection** (☎️0800 242 663; www.atsnz.com) also links Hanmer Springs to Christchurch.

Methven

Methven is busiest in winter, when it fills up with snow-sports fans heading to nearby Mt Hutt. In summer, Methven town is a laid-back option with quieter (and usually cheaper) accommodation than elsewhere in the country, and a 'what shall I do today?' range of warm-weather activities.

🏃 Activities

AORAKI BALLOON SAFARIS   Ballooning
(☎️0800 256 837, 03-302 8172; www.nz ballooning.co.nz; flights $385) Early morning combos of snowcapped peaks and a champagne breakfast.

METHVEN HELISKIING   Skiing
(☎️03-302 8108; www.methvenheli.co.nz; Main St; 5-run day trips $950; ⏰May-Oct) Trips include guide service, safety equipment and lunch.

SKYDIVING NZ   Skydiving
(☎️03-302 9143; www.skydivingnz.com; Pudding Hill Airfield) Offers tandem jumps from 3600m ($440).

🛏️ Sleeping

BELUGA LODGE   B&B $$
(☎️03-302 8290; www.beluga.co.nz; 40 Allen St; d incl breakfast $165-260; @) Highly relaxing B&B with king-sized beds, fluffy bathrobes, luscious bathrooms and private decks. Extreme privacy-seekers should consider the garden suite, with its own patio and barbecue. A four-bedroom cottage is also available ($275 to

The Southern Alps, near Methven
DAVID WALL / LONELY PLANET IMAGES ©

$375 per night; minimum three-night stay from June to October).

GLENTHORNE STATION Lodge $$
(☎0800 926 868, 03-318 5818; www.glenthorne. co.nz; lodges per person $25-35, holiday house per person $50) This beautifully isolated 258-sq-km sheep station is 60km north-west of Methven, on the northern shore of Lake Coleridge. The high-country accommodation ranges from budget lodges to a self-contained holiday house.

❶ Information

Methven i-SITE (☎03-302 8955; www. methveninfo.co.nz; 160 Main St; ◷9am-5pm; @) Books accommodation, skiing packages, transport and activities.

❶ Getting There & Around

Methven Travel (☎0800 684 888, 03-302 8106; www.methventravel.co.nz; 93 Main St; ◷Mon, Wed, Fri & Sat in summer, up to three times daily in winter) picks up from Christchurch (one hour). Christchurch airport departures are also available.

Shuttles operate from Methven to Mt Hutt ski field in winter ($38).

SOUTH CANTERBURY
Lake Tekapo

At the southern end of its namesake lake, this town has unobstructed views across turquoise water and a backdrop of rolling hills and mountains.

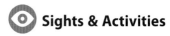 **Sights & Activities**

Popular walks include the track to the summit of **Mt John** (three hours return), accessible from just beyond the camping ground. Other walks are detailed in the brochure *Lake Tekapo Walkway* ($1). In winter, Lake Tekapo is a base for **downhill skiing** at Mt Dobson or Round Hill, and **cross-country skiing** on the Two Thumb Range.

 **Sleeping**

GLACIER ROCK BED AND BREAKFAST B&B $$
(☎03-680 6669; www.glacierrock.co.nz; 35 Lochinver Ave; d incl breakfast $195-250; @🛜) This architecturally designed home doubles as an art gallery. An artist's – or maybe an architect's – eye is evident in the spacious and airy rooms. Breakfast is served in sunny rooms with huge picture windows.

PEPPERS BLUEWATER RESORT Motel $$
(☎0800 275 373; www.peppers.co.nz; SH8; d from $140; 🛜) A sprawling resort arrayed around rocky pools and tussocky gardens. Rooms are chic and modern – if sometimes on the small side – but last-minute online discounts make this a place worth considering.

❶ Information

Lake Tekapo i-SITE (☎03-680 6579; www. laketekapountouched.co.nz; Godley Hotel, SH8; ◷9am-6pm) Accommodation, activites and transport information.

❶ Getting There & Away

Southbound services to Queenstown (four hours) and Wanaka (three hours via Tarras), and northbound services to Christchurch (four hours), are offered by Atomic Shuttles (www. atomictravel.co.nz), InterCity (www.intercity. co.nz) and Southern Link Coaches (☎0508 458 835; www.southernlinkcoaches.co.nz).

Cook Connection (☎0800 266 526; www. cookconnect.co.nz) operates to Mt Cook (two hours) and Twizel (one hour). Travel can be over more than one day.

Aoraki/Mt Cook National Park

Of the 27 NZ mountains over 3050m, 22 are in this park. The highest is the mighty Mt Cook – at 3754m it's the tallest peak in Australasia.

Mt Cook is a wonderful sight, assuming there's no cloud in the way. Most visitors arrive on tour buses, stop at the Hermitage hotel for photos, and then zoom off back down SH80. Hang around to soak up this awesome peak and the surrounding landscape and to try the excellent short walks. On the trails, look for the thar, a goatlike creature and excellent climber; the chamois, smaller and of lighter build than the thar; and red deer. Summertime brings the large mountain buttercup (the Mt Cook lily), and mountain daisies, gentians and edelweiss.

Sights

SIR EDMUND HILLARY
ALPINE CENTRE   Museum, Planetarium
(www.hermitage.co.nz; The Hermitage; 1 movie adult/child $18/8, 6 movies adult/child/family $27/13.50/54; ☺7.30am-8.30pm) The centre includes a full-dome digital planetarium showing four different digital presentations, and a cinema screen showing the *Mt Cook Magic* 3D movie and a fascinating 75-minute documentary about Sir Ed's conquest of Mt Everest.

 Activities

KEA POINT   Tramping
The trail to Kea Point (two hours return from the village) is lined with native plant life and ends at a platform with excellent views of Mt Cook, the Hooker Valley and the ice faces of Mt Sefton and the Footstool.

HOOKER VALLEY   Tramping
The walk up the Hooker Valley (three hours return) crosses a couple of swing bridges to Stocking Stream and the terminus of the Hooker Glacier. After the second swing bridge, Mt Cook totally dominates the valley.

TASMAN GLACIER VIEW
TRACK   Tramping
The Tasman Valley walks are popular for their views of the Tasman Glacier. Walks start at the end of the unsealed Tasman Valley Rd, 8km from the village. The Tasman Glacier View Track (50 minutes

Aoraki/Mt Cook National Park

JOHN ELK III / LONELY PLANET IMAGES ©

Aoraki/Mt Cook National Park

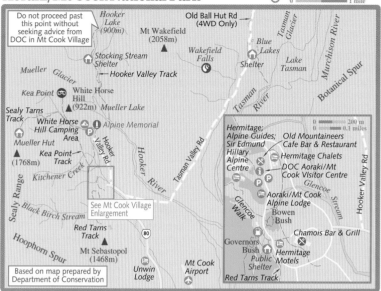

return) leads to a viewpoint on the moraine wall, passing the Blue Lakes (more green than blue these days) on the way.

GLACIER EXPLORERS   Boat Tour
(☎0800 686 800, 03-435 1809; www.glacier explorers.com; per person $145) Heads out on the terminal lake of the Tasman Glacier.

**MOUNT COOK SKI
PLANES**   Scenic Flights
(☎0800 800 702, 03-430 8034; www. mtcookskiplanes.com) Based at Mt Cook Airport, offering 40-minute (adult/child $405/295) and 55-minute (adult/child $530/405) flights, both with snow landings. Flightseeing without a landing is a cheaper option; try the 25-minute Mini Tasman trip (adult/child $275/255).

 Sleeping

**AORAKI/MT COOK
ALPINE LODGE**   Lodge $$
(☎03-435 1860; www.aorakipinelodge.co.nz; Bowen Dr; d $159-189, tr & q $164, f $220-240; @🛜) This modern lodge – with twin,

double and family rooms – is the best place to stay in the village. With Turkish rugs and underfloor heating, the place ensures a warm welcome.

HERMITAGE   Hotel $$$
(☎0800 686 800, 03-435 1809; www.hermit age.co.nz; Terrace Rd; r $209-575; @🛜) This sprawling complex has long monopolised Mt Cook accommodation in the village. Rooms in well-equipped A-frame chalets (double $269) sleep up to four and include a kitchen. Also available are motel units ($239) and refurbished rooms in various wings of the hotel proper. The higher-end hotel rooms are very smart indeed, and include cinematic views of Mt Cook through huge picture windows.

Eating & Drinking

**OLD MOUNTAINEERS CAFÉ,
BAR & RESTAURANT**   Cafe $$
(www.mtcook.com; Bowen Dr; lunch mains $17-24, dinner mains $22-35; @🛜) Cosy in winter, with mountain views from outside tables

in summer, this place delivers top-notch burgers, pizza, pasta and salad, and is a good-value alternative to the eateries at the Hermitage.

CHAMOIS BAR & GRILL Pub
Chamois Bar & Grill is upstairs in Mt Cook Backpackers, 500m from the YHA, where it entertains with a pool table, big-screen TV, and the occasional live gig.

 Information

DOC Aoraki/Mt Cook Visitor Centre (Department of Conservation; ☎03-435 1186; www.doc.govt.nz; 1 Larch Gr; ⏱8.30am-5pm Oct-Apr, to 4.30pm May-Sep) Advises on weather conditions, guided tours and tramping routes, and hires out beacons for trampers ($35).

 Getting There & Away

InterCity (www.intercity.co.nz) links Mt Cook to Christchurch (five hours), Queenstown (four hours) and Wanaka (with a change in Tarras; 4¼ hours).

The **Cook Connection** (☎0800 266 526; www.cookconnect.co.nz) has services to Twizel (one hour) and Lake Tekapo (two hours). Bus services in these towns link to Christchurch, Queenstown, Wanaka and Dunedin.

If you're driving, fill up at Lake Tekapo or Twizel.

THE WEST COAST
Greymouth

Welcome to the 'Big Smoke' of Westland. On the main road and rail route through Arthur's Pass and across the Southern Alps from Christchurch, Greymouth sees its fair share of travellers. The town is well-geared to look after them, with all the necessary services and the odd tourist attraction, the most famous of which is Shantytown.

 Sights & Activities

SHANTYTOWN Museum
(www.shantytown.co.nz; Rutherglen Rd, Paroa; adult/child/family $31.50/15.50/74; ⏱8.30am-5pm) Eight kilometres south of Greymouth

and 2km inland from SH6, Shantytown re-creates an 1860s gold-mining town, complete with steam-train rides, post office, pub and Rosie's House of Ill Repute.

MONTEITH'S BREWING CO Guided Tour
(www.monteiths.co.nz; cnr Turumaha & Herbert Sts) By the time you read this, Monteith's brand new brewery will be open: testatment to the power of a loyal public. Tours and tastings are available: ask for details at the i-SITE or just turn up at the front door.

 Sleeping

ARDWYN HOUSE B&B $
(☎03-768 6107; ardwynhouse@hotmail.com; 48 Chapel St; s/d incl breakfast from $55/85; 🛜) This old-fashioned B&B nestles amid steep gardens on a quiet dead-end street. Mary, the well-travelled host, cooks a splendid breakfast.

COLERAINE MOTEL Motel $$
(☎03-768 077, 0800 270 0027; www.coleraine motel.co.nz; 61 High St; d $152-225; @🛜) Rattan furniture, spa baths and king-sized beds add up to the smartest luxury rooms in town. Cheaper one- and two-bedroom studios are not far behind. Extra-mile courtesy is shown in the provision of a communal guest lounge.

 Eating & Drinking

DP:ONE CAFE Cafe $
(104 Mawhera Quay; meals $6-15; ⏱9am-9pm; @🛜) A stalwart of the Greymouth cafe scene, this hip cafe cups up the best espresso in town, along with good-value grub. Groovy NZ tunes, wi-fi, a relaxed vibe and quayside tables make this a great place for a meet-up to while away a grey day.

FRANK'S LATE NIGHT LOUNGE International $$
(☎03-768 9075; 115 Mackay St; mains $19-28; ⏱5pm-late Thu-Sat; 🍴) This effortlessly

PAUL KENNEDY / LONELY PLANET IMAGES ©

Don't Miss Punakaiki & Paparoa National Park

Paparoa National Park is blessed with sea cliffs, a dramatic mountain range, gorgeous limestone river valleys, diverse flora and a Westland petrel colony, the world's only nesting site of this rare sea bird.

Punakaiki is famous for its fantastic **Pancake Rocks and blowholes**. Through a layering-weathering process called stylobedding, the Dolomite Point limestone has formed into what looks like piles of thick pancakes. When the tide is high (tide times are posted at the visitor information centre), the sea surges into caverns and booms menacingly through blowholes. See it on a wild day and be reminded that Mother Nature really is the boss. An easy 15-minute walk loops from the highway out to the rocks and blowholes.

The **Paparoa National Park visitor information centre and i-SITE** has information on the park and track conditions, and handles bookings for local attractions and accommodation including hut tickets. See also www.punakaiki.co.nz.

NEED TO KNOW

Paparoa National Park visitor information centre and i-SITE (☎ 03-731 1895; www.doc. govt.nz; SH6; ⏰ 9am-5pm Oct-Nov, to 6pm Dec-Mar, to 4.30pm Apr-Sep)

---

cool, retro late-night lounge-bar-cafe is your best bet for getting a groove on. Art-deco architecture, eclectic decoration and excellent fresh food (including stellar fish dishes and salads) are just a few reasons to visit. Regular gigs, and it's family friendly. Nice one, Frank.

ℹ Information

Greymouth i-SITE (☎ 03-768 5101; www. greydistrict.co.nz; Railway Station, 164 Mackay St; ⏰ 8.30am-7pm Mon-Fri, 9am-6pm Sat, 10am-5pm Sun Nov-Apr, reduced hours May-Oct; @)

MERTEN SNIJDERS / LONELY PLANET IMAGES ©

Don't Miss **The TranzAlpine**

The *TranzAlpine* is one of the world's great train journeys, traversing the Southern Alps between Christchurch and Greymouth, from the Pacific Ocean to the Tasman Sea – a sequence of unbelievable landscapes. Leaving Christchurch at 8.15am, it speeds across the flat, alluvial Canterbury Plains to the Alps' foothills. Here it enters a labyrinth of gorges and hills called the Staircase, a climb made possible by three large viaducts and a plethora of tunnels.

The train emerges into the broad Waimakariri and Bealey Valleys and (on a good day) the vistas from the new carriages with their panoramic windows are stupendous.

The western side is just as stunning, with the Otira, Taramakau and Grey River valleys, patches of podocarp forest, and the trout-filled Lake Brunner, fringed with cabbage trees. The train rolls into Greymouth at 12.45pm, heading back to Christchurch an hour later, arriving at 6.05pm.

This awesome journey is diminished only when the weather's bad, but if it's raining on one coast, it's probably fine on the other.

NEED TO KNOW

☎0800 872 467, 03-768 7080; www.tranzscenic.co.nz; adult/child 1 way from $89/62

ⓘ Getting There & Around

Sharing the old railway station with the i-SITE, the West Coast Travel Centre (☎03-768 7080; www.westcoasttravel.co.nz; Railway Station, 164 Mackay St; ⊙9am-5pm Mon-Fri, 10am-4pm Sat & Sun; @ 📶) books all forms of transport, including buses, trains and interisland ferries, and has luggage-storage facilities.

Bus

InterCity (☎03-365 1113; www.intercity.co.nz) has daily buses north to Westport (from $17, two hours) and Nelson (from $40, six hours), and south to Franz Josef (from $29, 3½ hours) and Fox (from $31, 4¼ hours) Glaciers.

Naked Bus (www.nakedbus.com) runs north to Nelson and south to Queenstown stopping at Hokitika, Franz Josef and Fox Glaciers, Haast and Wanaka.

Atomic Shuttles (www.atomictravel.co.nz) runs daily to Queenstown ($70, 10½ hours) stopping at Hokitika (from $13, one hour), Franz Josef (from $30, 3½ hours) and Fox Glaciers (from $35, 4¼ hours), Haast ($65, 5¾ hours) and Wanaka ($65, nine hours). It also heads north daily to Nelson ($54, 6¼ hours) on the InterCity service, via Westport ($24, 2¾ hours).

WESTLAND TAI POUTINI NATIONAL PARK

Literally the biggest highlights of the Westland Tai Poutini National Park are the Franz Josef and Fox Glaciers. Nowhere else at this latitude do glaciers come so close to the ocean.

Some say Franz Josef is the superior ice experience, and while it's visually more impressive, the walk to Fox is shorter, more interesting and often gets you closer to the ice.

Franz Josef Glacier

The early Maori knew Franz Josef as Ka Roimata o Hine Hukatere (Tears of the Avalanche Girl). Legend tells of a girl losing her lover who fell from the local peaks, and her flood of tears freezing into the glacier. The glacier is 5km from Franz Josef village; the terminal face is a 40-minute walk from the car park.

◎ Sights & Activities

Independent Walks

Courtesy of DOC, the new **Te Ara a Waiau Walkway/Cycleway** provides pleasant rainforest trail access to the glacier car park. Pick up the track at the DOC Visitor Centre. It's an hour each way to walk.

Several glacier viewpoints are accessed from the car park, including **Sentinel** Rock (20 minutes return) and the **Ka Roimata o Hine Hukatere Walk** (1½ hours return), leading you to the terminal face (read the signs; respect the barriers).

Other longer walks include the **Douglas Walk** (one hour return), off the Glacier Access Rd, which passes moraine from the 1750 advance and Peter's Pool, a small kettle lake. The **Terrace Track** (30 minutes return) is an easy amble over bushy terraces behind the village, with Waiho River views.

Guided Walks

Small-group walks with experienced guides (boots, jackets and equipment supplied) are offered by **Franz Josef Glacier Guides** (☏0800 484 337, 03-752 0763; www.franzjosefglacier.com). Half-/full-day walks are $123/180 per adult (slightly cheaper for children). Full-day trips have around six hours on the ice, half-day trips up to two hours.

Aerial Sightseeing

A 20-minute flight to the head of Franz Josef (or Fox Glacier) costs around $200. Flights past both of the glaciers and to Mt Cook cost from $300 to $380.

AIR SAFARIS   Scenic Flights
(☏03-752 0716, 0800 723 274; www.airsafaris. co.nz) Fixed wing.

MOUNTAIN HELICOPTERS   Scenic Flights
(☏0800 369 432, 03-752 0046; www.mountain helicopters.co.nz)

Other Activities

 **WEST COAST WILDLIFE CENTRE**   Wildlife
(www.wildkiwi.co.nz; cnr Cron & Cowan Sts; day pass adult/child/family $25/15/75, backstage pass $20/15/60; ☏) This feel-good attraction ticks all the right boxes (exhibition, cafe and retail, wi-fi), then goes a whole lot further by actually breeding the rarest kiwi in the world, the rowi. The day-pass is well worthwhile by the time you've viewed the conservation, glacier and heritage

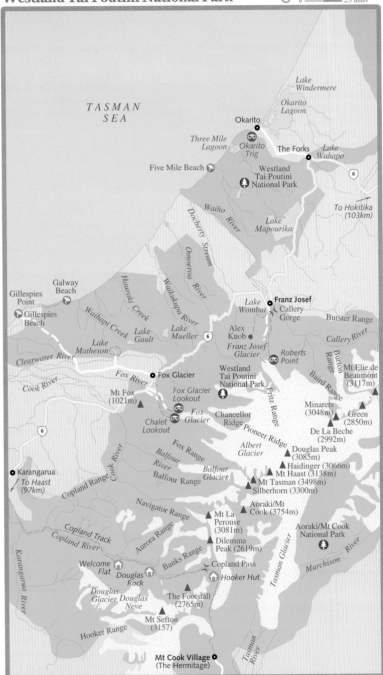

0 — 5 km
0 — 2.5 miles

TASMAN
SEA

Lake
Windermere

Okarito
Lagoon

Okarito

Three Mile
Lagoon

Okarito
Trig

The Forks

Lake
Wahapo

Westland
Tai Poutini
National Park

Five Mile Beach

To Hokitika
(103km)

Waiho River

Lake
Mapourika

Docherty Stream

Omoeroa River

Galway
Beach

Gillespies
Point

Gillespies
Beach

Hauraki Creek

Waitukupa River

Lake
Wombat

Franz Josef

Callery
Gorge

Burster Range

Callery River

Waihapi Creek

Lake
Gault

Lake
Mueller

Alex
Knob

Franz Josef
Glacier

Roberts
Point

Mt Elie de
Beaumont
(3117m)

Lake
Matheson

Button Range

Baird Range

Clearwater River

Fox River

Fox Glacier

Minarets
(3048m)

Green
(2850m)

Cook River

Mt Fox
(1021m)

Fox Glacier
Lookout

Westland
Tai Poutini
National Park

Fritz Range

De La Beche
(2992m)

Chalet
Lookout

Fox
Glacier

Chancellor
Ridge

Pioneer Ridge

Douglas Peak
(3085m)

Fox Range

Albert
Glacier

Haidinger (3066m)

Mt Haast (3138m)

Balfour
River

Balfour
Glacier

Mt Tasman (3498m)

Silberhorn (3300m)

Karangarua
To Haast
(97km)

Copland Range

Cook River

Balfour Range

Aoraki/Mt
Cook (3754m)

Navigator Range

Mt La
Perouse
(3081m)

Aoraki/Mt Cook
National Park

Aurora Range

Copland Track

Banks Range

Dilemma
Peak (2619m)

Copland River

Copland Pass

Tasman Glacier

Murchison River

Karangarua River

Welcome
Flat

Douglas
Rock

Hooker Hut

Douglas
Glacier Douglas
Neve

The Footstall
(2765m)

Hooker Range

Mt Sefton
(3157)

Tasman River

Mt Cook Village
(The Hermitage)

Detour:
Okarito

Twenty-three kilometres north of Franz Josef is the Forks, the turn-off to the tiny seaside hamlet of Okarito, 11km further away on the coast. It sits alongside **Okarito Lagoon**, the largest unmodified wetland in NZ.

Okarito Nature Tours (☎0508 652 748, 03-753 4014; www.okarito.co.nz; kayak rental half/full day $55/65; 🛜) hires out kayaks for paddles into the lagoon and up into the stunning rainforest channels where all sorts of birds hang out. Guided tours are available (from $75), and overnight rentals ($80) allow experienced paddlers to check out deserted North Beach or Lake Windemere.

The lagoon can also be explored with **Okarito Boat Tours** (☎03-753 4223; www.okaritoboattours.co.nz) on morning and afternoon sightseeing tours starting at $45. **Okarito Kiwi Tours** (☎03-753 4330; www.okaritokiwitours.co.nz; 2-3hr tours $75) run nightly expeditions to spot the rare bird (95% success rate) with an interesting education along the way.

displays, and hung out with real, live kiwi in their ferny enclosure.

GLACIER HOT POOLS Bathhouse
(www.glacierhotpools.co.nz; 63 Cron St; adult/child $23/16.50; ⏰noon-10pm) Setting a new standard for outdoor hot pools, this complex has been skilfully built within dense rainforest. Perfect après-hike or on a rainy day. Enjoy the communal pools, or private ones ($42 per 45 minutes) and massages ($85 per half-hour) if you want to really indulge.

SKYDIVE FRANZ Skydiving
(☎0800 458 677, 03-752 0714; www.skydivefranz.co.nz; Main Rd) Claiming NZ's highest jump (18,000ft, 75 seconds freefall, $549), this company also offers 15,000 for $399, and 12,000 for $299. With Aoraki/Mt Cook in your sights, this could be the most scenic jump you ever do.

 Sleeping

TE WAONUI FOREST RETREAT Hotel $$$
(☎0800 696 963, 03-752 0555; www.tewaonui.co.nz; 3 Wallace St; s/d $620/795; @🛜) The damp, earthy surrounds and unflashy exterior of Franz' fancy new hotel hide

the fact that inside is porter service, *degustation* dinners (included, along with breakfast, in the price) and a snazzy bar. The interior is dark – there's definitely a rainforest feel to the place – but you'll sleep like a log in the luxurious beds, and appreciate the modern-styled rooms, all natural tones textured in wood and stone.

58 ON CRON Motel $$
(☎0800 662 766, 03-752 0627; www.58oncron.co.nz; 58 Cron St; d $175-245; 🛜) No prizes for the name, but this newish motel will impress with refreshed furnishings and all mod cons. A smart, clean, consistent performer.

GLENFERN VILLAS Apartments $$$
(☎0800 453 633, 03-752 0054; www.glenfern.co.nz; SH6; d $210-266; 🛜) A handy 3km out of the tourist hubbub, these delightful one- and two-bedroom villas sit amid nikau palms and have top-notch beds, full kitchens, and private decks with views. This is the sort of place that says 'holiday', not 'stop-off'.

🍴 **Eating & Drinking**

ALICE MAY Modern NZ $$
(cnr Cowan & Cron Sts; mains $18-33; ⏰4pm-late) Resembling an old staging post,

Below: Inside an ice cave, Fox Glacier; **Right:** Mt Cook and Lake Matheson (p262)

(BELOW) OLIVER STREWE / LONELY PLANET IMAGES ©; (RIGHT) ANDERS BLOMQVIST / LONELY PLANET IMAGES ©

this sweet dining room serves up meaty, home-style meals such as pork ribs and venison casserole. Park yourself outside and enjoy mountain views and bar snacks during happy hour (4pm to 7pm).

SPEIGHTS LANDING BAR & RESTAURANT   Pub $$
(SH6; mains $19-39; ☽7.30am-late) A slighty frenzied but well-run pub serving up mega-portions of crowd-pleasing food; think big burgers, steaks and pizzas. The patio – complete with heaters and umbrellas – is a good place to unwind after a day on the ice.

ℹ Information

Scott Base Tourist Information Centre (☎03-752 0288; SH6; 9am-9pm; @ 🛜)

Westland Tai Poutini National Park Visitor Centre & i-SITE (☎03-752 0796; www.glaciercountry.co.nz; SH6; ☽8.30am-6pm Oct-Apr, to 5pm May-Sep) Regional DOC office with good exhibits, weather information and track updates.

ℹ Getting There & Around

InterCity (☎03-365 1113; www.intercity.co.nz) has daily buses south to Fox Glacier (from $10, 35 minutes) and Queenstown (from $62, eight hours); and north to Nelson (from $56, 10 hours).

Atomic Shuttles (☎03-349 0697; www.atomictravel.co.nz) has services Sunday to Thursday south to Queenstown ($50, 6½ hours) via Fox Glacier ($15, 35 minutes), and north to Greymouth ($30, four hours). Book at the Scott Base Tourist Information Centre.

Glacier Valley Eco Tours (☎03-752 0699, 0800 999 739; www.glaciervalley.co.nz) runs scheduled shuttle services to the glacier car park (return trip $12.50).

Naked Bus (www.nakedbus.com) runs north to Hokitika, Greymouth and Nelson, and south to Fox Glacier.

Fox Glacier

Fox is smaller and quieter than Franz Josef, with a farmy feel and more open aspect. Beautiful Lake Matheson is a highlight, as is the beach and historic walk down at Gillespies Beach.

 Sights & Activities

Glacier Valley Walks

It's 1.5km from Fox Village to the glacier turn-off, and a further 2km to the car park. Thanks to DOC you can now reach the car park under your own steam via the new **Te Weheka Walkway/Cycleway**, a pleasant rainforest trail starting just south of the Bella Vista motel.

From the car park, the terminal face is 30 to 40 minutes' walk. How close you can get to it depends on conditions. Obey all signs: this place is dangerously dynamic.

Short walks near the glacier include the **Moraine Walk** (over a major 18th-century advance) and **Minnehaha Walk**. The **River Walk** extends to the **Chalet Lookout Track** (1½ hours return) leading to a glacier lookout. The fully accessible **River Walk Lookout Track** (20 minutes return) starts from the Glacier View Rd car park and allows people of all abilities the chance to view the glacier.

Guided walks (equipment provided) are organised by **Fox Glacier Guiding** (✆ 0800 111 600, 03-751 0825; www.foxguides. co.nz; 44 Main Rd). Half-day walks cost $115/95 per adult/child; full-day walks are $165 (over-13s only). There are also easy-going two-hour interpretive walks to the glacier (adult/child $49/35).

Skydiving & Aerial Sightseeing

With Fox Glacier's backdrop of Southern Alps, rainforest and ocean, it's hard to imagine a better place to jump out of a plane. **Skydive Glacier Country**

(03-751 0080, 0800 751 0080; www.
skydivingnz.co.nz; Fox Glacier Airfield, SH6)
is a professional outfit that challenges
Isaac Newton, with thrilling leaps from
16,000ft ($399) or 12,000ft ($299).
Also try **Fox & Franz Josef Heliservices**
(03-751 0866, 0800 800 793; www.scenic-
flights.co.nz) for a bird's-eye view.

Other Sights & Activities

LAKE MATHESON   Lake
The famous 'mirror lake' can be found
about 6km down Cook Flat Rd. Taken
slowly (as it should be), the circuit takes
1½ hours to complete. At the far end – on
a clear day – you *may* get the money shot,
but failing that you can buy a postcard at
the excellent gift store in the car park.

Sleeping & Eating

FOX GLACIER LODGE   B&B $$$
(0800 369 800, 03-751 0888; www.foxglacier
lodge.com; 41 Sullivan Rd; d $195-225;)
Beautiful timber adorns the exterior and
interior of this attractive property, impart-
ing a mountain chalet vibe. Similarly
woody self-contained mezzanine apartments with spa baths are also available.

WESTHAVEN   Motel $$
(0800 369 452, 03-751 0084; www.thewest
haven.co.nz; SH6; d $125-185;) These
architecturally precise suites are a classy
combo of corrugated steel and local
stone amid burnt red and ivory walls. The
deluxe king rooms have spas, and there
are bikes to hire for the energetic (half/
full day $20/40).

MATHESON CAFÉ   Modern NZ $$
(www.lakematheson.com; Lake Matheson
Rd; breakfast & lunch $9-19, dinner $24-36;
7.30am-late Nov-Mar, 8am-4pm Apr-Oct)
Near the shores of Lake Matheson, this
cafe does everything right: slick interior
design, inspiring mountain views, strong
coffee and upmarket Kiwi fare. Get your
sketchpad out and while away the afternoon. Next door is the ReflectioNZ Gallery
stocking quality, primarily NZ-made art
and souvenirs.

Large ice blocks at Fox Glacier

OLIVER STREWE / LONELY PLANET IMAGES ©

ℹ Information

Department of Conservation South Westland Weheka Area Office (DOC; ☎03-751 0807; SH6; ⏱9am-noon & 1-4.30pm Mon-Fri) This is no longer a general visitor information centre, but has the usual DOC information, hut tickets and weather/track updates.

Fox Glacier Guiding (☎0800 111 600, 03-751 0825; www.foxguides.co.nz; 44 Main Rd) Books Atomic Shuttles, and provides postal and currency-exchange services.

ℹ Getting There & Around

InterCity (☎03-365 1113; www.intercity.co.nz) runs two buses a day north to Franz Josef (from $10), the morning bus continuing to Nelson (from $57). Daily southbound services run to Queenstown (from $58).

Atomic Shuttles (☎03-349 0697; www.atomictravel.co.nz) runs daily services to Franz Josef ($15), continuing to Greymouth (from $35). Southbound buses run daily to Queenstown ($45).

Fox Glacier Shuttles & Tours (☎0800 369 287) will drive you to destinations such as Lake Matheson, Gillsepies Beach, the glaciers or beyond (from $10 return).

Naked Bus (www.nakedbus.com) runs north to Franz Josef Glacier, Hokitika, Greymouth, Westport and Nelson, and south to Queenstown, stopping at Haast and Wanaka.

Queenstown & the South

With a cinematic background of mountains and lakes you actually might have seen in the movies, and a 'what can we think of next' array of adventure activities, it's little wonder Queenstown tops many travellers' Kiwi itineraries.

You can slow down (slightly) in Wanaka, Queenstown's junior cousin, which also has good bars and outdoor adventures on tap.

To the east, Otago is overflowing with picturesque scenery. The region's historic heart is Dunedin, with excellent restaurants and cafes, and a vibrant student-based culture. If you're seeking wildlife, head to the Otago Peninsula, where penguins, albatross, sea lions and seals are easily sighted.

The bottom end of the South Island offers some of the country's most spectacular landscapes: Fiordland National Park, with jagged, misty peaks, glistening lakes and Milford and Doubtful Sounds; and the peaceful Catlins, showcasing bird-rich native forests and a rugged, windswept coastline.

Lake Te Anau (p305)

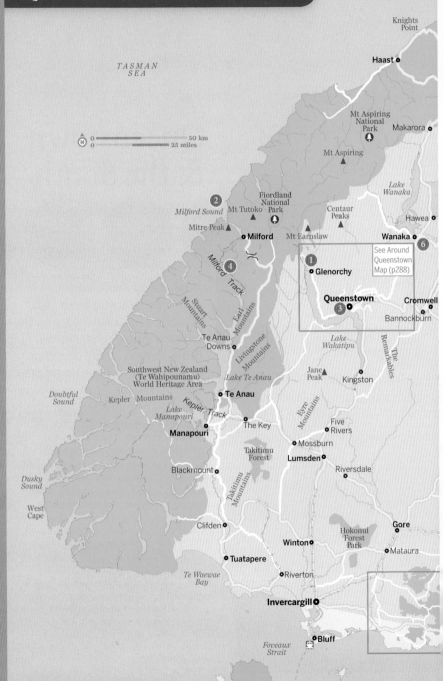

Queenstown & the South

Knights Point

Haast ○

Mt Aspiring National Park

Makarora ○

Mt Aspiring ▲

Lake Wanaka

0 ——— 50 km
0 ——— 25 miles

2 Milford Sound

Mt Tutoko ▲

Fiordland National Park

Centaur Peaks ▲

Hawea ○

Mitre Peak ▲

Milford ○ **Milford**

Mt Earnslaw ▲

Wanaka ○ **6**

4 Milford Track

1

○ **Glenorchy**

See Around Queenstown Map (p288)

Stuart Mountains

Earl Mountains

Queenstown
3

Cromwell ○

Bannockburn ○

Te Anau Downs ○

Livingstone Mountains

Lake Wakatipu

The Remarkables

Southwest New Zealand (Te Wahipounamu) World Heritage Area

Lake Te Anau

Jane Peak ▲

Kingston ○

Doubtful Sound

Kepler Mountains

Te Anau ○

Eyre Mountains

Lake Manapouri

Kepler Track

The Key ○

Five Rivers ○

Manapouri

○ Mossburn

Takitimu Forest

Lumsden ●

Dusky Sound

Takitimu Mountains

Blackmount ○

Riversdale ○

West Cape

Hokonui Forest Park

Gore ○

Clifden ○

Winton ○

Mataura ○

Tuatapere ○

Te Waewae Bay

○ **Riverton**

Invercargill ○

Foveaux Strait

○ **Bluff**

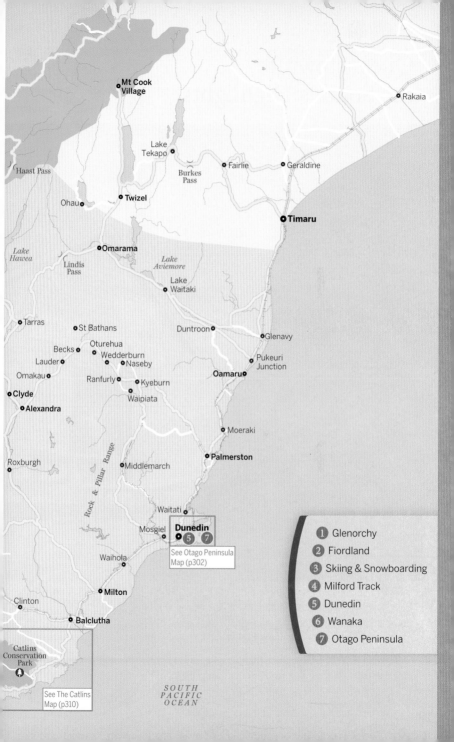

Mt Cook
Village

Rakaia

Lake
Tekapo

Burkes
Pass

Fairlie

Geraldine

Haast Pass

Ohau

Twizel

Timaru

Lake
Hawea

Omarama

Lake
Aviemore

Lindis
Pass

Lake
Waitaki

Tarras

St Bathans

Duntroon

Glenavy

Becks

Oturehua

Wedderburn

Pukeuri
Junction

Lauder

Naseby

Omakau

Ranfurly

Kyeburn

Oamaru

Clyde

Waipiata

Alexandra

Moeraki

Roxburgh

Middlemarch

Palmerston

Rock & Pillar Range

Waitati

Mosgiel

Dunedin

5

7

See Otago Peninsula
Map (p302)

Waihola

Milton

Clinton

Balclutha

Catlins
Conservation
Park

See The Catlins
Map (p310)

SOUTH
PACIFIC
OCEAN

1 Glenorchy

2 Fiordland

3 Skiing & Snowboarding

4 Milford Track

5 Dunedin

6 Wanaka

7 Otago Peninsula

Queenstown & the South's Highlights

1 Glenorchy Area

Blessed with good weather, the area around Glenorchy, northwest of Queenstown on Lake Wakatipu, has magical, end-of-the-world appeal. With majestic mountains and laconic locals, the area was a holiday destination long before the road arrived from Queenstown in 1962: before then, access was along the lake by boat.

Above: Glenorchy boathouse

Need to Know

ACTIVITIES Tramping, swimming, kayaking, horse treks, jetboating, fishing **BEST TIME TO VISIT** Summer days for tramping; winter for magical snows **For further coverage, see p287**

Glenorchy Area Don't Miss List

BY JANE CAMPION, FILM DIRECTOR AND SCREENWRITER

1 GLENORCHY
Glenorchy offers jetboating on the Dart River (p288) and coffee and home-baked bread at the Glenorchy Café (p289), but the best thing to do is to take yourself on a bush walk. I recommend the two-hour loop to Lake Sylvan: it's a fairly short walk for this scale of landscape, but it immediately gives you a sense of the delight and intimacy of the bush. And the lake is phenomenal for swimming!

2 LAKE RERE WALK
My favourite day walk in the area is Lake Rere (p287), a loop walk from Greenstone about an hour from Glenorchy. The walk takes about five hours, but allow six or seven to picnic at the lake, a magical place where I am yet to see a sand fly (both the curse and protector of this area: reasonably rare in Glenorchy, they proliferate in the bush).

3 ROUTEBURN TRACK
The legendary, four-day Routeburn Track (p290) also starts near Glenorchy. The track here is very well maintained – a highway for walkers. For a day walk, go about 2½ hours in to the flats and loll about amid the yellow tussocks.

4 HORSE TREKKING
Horse treks at Dart Stables (p288) here are excellent – the horses are well cared for, and the landscape is magnificent. I had a horse as a kid, so organised treks are a little bit tame for me, but I have ridden the Dart River horses on some stunning rides along the riverbanks.

5 PLACES TO STAY
My favourite place to stay up here is Paradise (p287), which has some extremely low-tech, genuinely old huts; the best is called 'Eden'. There's no electricity – it's all candles and wood-fire cookers. There are deer in the hills and glow-worms to inspect. Kinloch Lodge (p289), a fantastic place across the lake, has all sorts of accommodation, from backpackers to en-suite rooms. The food here is wonderful – unexpected for such a remote place.

Fiordland

Fiordland is a bit like Timbuktu: lots of people know it's there, but they're not sure what it's all about. It's so diverse and across such a large area. If the weather's fine, an aerial overview is the best way to see it, but boat trips, road journeys and tramping are also really good.

Below: Mitre Peak, Milford Sound (p307)

Need to Know

PHOTO OP Mitre Peak rising over Milford Sound **ACTIVITIES** Tramping, scenic flights, sea kayaking, jetboating **BEST TIME TO VISIT** Summer **For further coverage, see p305**

Fiordland Don't Miss List

BY KIM HOLLOWS,
HELICOPTER PILOT

1 MILFORD SOUND

Dominated by Mitre Peak, iconic Milford Sound (p307) has a real steepness about it. It's the best known of Fiordland's sounds, largely due to the fact that it's the only fiord you can access by road. It's also the end point of the famous Milford Track (p307), which sees around 14,000 hikers a year. Kayaking or boating on the Sound is a great day out. Left: Waterfall on Milford Track (p307)

2 DOUBTFUL SOUND

A superb wilderness area, Doubtful Sound (p308) is a broad, open waterway. The sound's name dates back to 1770, when Captain Cook spied it from the coast: he was 'doubtful' whether the winds in the sound would be sufficient to blow his ship back out to sea. You can only visit the sound on a tour, many of which depart from Manapouri. Below left: Cruise boat on Doubtful Sound

3 TUATAPERE HUMP RIDGE TRACK

It's a very exposed piece of real estate down there, but the three-day/two-night Tuatapere Hump Ridge Track (p309) is a unique way to experience Fiordland's forests, geology and coastline. It's really growing in popularity, and is a real credit to the Hump Ridge Trust: what they've achieved in developing the track is fantastic.

4 FIORDLAND'S UNIQUE WEATHER

In Fiordland, we're at the whim of a large expanse of ocean from the polar cap – we certainly get climatic extremes. However, the mountains actually create two different weather patterns: it can be raining in Milford Sound but fine in Te Anau, where we actually get less rain than in Auckland.

Ski the South

The Southern Alps jag up high and mighty down here, and with rain-weighty clouds streaming in from the Tasman Sea, expect plenty of winter snow. Queenstown (p278) has, of course, long been a hot spot for powder-hounds. Coronet Peak and the Remarkables are the main ski spots near here, but there's also Treble Cone and Cardrona, and great Nordic (cross-country) and snowboarding near Wanaka (p290). Below: Coronet Peak (p279)

③

DAVID WALL / LONELY PLANET IMAGES ©

Milford Track

④

Wandering into the rain-hazed wilderness mightn't be on your hit-list if you're only in NZ for a few weeks... But trust us, the Milford Track (p307) in photogenic Fiordland National Park will linger in your memories for years to come. Not convinced? Take the drive from Te Anau to Milford (p307) and see what we're talking about: all around are mountains, forests and mirror-perfect waterways. It's even beautiful in the rain!

ANDREW BAIN / LONELY PLANET IMAGES ©

Dunedin After Dark

Dunedin's nocturnal bar, pub and live-music scene (p301) is much cooler and more progressive than you'd expect in a small city at this latitude. Actually, given the vast numbers of students living here, maybe you would expect it... But either way, you'll be able to find lots of grungy pub rock, plus reggae, dub and chilled-out house resonating off the stage, all washed down with quality southern micro- and macrobrewed beers.

Wanaka

Queenstown gets the publicity for its bungy jumps, après-ski nightlife and ritzy restaurants, but Wanaka (p290), about 120km to the northwest, is just as hip without the hype. The extreme activities are all here: jetboating, rafting, skydiving, paragliding, plus there are some cool places to stay, great eateries and even a little art-house cinema. Wanaka rocks!

Otago Peninsula

Like a Jackson Pollock paint spillage on the map, the Otago Peninsula (p303) makes a brilliant day trip from Dunedin. Jump in a rental car and meander around the convoluted bays, headlands and inlets. En route you can check out some southern wildlife – royal albatrosses, sea lions and yellow-eyed penguins are all here, happily soaring, grunting and waddling. Above: Taiaroa Head (p304)

Queenstown & the South's Best…

Wild Rides

○ **Queenstown bungy jumping** (p279) The original is still the best

○ **Wanaka paragliding** (p292) Float down off the top of Treble Cone under a paraglide plume

○ **Otago Central Rail Trail** (p304) Mountain bike 150km through the Otago countryside, with plenty of interesting detours and B&B pit stops

○ **Helicopter sightseeing** (p306) Sound-out Milford Sound from above

Snow Zones

○ **Coronet Peak** (p349) Queenstown region's oldest ski field…also has night skiing!

○ **The Remarkables** (p279) Downhill for all comers; tackle the remarkable, sweeping 'Homeward Bound' run

○ **Snow Park** (p292) New Zealand's only dedicated freestyle ski and snowboard area

○ **Snow Farm New Zealand** (p292) Spectacular cross-country (Nordic) skiing high above Lake Wanaka

Urban Moments

○ **Eating out in Queenstown** (p283) From fine dining to perfect pizza, Queenstown serves it up

○ **Tune-in to Dunedin** (p301) The live-music scene in Dunedin is pumping

○ **Art-house cinema** (p294) Fab flicks at duelling art-house cinemas in Wanaka

○ **Caffeine fix** (p301) Dunedin's cool cafes keep the southern chills at bay

Need to Know

Natural Splendours

- **Milford Sound** (p307)
Tranquil, reflective, serene...
We hope your cruise boat is
quiet!

- **Doubtful Sound** (p308)
Like Milford, but much bigger
with less tourists

- **Otago Peninsula** (p303)
Wildlife havens and harbour
inlets near Dunedin

- **The Catlins** (p309)
Compact wilderness with
waterfalls, forests and wild
coast

ADVANCE PLANNING

- **One month before**
Book internal flights, car
hire and accommodation
(especially in summer
around Milford Sound,
and in Queenstown
and Wanaka during ski
season)

- **Two weeks before** Book
a cruise or a kayak on
Milford Sound or Doubtful
Sound, or a tour through
the underrated Catlins

- **One week before** Book
a death-defying bungy
jump in Queenstown,
check www.dunedinmusic.
co.nz to see who's rocking
Dunedin, and reserve a
table for a top-shelf dinner
in Queenstown

RESOURCES

- **Queenstown i-SITE**
(www.queenstownnz.co.nz)

- **Queenstown
Department of
Conservation Visitor
Centre** (www.doc.govt.nz,
queenstownvc@doc.govt.nz)

- **Lake Wanaka i-SITE**
(www.lakewanaka.co.nz)

- **Dunedin i-SITE** (www.
dunedinnz.com)

- **Otago Daily Times**
(www.odt.co.nz) Your best
news and current-affairs
source down south

- **Ski & Snowboard new
Zealand** (www.brownbearski.
co.nz) Online info for all the
southern ski resorts

GETTING AROUND

- **Cruise** Across the
mirror-flat waters of
Milford Sound

- **Drive** Along the
superscenic Te Anau–
Milford Hwy (keep at least
one hand on the wheel as
you snap photos)

- **Sea kayak** Around the
shores of Doubtful Sound

- **Minibus** Through the
Catlins on a guided tour

- **Hike** Along the 53.5km
Milford Track

BE FOREWARNED

- **Queenstown
in Summer** Sure,
Queenstown is a
happening ski town, but
don't arrive in summer
expecting to have the pace
all to yourself: mountain
bikers and hikers are
here in their hundreds.
Accommodation books
out and prices rocket
during both seasons; book
well in advance

- **Royal Albatross Centre,
Otago Peninsula** No
viewing mid-September
to late November; limited
sightings late November to
December

Left: Tramping by the Remarkables (p279);
Above: Skiing at Coronet Peak (p279)

Queenstown & the South Itineraries

Everyone in Queenstown is from somewhere else. They're all here to bungy jump, jetboat, ski and party. Beyond 'QT' are the sublime wilderness areas of Fiordland and the Catlins, with student-cool Dunedin to the east.

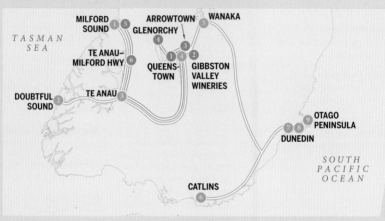

<table>
</table>

Map labels: MILFORD SOUND, ARROWTOWN, WANAKA, GLENORCHY, TASMAN SEA, TE ANAU–MILFORD HWY, QUEENSTOWN, GIBBSTON VALLEY WINERIES, DOUBTFUL SOUND, TE ANAU, OTAGO PENINSULA, DUNEDIN, SOUTH PACIFIC OCEAN, CATLINS

3 DAYS

QUEENSTOWN TO MILFORD SOUND
Queenstown & Around

Kick-start your **(1) Queenstown** experience with a hefty breakfast at Vudu Cafe & Larder, then devote the day to bungy jumping, hang gliding, downhill skiing, paragliding, skydiving, mountain biking, white-water rafting...whichever white-knuckle ride suits your mood (or season). In the evening, chow down at Fishbone Bar & Grill (how can seafood this far inland be so good?), then head to Atlas Beer Cafe for some mellow tunes and a nocturnal tipple.

On day two, take things a bit more slowly with a leisurely hot-air balloon flight, an indulgent cellar-door tour of the nearby **(2) Gibbston Valley wineries**, or a visit to the local shops and Chinese settlement in **(3) Arrowtown**. Alternatively, drive around Lake Wakatipu to tiny **(4) Glenorchy** for lunch at the Glenorchy Café and a short walk in the area.

Get up early on day three and prep yourself for a real highlight: a boat cruise across the hushed, mesmerising waters of **(5) Milford Sound** is an experience that will have you reaching for your camera (if you haven't already filled your memory card along the **(6) Te Anau–Milford Highway**).

MILFORD SOUND TO OTAGO PENINSULA
The Sounds of Silence

5 DAYS

Fiordland National Park is just so darn *pure*... Do places like this really still exist?

South of **(1) Milford Sound** the coastline fractures: **(2) Doubtful Sound** is one of Fiordland's biggest and most spectacular sounds, with waterfalls, thick forest and glass-flat waters. Book a cruise, overnight adventure or kayaking trip.

Backtrack for an evening in laid-back **(3) Te Anau**, or drive further for a night's drinking and carousing in **(4) Queenstown** or an art-house movie in **(5) Wanaka**.

Veering back southeast into Southland for a day or two, explore the beautiful, lonesome **(6) Catlins** region, either on a tour or under your own steam.

Trundle north to **(7) Dunedin** for some reggae, rock and coffee (the three pillars of modern civilisation). If the sun is shining, surfing at the local **(8) St Clair and St Kilda beaches** is awesome! Warm up afterwards at a Dunedin cafe, then lurch into the night for some bar-hopping and live tunes.

On day five, day-trip to **(9) Otago Peninsula** east of Dunedin, exploring little beaches and fishing towns and ogling fur seals, penguins and seabirds up close.

Hollyford River, Fiordland (p305)

Discover Queenstown & the South

Skyline Gondola, Queenstown
GERARD WALKER / LONELY PLANET IMAGES ©

QUEENSTOWN REGION

Queenstown

No one's ever visited Queenstown and said, 'I'm bored'. Looking like a small town, but with the energy of a small city, Queenstown offers a mountain of activities.

Maximise bragging rights in the town's atmospheric restaurants, laid-back cafes and bustling bars.

👁 Sights

SKYLINE GONDOLA   Cable Car
(Map p280; www.skyline.co.nz; Brecon St; adult/child/family return $25/14/71) Hop on the Gondola for fantastic views. At the top are a cafe, a restaurant with regular Maori cultural shows (p285), and souvenir shops. Walking trails include the loop track (30 minutes return), or try the Luge or new mountain-bike trails.

KIWI BIRDLIFE PARK   Wildlife
(Map p284; www.kiwibird.co.nz; Brecon St; adult/child $38/19; ⊙9am-5pm, shows 11am & 3pm) Here's your best bet to spy a kiwi. There are also 10,000 native plants and scores of birds, including the rare black stilt, kea, morepork and parakeets. Stroll around, watch the conservation show, and tiptoe into darkened kiwi houses.

🏃 Activities

Purchase discounted combination tickets from **Queenstown Combos** (☎03-442 7318, 0800 423 836; www.combos.co.nz).

Bungy Jumping

Queenstown is famous for bungy jumping and **AJ Hackett Bungy** (📞 03-442 7100; www.bungy.co.nz; The Station, cnr Camp & Shotover Strs) is the activity's best-known representative. Prices include transport out of town and gonola rides where relevant.

KAWARAU BRIDGE   Bungy

(Map p288; per person $180) The historic 1880 Kawarau Bridge, 23km from Queenstown, became the world's first commercial bungy site in 1988 and allows you to leap 43m.

LEDGE BUNGY   Bungy

(Map p280; per person $180) The 47m-high Ledge Bungy also operates after dark.

NEVIS HIGHWIRE   Bungy

(Map p288; per person $260) Jump from a 134m-high pod above the Nevis River.

Jetboating

SHOTOVER JET   Jetboating

(📞 0800 746 868; www.shotoverjet.co.nz; adult/child $119/69) Half-hour trips through the rocky Shotover Canyons, with lots of thrilling 360-degree spins.

KAWARAU JET   Jetboating

(Map p284; 📞 0800 529 272, 03-442 6142; www.kjet.co.nz; Queenstown Bay Jetty; adult/child $110/65) Does one-hour trips on the Kawarau and Lower Shotover Rivers.

SKIPPERS CANYON JET   Jetboating

(📞 0800 226 996, 03-442 9434; www.skipperscanyon.co.nz; adult/child $129/79) Includes a 30-minute blast in the narrow gorges of Skippers Canyon in three-hour trips that also cover the region's gold-mining history.

White-Water Rafting

QUEENSTOWN RAFTING   Rafting

(📞 03-442 9792, 0800 723 8464; www.rafting.co.nz; rafting/helirafting $195/279) One of the most established rafting companies.

EXTREME GREEN RAFTING   Rafting

(📞 03-442 8517; www.nzraft.com; rafting/helirafting $195/279) Trips on both the Kawarau and Shotover rivers.

FAMILY ADVENTURES   Rafting

(📞 03-442 8836, 0800 4723 8464; www.familyadventures.co.nz; adult/child $179/120; ⏱summer) Gentler (Grade I to II) trips on the Shotover suitable for children three years and older.

Flying, Gliding & Skydiving

TANDEM PARAGLIDING   Paragliding

(Map p280; 📞 0800 759 688, 03-441 8581; www.nzgforce.com; per person $199) Tandem paragliding from the top of the gondola or from Coronet Peak (9am departures are $20 cheaper).

SKYTREK HANG GLIDING   Hang Gliding

(📞 0800 759 873; www.skytrek.co.nz; from $210) Soar on tandem flights from Coronet Peak or the Remarkables.

NZONE   Skydiving

(📞 03-442 5867, 0800 376 796; www.nzone.biz; from $269) Jump out of an airplane with a tandem skydiving expert.

Skiing & Snowboarding

CORONET PEAK

(📞 03-450 1970; www.nzski.com; daily lift pass adult/child $95/52) Snow-making systems and treeless slopes provide excellent skiing and snowboarding for all levels.

THE REMARKABLES

(📞 03-450 1970, www.nzski.com; daily lift pass adult/child $91/49) This ski field is 28km from Queenstown, with shuttle buses in ski season. It has a good set of intermediate and advanced runs (only 10% beginner).

Tramping

Pick up the *Wakatipu Walks* brochure ($2) from DOC for local tramping tracks ranging from one-hour strolls to eight-hour slogs.

QUEENSTOWN HILL   Walking

A short climb is up 900m Queenstown Hill (two to three hours return). Access is from Belfast Tce.

**ENCOUNTER GUIDED
DAY WALKS**   Tramping

(📞 03-442 8200; www.ultimatehikes.co.nz; Routeburn Track: adult/child $145/85, Milford

Queenstown

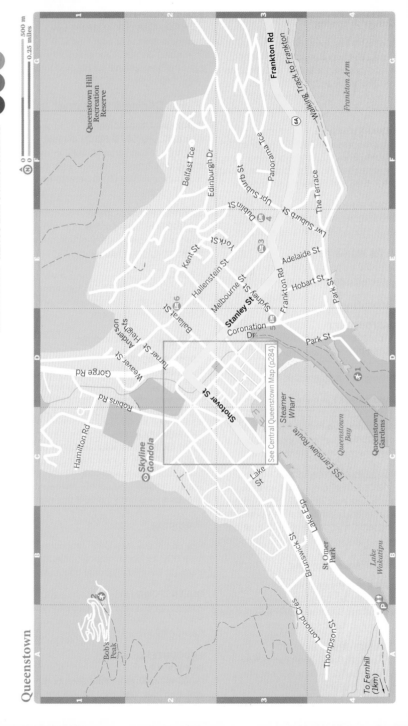

N

500 m
0.25 miles

Queenstown Hill Recreation Reserve

Frankton Rd

Walking Track to Frankton

Frankton Arm

Belfast Tce

Edinburgh Dr

Upr Suburb St

Panorama Tce

Dublin St

The Terrace

Kent St

York St

Lwr Suburb St

Hallenstein St

Adelaide St

Melbourne St

Hobart St

Ballarat St

Sydney St

Frankton Rd

Park St

St Helen's St

Anderson St

Stanley St

Coronation Dr

Turner St

Weaver St

Gorge Rd

Park St

Robins Rd

Shotover St

See Central Queenstown Map (p284)

Skyline Gondola

Steamer Wharf

Queenstown Bay

Queenstown Gardens

Hamilton Rd

Lake St

Lake Esp

TSS Earnslaw Route

Brunswick St

St Omer Park

Lake Wakatipu

Bob's Peak

Lomond Cres

Thompson St

To Fernhill (1km)

Track: adult/child $165/95, Mt Cook: adult/child $105/65; ⏱ Oct-Apr) Day walks on the Routeburn Track, the Milford Track and near Mt Cook, as well as multiday tramps.

GUIDED NATURE WALKS Walking
(☏03-442 7126; www.nzwalks.com; adult/child from $105/65) Excellent walks in the Queenstown area, including a Walk and Wine option and snow-shoeing in winter.

 Tours

OVER THE TOP HELICOPTERS Scenic Flights
(☏0800 123 359, 03-442 2233; www.flynz.co.nz; from $265) Queenstown and beyond.

SUNRISE BALLOONS Scenic Flights
(☏0800 468 247; 03-442 0781; www.balloon ingnz.com; adult/child $445/295) One-hour rides including a champagne breakfast.

NOMAD SAFARIS 4WD Tour
(☏0800 688 222, 03-442 6699; www.nomad safaris.co.nz; adult/child from $130/65) Trips take in stunning scenery and hard-to-get-to backcountry around Skippers Canyon and Macetown. The operators will let you drive ($260), or ride a quad-bike ($245).

QUEENSTOWN WINE TRAIL Wine Tour
(☏03-441 3990, 0800 827 8464; www.queens townwinetrail.co.nz; adult $129, shorter tour with lunch $148) Choose from a five-hour tour with tastings at four wineries or a shorter tour with lunch included.

 Sleeping

THE DAIRY B&B $$$
(Map p284; ☏03-442 5164, 0800 333 393; www. thedairy.co.nz; 10 Isle St; s/d incl breakfast from $435/465, Jun-Aug 3-night packages d $900-990; P @ ☎) Once a corner store, the Dairy is now a luxury B&B with 13 rooms packed with classy touches like designer bed linen, silk cushions and luxurious mohair rugs. Rates also include freshly baked afternoon tea.

CHALET QUEENSTOWN B&B B&B $$$
(Map p280; ☏0800 222 457, 03-442 7117; www. chaletqueenstown.co.nz; 1 Dublin St; d $195-225; P ☎) This chic and friendly B&B is one of the best boutique accommodation options in Queenstown. Perfectly appointed rooms sparkle with flat-screen TVs, interesting original artworks and quality bed linen. Book well ahead to secure one of the rooms with a lake view – easily one of the best vistas in town.

AMITY LODGE Motel $$
(Map p280; ☏0800 556 000; www.amitylodge. co.nz; 7 Melbourne St; d from $165; P ☎) In a quiet street around five minutes' (uphill) walk from central Queenstown, Amity Lodge combines older, but recently renovated units, and more comfortable and modern two-bedroom units. The friendly owners are a wealth of local information, and in an expensive destination, Amity Lodge is good value.

HISTORIC STONEHOUSE Apartments $$$
(Map p280; ☏03-442 9812; www.historicstone house.co.nz; 47 Hallenstein St; d $225-395; P) One of Queenstown's loveliest old private residences – built in 1874 – now houses three very comfortable self-contained apartments. Formerly the mayor's digs, the apartments are surrounded by established gardens and trimmed with antique furniture and a heritage vibe.

WILL SALTER / LONELY PLANET IMAGES ©

Don't Miss Mountain-Biking Mecca

With the opening of the Queenstown Bike Park, the region is now firmly established as an international focus for the sport. See also www.wakatiputrails.co.nz for details on the ongoing development of new mountain-bike trails around the area.

The Queenstown Trail More than 90km in total – links five scenic smaller trails showcasing Queenstown, Arrowtown, the Gibbston Valley, Lake Wakatipu and Lake Hayes. Overall the trail is technically easy and suitable for cyclists of all levels.

Queenstown Bike Park (Map p280; ☏ 03-441 0101; www.skyline.co.nz; Brecon St; ☾ half-day pass adult/child/family $45/25/115, day pass adult/child/family $60/30/150) Nine different trails – from easy to extreme – traverse Bob's Peak high above the lake. Once you've descended on two wheels, simply jump on the gondola and do it all over again. The best trail for novice riders is the 6km-long Hammy's Track, studded with lake views and picnic spots all the way down.

Vertigo (Map p284; ☏ 0800 837 8446, 03-442 8378; www.vertigobikes.co.nz; 4 Brecon St; rental per day from $79) Options include downhill rides into Skippers Canyon ($169) and a Remarkables helibike option ($399).

Fat Tyre Adventures (☏ 0800 328 897; www.fat-tyre.co.nz; from $199) Tours cater to different abilities with day tours, multiday tours, helibiking and singletrack riding. Bike hire and trail snacks are included.

CORONATION LODGE　　　　Motel $$
(Map p280; ☏ 0800 420 777, 03-442 0860; www. coronationlodge.co.nz; 10 Coronation Dr; d $150-220; @ ☜) Right beside the Queenstown Gardens, this lodge has plush bed linen, cosy wooden floors, and Turkish rugs. In a town that's somewhat lacking in good midrange accommodation, Coronation Lodge is recommended. Larger rooms have kitchenettes, and some of Queenstown's best restaurants and bars are a short stroll downhill.

LITTLE PARADISE LODGE   Lodge $$

(Map p288; ☎03-442 6196; www.littleparadise.co.nz; Glenorchy-Queenstown Rd; s $45, d $120-160; ☒) Wonderfully eclectic, this slice of arty paradise is the singular vision of the Swiss owner. Each rustic room features wooden floors, quirky artwork and handmade furniture. Outside the fun continues with a back-to-nature swimming hole and well-crafted walkways along a nearby hillside.

LOMOND LODGE   Lodge $$

(Map p284; ☎03-442 8235; www.lomondlodge.com; 33 Man St; d $138-169; P @ 🛜) A recent makeover has modernised Lomond Lodge's cosy decor. Share your on-the-road stories with fellow travellers in the communal kitchen and around the garden barbecue. Larger family apartments ($270 for up to four people) are also available.

 # Eating

FISHBONE BAR & GRILL   Seafood $$

(Map p284; ☎03-442 6768; www.fishbonequeenstown.co.nz; 7 Beach St; mains $26-32) Queenstown's more than a few miles inland, but that doesn't stop Fishbone from sourcing the best of NZ seafood. Everything from scallops to snapper is treated with a light and inventive touch. Try the zingy prawn tacos on handmade tortillas or the robust South Indian–style seafood curry.

VUDU CAFE & LARDER   Cafe $

(Map p284; 16 Rees St; mains $10-18) Excellent home-style baking – try the pork and fennel sausage rolls or the delicate mini-pavlovas – features at this cosmopolitan cafe. Top-notch breakfast and lunch options include buttermilk pancakes and a cheesy quesadilla. Check out the huge photo inside of a much less-populated Queenstown, or head through to the rear garden for lake and mountain views.

BELLA CUCINA   Italian $$

(Map p284; ☎03-442 6762; www.bellacucina.co.nz; 6 Brecon St; pizza & pasta $29, mains $29-34; ⏲5pm-late) Fresh pasta and risotto are highlights at Bella Cucina, while the

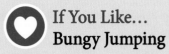

If You Like...
Bungy Jumping

If you like hurling yourself off high platforms into godless oblivion, try these variations on the bungy theme around Queenstown:

1 SHOTOVER CANYON SWING
(☎0800 279 464, 03-442 6990; www.canyonswing.co.nz; per person $199, additional swings $39) Be released loads of different ways – backwards, in a chair, upside down... From there it's a 60m free fall and a wild swing across the canyon at 150km/h.

2 NEVIS ARC
(☎0800 286 4958; www.nevisarc.co.nz) Fly in tandem ($320) or go it alone ($180) on the planet's highest swing.

3 LEDGE SKY SWING
(Map p280; ☎0800 286 4958; www.bungy.co.nz; $150) The Ledge offers a shorter swing than at the Nevis Arc, but equally stunning views of Queenstown.

rustic woodfired pizzas are perfect for sharing. Beautifully simple food done just right and a perfectly concise wine list, all served in one of Queenstown's cosiest and most romantic dining rooms.

@THAI   Thai $$

(Map p284; www.atthai.co.nz; 3rd fl, 8 Church St; mains $16-24) Head up the semi-hidden set of stairs for pad thai worth writing home about, and the *hor-mok* seafood red curry will blow your mind. Definitely kick off your meal with the coconut prawns ($12) and an icy Singha beer.

FERGBURGER   Burgers $

(Map p284; www.fergburger.com; 42 Shotover St; burgers $10-17; ⏲8.30am-5am) Queenstown's iconic Fergburger has now become a tourist attraction in itself, forcing a few locals to look elswhere for their regular gourmet burger fix. Ferg's was the innovative original in town though, and an international bunch of travellers of all ages still crowd in for their burger fix.

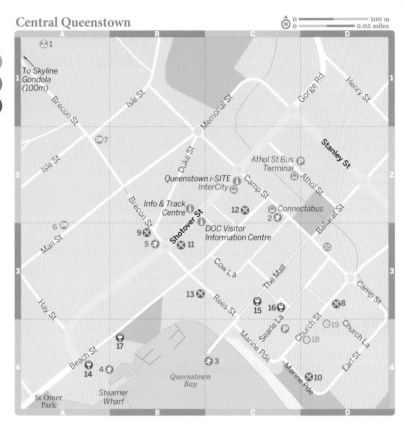

 Drinking

ATLAS BEER CAFE   Craft Beer
(Map p284; Steamer Wharf, Beach St; ⏰10am-2am) Perched at the end of Steamer Wharf this pint-sized bar specialises in beers from Dunedin's Emerson's Brewery and regular guest beers from further afield. A concise but tasty food menu includes good-value sandwiches and wraps for lunch (around $10), and shared plates and tapas ($10 to $15) for dinner.

BALLARAT TRADING COMPANY   Pub
(Map p284; www.ballarat.co.nz; 7-9 The Mall) Stuffed bears, rampant wall-mounted ducks and a recreated colonial general store – there's really no competition for the title of Queenstown's most eclectic decor. Beyond the grab bag of infuences, Ballarat's gastro pub combo is quite a traditional spot, with gleaming beer taps, occasional lapses into 1980s music, and robust meals, including confit duck leg, lamb pie, burgers and steaks.

PUB ON WHARF   Pub
(Map p284; www.pubonwharf.co.nz; Steamer Wharf) Ubercool interior design combines with handsome woodwork and lighting fit for a hipster hideaway. Stuffed animal heads reinforce you're still in NZ, and Mac's beers on tap, scrummy nibbles and a decent wine list make this a great place to settle in for the evening. Check the website for live-music listings.

BARDEAUX   Wine Bar
(Map p284; Eureka Arcade, 11 The Mall; ⏰6pm-late) This small, low-key wine bar is all

Central Queenstown

class. Under a low ceiling await plush leather armchairs and a fireplace made from Central Otago's iconic schist rock. Come along for one of Queenstown's best wine selections, many also from Central Otago.

 Entertainment

SUBCULTURE   Club
(Map p284; www.subculture.net.nz; downstairs 12-14 Church St) Drum and bass, hip-hop, dub and reggae noises that get the crowds moving.

DUX DE LUX   Live Music
(Map p284; 14 Church St) Lots of live bands and DJs with everything from reggae to drum and bass. Look forward to occasional summer visits from NZ's biggest touring acts. The 'Dux' also brews its own beers.

KIWI HAKA   Traditional Dance
(Map p280; ☎03-441 0101; www.skyline.co.nz; Brecon St; adult/child/family incl gondola $59/32/166; ◷from 5.15pm) For traditional Maori dancing and singing, come watch this group at the top of the gondola. There are four 30-minute shows nightly, but bookings are essential.

ⓘ Information

Tourist Information

Queenstown i-SITE (☎03-442 4100, 0800 668 888; www.queenstownnz.co.nz; Clocktower Centre, cnr Shotover & Camp Sts; ◷8am-6.30pm) Booking service, accommodation and information on Queenstown, Arrowtown and Glenorchy.

DOC Visitor Centre (Department of Conservation; ☎03-442 7935; www.doc.govt.nz; 38 Shotover St; ◷8.30am-5.30pm)

ⓘ Getting There & Away

Air

Air New Zealand (☎03-441 1900; www.airnewzealand.co.nz; 8 Church St) links Queenstown to Auckland, Wellington and Christchurch, and Sydney and Melbourne. Virgin Australia has flights between Queenstown and Sydney and Brisbane. **Jetstar** (☎0800 800 995; www.jetstar.com) links Queenstown with Auckland, Christchurch and Wellington, and Sydney, Melbourne and the Gold Coast.

Bus

InterCity (www.intercity.co.nz) Book at the i-SITE. Travels to Christchurch, Te Anau, Milford Sound, Dunedin and Invercargill, plus a daily West Coast service to the glaciers and Haast.

Naked Bus (www.nakedbus.com) To the West Coast, Te Anau, Christchurch, Dunedin, Cromwell, Wanaka and Invercargill.

Atomic Shuttles (www.atomictravel.co.nz) To Wanaka, Christchurch, Dunedin and Greymouth.

Catch-a-Bus (☎03-479 9960; www.catchabus.co.nz) To Dunedin and Central Otago – also links to the Taeri Gorge Railway.

Bottom Bus (03-477 9083; www.bottombus. co.nz) Does a loop service around the south of the South Island.

Wanaka Connexions (03-443 9120; www. alpinecoachlines.co.nz) Links Queenstown with Wanaka and the Rail Trail towns of Central Otago.

ⓘ Getting Around

To/From the Airport

Queenstown Airport (ZQN; 03-450 9031; www.queenstownairport.co.nz; Frankton) is 8km east of town. **Super Shuttle** (0800 748 885; www.supershuttle.co.nz) picks up and drops off in Queenstown (around $20). **Connectabus** (03-441 4471; www.connectabus.com; cnr Beach & Camp Sts) runs to to the airport ($6) every 15 minutes from 6.50am to 10.20pm. **Alpine Taxis** (0800 442 6666) or **Queenstown Taxis** (03-442 7788) charge around $30.

Arrowtown

Beloved by day-trippers from Queenstown, exceedingly quaint Arrowtown sprang up in the 1860s following the

discovery of gold in the Arrow River. Today the town retains more than 60 of its original wooden and stone buildings, and has pretty, tree-lined avenues, excellent galleries and an expanding array of fashionable shopping opportunities.

◎ Sights & Activities

Try your luck **gold panning** on the Arrow River. Rent pans from the visitor information centre ($3) and head to the northern edge of town.

CHINESE SETTLEMENT   Historical Site (admission by gold coin donation; ⏱24hr) Arrowtown has NZ's best example of a gold-era Chinese settlement. Interpretive signs explain the lives of Chinese 'diggers' during and after the gold rush, while restored huts and shops make the story more tangible. Subjected to significant racism, the Chinese often had little choice but to rework old tailings rather than seek new claims. The Chinese

Left: Paragliding (p279), Lake Wakatipu; **Below:** Amisfield Winery (p289)

(LEFT) ED NORTON / LONELY PLANET IMAGES ©; (BELOW) GERARD WALKER / LONELY PLANET IMAGES ©

settlement is off
Buckingham St.

ℹ Information

Arrowtown Visitor Information Centre (☎ 03-442 1824; www.arrowtown.com; 49 Buckingham St; ⏱ 8.30am-5pm; @ 🛜) Shares premises with the Lake District Museum and Gallery.

ℹ Getting There & Away

From Queenstown, **Connectabus** (☎ 03-441 4471; www.connectabus.com) runs regular services (7.45am to 11pm) on its No 10 route from Frankton to Arrowtown. You'll need to catch a No 11 bus from Queenstown to the corner of Frankton and Kawarau Rd, and change to a No 10 bus there. The cheapest way is a one-day pass (adult/child $17/12).

The **Double-Decker Bus Tour** (Map p284; ☎ 03-441 4421; www.doubledeckerbus.co.nz; $48) does a three-hour round-trip tour to Arrowtown (departs Queenstown at 9.30am).

Arrowtown Scenic Bus (☎ 03-442 1900; www.arrowtownbus.co.nz) runs a daily four-hour round trip from Queenstown at 10am ($69).

Glenorchy

Set in achingly beautiful surroundings, postage-stamp-sized Glenorchy is the perfect low-key antidote to Queenstown. Glenorchy lies at the head of Lake Wakatipu, a scenic 40-minute (68km) drive northwest from Queenstown.

Activities

The DOC brochure *Heads of Lake Wakatipu* ($2) details an easy waterside walk around the outskirts of town, and other tramps from two hours to two days, taking in the Routeburn Valley, Lake Sylvan, Dart River and Lake Rere.

Those with sturdy wheels can explore the superb valleys north of Glenorchy. **Paradise** lies 15km northwest of town, just before the start of the Dart Track. You can also explore the Rees Valley or take

287

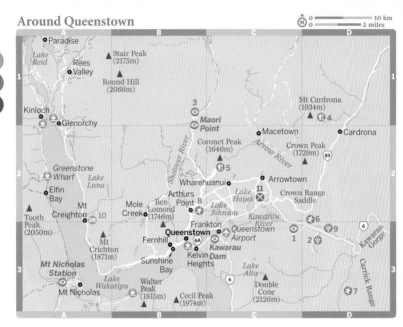

Around Queenstown

the road to Routeburn, which goes via the Dart River Bridge.

GLENORCHY BASE   Tramping
(☏ 03-409 0960; www.glenorchybase.co.nz; adult/child from $60) Specialising in guided walks around the Glenorchy area (from two hours to one day). Highlights include birdwatching around Lake Sylvan and a Routeburn Track day walk.

DART RIVER SAFARIS   Jetboating
(☏ 0800 327 8538, 03-442 9992; www.dartriver. co.nz; adult/child $219/119) Journeys into the heart of the spectacular Dart River wilderness, followed by a short nature walk and a 4WD trip. The round trip from Glenorchy takes three hours.

KAYAK KINLOCH   Kayaking
(☏ 03-442 4900; www.kayakkinloch.co.nz; adult $40-80, child $35-50) Excellent guided trips exploring the lake. Trips depart from Queenstown, Glenorchy or Kinloch.

DART STABLES   Horse Riding
(☏ 0800 474 3464, 03-442 5688; www.dartsta bles.com) Offer a two-hour ride ($129), a full-day trot ($279) and a 1½-hour Ride of the Rings trip ($169) for Hobbitty types. If you're really keen, consider the overnight two-day trek with a sleepover in Paradise ($695). All trips can be joined in Queenstown.

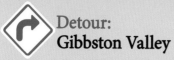

Detour:
Gibbston Valley

Gung-ho visitors to Queenstown might be happiest dangling off a giant rubber band, but as they're plunging towards the Kawarau River, they'll be missing out on some of Central Otago's most interesting winemaking areas just up the road in the stunning Gibbston Valley.

On a spectacular river terrace near the Kawarau Bridge, AJ Hackett's original bungy partner Henry van Asch set up the **Winehouse & Kitchen** (☎03-442 7310; www.winehouse.co.nz; mains $15-30; ⊙10am-5pm). A restored wooden villa includes a garden cafe, and in early 2012, the Winehouse's annual Summer Playgound Series music festival was also launched from January to April.

Almost opposite, a winding and scenic road leads to beautiful **Chard Farm** (☎03-442 6110; www.chardfarm.co.nz; ⊙11am-5pm), and a further 700m along is **Gibbston Valley Wines** (www.gvwines.co.nz) the area's largest wine producer.

A further 4km along SH6, **Peregrine** (☎03-442 4000; www.peregrinewines.co.nz; ⊙10am-5pm) produces excellent sauvignon blanc, pinot noir and pinot gris, and hosts occasional outdoor concerts during summer, sometimes featuring international names.

Further west near the shores of Lake Hayes, the **Amisfield Winery & Bistro** (☎03-442 0556; www.amisfield.co.nz; small plates $16.50; ⊙11.30am-8pm Tue-Sun) is regularly lauded by NZ's authoritative *Cuisine* magazine.

Ask at the Queenstown i-SITE for maps and information about touring the Gibbston Valley. Visit www.gibbstonvalley.co.nz for more info about this compact wine-growing area with its own unique microclimate.

Sleeping & Eating

KINLOCH LODGE　　　　Lodge **$$**
(☎03-442 4900; www.kinlochlodge.co.nz; Kinloch Rd; dm $33, d $82-120, r $175-195) Across Lake Wakatipu from Glenorchy, this is a great place to unwind or prepare for a tramp. Rooms in the bunkhouse are comfy and colourful, and there's a post-tramp hot tub. The 19th-century Heritage Rooms are small but plusher, and come with breakfast and dinner ($278 to $298). A bar and a good restaurant are on-site. Kinloch is a 26km drive from Glenorchy, or you can organise a five-minute boat ride across the lake.

GLENORCHY CAFÉ　　　　Cafe **$$**
(Mull St; breakfast & lunch mains $15-20, pizza $25; ⊙8am-5pm May-Oct, dinner Nov-Apr) Perennial favourites like pizza and breakfast stacks keep locals coming back time after time.

❶ Information

The best place for local information, updated weather, track information and hut passes is the Glenorchy Visitor Information Centre (☎03-409 2049; www.glenorchy-nz.co.nz; Oban St) in the Glenorchy Hotel.

❶ Getting There & Away

With sweeping vistas and gem-coloured waters, the sealed Glenorchy-to-Queenstown road is wonderfully scenic. Its constant hills are a killer for cyclists. Pick up the *Queenstown to Glenorchy Road* leaflet from the Queenstown i-SITE for points of interest along the way.

Lake Wakatipu Region

The mountainous region at the northern head of Lake Wakatipu showcases gorgeous, remote scenery, best viewed while tramping along the famous Routeburn and lesser-known Greenstone, Caples and Rees-Dart Tracks. For shorter tracks, see the DOC brochure *Wakatipu Walks* ($5). Glenorchy is a convenient base for all these tramps.

Ultimate Hikes (☏03-442 8200; www.ultimatehikes.co.nz) has a three-day guided tramp on the Routeburn ($1125/1270 low/high season); a six-day Grand Traverse ($1560/1765), combining walks on the Routeburn and Greenstone Tracks; and a one-day Routeburn Encounter ($169), available from November to mid-April.

Routeburn Track

Passing through a huge variety of landscapes with fantastic views, the 32km-long, three- to four-day Routeburn Track is one of the most popular rainforest/subalpine tracks in NZ. Reservations are required throughout the main season (October to April). Book huts or campsites online at www.doc.govt.nz or at a DOC office prior to the trip.

There are car parks at the Divide and Glenorchy ends of the Routeburn, but they're unattended, so don't leave any valuables in your car.

The track can be started from either end. Many people travelling from Queenstown try to reach the Divide in

Trampers in Routeburn Gorge

time to catch the bus to Milford and connect with a cruise on the sound. En route, you'll take in breathtaking views from Harris Saddle and the top of nearby Conical Hill, from where you can see waves breaking at Martins Bay. From Key Summit, there are panoramic views of the Hollyford Valley and the Eglinton and Greenstone River Valleys.

WANAKA REGION
Wanaka

Beautiful scenery, tramping and skiing opportunities, and a huge roster of adrenaline-inducing activities have transformed the lakeside town of Wanaka into a year-round tourist destination.

 Sights

WARBIRDS & WHEELS   Museum
(www.warbirdsandwheels.com; Wanaka Airport, 11 Lloyd Dunn Av; adult/child/family $20/5/45; ⏱9am-5pm) Dedicated to NZ combat pilots, their aircraft, and the sacrifices they made, this excellent mueseum features

Wanaka

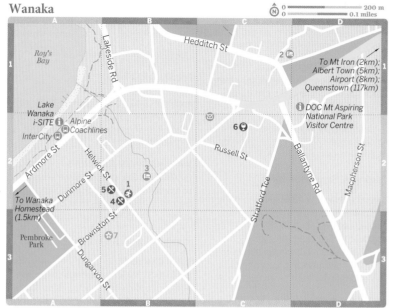

Hawker Hurricanes, a de Havilland Vampire and vintage Soviet fighter planes. Classic cars make up the 'wheels' part.

WANAKA BEERWORKS *Brewery*
(www.wanakabeerworks.co.nz; SH6; tours & tasting $10; ⊙9am-4pm) This small brewery's three main beers, a Vienna lager, a German-style black beer, and a hops-laden Bohemian pilsner are complemented by up to 12 different seasonal brews each year. Dave the owner is a real deal Belgian brewing supremo, and is usually available for tastings and brewery tours.

🏃 Activities

Wide valleys, alpine meadows, more than 100 glaciers and sheer mountains make **Mt Aspiring National Park** an outdoor enthusiast's paradise.

Tramping

While the southern end of Mt Aspiring National Park is well trafficked and includes popular tramps such as the Routeburn

Track, there are great short walks and more demanding multiday tramps in the Matukituki Valley, close to Wanaka; see the DOC brochure *Matukituki Valley Tracks* ($2). The dramatic **Rob Roy Valley Track** (two to three hours return) takes in glaciers, waterfalls and a swing bridge. The **West Matukituki Valley** track goes on to Aspiring Hut (four to five hours return), a scenic walk over mostly grassy flats.

291

For walks closer to town, pick up the DOC brochure *Wanaka Outdoor Pursuits* ($3.50). Many outfits offer guided walking tours, some into Mt Aspiring National Park.

ALPINISM & SKI WANAKA   Tramping
(☎ 03-442 6593; www.alpinismski.co.nz; from $200) Day walks and overnight tramps.

ECO WANAKA ADVENTURES   Tramping
(☎ 0800 926 326; www.ecowanaka.co.nz; half-/ full day from $105/170) Day, half-day and multiday trips.

Skiing & Snowboarding

SNOW FARM NEW ZEALAND   Skiing
(☎ 03-443 7542; www.snowfarmnz.com; daily trail pass adult/child $40/20) NZ's only commercial cross-country ski area is 35km from Wanaka on the Pisa Range. There are 50km of groomed trails, huts with facilities, and thousands of hectares of snow.

SNOW PARK NZ   Skiing
(☎ 03-443 9991; www.snowparknz.com; daily lift pass adult/child $88/41) NZ's only dedicated freestyle ski and snowboard area, with a plethora of pipes, terrain parks, boxes and rails and snow-making facilities. It's 34km from Wanaka.

Jetboating & Rafting

PIONEER RAFTING   Rafting
(☎ 03-443 1246; www.ecoraft.co.nz; half day adult/child $145/85, full day $195/105) Ecorafting on the high-volume Clutha, with Grade II to III rapids, gold panning and birdwatching.

WANAKA RIVER JOURNEYS   Jetboating
(☎ 0800 544 555; www.wanakariverjourneys. co.nz; adult/child $240/145) Combination bush walk (50 minutes) and jetboat ride in the stunning Matukituki Valley.

Canyoning & Kayaking

DEEP CANYON   Canyoning
(☎ 03-443 7922; www.deepcanyon.co.nz; from $240; ☉ mid-Nov–Apr) Loads of climbing, swimming and waterfall-abseiling through confined, wild gorges.

ALPINE KAYAK GUIDES   Kayaking
(☎ 03-443 9023; www.alpinekayaks.co.nz; half/full day $149/195; ☉ Nov-May) Down the Hawea, Clutha and Matukituki Rivers. Kids can join a more leisurely half-day Grandview trip (two adults, two kids $450).

Skydiving & Paragliding

SKYDIVE LAKE WANAKA   Skydiving
(☎ 03-443 7207; www.sky divewanaka.com; from $299) Jumps from 12,000ft and a scary 15,000ft; the latter lets you fall for 60 seconds.

WANAKA PARAGLIDING   Paragliding
(☎ 0800 359 754; www. wanakaparagliding.co.nz; $189) Count on around 20 minutes soaring on the Central Otago thermals.

Kayaking, Clutha River
JOHN ELK III / LONELY PLANET IMAGES ©

Mountain Biking

Many tracks and trails in the region are open to cyclists. Pick up the DOC brochure *Wanaka Outdoor Pursuits* ($3.50), describing mountain-bike rides ranging from 2km to 24km, including the Deans Bank Loop Track (11.5km).

The *Bike Wanaka Cycling Map* ($2) is available at local cycle shops and features forested tracks for more adventurous riders. To hire a bike and get local track information head to **Thunderbikes (cnr Helwick & Bronwston St)**.

FREERIDE NZ — Mountain Biking
(☎0800 743 369, 021 712 996; www.freeridenz. com; per person from $185) Guided full-day trips including helibiking options, and a three-day ($1370) Central Otago adventure. Self-guided tours and rental is $95.

 Tours

WANAKA FLIGHTSEEING — Scenic Flights
(☎03-443 8787; www.flightseeing.co.nz; adult/child from $200/120) Spectacular flyovers of Mt Aspiring, Milford Sound and Mt Cook.

ASPIRING HELICOPTERS — Scenic Flights
(☎03-443 7152; www.aspiringhelicopters.co.nz) Also flights to Milford Sound.

LAKE WANAKA CRUISES — Boat Cruise
(☎03-443 1230; www.wanakacruises.co.nz; from $70) Lake cruising aboard a catamaran with overnight options.

 **Sleeping**

RIVERSONG — B&B $$
(☎03-443 8567; www.riversongwanaka.co.nz; 5 Wicklow Tce; d $160-180) On the banks of the Clutha River in nearby Albert Town, Riversong has two rooms in a lovely heritage B&B. The well-travelled owners may have the best nonfiction library in NZ, and if you can tear yourself away, there's excellent trout fishing just metres away. Dinner including wine is $55 per person.

WANAKA HOMESTEAD — Lodge $$$
(☎03-443 5022; www.wanakahomestead.co.nz; 1 Homestead Close; d $265, cottages $410-525; @ ☎) Wooden interiors, oriental rugs and local artwork punctuate this boutique lodge, which has won awards for its ecofriendly approach to sustainability. Despite the focus on green good deeds, it's still luxurious, with underfloor heating and an under-the-stars hot tub. Choose from rooms in the main lodge or in self-contained cottages.

ARCHWAY MOTELS — Motel $$
(☎0800 427 249, 03-443 7698; www.archway motels.co.nz; 64 Hedditch St; $105-150; ☎) This older motel with clean and spacious units and chalets is a short uphill walk from the lakefront. Helpful owners, new flat-screen TVs, and cedar hot tubs with mountain views make Archway great value in a sometimes expensive town.

BROOK VALE — Motel $$
(☎0800 438 333, 03-443 8333; www.brookvale. co.nz; 35 Brownston St; d $145-185; ☎ ☒) Self-contained studio and family units with a few classy touches and patios that open onto a grassy lawn complete with a gently flowing creek. You'll also find a barbecue, a spa and a swimming pool .

 Eating

FEDERAL DINER — Cafe $
(www.federaldiner.co.nz; 47 Helwick St; snacks & mains $10-20; ⏲7.30am-4pm, open later for tapas in summer) Seek out this cosmopolitan cafe tucked away off Wanaka's main shopping street. The all-day menu delivers robust spins on breakfast, excellent coffee and chunky gourmet sandwiches. Beers and wines are proudly local, and there's occasional live music with a blues or folk flavour on Friday nights.

SPICE ROOM — Indian $$
(www.spiceroom.co.nz; 43 Helwick St; mains $20-25; ☛) The combo of an authentic curry, crispy garlic naan and cold beer is a great way to recharge after a day's snowboarding or tramping. Beyond the spot-on

Right: Campervanning, near Wanaka; **Below:** Heliskiers, Mt Aspiring National Park (p291)

(RIGHT) DAVID WALL / LONELY PLANET IMAGES ©; (BELOW) JOHN HAY /LONELY PLANET IMAGES ©

renditions of all your subcontinental favourites, the Spice Room springs a few surprises with starters including a zingy scallops masala salad.

BOTSWANA BUTCHERY
Modern NZ $$$

(☎ 03-443 6745; Post Office Lane; mains $30-45; ⏲5pm-late) In a sophisticated dining room, locally inspired dishes like Central Otago hare and Cardrona Merino lamb shoulder go head to head with Botswana Butchery's signature aged beef steaks. Definitely food for grown-ups, as is the serious Central Otago–skewed wine list.

🍷 Drinking & Entertainment

BARLUGA
Bar

(Post Office Lane; ⏲4pm-late) In the funky Post Office Lane area, Barluga's leather armchairs and coolly retro wallpaper at first make you think of a refined gentlemen's club. Wicked cocktails and killer back-to-back beats soon smash that illusion.

CINEMA PARADISO
Cinema

(☎ 03-443 1505; www.paradiso.net.nz; 72-76 Brownston St; adult/child $16/10; @) Wanaka's original Cinema Paradiso in Ardmore St was a true NZ icon, and it re-opened at these more modern and spacious premises in March 2012. Look forward to an entertaining slice of the old Paradiso magic with comfy couches and extra cushions on the floor to stretch out on. The best of Hollywood and art-house flicks run across three screens.

RUBY'S
Cinema

(www.rubyscinema.co.nz; 50 Cardrona Valley Rd; adult/child $18.50/12.50) Channelling a lush New York or Shanghai vibe, this hip art-house-cinema-meets-chic-cocktail-bar is a real surprise in outdoorsy Wanaka.

Luxuriate in the huge cinema seats, or chill out in the red velvet lounge with craft beers, classic cocktails and sophisticated bar snacks ($6 to $14).

ℹ Information

DOC Mt Aspiring National Park Visitor Centre (Department of Conservation; ☎ 03-443 7660; www.doc.govt.nz; Ardmore St; ⊙ 8am-5pm Nov-Apr, 8.30am-5pm Mon-Fri, 9.30am-4pm Sat May-Oct) Enquire about tramps, and there's a small museum (admission free) on Wanaka geology, flora and fauna.

Lake Wanaka i-SITE (☎ 03-443 1233; www. lakewanaka.co.nz; 100 Ardmore St; ⊙ 8.30am-5.30pm, to 7pm in summer) In the log cabin on the lakefront.

ℹ Getting There & Away

Air

Air New Zealand (☎ 0800 737 000; www. airnewzealand.co.nz) has daily flights between Wanaka and Christchurch (from $99).

Bus

InterCity (www.intercity.co.nz) Wanaka receives daily buses from Queenstown (two hours), which motor on to Franz Josef (six hours) via Haast Pass (three hours). For Christchurch (6½ hours) you'll need to change at Tarras.

Atomic Shuttles (www.atomictravel.co.nz) Services to Christchurch (seven hours), Dunedin (4½ hours) and the West Coast.

Catch-a-Bus (☎ 03-479 9960; www.catchabus. co.nz) Links Wanaka with Dunedin and the Rail Trail towns of Central Otago

Naked Bus (www.nakedbus.com) Services to Queenstown, Christchurch, Cromwell and the West Coast.

Connectabus (☎ 0800 405 066; www. connectabus.com; one-way/return $35/65) Handy twice-daily service linking Wanaka with Queenstown airport and Queenstown.

Wanaka Connexions (☎ 03-443-9120; www. alpinecoachlines.co.nz) Links Wanaka with Queenstown and the Rail Trail towns of Central Otago

Detour:
Cardrona

The sealed **Crown Range Road** from Wanaka to Queenstown via Cardrona is shorter than the route via Cromwell, but it's a narrow, twisting-and-turning mountain road that needs to be tackled with care, especially in poor weather.

With views of lush valleys, foothills and countless snowy peaks, this is one of the South Island's most scenic drives. The road passes through tall, swaying tussock grass in the **Pisa Conservation Area**, which has a number of short walking trails. There are plenty of **rest stops** to drink in the view. Particularly good ones are at the Queenstown end of the road, as you switchback down towards Arrowtown.

The unpretentious-looking **Cardrona Hotel** (☏03-443 8153; www.cardronahotel. co.nz; Crown Range Rd; d $135-185) first opened its doors in 1863. Today you'll find lovingly restored, peaceful rooms with snug, country-style furnishings and patios opening onto a garden. You'll also find a deservedly popular pub with a good **restaurant** (mains $15-20) and a great garden bar.

🛈 Getting Around

Alpine Coachlines (☏03-443 7966; www.alpinecoachlines.co.nz; Dunmore St) meets and greets flights at Wanaka Airport ($15), and in summer has twice-daily shuttles for trampers ($35) to Mt Aspiring National Park and Raspberry Creek. **Wanaka Taxis** (☏0800 272 2700) also looks after airport transfers, while **Adventure Rentals** (☏03-443 6050; www.adventurerentals.co.nz; 20 Ardmore St) hires cars and 4WDs, and **Yello** (☏0800 443 5555; www.yello.co.nz) provide charter transport, airport transfers and regional sightseeing.

DUNEDIN & OTAGO
Dunedin

Dunedin's compact town centre blends the historic and the contemporary, reflected in its alluring museums and tempting bars, cafes and restaurants. Weatherboard houses ranging from stately to ramshackle pepper its hilly suburbs, and bluestone Victorian buildings punctuate the centre. The country's oldest university provides loads of student energy to sustain thriving theatre, live-music and after-dark scenes.

Sights

OTAGO MUSEUM — Museum

(www.otagomuseum.govt.nz; 419 Great King St; admission by donation; ⏰10am-5pm) Explores Otago's cultural and physical past and present, from geology and dinosaurs to the modern day. The Tangata Whenua Maori gallery houses an impressive *waka taua* (war canoe), wonderfully worn old carvings and some lovely *pounamu* (greenstone) works. Join themed guided tours ($12, see website for times and themes).

RAILWAY STATION — Historic Building

(Anzac Ave) Featuring mosaic-tile floors and glorious stained-glass windows, Dunedin's striking Edwardian Railway Station claims to be NZ's most-photographed building. The station houses the NZ Sports Hall of Fame, hosts the Dunedin Farmers Market, and is the departing point for the Taieri Gorge Railway.

FREE **PUBLIC ART GALLERY** — Gallery

(www.dunedin.art.museum; 30 The Octagon; ⏰10am-5pm) Explore NZ's art scene at Dunedin's expansive and airy Public Art Gallery. Climb the iron staircase for great city views.

BALDWIN STREET
Street

The world's steepest residential street (or so says the *Guinness Book of World Records*), Baldwin St has a gradient of 1 in 1.286 (19 degrees). The annual 'Gutbuster' race in February sees up to 1000 athletes run to the top of Baldwin St and back. The record is just under two minutes.

Activities

St Clair and St Kilda are both popular **swimming** beaches (though you need to watch for rips at St Clair). Both have consistently good left-hand breaks, and you'll also find good **surfing** at Blackhead further south, and at Aramoana on Otago Harbour's North Shore.

The **Esplanade Surf School** (☏455 8655; www.espsurfschool.co.nz; lessons from $60), based at St Clair Beach, provides equipment and lessons.

The **Tunnel Beach Walkway** (5 min return; ⊙closed 20 Aug-31 Oct for lambing) crosses farmland before descending the sea cliffs to Tunnel Beach. Sea stacks, arches and unusual rock shapes have been carved out by the wild Pacific, and a few fossils stud the sandstone cliffs.

The walk is southwest of central Dunedin.

CYCLE SURGERY
Bicycle Rental

(www.cyclesurgery.co.nz; 67 Lower Stuart St; per day $40) Rents out bikes and has mountain-biking information.

Tours

FIRST CITY TOURS
Bus Tour

(adult/child $20/10; ⊙buses depart The Octagon 9am, 10.15am, 1pm, 2.15pm & 3.30pm) Hop-on/hop-off double-decker bus tour

that loops around the city. Stops include the Otago Museum, Speight's, Botanic Gardens and Baldwin St.

WALK DUNEDIN
Walking Tour

(☏03-477 5052; 2hr walk $20; ⊙10am) History-themed strolls around the city, organised by the Otago Settlers Museum. Book at the i-SITE, or pick up a self-guided tour brochure ($4).

WINE TOURS OTAGO
Wine Tasting

(☏021 070 1658, 03-453 1455; www.winetours otago.co.nz; per person $159) Wine-tasting excursions exploring Central Otago or the Waitaki Valley.

Sleeping

GRANDVIEW BED & BREAKFAST
B&B $$

(☏0800 749 472, 03-474 9472; www.grandview. co.nz; 360 High St; d incl breakfast $125-200; **P @ 🛜**) Bold colours, exposed brick walls and snazzy art-deco bathrooms are the highlights at this family-owned B&B.

House on Baldwin Street
JOHN ELK III / LONELY PLANET IMAGES ©

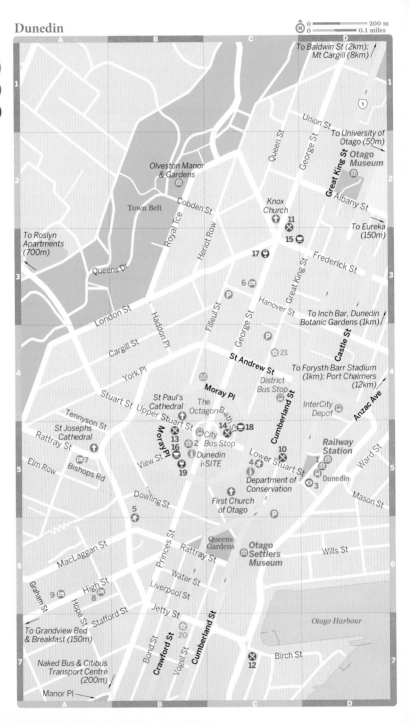

To Baldwin St (2km);
Mt Cargill (8km)

Union St

To University of
Otago (50m)

Otago
Museum

Queen St

George St

Great King St

Albany St

Olveston Manor
& Gardens

Cobden St

Knox
Church

To Eureka
(150m)

Town Belt

11

15

Royal Tce

Heriot Row

17

Frederick St

To Roslyn
Apartments
(700m)

Queens Dr

Great King St

6

Castle St

London St

Hanover St

To Inch Bar, Dunedin
Botanic Gardens (1km)

Filleul St

George St

Haddon Pl

Cargill St

21

St Andrew St

To Forysth Barr Stadium
(1km); Port Chalmers
(12km)

York Pl

Moray Pl

District
Bus Stop

InterCity
Depot

Anzac Ave

Stuart St

Bath St

Cumberland St

Upper Stuart St

St Paul's
Cathedral

The
Octagon

14

18

Tennyson St

St Josephs
Cathedral

Moray Pl

13

City
Bus Stop

2

Railway
Station

Rattray St

16

Dunedin
i-SITE

1

Ward St

Elm Row

View St

19

Lower Stuart St

10

Dunedin

Bishops Rd

7

Mason St

4

Department of
Conservation

3

Dowling St

First Church
of Otago

5

MacLaggan St

Princes St

Rattray St

Queens
Gardens

Otago
Settlers
Museum

Wills St

Water St

Graham St

High St

9

8

Liverpool St

Hope St

Stafford St

Jetty St

To Grandview Bed
& Breakfast (150m)

Bond St

Crawford St

20

Vogel St

Cumberland St

Otago Harbour

Naked Bus & Citibus
Transport Centre
(200m)

Birch St

12

Manor Pl

Dunedin

The building dates back to 1861, there are superb harbour views from the barbecue and deck area, and lots of sunny shared spaces. The larger rooms have private spa baths, and there's even a gym and sauna.

ROSLYN APARTMENTS Apartments $$

(☎03-477 6777; www.roslynapartments.co.nz; 23 City Rd; d $150-300; [P] [🛜]) Modern decor and brilliant city and harbour views are on tap at these chic apartments just a short walk from the restaurants and cafes of Roslyn Village. Leather furniture and designer kitchens add a touch of class, and it's a 10-minute downhill walk to the Octagon.

315 EURO Motel $$

(☎0800 387 638, 03-477 9929; www.eurodunedin.co.nz; 315 George St; d $150-250; [P] [🛜]) This sleek complex is in the absolute heart of George St's daytime retail strip and after-dark eating and drinking hub. Choose from modern studio apartments or larger one-bedroom apartments with full kitchens. Access via an alleyway is a bit odd, but soundproofing and double-glazed windows keeps George St's irresistible buzz at bay.

BROTHERS BOUTIQUE HOTEL Boutique Hotel $$$

(☎0800 477 004, 03-477 0043; www.brothershotel.co.nz; 295 Rattray St; d incl breakfast $170-320; [P] [@] [🛜]) Rooms in this distinctive old 1920s Christian Brothers residence have been refurbished beyond any monk's dreams, while still retaining many unique features. The chapel room ($320) includes the original arched stained-glass windows of its past life. There are great views from the rooftop units.

DUNEDIN PALMS MOTEL Motel $$

(☎0800 782 938, 03-477 8293; www.dunedinpalmsmotel.co.nz; 185-195 High St; d $170-210; [P] [@] [🛜]) A short stroll from the Speight's Ale House, the art-deco-style Palms has smartly decorated studios and one- and two-bedroom units arrayed around a central courtyard. You're handily just out of the centre, but don't have to endure a long walk uphill.

FLETCHER LODGE B&B $$$

(☎03-477 5552; www.fletcherlodge.co.nz; 276 High St; d $325-595, apt $650-750; [P] [@] [🛜]) Originally home to one of NZ's wealthy industrialist families, this gorgeous redbrick manor is just minutes from the city, but the secluded gardens feel wonderfully remote.

Detour:
Moeraki

About 76km north of Dunedin, stop to check out the **Moeraki Boulders** (Te Kaihinaki), a collection of large spherical boulders on a stunning stretch of beach, scattered about like a giant kid's discarded marbles. Try to time your visit with low tide.

Moeraki township is a charming fishing village. It's a nice 1½-hour walk along the beach between the village and the boulders. Head in the other direction towards the Kaiks wildlife trail and a cute old wooden lighthouse – a great spot to see yellow-eyed penguins and fur seals.

Fleur's Place (☎03-439 4480; www.fleursplace.com; Old Jetty; mains $25-38; ⊗10.30am-late Wed-Sat) has a rumble-tumble look about it, but this stylish timber hut serves up some of the South Island's best food. The speciality is seafood, fresh off Moeraki's fishing boats.

Rooms are elegantly trimmed with antique furniture and ornate plaster ceilings.

Eating

PLATO
Modern NZ $$

(☎03-477 4235; www.platocafe.co.nz; 2 Birch St; brunch mains $15-23, dinner mains $27-33; ⊗6pm-late Mon-Sat, 11am-late Sun) A regular contender in *Cuisine* magazine's Best of NZ gongs, Plato has a retro-themed location near the harbour and a strong beer and wine list. Try standouts like the Indian seafood curry or grilled salmon on potato gnocchi. Sunday brunch is worth the shortish trek from the centre. Bookings are recommended.

SCOTIA
Restaurant $$

(☎03-477 7704; www.scotiadunedin.co.nz; 199 Upper Stuart St; mains $18-32; ⊗lunch Mon-Fri, dinner Mon-Sat) Occupying a cosy heritage townhouse, Scotia toasts all things Scottish with a wall full of single malt whisky, and hearty fare such as smoked salmon and Otago rabbit. The two Scottish Robbies – Burns and Coltrane – look down approvingly on a menu that also includes haggis, and duck and whisky pâté.

BEST CAFE
Fish & Chips $$

(30 Stuart St; from $8; ⊗lunch & dinner, takeaway until late) Serving up fish and chips since 1932, this local icon has its winning formula down pat, complete with vinyl tablecloths, hand-cut chips and curls of butter on white bread. If there's two or more of you, try the 'Old School' platter with juicy oysters, whitebait, scallops, squid rings and fish of your choice ($29.50, or $35 with Bluff oysters).

PERC
Cafe $

(142 Lower Stuart St; mains $10-18) Always busy, and for good reason – the Perc is a grand place to kick-start your day. The decor's kinda retro and kinda art deco, and there's hearty cafe fare ranging from salmon bagels and *panini* to warming porridge.

GOVERNORS
Cafe $

(438 George St; mains $9-16) Popular with students, Governors does a nice line in early morning pancakes and other light meals. If you're feeling a little off the pace after the previous night, a strong coffee and an eggy omelette are just what the doctor ordered.

DUNEDIN FARMERS MARKET
Farmers Market $

(www.otagofarmersmarket.org.nz; Dunedin Railway Station, off Anzac Ave; ⊗8am-12.30pm Sat) The thriving Dunedin Farmers Market is all local, all eatable (or drinkable) and mostly organic. Grab felafels or espresso to sustain you while you browse, and stock up on fresh meats, seafood, vegies and cheese for your journey. Also pick up some locally brewed Green Man organic beer. Sorted.

Drinking & Entertainment

MOU VERY
Bar

(www.mouvery.co.nz; 357 George St)
Welcome to one of the world's smallest bars – it's only 1.8m wide, but is still big enough to host regular funk and soul DJ sessions most Fridays from 5pm. There are just six bar stools, so Mou Very's boho regulars usually spill out into an adjacent laneway. By day, it's a handy refuelling spot for your morning or afternoon espresso.

EUREKA
Bar

(www.eurekadunedin.co.nz; 116 Albany St)
Despite its proximity to occasional student sofa burnings around the corner on Hyde St, Eureka attracts a diverse crowd from first-year university newbies to their more grizzled tutors and other academics. The food's hearty and good value, and it's yet another Dunedin bar showcasing Kiwi microbreweries.

PEQUENO
Bar

(www.pequeno.co.nz; alleyway behind 12 Moray Pl; ⊙Mon-Sat) Down the alleyway opposite the Rialto cinema, Pequeno attracts a more sophisticated crowd with leather couches, a cosy fireplace and an excellent wine and tapas menu. Music is generally laid-back and never too loud to intrude on conversation.

XIIB
Bar

(www.bennu.co.nz/xiib.html; alleyway behind 12 Moray Pl; ⊙Tue-Sat) XIIB (aka 12 Below) is an intimate underground bar with comfy seats and couches, and cosy nooks aplenty. There's also floor space for live-music acts (look forward to lots of funk and reggae), or to wriggle along to hip-hop and drum and bass.

If You Like…
Dunedin's Caffeine Scene

If you like the coffee at Governors, here are a few other spots in Dunedin to kick-start your heart:

1 FIX
(15 Frederick St; ⊙closed Sun) Wage slaves queue at the pavement window every morning, while students and others with time on their hands relax in the courtyard. Fix doesn't serve food, but you can bring along your own food or takeaways.

2 MAZAGRAN ESPRESSO BAR
(36 Moray Pl; ⊙closed Sun) The godfather of Dunedin's coffee scene, this compact wood-and-brick coffee house is the source of the magic bean for many of the city's restaurants and cafes.

3 STRICTLY COFFEE
(23 Bath St; ⊙8am-4pm Mon-Fri) Stylish retro coffee bar hidden down grungy Bath St. Different rooms provide varying views and artworks to enjoy while you sip and sup.

URBAN FACTORY
Club

(www.urbanfactory.co.nz; 101 Great King St) The hippest of NZ's touring bands, regular DJ sessions and carefully-crafted cocktails.

SAMMY'S
Live Music

(65 Crawford St) Dunedin's premier live-music venue draws an eclectic mix of genres from noisy-as-hell punk to chilled reggae and gritty dubstep. It's also usually venue of choice for visiting Kiwi bands and up-and-coming international acts.

CHICK'S HOTEL
Live Music

(Map p302; Search Facebook for 'Friends of Chicks'; 2 Mount St; ⊙hours vary) Across in Port Chalmers, Chick's is the archetypal rock-and-roll pub, hosting everything from US alt-country bands to local metal noise merchants. Catch bus 13 or 14 from Cumberland St in Dunedin.

Otago Peninsula

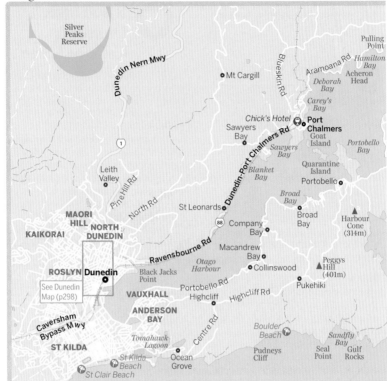

ℹ️ Information

Dunedin Hospital (📞03-474 0999, emergency department 0800 611 116; www.southerndhb. govt.nz; 201 Great King St)

Urgent Doctors & Accident Centre (📞03-479 2900; 95 Hanover St; 🕐8am-11.30pm) Also a pharmacy open outside normal business hours.

DOC (Department of Conservation; 📞03-477 0677; www.doc.govt.nz; 1st fl, 77 Lower Stuart St; 🕐8.30am-5pm Mon-Fri) Information and maps on regional walking tracks and Great Walks bookings.

Dunedin i-SITE (📞03-474 3300; www. dunedinnz.com; 26 Princes St; 🕐8.30am-5pm Mon-Fri, 8.45am-5pm Sat & Sun) Accommodation, activities, transport and walking tours.

ℹ️ Getting There & Away

Air

Air New Zealand (📞0800 737 000; www. airnewzealand.co.nz) flies from Dunedin to Christchurch, Wellington and Auckland. Australian destinations are Brisbane, Sydney and Melbourne. Pacific Blue links Dunedin to Melbourne and Brisbane, and Jetstar flies to Auckland.

Bus

InterCity (📞03-471 7143; www.intercity.co.nz; 205 St Andrew St; 🕐ticket office 7.30am-5pm Mon-Fri, 11am-3pm Sat, 11am-5.15pm Sun, tickets by phone 7am-9pm daily) has services to Oamaru (one hour 40 minutes), Christchurch (six hours), Queenstown (4½ hours), Te Anau (4½ hours) and Invercargill – via Gore (four hours). Buses leave from St Andrew St.

0 _____ 5 km
0 _____ 2.5 miles

Aramoana ●   **Royal Albatross**
Pilot Beach ●   **Centre**
(88)   Harrington ●   Taiaroa
  Point   Head
Te Rauone Beach   **Yellow-Eyed**
  Penguin
Otago   **Otakou**   **Conservation**
Harbour   **Marae**   **Reserve**
   Pipikaretu
   Beach
Harwood
Harrington Point Rd
   Wickliffe
   Bay
Weir Rd   Dick Rd
   Victory
   Beach
Papanui Inlet
Mckay Rd
Cape Saunders Rd
Mt Charles   Papanui
(408m)   Beach
Hoopers
Inlet   Allans Beach Rd
Allans   Cape
Beach   Saunders
Lighthouse

Chasm   SOUTH PACIFIC
    OCEAN

Naked Bus (www.nakedbus.com) connects Dunedin with Christchurch (six hours) and Invercargill (four hours). Buses leave from the **Citibus Transport Centre** (630 Princes St).

Southern Link (✆0508 458 835; www. southernlinkcoaches.co.nz) connects Dunedin to Christchurch (six hours), Oamaru (one hour 50 minutes) and Invercargill (three hours 40 minutes).

A couple of services connect Dunedin to the Catlins and Southland. The **Bottom Bus** (✆03-477 9083; www.bottombus.co.nz) does a circuit from Dunedin through the Catlins to Invercargill, Te Anau, Queenstown and back to Dunedin. **Catlins Coaster** (✆03-477 9083; www. catlinscoaster.co.nz) connects Dunedin with Invercargill, returning via the scenic Catlins.

Other services:

Atomic Shuttles (✆03-349 0697; www.atomic travel.co.nz) To/from Christchurch (six hours),

Oamaru (two hours), Invercargill (four hours), and Queenstown and Wanaka (both four hours).

Trail Journeys (✆03-449-2024; www. trailjourneys.co.nz) Door-to-door daily between Dunedin and Wanaka stopping at Otago Central Rail Trail towns along the way. Bikes can be transported.

Wanaka Connexions (✆03-443 9120; www. alpinecoachlines.co.nz) Shuttles between Dunedin and Wanaka (four hours) and Queenstown (four hours).

❶ Getting Around

To & From the Airport

Dunedin Airport (DUD; ✆03-486 2879; www. dnairport.co.nz) is 27km southwest of the city. A door-to-door shuttle is around $15 per person. Try **Kiwi Shuttles** (✆03-487 9790; www. kiwishuttles.co.nz), **Super Shuttle** (✆0800 748 885; www.supershuttle.co.nz) or **Southern Taxis** (✆03-476 6300; www.southerntaxis.co.nz). There is no public bus service.

A standard taxi ride between the city and the airport costs around $80.

Bus

City buses (✆03-474 0287; www.orc.govt.nz) Buses run regularly during the week, but services are greatly reduced (or nonexistent) on weekends and holidays.

Taxi

Dunedin Taxis (✆03-477 7777, 0800 50 50 10; www.dunedintaxis.co.nz)

Otago Taxis (✆03-477 3333).

Otago Peninsula

Otago Peninsula has the South Island's most accessible diversity of wildlife. Albatross, penguins, fur seals and sea lions provide a natural background to rugged countryside, wild walks and beaches, and interesting historical sites. Get the *Otago Peninsula* brochure and map from the Dunedin i-SITE and visit www.otago -peninsula.co.nz.

Sights

FREE **ROYAL ALBATROSS CENTRE** Wildlife Reserve
(✆03-478 0499; www.albatross.org.nz; Taiaroa Head; ⊙9am-dusk summer, 10am-4pm winter) Taiaroa Head, at the peninsula's eastern tip, has the world's only mainland royal albatross colony. The best time to visit is from December to February, when one parent is constantly guarding the young while the other delivers food throughout the day. Sightings are most common in the afternoon when the winds pick up, and calm days don't see much bird action. The only public access is through the Royal Albatross Centre where 45-minute tours (adult/child/family $40/20/100) include viewing from a glassed-in hut overlooking the nesting sites. There's no viewing from mid-September to late November, and from late November to December the birds are nestbound so it's difficult to see their magnificent wingspan. Ask the staff whether the birds are flying before you pay.

YELLOW-EYED PENGUIN CONSERVATION RESERVE Wildlife Reserve
(✆03-478 0286; www.penguinplace.co.nz; McGrouther's Farm, Harington Point Rd; tours adult/child $49/12) Activities include building nesting sites, caring for sick and injured birds, and trapping predators. Ninety-minute tours focus on penguin conservation and close-up viewing from a system of hides.

 Activities

The peninsula's coastal and farmland walkways offer stunning views and the chance to see wildlife on your own. Pick up a free copy of the detailed *Otago Peninsula Tracks* from the Dunedin i-SITE. A popular walking destination is the beautiful **Sandfly Bay**, reached from Seal Point Rd (moderate; 40 minutes) or Ridge Rd (difficult; 40 minutes).

WILD EARTH ADVENTURES Kayaking
(✆03-489 1951; www.wildearth.co.nz; trips from $115) Offers trips in double sea kayaks, with wildlife often sighted en route. Trips run between four hours and a full day.

Otago Central Rail Trail

Stretching from Dunedin to Clyde, the Central Otago rail branch linked small, inland goldfield towns with the big city from the early 20th century through to the 1990s. After the 150km stretch from Middlemarch to Clyde was permanently closed, the rails were ripped up and the trail resurfaced. The result is a year-round trail that takes bikers, walkers and horseback riders along a historic route containing old rail bridges, viaducts and tunnels. With excellent trailside facilities (toilets, shelters and information), no steep hills, gob-smacking scenery and profound remoteness, the trail attracts well over 25,000 visitors annually.

The trail can be followed in either direction. The entire trail takes approximately four to five days to complete by bike (or a week on foot), but you can obviously choose to do as short or long a stretch as suits your plans. There are also easy detours to towns such as Naseby and St Bathans. Many settlements along the route offer accommodation and dining, including lodgings in restored cottages and rural farmhouses.

Mountain bikes can be rented in Dunedin, Middlemarch, Alexandra and Clyde. Any of the area's major i-SITEs can provide detailed information. See www.otagocentralrailtrail.co.nz and www.otagorailtrail.co.nz for track information, recommended timings, accommodation options and tour companies.

Some trips start in Dunedin and some on the peninsula.

Tours

BACK TO NATURE TOURS Wildlife
(📞0800 528 767, 03-478 0499; www.backtonaturetours.co.nz; adult/child $95/55) Good-value peninsula tours getting you up close and personal with yellow-eyed penguins, NZ fur seals and sea lions. From November to March an optional tour is a spectacular coastal hike (adult/child $85/45).

CITIBUS Wildlife
(📞03-477 5577; www.citibus.co.nz; adult/child from $95/47.50) Tours combining albatross and penguin viewing.

❶ Getting There & Around

Up to 10 buses travel each weekday between Dunedin's Cumberland St and Portobello Village, with one or two a day continuing on to Harington Point. Weekend services are more limited. Once on the peninsula, it's tough to get around without your own transport. Most tours will pick you up from your Dunedin accommodation.

There's a petrol station in Portobello, but opening hours are unpredictable. Fill up in Dunedin before driving out.

Central Otago

Rolling hills, grassy paddocks and a succession of tiny, charming gold-rush towns make this region worth exploring. Naseby and Clyde compete for the title of NZ's cutest towns, and rugged, laconic 'Southern Man' types can be seen propping up the bar in backcountry hotels. There are also fantastic opportunities for those on two wheels, whether mountain biking along old gold-mining trails, or taking it easy on the Otago Rail Trail.

FIORDLAND

Fiordland is NZ's rawest wilderness area, a jagged, mountainous, forested zone sliced by numerous deeply recessed sounds (which are technically fiords) reaching inland like crooked fingers from the Tasman Sea. Part of the Te Wahipounamu Southwest New Zealand World Heritage Area, it remains formidable and remote.

Te Anau

Peaceful, lakeside Te Anau township is a good base for trampers and visitors to Milford Sound, and an ideal place to recharge or get active in the surrounding landscapes.

 Activities

Tramping

Register your intentions at the **Department of Conservation Visitor Centre** (📞03-249 0200; www.doc.govt.nz; cnr Lakefront Dr & Manapouri Hwy; ⏰8.30am-4.30pm).

KEPLER TRACK

This 60km circular Great Walk starts less than an hour's walk from Te Anau and heads west into the Kepler Mountains, taking in the lake, rivers, gorges, glacier-carved valleys and beech forest. The walk can be done in four days, or three if you exit at Rainbow Reach. It's recommended that the track be done in the Luxmore–Iris Burn–Moturau direction.

During the main walking season (October to April), advance bookings must be made by all trampers online at www.doc.govt.nz or at any DOC visitor centre.

SHORT WALKS

Set out along the Kepler Track on free day walks. **Kepler Water Taxi** (📞03-249 8364; stevsaunders@xtra.co.nz; 1 way/return $25/50) will scoot you over to Brod Bay from where you can walk to Mt Luxmore (seven to eight hours) or along the southern lakeshore back to Te Anau (two to three hours). Regular shuttles leave Te Anau lakefront at 8.30am and 9.30am during summer.

During summer, **Trips'n'Tramps** (📞03-249 7081, 0800 305 807; www.tripsandtramps.com; ⏰Oct-Apr) offers small-group, guided hikes on sections of the Routeburn and Kepler and Hollyford Tracks. Some departures incorporate kayaking on Milford Sound. **Real Journeys** (📞0800 656 501; www.realjourneys.co.nz; ⏰9am-5pm) runs guided day hikes (adult/child $195/127, November to mid-April) along an 11km stretch of the Milford Track.

Grab a copy of *Fiordland National Park Day Walks* ($1 from the Fiordland i-SITE or free at www.doc.govt.nz).

Kayaking

FIORDLAND WILDERNESS
EXPERIENCES   Kayaking
(0800 200 434; www.fiordlandseakayak. co.nz; from $145) One-day and multiday kayaking explorations of Lake Te Anau and Lake Manapouri. Prices start at $145 per day.

 ## Tours

SOUTHERN LAKES
HELICOPTERS   Scenic Flights
(03-249 7167; www.southernlakeshelicopters. co.nz; Lakefront Dr) Flights over Te Anau for 25 minutes ($195), longer trips over Doubtful, Dusky and Milford Sounds (from $540), and a chopper/walk/boat option on the Kepler Track ($185).

WINGS & WATER
TE ANAU   Scenic Flights
(03-249 7405; www.wingsandwater.co.nz; Lakefront Dr) Ten-minute local flights (adult/child $95/55), and longer flights over the Kepler Track and Doubtful and Milford Sounds (from $225).

 ## Sleeping

TE ANAU LODGE B&B   B&B $$$
(03-249 7477; www.teanaulodge.com; 52 Howden St; d $240-350; @ 🖥) The former 1930s-built Sisters of Mercy Convent, relocated to a grand location just north of town, is a positively decadent accommodation option. Sip your drink in a Chesterfield in front of the fire, retire to your spa before collapsing on a king-size bed, then awaken to a fresh, delicious breakfast in the old chapel.

BLUE MOUNTAIN
COTTAGES   Lodge $$$
(03-249 9030; www.bluemountaincottages. co.nz; Hwy 95; cabins $260) These family-friendly self-contained cabins surrounded by farmland 8km south of town can sleep up to four. Fresh-baked goods, free-range eggs, and organic produce and vegies are often available for guests.

COSY KIWI   Motel $$
(0800 249 700, 03-249 7475; www.cosykiwi. com; 186 Milford Rd; d $150-210; @ 🖥) This smart motel with modern, well-appointed rooms is just a short stroll from bustling central Te Anau. Breakfast is included, and host Eleanor usually offers a couple of cooked options.

 ## Eating & Drinking

FAT DUCK   Restaurant $$
(03-249 8480; 124 Town Centre; breakfast $10-17, lunch & dinner mains $22-38; 🕐 8.30am-late; 🖥) Dishes are tasty and hearty in proportions, with imaginative variations on crispy duck, pork belly and salmon. There's a bar as long as Doubtful Sound if you just want a drink before kicking on somewhere else.

REDCLIFF BAR &
RESTAURANT   Restaurant $$$
(03-249 7431; 12 Mokonui St; mains $29-42; 🕐 5pm-late) Housed in a replica old settler's cottage, Redcliff showcases locally sourced produce in a convivial atmosphere. Try the wild Fiordland venison or tender herby hare. There's occasional live music and a permanent friendly vibe with excellent service.

RANCH BAR & GRILL   Pub
(Town Centre) Look forward to happy hour from 8pm to 9pm and good-value Sunday-night roast dinners ($15). It's the locals' choice for the best pub meals in town.

ℹ️ Information

DOC Visitor Centre (Department of Conservation; 03-249 0200; www.doc.govt.nz; cnr Lakefront Dr & Manapouri Hwy; 🕐 8.30am-4.30pm) Includes the Great Walks counter for bookings and confirmed tickets for the Milford, Routeburn and Kepler Tracks.

Fiordland i-SITE (☏03-249 8900; www.fiordland. org.nz; 85 Lakefront Dr; ⊙8.30am-5.30pm) Activities, accommodation and bus bookings.

Real Journeys (☏0800 656 501; www. realjourneys.co.nz; ⊙9am-5pm) Fiordland-focused tours and activities.

Getting There & Away

InterCity (www.intercity.co.nz) has daily bus services between Te Anau and Queenstown (2½ hours), Invercargill (2½ hours) and Dunedin (4¾ hours).

Bottom Bus (☏03-477 9083; http:// travelheadfirst.com/bottom-bus/) is a hop-on, hop-off bus service linking Te Anau to Queenstown, Invercargill and Milford Sound (1½ hours), and **Naked Bus** (www.nakedbus.com) links Te Anau with Queenstown (2½ hours), Invercargill (2½ hours) and Milford Sound (1½ hours).

From November to April, **Topline Tours** (☏03-249 8059; www.toplinetours.co.nz) run a Te Anau–Queenstown shuttle.

Te Anau–Milford Hwy

If you don't have the opportunity to hike into Fiordland's wilderness, the 119km road from Te Anau to Milford is the most easily accessible taste of its vastness and beauty.

The trip takes two to 2½ hours if you drive straight through, but take time to stop and experience the majestic landscape.

Milford Track

The 53.5km Milford Track is one of the world's finest walks. The number of walkers is limited in the Great Walks season (late October to late April), and you must follow a one-way, four-day set itinerary. Accommodation is only in huts (camping isn't allowed).

You can walk the track independently or with a guided tour. For independent bookings, contact DOC in Te Anau or book online at www.doc.govt.nz.

The track must be booked during the Great Walks season (late October to late April).

Ultimate Hikes (☏03-450 1940, 0800 659 255; www.ultimatehikes.co.nz; adult/child Dec-

Mar from $1995/1790, Apr & Nov $1830/1640) has five-day guided walks staying at private lodges. A one-day 11km sampler is also available (adult/child $195/123).

 **Sleeping**

MILFORD SOUND LODGE   Lodge $$
(☏03-249 8071; www.milfordlodge.com; just off SH94; sites per person from $18, dm $30-33, d $85) Alongside the Cleddau River, this simple but comfortable lodge has an un-hurried, ends-of-the-earth air. There's no TV, and travellers and trampers relax in the large lounges to discuss their experiences. There's a tiny shop-cafe-bar and a free shuttle to Milford Sound, just 1.5km away. Very comfortable chalets ($255) enjoy an absolute riverside location.

KNOB'S FLAT   Motel $$
(☏03-249 9122; www.knobsflat.co.nz; sites per person $10, studio/motel units $120/150) In the grassy Eglinton Valley, 63km from Te Anau, Knob's Flat has comfortable units catering to walkers and anglers. TV, email and stress have no place here, and mountain bikes can be hired.

Milford Sound

The first sight of Milford Sound is stunning. Sheer rocky cliffs rise out of still, dark waters, and forests clinging to the slopes sometimes relinquish their hold, causing a 'tree avalanche' into the waters. The spectacular, photogenic 1692m-high Mitre Peak rises dead ahead.

 Activities

ROSCO'S MILFORD KAYAKS   Kayaking
(☏0800 476 726, 03-249 8500; www.roscosmil fordkayaks.com; trips $130-175) Recommended excursions include the 'Morning Glory', a challenging early-morning kayak (around five hours in the boat) the full length of the fiord to Anita Bay, and the 'Stirling Sunriser', which includes kayaking under the 151m-high Stirling Falls. Another option includes a 20-minute paddle around Deepwater Basin to Sandfly

MICAH WRIGHT / LONELY PLANET IMAGES ©

Don't Miss **Doubtful Sound**

Massive, magnificent Doubtful Sound is a wilderness area of rugged peaks, dense forest and thundering post-rain waterfalls. It's one of NZ's largest sounds: three times the length and 10 times the area of Milford Sound. Doubtful is also much, *much* less trafficked. If you have the time and the money, it's an essential experience. Fur seals, dolphins, Fiordland crested penguins and seals are also regular visitors.

Doubtful Sound is only accessible by tour. **Real Journeys** has a Wilderness Cruise day trip (adult/child $235/65), beginning with a 45-minute boat ride across Lake Manapouri to West Arm power station, followed by a bus ride over Wilmot Pass to the sound, which you explore on a three-hour cruise. Pick-up options from Te Anau or Queenstown are also available. From September to May, Real Journeys also runs a Doubtful Sound overnight cruise.

Other options include **Adventure Kayak & Cruise**, which offers kayaking day trips ($239) and overnight kayaking and camping trips ($269). **Deep Cove Charters** runs intimate overnight cruises with a maximum of 12 passengers. This includes meals, and you can fish for your own dinner. **Fiordland Explorer Charters** offers a day cruise with maximum of 20 people, which includes power-station tour and three hours on the sound.

NEED TO KNOW

Real Journeys (☎0800 656 501; www.realjourneys.co.nz); **Adventure Kayak & Cruise** (☎0800 324 966; www.fiordlandadventure.co.nz; ◷late Sep-May); **Deep Cove Charters** (☎0800 249 682; www.doubtful-sound.com; bunk beds per person $500, private cabin $1200); **Fiordland Explorer Charters** (☎0800 434 673; www.doubtfulsoundcruise.com; day cruise adult/child $220/80)

Point and a 3½-hour walk on the Milford Track ($89).

FIORDLAND WILDERNESS EXPERIENCES Kayaking
(0800 200 434, 03-249-7700; www.seakayak fiordland.co.nz; per person $145; Sep-Apr) Guided six-hour paddles on Milford Sound.

 Tours

REAL JOURNEYS Boat Tour
(Map p284; 0800 656 501; 03-249 7416; www. realjourneys.co.nz; adult/child from $68/22) Lots of cruises from this big company including 1¾-hour scenic cruises (adult $68 to $90, child $22). The company also does 2½-hour nature cruises (adult $75 to $95, child $22) with a nature guide for commentary and Q&A.

JUCY CRUIZE Boat Tour
(0800 500 121; www.jucycruize.co.nz; adult/ child from $65/15) A smaller, less-crowded experience with 1½-hour trips on a comfortable boat with lots of deck space.

MITRE PEAK CRUISES Boat Tour
(0800 744 633, 03-249 8110; www.mitrepeak. com; adult/child from $68/16.50) Cruises in smallish boats with a maximum capacity of 75. The 4.30pm cruise is good because many larger boats are heading back at this time.

 Eating & Drinking

BLUE DUCK CAFÉ & BAR Cafe $$
(snacks $5-15, buffet lunch $17-21; cafe 8.30am-4pm, bar 4pm-late; @ P) Serving sandwiches and a lunch buffet, and at night the attached bar sees a mix of travellers and trampers tucking in to the $25 beer and pizza deal.

 Getting There & Away

Bus

InterCity (www.intercity.co.nz) runs daily bus services from Queenstown (4½ hours) and Te Anau

(1½ hours). **Naked Bus** (www.nakedbus.com) also runs from Te Anau to Milford Sound. Many bus trips include a boat cruise on the sound; most are around $150 from Te Anau (or around $200 from Queenstown).

SOUTHLAND
Southern Scenic Route

The quiet, unhurried Southern Scenic Route begins in Queenstown and heads south via Te Anau to Tuatapere, Riverton and Invercargill. From Invercargill it continues north through the Catlins to Dunedin. See www.southernscenicroute. co.nz or pick up *Southern Scenic Route* free map.

Tuatapere Hump Ridge Track

The excellent 53km Tuatapere Hump Ridge Track climbs to craggy subalpine heights with views north to Fiordland and south to Stewart Island, and then descends through lush native forests of rimu and beech to the rugged coast. En route the path crosses a number of towering historic wooden viaducts, including NZ's highest. Beginning and ending at Bluecliffs Beach on Te Waewae Bay, 20km from Tuatapere, the track takes three fairly long days to complete.

It's essential to book for this track, which is administered privately rather than by DOC. Contact **Tuatapere Hump Ridge Track** (03-226 6739; www. humpridgetrack.co.nz). No-frills summer bookings cost from $130 for two nights, and there are also guided, jetboating and helihiking options.

The Catlins

If you veer off SH1 and head for the coastal route between Invercargill and Dunedin (via SH92), you wind through the enchanting Catlins, a region that combines lush farmland, native forests and rugged bays. With bushwalks, wildlife-spotting opportunities and lonely beaches to explore, the Catlins is well worth a couple of days.

Activities

CATLINS
ADVENTURES Adventure Tour

(☎03-415 8339, 027 416 8822; www.catlins
adventures.co.nz; 5 Ocean Gr; per person 1/2
days $175/295) Energetic, switched-on
operators offering one- and two-day
Catlins scenic tours, river walking ($75
per person), rainforest kayaking ($75 per
person) and yellow-eyed penguin viewing
($89 per person). Catlins Adventures
have exclusive access to certain areas
of the Catlins, and mountain bikes and
kayaks are also available for hire.

CATLINS
WILDLIFE TRACKERS Wildlife

(☎0800 228 5467, 03-415 8613; www.catlins
-ecotours.co.nz) Papatowai-based Catlins
Wildlife Trackers offer eco-centric guided
walks and tours (three days/two nights
$800),including all food, accommoda-
tion and transport. Guided trips focusing
on wildlife are also available.

Tours

BOTTOM BUS Tour

(☎03-477 9083; www.bottombus.co.nz; from
$175) Does a regular loop from Queenstown
to Dunedin, south through the Catlins to Invercargill, along the Southern Scenic Route
to Te Anau, then back to Queenstown. It
stops at all main points of interest, and you
can hop off and catch the next bus coming
through. There are lots of pass options.
The Southlander pass ($375) lets you
start anywhere on the loop and includes a
Milford Sound cruise.

CATLINS COASTER Tour

(☎03-477 9083; www.catlinscoaster.co.nz; from
$210) Run by Bottom Bus and offering
day tours and trips through the Catlins
from Dunedin and Invercargill. Check the
website for details. Departures are more
limited in winter.

ℹ Information

Contact the main Catlins information centre
(☎03-415 8371; www.cluthacountry.co.nz;
20 Ryley St; ⊙9.30am-1pm & 1.30-4.30pm
Mon-Fri, 10am-4pm Sat & Sun) in Owaka or the
smaller Waikawa visitors centre (☎03-205
8006; waikawamuseum@hyper.net.nz; Main Rd;
⊙10am-5pm; @). The i-SITEs in Invercargill
and Balclutha also have lots of Catlins
information. Online see www.catlins.org.nz and
www.catlins-nz.com.

The Best of the Rest

Bay of Islands (p312)

Much more than a gorgeous bay festooned with islands and dolphins, this part of Northland is where both Maori and pakeha New Zealanders have their roots.

Taranaki (p318)

New Zealand's best-looking peak is well worth checking out. Down on the coast is New Plymouth with its impressive museum, art gallery and caffeine scene.

Stewart Island (p322)

New Zealand's third-biggest island is oft overlooked... But if you're looking for quirky, far-flung wilderness and wildlife experiences, you're in for a treat.

Top: Tramping above Mason Bay, Rakiura National Parkl (p322)
Left: Mt Taranaki (p321)

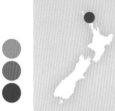

Bay of Islands

HIGHLIGHTS

1 **Sailing & Cruising (p312)** Count dolphins and gorgeous uninhabited islands.

2 **Russell (p314)** Hell-hole turned holiday haven.

3 **Waitangi Treaty Grounds (p316)** The birthplace of modern NZ.

Dolphin, Bay of Islands
BEN LEWIS/ALAMY ©

Undeniably pretty, the Bay of Islands ranks as one of NZ's top tourist drawcards. The footage that made you want to come to NZ in the first place no doubt featured lingering shots of lazy, sun-filled days on a yacht floating atop these turquoise waters punctuated by around 150 undeveloped islands.

 Activities

DIVE NORTH Diving
(09-402 5369; www.divenorth.co.nz; reef & wreck $220) Experienced operators based in Kerikeri but offering free pick-ups from Paihia. Covers all the local dive sites and offers PADI courses.

COASTAL KAYAKERS Kayaking
(0800 334 661; www.coastalkayakers.co.nz; Te Karuwha Pde, Paihia) Runs guided tours (half/full day $75/95, minimum two people) and multiday adventures. Kayaks (per hour/half/full day $15/40/50) and snorkelling gear (per day $15) can also be rented.

SKYDIVE ZONE Skydiving
(09-407 7057; www.skydivezoneboi .co.nz; Kerikeri Airport; tandem jump from 16,000/12,000/8000ft $395/325/265) At the time of research, this operator offered the highest tandem jump on the North Island and one of the most scenic.

FLYING KIWI PARASAIL Parasailing
(09-402 6068; www.parasail-nz.co.nz; solo $99, tandem $89) Departs from both Paihia and Russell wharves for NZ's highest parasail (1200ft).

 Tours

Boat

Of all the bay's islands, perhaps the most striking is **Piercy Island (Motukokako)** off Cape Brett, at the bay's eastern edge. This steep-walled rock fortress is rent by a vast natural arch – the famous **Hole in the Rock**.

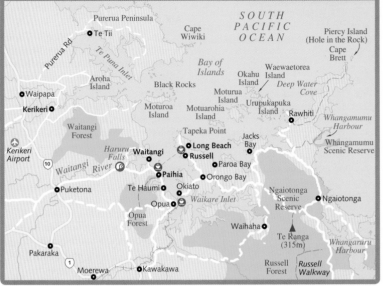

The best way to explore the bay is under sail. In most cases you can either help crew the boat (no experience required), or just spend the afternoon island-hopping, sunbathing, swimming, snorkelling, kayaking and fishing.

EXPLORE NZ
Cruises, Sailing

(09-402 8234; www.explorenz.co.nz; cnr Marsden & Williams Rds, Paihia) This outfit's swim with the Dolphins Cruise (adult/child $89/45) is a four-hour trip departing at 8am and 12.30pm, with an additional $30 payable if you choose to swim. If you'd like to see dolphins but prefer to stay dry, the four-hour Discover the Bay Cruise (adult/child $95/48) departs at 9am and 1.30pm, heading to the Hole in the Rock and stopping at Urupukapuka Island. This cruise is combined with a trip to Kerikeri Basin in the seven-hour Day Discovery Cruise (adult/child $109/45).

If you've a taste for speed, Ocean Adventure (adult/child $95/48) is a 2½-hour blast on a rigid-hulled inflatable to the Hole in the Rock.

FULLERS GREAT SIGHTS
Cruises

(0800 653 339; www.dolphincruises.co.nz; Paihia Wharf) The four-hour Dolphin Cruise (adult/child $95/48) departs daily at 9am and 1.30pm, actively seeking out dolphins and any other marine mammals en route to the Hole in the Rock, stopping at Urupukapuka Island on the way back.

A glamorous option for an overnight cruise is the launch **Ipipiri** (www.overnight cruise.co.nz; s/d $563/750). On this floating hotel the accommodation is by way of en-suite state rooms. All meals are included, and if you get sick of lazing around the bar on the sundeck, you can partake in kayaking, snorkelling or island walks.

TUCKER THOMPSON
Sailing

(09-402 8430; www.tucker.co.nz) Run by a charitable trust with an education focus, the *Tucker* is a majestic tall ship offering day sails (adult/child $145/73, including a barbecue lunch) and late afternoon cruises (adult/child $69/35). Talking like a pirate is optional.

CARINO
Dolphin Swimming

(☎09-402 8040; www.sailingdolphins.co.nz; adult/child $114/69) This 50ft catamaran is the only yacht licensed for swimming with dolphins. A barbecue lunch is available for $6.

ECOCRUZ
Sailing

(☎0800 432 627; www.ecocruz.co.nz; dm/d $595/1350) A highly recommended three-day/two-night sailing cruise aboard the 72ft ocean-going yacht *Manawanui,* with an emphasis on the marine environment. Prices include accommodation, food, fishing, kayaking and snorkelling.

GUNGHA II
Sailing

(☎0800 478 900; www.bayofislandssailing. co.nz; day sail $90) A beautiful 65ft ocean yacht with a friendly crew; lunch included.

MACK ATTACK
Jetboating

(☎0800 622 528; www.mackattack.co.nz; 9 Williams Rd, Paihia; adult/child $89/40) Fasten your seatbelt for a high-speed 1½-hour Hole in the Rock trip on board a jetboat – good fun and handy if you're short on time.

Maori

NATIVE NATURE TOURS
Cultural, Tramping

(☎0800 668 873; www.nativenaturetours. co.nz; 581 Tipene Rd, Motatau; day tramps $190, overnight $375) A local couple formally welcome you to their *marae* and lead you on tramps into their ancestral lands, including visits to sacred sites and an introduction to Maori food and medicine. Overnight stays include a traditional *hangi* (earth-cooked meal) and glowworm spotting.

Other

SALT AIR
Scenic Flights

(☎09-402 8338; www.saltair.co.nz; Marsden Rd, Paihia) Offers a range of scenic flights, including a five-hour light aircraft and 4WD tour to Cape Reinga and Ninety Mile Beach ($425) and helicopter flights out to the Hole in the Rock ($220).

Getting There & Around

AIR

Air New Zealand (☎0800 737 000; www.airnz .co.nz) Daily flights from Auckland to Whangarei (35 minutes), Kerikeri (40 minutes) and Kaitaia (45 minutes), and from Wellington to Whangarei (2½ hours).

Salt Air Xpress (☎09-402 8338; www.saltair .co.nz) Flies from Kerikeri to Whangarei (20 minutes) and then on to Auckland's North Shore (30 minutes), every day except Saturday.

BUS

InterCity (☎09-583 5780; www.intercity.co.nz) InterCity and associated Northliner services head from Auckland to Kerikeri via Waipu, Whangarei and Paihia; and from Paihia to Kaitaia via Kerikeri, Mangonui and Coopers Beach.

Naked Bus (☎per min $1.99 0900 625 33; www.nakedbus.com) Has daily buses from Auckland to Paihia (3¾ hours), via Warkworth, Waipu, Whangarei and Kawakawa.

Russell

Although it was once known prosaically as 'the hellhole of the Pacific', those coming to Russell for debauchery will be sadly disappointed: they've missed the orgies on the beach by 170 years. Instead they'll find a sweetly historic town that is a bastion of gift shops and B&Bs.

Sights

CHRIST CHURCH
Church

(Church St) Creationists may be surprised to learn that Charles Darwin made a donation towards the cost of the construction of this, the country's oldest church (1836).

RUSSELL MUSEUM
Museum

(www.russellmuseum.org.nz; 2 York St; adult/ child $7.50/2; ⏰10am-4pm) This small, modern museum has a well-presented Maori section, a large 1:5-scale model of Captain Cook's *Endeavour* and a 10-minute video on the town's history.

Tours

RUSSELL MINI TOURS Minibus
(☎0800 64 64 86; www.dolphincruises.co.nz;
cnr The Strand & Cass St; adult/child $29/14;
⏱10am, 11am, 1pm, 2pm, 3pm & 4pm) Minibus
tour with commentary.

 Sleeping

ARCADIA LODGE B&B $$$
(☎09-403 7756; www.arcadialodge.co.nz; 10
Florance Ave; d $195-310; 🛜) The character-
ful rooms of this 1890 hillside house are
decked out with interesting antiques and
fine linen, while the breakfast is probably
the best you'll eat in town – organic, deli-
cious and complemented with spectacu-
lar views from the deck.

COMMODORE'S LODGE Motel $$$
(☎09-403 7899; www.commodoreslodgemotel
.co.nz; 28 The Strand; units $200-295; 🛜🏊)
Being the envy of every passer-by
makes up for the lack of privacy in the
front apartments facing the waterfront
promenade. Spacious, nicely presented
units are the order of the day here,
along with a small pool and free kayaks,
dinghies and bikes.

**HANANUI LODGE &
APARTMENTS** Motel $$$
(☎09-403 7875; www.hananui.co.nz; 4 York
St; units $190-320; 🛜) Choose between
sparkling motel-style units in the trim
waterside lodge or apartments in the
newer block across the road. Pick of the
bunch are the upstairs waterfront units
with views straight over the beach.

**DUKE OF
MARLBOROUGH** Historic Hotel $$
(☎09-403 7829; www.theduke.co.nz; 35 The
Strand; r $165-360; 🛜) Holding NZ's oldest
pub license, the Duke boasts about 'serving rascals and reprobates since 1827',
although the building has burnt down
twice since then. The upstairs accommodation ranges from small, bright rooms
in a 1930s extension to snazzy, spacious
doubles facing the water.

The Gables restaurant (p316), Russell

JOHN ELK III/LONELY PLANET IMAGES ©

PAUL KENNEDY/LONELY PLANET IMAGES ©

Don't Miss **Waitangi Treaty Grounds**

It was here on 6 February 1840 that the first 43 Maori chiefs, after much discussion, signed the Treaty of Waitangi with the British Crown (eventually more than 500 would sign it).

The **Treaty House** was built in 1832 as the four-room home of British resident James Busby. It's now preserved as a memorial and museum containing displays, which include a copy of the treaty. Just across the lawn, the magnificently detailed **whare runanga** (meeting house) was completed in 1940 to mark the centenary of the treaty.

International visitors will get more out of what is already quite a pricy admission fee if they pay extra for a guided tour or cultural performance (adult/child $18/10 for each; check the website or call for times).

Finally, the two-hour **Culture North Night Show** is a dramatisation of Maori history held in the *whare runanga*. Free transfers from Paihia are included in the price.

NEED TO KNOW

Waitangi Treaty Grounds (☎09-402 7437; www.waitangi.net.nz; 1 Tau Henare Dr; adult/child $25/12; ⊗9am-5pm Apr-Sep, 9am-7pm Oct-Mar); **Culture North Night Show** (☎09-402 5990; www.culturenorth.co.nz; admission $65; ⊗7.30pm when numbers allow)

 Eating

GABLES   Modern NZ $$
(☎09-403 7670; www.thegablesrestaurant.co.nz; 19 The Strand; mains $27-42) Serving an imaginative take on Kiwi classics (lamb, beef and lots of seafood), the Gables occupies an 1847 building on the waterfront, built using whale vertebrae for foundations. Ask for a table by the windows for watery views.

TUK TUK   Thai $$
(19 York St; mains $15-24; ⊗10.30am-11pm; ☞) Thai fabrics adorn the tables and Thai favourites fill the menu. In clement weather grab a table out front and watch Russell's little world go by.

ℹ️ Information

ℹ️ Getting There & Away

The quickest way to reach Russell by car is via the car ferry (car/motorcycle/passenger $11/5.50/1), which runs every 10 minutes from Opua (5km from Paihia) to Okiato (8km from Russell), between 6.40am and 10pm.

Paihia & Waitangi

The birthplace of NZ (as opposed to Aotearoa), Waitangi inhabits a special, somewhat complex place in the national psyche – aptly demonstrated by the mixture of celebration, commemoration, protest and apathy that accompanies the nation's birthday (Waitangi Day, 6 February).

It was here that the long-neglected and much-contested Treaty of Waitangi was first signed between Maori chiefs and the British Crown, establishing British sovereignty or something a bit like it, depending on whether you're reading the English or Maori version of the document.

Joined to Waitangi by a bridge, Paihia would be a fairly nondescript coastal town if it wasn't the main entry point to the Bay of Islands.

Tuck into fresh fish and chips, served as the good lord intended them – in newspaper with a cold beverage in hand – onboard a permanently moored 19th-century tall ship. The views from **Shippey's** (www.shippeys.com; Waitangi Bridge; mains $6-12; 🕐10am-late) over the inlet and bay are magical, particularly at sunset.

The **Bay of Islands i-SITE** (📞09-402 7345; www.visitnorthland.co.nz; Marsden Rd; 🕐8am-5pm Mar–mid-Dec, 8am-7pm mid-Dec–Feb; @ 🛜) offers information and internet access.

Taranaki

HIGHLIGHTS

1. **Mt Taranaki (p321)** So pretty it hurts.
2. **Puke Ariki (p318)** Innovative, contemporary and socially astute museum.
3. **Govett-Brewster Art Gallery (p318)** One of the best regional art galleries in NZ.

Dawson Falls (p321), Egmont National Park
STEPHEN BELCHER/FOTO NATURA/GETTY IMAGES ©

New Plymouth

Dominated (in the best possible way) by Mt Taranaki and surrounded by lush farmland, New Plymouth is this part of NZ's only international deep-water port. The city has a bubbling arts scene, some fab cafes and a rootsy, outdoorsy focus, with good beaches and Egmont National Park a short hop away.

 Sights

FREE **PUKE ARIKI** Museum
(www.pukeariki.com; 1 Ariki St; ⊘9am-6pm Mon, Tue, Thu & Fri, 9am-9pm Wed, 9am-5pm Sat & Sun) Translating as 'Hill of Chiefs', Puke Ariki is home to the i-SITE, a museum, library, a cafe and the fabulous Arborio restaurant. The excellent museum has an extensive collection of Maori artefacts, plus colonial and wildlife exhibits (...we hope the shark suspended above the lobby isn't life-size). The regular 'Taranaki Experience' show tells the history of the province while the audience sits in podlike seats that rumble and glow.

FREE **GOVETT-BREWSTER ART GALLERY** Gallery
(www.govettbrewster.com; 42 Queen St; ⊘10am-5pm) The Govett-Brewster Art Gallery is arguably the country's best regional art gallery. Presenting contemporary – often experimental – local and international shows, it's most famous for its connection with NZ sculptor, filmmaker and artist Len Lye (1901–80).

 Activities

Surfing

The black, volcanic-sand beaches of Taranaki are world renowned for surfing. Close to the eastern edge of town are **Fitzroy Beach** and **East End Beach** (allegedly the cleanest beach in Oceania).

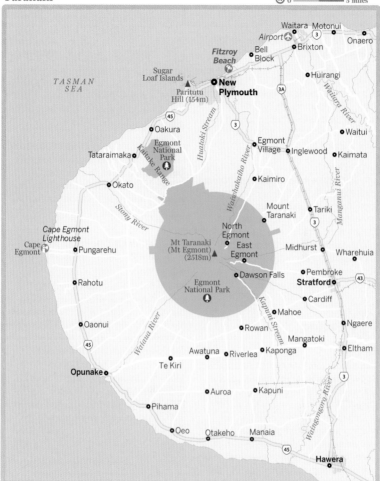

BEACH STREET SURF SHOP   Surfing
(☏ 06-758 0400; www.taranakisurf.com; 39
Beach St; 2hr lesson $75; ⊙ 9am-6pm) Close
to Fitzroy Beach, this surf shop offers lessons, gear hire and surf tours.

Tramping

The excellent **Coastal Walkway** (13km)
from Bell Block to Port Taranaki, gives you
a surf-side perspective on New Plymouth
and crosses the sexy new **Te Rewa Rewa
Bridge**.

Sleeping

FITZROY BEACH MOTEL   Motel $$
(☏ 06-757 2925; www.fitzroybeachmotel.co.nz;
25 Beach St; s/d $130/150, 2br unit $190; 🛜)
This quiet, old-time motel (just 160m
from Fitzroy Beach) has been thoroughly
redeemed with a major overhaul and
extension. Highlights include quality
carpets, double glazing, lovely bath-
rooms, LCD TVs, and an absence of

poky studio-style units (all one- or two-bedroom). Free bikes too. Winner!

ISSEY MANOR
Boutique Hotel $$

(☏06-758 2375; www.isseymanor.co.nz; 32 Carrington St; d $150-210) Friendly Issey is hard to miss(ey): two conjoined Victorian timber houses (1875 and 1910) painted with startling panels of white, orange and black. Inside are four stylish units (two with spa), a guest kitchen, and far more designer touches than you'd expect at these prices. Fab!

WATERFRONT
Hotel $$$

(☏06-769 5301; www.waterfront.co.nz; 1 Egmont St; r $190-550; @🛜) Sleek and snazzy, the Waterfront is *the* place to stay, particularly if the boss is paying. The minimalist studios are pretty flash, while the penthouses steal the show with big TVs and little balconies. It's got terrific views from some – but not all – rooms, but certainly from the curvy-fronted bar and restaurant.

 Eating

ARBORIO
Mediterranean $$

(www.arborio.co.nz; Puke Ariki, 1 Ariki St; mains $13-34; ☺breakfast, lunch & dinner) Despite looking like a cheese grater, Arborio, in the Puke Ariki building, is the star of New Plymouth's local food show. The Mediterranean-influenced menu ranges from an awesome Moroccan lamb pizza to pastas, risottos and barbecued chilli squid with lychee-and-cucumber noodle salad. Cocktails and NZ wines are also available.

FREDERIC'S
Tapas $$

(www.frederics.co.nz; 34 Egmont St; plates $10-19, mains $20-25; ☺2pm-late Mon-Thu, 11am-late Fri-Sun) Freddy's is a fab gastro-bar with quirky interior design (rusty medieval chandeliers, peacock-feather wallpaper, religious icon paintings), serving generous share-plates. Order some meatballs with bell-pepper sauce, or some green-lipped mussels with coconut cream, chilli and coriander to go with your beer.

ELIXIR
Cafe $$

(www.elixircafe.co.nz; 117 Devon St E; brunch $7-18, dinner $18-31; ☺7am-4.30pm Mon, 7am-late Tue-Sat, 8am-4pm Sun) Behind a weird louvered wall facing onto Devon St, Elixir fosters an American-diner vibe, serving up everything from coffee, cake, bagels and eggs on toast, through to more innovative evening fare.

ℹ Information

New Plymouth i-SITE (☏06-759 6060, 0800 639 759; www.visitnewplymouthnz.co.nz; Puke Ariki, 1 Ariki St; ☺9am-6pm Mon, Tue, Thu & Fri, 9am-9pm Wed, 9am-5pm Sat & Sun) In the Puke Ariki building, with a fantastic interactive tourist-info database.

ℹ Getting There & Away

Air

New Plymouth Airport (☏06-755 2250; www.newplymouthairport.com; Airport Dr) is 11km east of the centre off SH3. **Scott's Airport Shuttle** (☏06-769 5974, 0800 373 001; www.np airportshuttle.co.nz; adult from $25) operates a door-to-door shuttle to/from the airport.

Air New Zealand (☏0800 737 000, 06-757 3300; www.airnewzealand.co.nz; 12 Devon St E; ☺9am-5pm Mon-Wed & Fri, 9.30am-5pm Thu) Daily direct flights to/from Auckland, Wellington and Christchurch, with onward connections.

Bus

InterCity (☏09-583 5780; www.intercity.co.nz) services numerous destinations including Auckland ($70, 6¼ hours, four daily), Hamilton ($58, four hours, four daily), Palmerston North ($30, four hours, two daily), Wellington ($41, seven hours, two daily) and Whanganui ($38, three hours, two daily).

Naked Bus (☏0900 625 33; www.nakedbus.com) services run to the following destinations (among many others): Auckland ($30, 6½ hours, one daily), Hamilton ($27, four hours, one daily), Palmerston North ($20, 3½ hours, one daily), Wellington ($26, 6¼ hours, one daily) and Whanganui ($18, 2½ hours, one daily).

Mt Taranaki (Egmont National Park)

A classic 2518m volcanic cone dominating the landscape, Mt Taranaki is a magnet to all who catch his eye. With the last eruption more than 350 years ago, experts say that the mountain is overdue for another go. But don't let that put you off – this mountain is an absolute beauty and the highlight of any visit to the region.

 Activities

Tramping

From North Egmont, the main walk is the scenic **Pouakai Circuit**, a two- to three-day, 25km loop through alpine, swamp and tussock areas with awesome mountain views. Short, easy walks from here include the **Ngatoro Loop Track** (one hour), **Veronica Loop** (two hours) and **Connett Loop** (40 minutes return).

East Egmont has **Potaema Track** (30 minutes return) and **East Egmont Lookout** (30 minutes return); a longer walk is the steep **Enchanted Track** (two to three hours return).

At Dawson Falls you can do several short walks including **Wilkies Pools Loop** (one hour return) or the excellent but challenging **Fanthams Peak Return** (five hours return), which is snowed-in during winter. The **Kapuni Loop Track** (one-hour loop) runs to the impressive 18m **Dawson Falls** themselves.

Scenic Flights

HELIVIEW — Scenic Flights
(☏06-753 0123, 0800 435 426; www.heliview.co.nz; flights from $110) A 20-minute summit flight costs $200 per passenger.

NEW PLYMOUTH AERO CLUB — Scenic Flights
(☏06-755 0500; www.airnewplymouth.co.nz; flights from $69) A 50-minute, fixed-wing Mt Taranaki summit buzz costs $159 per person (minimum three people).

 Sleeping

ALPINE LODGE — B&B $$
(☏06-765 6620; www.andersonsalpinelodge.co.nz; 922 Pembroke Rd; s/tw/d incl breakfast from $50/100/140; P☏) With picture-postcard mountain views, this lovely Swiss-style lodge is on the Stratford side of the mountain. Inside are four rooms (three with en suite) and lots of nifty timberwork; outside are billions of birds, a hot tub and some wandering black-faced sheep.

MOUNTAIN HOUSE — Lodge $$
(☏06-765 6100; www.stratfordmountainhouse.co.nz; Pembroke Rd; s & d $155) This upbeat lodge, on the Stratford side of the mountain (15km from the SH3 turn-off and 3km to the Manganui ski area), has recently renovated, motel-style rooms and a European-style **restaurant/cafe** (Pembroke Rd; mains $30-35; ☉breakfast, lunch & dinner). DB&B packages available.

❶ Information

North Egmont Visitor Centre (☏06-756 0990; www.doc.govt.nz; Upper Manaia Rd; ☉8am-4.30pm) Current and comprehensive national park info, plus a greasy-spoon cafe (meals $10 to $18).

Dawson Falls Visitor Centre (☏027 443 0248; www.doc.govt.nz; Manaia Rd; ☉daily Dec-Feb, 9am-4pm Thu-Sun Mar-Nov)

❶ Getting There & Away

There are no public buses to the national park but numerous shuttle-bus/tour operators will gladly take you there for around $40/55 one-way/return:

Outdoor Gurus (☏06-758 4152, 027 270 2932; www.outdoorgurus.co.nz) Pick-up points (New Plymouth) and times to suit; gear hire available.

Taranaki Tours (☏06-757 9888, 0800 886 877; www.taranakitours.com) New Plymouth to North Egmont return. Tours also available.

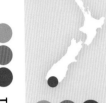

Stewart Island

HIGHLIGHTS

1 **Rakiura Track (p323)** One of NZ's greatest 'Great Walks'.

2 **Spotting a Kiwi (p323)** Wait! What's that, there... In the bushes...

3 **Meeting the Locals (p325)** Bend an elbow at the bar with some islanders.

Coast of Stewart Island
TIM MOORE/ALAMY ©

Travellers who undertake the short jaunt to Stewart Island will be rewarded with a warm welcome from both the local kiwi and the local Kiwis. NZ's 'third' island is a good place to spy the country's shy, feathered icon in the wild, and the close-knit community of Stewart Islanders (population 420) are relaxed hosts.

Once you've said g'day to the locals, there's plenty of active adventure on offer including kayaking and setting off on a rewarding tramp in Stewart Island's Rakiura National Park.

Sights

ULVA ISLAND   Island
An early naturalist, Charles Traill, was honorary postmaster here. His postal service was replaced by one at Oban in 1921, and in 1922 Ulva Island was declared a bird sanctuary. The air is alive with the song of tui and bellbirds, and you'll also see kaka, weka, kakariki and kereru (NZ pigeon). Good walking tracks in the island's northwest are detailed in *Ulva: Self-Guided Tour* ($2), available from the Department of Conservation (DOC). During summer, water taxis depart from Golden Bay wharf to Ulva Island.

RAKIURA MUSEUM   Museum
(Ayr St, Oban; adult/child $2/50c; ⊙10am-1.30pm Mon-Sat, noon-2pm Sun) Models of various ferries from over the years, Maori artefacts, and exhibitions on whaling and early European settlement.

Activities

Tramping

There are a number of tramps, ranging from half an hour to seven hours; the majority are easily accessed from Halfmoon Bay. Pick up *Day Walks* ($2) from DOC Rakiura National Park Visitor Centre. The walk to **Observation Rock** (30 minutes return) has good views over Paterson Inlet. Continue past the old stone house at Harrold Bay to **Acker's Point Lighthouse**

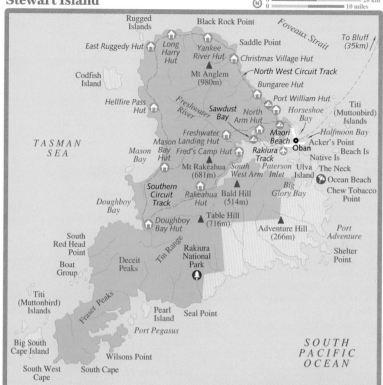

(three hours return), for good views of Foveaux Strait and the chance to see blue penguins and a colony of titi.

RAKIURA TRACK   Tramping

(www.doc.govt.nz) The 30km, three-day Rakiura Track is a well-defined, easy circuit starting and ending at Oban with copious bird life, beaches and lush bush en route. It requires a moderate level of fitness and is suitable for tramping year-round. The entire circuit is 37km in total (including the road sections) and showcases spectacular scenery.

The Rakiura Track is one of New Zealand's Great Walks and bookings are required all year round to stay in the huts and at campsites. These must be made in advance, either online at www.doc.govt.nz or at the DOC Rakiura National Park Visitor Centre on Stewart Island.

Kiwi-Spotting

The Stewart Island kiwi (*Apteryx australis lawryi*) is a distinct subspecies, with a larger beak and longer legs than its northern cousins. Kiwi are common over much of Stewart Island, particularly foraging around beaches for sand hoppers under washed-up kelp.

BRAVO ADVENTURE
CRUISES   Birdwatching

(☏ 03-219 1144; www.kiwispotting.co.nz) To see a kiwi in the wild, Bravo Adventure Cruises runs twilight tours ($140). In order to protect the kiwi, numbers are limited so make sure you book *well* ahead. Kiwi-spotting is also available with Ruggedy Range.

Other Activities

RUGGEDY RANGE WILDERNESS EXPERIENCE — Tours, Birdwatching

(📞 0508 484 337, 03-219 1066; www.ruggedy range.com; cnr Main Rd & Dundee St) Excellent guide Furhana Ahmad takes small groups on guided walks with an ecofriendly, conservation angle. A very popular excursion is the half-day trip to Ulva Island ($110); one- and two-night expeditions to see kiwi in the wild ($470 to $860) are also available. Guided sea kayaking starts at $95, and you can also buy tramping and camping gear.

RAKIURA KAYAKS — Kayaking

(📞 027 868 0318; www.rakiura.co.nz) Paterson Inlet consists of 100 sq km of sheltered, kayak-friendly waterways, with 20 islands, DOC huts and two navigable rivers. A popular trip is a paddle to Freshwater Landing (7km upriver from the inlet) followed by a three- to four-hour walk to Mason Bay to see kiwi in the wild. Rakiura Kayaks rents kayaks (half/full day $50/65) and also runs guided paddles around the inlet ($65 to $105).

STEWART ISLAND EXPERIENCE — Guided Tours

(📞 0800 000 511; www.stewartislandexperience .co.nz) Runs 2½-hour Paterson Inlet cruises (adult/child $85/22) via Ulva Island; 1½-hour minibus tours of Oban and the surrounding bays ($45/22); and 45-minute semisubmersible cruises ($85/42.50).

🛏 Sleeping

OBSERVATION ROCK LODGE — Lodge $$$

(📞 03-219 1444, 027 444 1802; www.observation rocklodge.co.nz; 7 Leonard St; d from $195) Tucked away in native bush with views south to Golden Bay, this luxury lodge is run by the lovely Annett Eiselt from Perfect Dinner. A sauna, hot tub, and plenty of hidden sanctuaries around the bird-studded property add up to a relaxing island escape.

PILGRIM COTTAGE — Rental House $$

(📞 03-219 1144; www.kiwispotting.co.nz; 8 Horseshoe Bay Rd; d $140) This quaint, weatherboard cottage in a leafy oasis near town has wooden furnishings, a potbelly stove and a well-equipped kitchen. Expect lots of bird life.

PORT OF CALL B&B — B&B $$$

(📞 03-219 1394; www.portof call.co.nz; Leask Bay Rd; s/d incl breakfast $345/385) Take in ocean views, get cosy before an open fire, or explore an isolated beach. Port of Call is 1.5km southwest of Oban on the way to Acker's Point. It has a two-night minimum stay, and guided walks and water-taxi trips can also be arranged.

Kiwi (p323)
TERRY WHITTAKER/ALAMY ©

BAY MOTEL
Motel $$

(☏03-219 1119; www.baymotel.co.nz; 9 Dundee St; d $165-185) Modern, comfortable units with lots of light and views over the harbour. Some units have big spa tubs, all rooms have full kitchens and two are wheelchair-accessible. When you've exhausted the island's bustling after-dark scene, Sky TV's on hand for on-tap entertainment.

TE TAHI BED & BREAKFAST
B&B $$$

(☏03-219 1487, 0800 725 487; www.rakiura charters.co.nz; 14 Kaka Ridge Rd; d $200) A sunny conservatory immersed in verdant bush, ocean views and colourfully decorated bedrooms are the standouts at this friendly B&B just five minutes' walk from the bustling hub of Oban and Halfmoon Bay.

 Eating & Drinking

SOUTH SEA HOTEL
Pub $$

(26 Elgin Tce; mains $20-30; ⊘7am-9pm; 🕾) This cafe-style spot does superb fish and robust seafood chowder. The attached pub is the town's main drinking hole, enlivened by occasional weekend bands and a loads-of-fun pub quiz that kicks off at 6.30pm on Sunday nights.

PERFECT DINNER
International $$

(☏027 444 1802, 03-219 1444; perfect dinner@observationrocklodge.co.nz; 3-course menu per person $89; ⊘Oct-May) Relocated from Germany, Annett Eiselt specialises in 'moveable feasts'. She's available to provide three-course menus or gourmet platters ($69) wherever you desire on the island; at your accommodation, on a beach, or somewhere else with equally terrific views. Produce is always seasonal, and ideally organic and sourced locally.

ℹ Information

The Invercargill i-SITE has a wide range of information. Online, see www.stewartisland.co.nz.

There are no banks on Stewart Island.

DOC Rakiura National Park Visitor Centre (☏03-219 0002; www.doc.govt.nz; Main Rd; ⊘8am-5pm daily Jan-Mar, 8.30am-4.30pm Mon-Fri & 10am-2pm Sat-Sun Apr-late Oct, 8am-5pm Mon-Fri late Oct-Dec) Visit the free exhibition here to understand Stewart Island's flora and fauna.

Post office (Elgin Tce) At Stewart Island Flights.

Stewart Island Experience (☏03-219 1456; www.stewartislandexperience.co.nz; 12 Elgin Tce; ⊘8.30am-6pm) In the big red building; books accommodation and activities. Also handles sightseeing tours and rents scooters, cars, fishing rods, dive gear and golf clubs.

ℹ Getting There & Away

Air

Rakiura Helicopters (☏03-219 1155; www.rakiura helicopters.co.nz; 151 Main Rd) Available for transfers from Bluff ($250 per person), scenic flights ($50 to $785 per person) and charter flights for hunters and trampers.

Stewart Island Flights (☏03-218 9129; www.stewartislandflights.co.nz; Elgin Tce; adult/child one-way $115/75, return $195/115) Flies between the island and Invercargill three times daily.

Boat

Stewart Island Experience (☏03-212 7660, 0800 000 511; www.stewartislandexperience.co.nz; Main Wharf) The passenger-only ferry runs between Bluff and Oban (adult/child $69/34.50) around three times daily. Book a few days ahead in summer. The crossing takes one hour and can be a rough ride. Cars and campervans can be stored in a secure car park at Bluff for an additional cost.

ℹ Getting Around

Water taxis offer pick-ups and drop-offs to remote parts of the island – a handy service for trampers. Try **Stewart Island Water Taxi & Eco Guiding** (☏03-219 1394), **Aihe Eco Charters & Water Taxi** (☏03-219 1066; www.aihe.co.nz) or **Sea View Water Taxi** (☏03-219 1014; www.seaview watertaxi.co.nz).

Rent a scooter (per half/full day $60/70) or a car (per half/full day $70/115) from Stewart Island Experience.

New Zealand

In Focus

Rata blossoms
PHOTOGRAPHER: SCIENCE PHOTO LIBRARY / GETTY IMAGES ©

New Zealand Today

Family tramping at Aoraki/Mt Cook (p251)

where they live
(% of New Zealanders)

63	20	10	5	2
North Island	South Island	Australia	Rest of the World	Travelling

if New Zealand were 100 people

69 would be European
14 would be Maori
9 would be Asian
7 would be Pacific Islanders
1 would be other

population per sq km

≈ 3 people

NEW ZEALAND   AUSTRALIA   USA

Shaky Isles

There's no denying it: New Zealand has had it tough over the last few years. The country may be a long way away from just about everywhere, but it's not immune to the vagaries of the global economy. In September 2010, just as it was edging out of its worst recession in 30 years, a magnitude 7.1 earthquake struck near Christchurch, the nation's second-largest city. The damage was extensive but miraculously no lives were lost, partly because it occurred in the early hours of the morning when people were in their beds (by way of comparison, Haiti's slightly smaller earthquake earlier that year killed more than 316,000 people).

While the clean-up was continuing on the East Coast, tragedy struck on the West Coast when an explosion at the Pike River coalmine, near Greymouth, sealed 29 men inside. All hope of rescue ended on 24 November when a second large explosion ripped through the mine.

Pause, Engage

In the midst of all this doom and gloom, New Zealanders have soldiered on stoically, with the people of Christchurch proving remarkably resilient in the face of what is still an ongoing event.

Throughout September and October 2011, the influx of tourists for the Rugby World Cup provided a welcome distraction. Kiwis love sharing their spectacular country with visitors and in turn seeing it anew through foreign eyes. They never tire of being reminded of the rugged beauty of their beaches, mountains, fiords, glaciers, native forests and thermal regions. Although Christchurch missed out on hosting any games (its brand new stadium, constructed for the event, lay in ruins), its rattled residents couldn't help but be cheered by the feel-good success of the tournament – and, of course, the national team's victory.

In the face of all that's occurred, you might be surprised by the extent to which the average Kiwi will genuinely want you to have a really, really good time during your stay. It's in these interactions with everyday, eager-to-please Kiwis that lasting memories are made. In the words of an enduring Maori proverb: *He aha te mea nui o te ao? He tangata! He tangata! He tangata!* (What is the most important thing in the world? It is people! It is people! It is people!).

Then, in the early afternoon of 22 February 2011, a magnitude 6.3 earthquake struck Christchurch. This time the city wasn't so lucky and 181 people lost their lives. Canterbury has barely had a break since then, experiencing literally hundreds of aftershocks: a 6.4 magnitude earthquake killed an elderly man in June 2011; a 5.8 magnitude rattled Christmas shoppers on 23 December 2011; and a 5.5 magnitude got the new year off to a shaky start on 2 January 2012.

Just when it seemed that things couldn't get any worse, a fully loaded container ship hit the Astrolabe Reef in October 2011 and proceeded to leak heavy fuel oil into the Bay of Plenty. As we write, the recovery continues, with the fuel tanks drained and a substantial proportion of the containers removed – yet bad weather continues to wash debris and rotting food onto surrounding beaches.

History
By Professor James Belich

Early Maori *pa* site, north of Dunedin

DAVID WALL / LONELY PLANET IMAGES

New Zealand's history isn't long but it is fast. In less than a thousand years these islands have produced two new peoples: the Polynesian Maori and European New Zealanders. The latter are often known by their Maori name 'Pakeha' (though not all like the term). NZ shares some of its history with the rest of Polynesia, and with some other European settler societies, but also has its unique features.

Making Maori

The first settlers of NZ were the Polynesian forebears of today's Maori. Beyond that, there are a lot of question marks. Exactly where in east Polynesia did they come from: the Cook Islands, Tahiti, the Marquesas? When did they arrive? Did the first settlers come in one group or several?

Prime sites for first settlement were warm coastal gardens for the food plants brought from Polynesia (kumara or sweet

AD 1000–1200
Archaeological evidence suggests Maori arrived in NZ around AD 1200, but earlier dates have been suggested.

potato, gourd, yam and taro); sources of workable stone for knives and adzes; and areas with abundant big game. The first settlers spread far and fast, from the top of the North Island to the bottom of the South Island within the first 100 years. High-protein diets are likely to have boosted population growth.

By about 1400, however, with big-game supply dwindling, Maori economics turned from big game to small game – forest birds and rats – and from hunting to gardening and fishing. A good living could still be made, but it required detailed local knowledge, steady effort and complex communal organisation, hence the rise of the Maori tribes. Competition for resources increased, as did conflict, and this led to the building of increasingly sophisticated fortifications, known as *pa*.

The Maori had no metals and no written language (and no alcoholic drinks or drugs). But their culture and spiritual life was rich and distinctive. Below Ranginui (sky father) and Papatuanuku (earth mother) were various gods of land, forest and sea, joined by deified ancestors over time. The mischievous demigod Maui was particularly important.

Maori traditional performance art, the group singing and dancing known as *kapa haka*, has real power, even for modern audiences. Visual art, notably woodcarving, is something special – 'like nothing but itself' in the words of 18th-century explorer-scientist Joseph Banks.

For more on Maori culture, see p343.

Enter Europe

NZ became an official British colony in 1840, but the first authenticated contact between Maori and the outside world took place almost two centuries earlier in 1642, in Golden Bay at the top of the South Island. Two Dutch ships sailed from Indonesia to search for a southern land and anything valuable it might contain. If native people were encountered, the commander, Abel Tasman, was instructed to pretend that he was 'by no means eager for precious metals, so as to leave them ignorant of the value of the same'.

When Tasman's ships anchored in the bay, local Maori came out in their canoes to make the traditional challenge: friends or foes? Misunderstanding this, the Dutch

1642
First European contact: Abel Tasman arrives, but leaves without landing after a skirmish with Maori.

1769
James Cook and Jean de Surville visit; despite some violence, both communicate with Maori.

1790s
Whaling ships and sealing gangs arrive. Europeans depend on Maori for food, water and protection.

challenged back, by blowing trumpets. When a boat was lowered to take a party between the two ships, it was attacked. Four crewmen were killed. Tasman sailed away and did not come back; nor did any other European for 127 years. But the Dutch did leave a name: 'Nieuw Zeeland' or 'New Sealand'.

Contact between Maori and Europeans was renewed in 1769, when English and French explorers arrived, under James Cook and Jean de Surville. Relations were more sympathetic, and exploration continued, motivated by science, profit and great power rivalry. Cook made two more visits between 1773 and 1777, and there were further French expeditions.

Unofficial visits, by whaling ships in the north and sealing gangs in the south, began in the 1790s. The first mission station was founded in 1814, in the Bay of Islands, and was followed by dozens of others: Anglican, Methodist and Catholic. Surprisingly, the most numerous category of visitor was probably American. New England whaling ships favoured the Bay of Islands for rest and recreation; 271 called there between 1833 and 1839 alone. To whalers, 'rest and recreation' meant sex and drink. Their favourite haunt, the little town of Kororareka (now Russell), was known to the missionaries as 'the hellhole of the Pacific'.

One or two dozen bloody clashes dot the history of Maori–European contact before 1840, but given the number of visits, interracial conflict was modest. Europeans needed Maori protection, food and labour, and Maori came to need European articles, especially muskets. Whaling stations and mission stations were linked to local Maori groups by intermarriage, which helped keep the peace. Most warfare was between Maori and Maori: the terrible intertribal 'Musket Wars' of 1818–36.

Europe brought such things as pigs (at last) and potatoes, which benefited Maori, while muskets and diseases had the opposite effect. The Musket Wars killed perhaps 20,000 people, and new diseases did considerable damage too. By 1840, the Maori had been reduced to a population of about 70,000, a decline of at least 20%. Maori bent under the weight of European contact, but they certainly did not break.

1840
Treaty of Waitangi signed by 40 chiefs in a sovereignty settlement. NZ becomes a nominal British colony.

1853–56
Provincial and central elected governments are established, and the first elections held for the NZ parliament.

1860–61
Conflict with the government over Maori land at Waitara sparks the First Taranaki War; Waikato tribes get involved.

Making Pakeha

By 1840, Maori tribes described local Europeans as 'their Pakeha', and valued the profit and prestige they brought. Maori wanted more of both, and concluded that accepting nominal British authority was the way to get them. At the same time, the British government was overcoming its reluctance to undertake potentially expensive intervention in NZ. In 1840, the two peoples struck a deal, symbolised by the treaty first signed at Waitangi on 6 February that year. The Treaty of Waitangi now has a standing not dissimilar to that of the Constitution in the US, but is even more contested. The original problem was a discrepancy between British and Maori understandings of it. The English version promised Maori full equality as British subjects in return for complete rights of government. The Maori version also promised that Maori would retain their chieftainship, which implied local rights of government. The problem was not great at first, because the Maori version applied outside the small European settlements. But as those settlements grew, conflict brewed.

In 1840, there were only about 2000 Europeans in NZ, with the shanty town of Kororareka (now Russell) as the capital and biggest settlement. By 1850, six new settlements had been formed with 22,000 settlers between them. About half of these had arrived under the auspices of the New Zealand Company and its associates. The company was the brainchild of Edward Gibbon Wakefield, who also influenced the settlement of South Australia. From the 1850s, his settlers, who included a high proportion of upper-middle-class gentlefolk, were swamped by succeeding waves of immigrants that continued to wash in until the 1880s. These people were part of the great British and Irish diaspora that also populated Australia and much of North America. Small groups of Germans, Scandinavians and Chinese made their way in, though the last faced increasing racial prejudice from the 1880s, when the Pakeha population reached half a million.

Much of the mass immigration from the 1850s to the 1870s was assisted by the provincial and central governments, which also mounted large-scale public works schemes, especially in the 1870s under Julius Vogel. In 1876, Vogel abolished the provinces on the grounds that they were hampering his development efforts. The last imperial governor with substantial power was the talented but Machiavellian

The Best...
Historic Buildings

1 Auckland Art Gallery (p68)

2 Dunedin Railway Station (p296)

3 National Tobacco Company Building, Napier (p180)

4 Civic Theatre, Auckland (p60)

5 Embassy Theatre, Wellington (p171)

6 Antigua Boatsheds, Christchurch (p239)

1861

Gold is discovered in Otago; the regional population climbs from 13,000 to over 30,000 in six months.

1865–69

Second Taranaki War: Maori resist First Taranaki War land confiscations and come close to victory.

George Grey, who ended his second governorship in 1868. Thereafter, the governors (governors-general from 1917) were largely just nominal heads of state; the head of government (the premier or prime minister) had more power. The central government, originally weaker than the provincial governments, the imperial governor and the Maori tribes, eventually exceeded the power of all three.

The Maori tribes did not go down without a fight, however. The first clash took place in 1843 in the Wairau Valley, now a wine-growing district. In 1845, more serious fighting broke out in the Bay of Islands, when Hone Heke sacked a British settlement. Pakeha were able to swamp the few Maori living in the South Island, but the fighting of the 1840s confirmed that the North Island at that time comprised a European fringe around an independent Maori heartland.

In the 1850s, settler population and aspirations grew, and fighting broke out again in 1860. The wars burned on sporadically until 1872 over much of the North Island. In the early years, a Maori nationalist organisation, the King Movement, was the backbone of resistance. In later years, some remarkable prophet-generals, notably Titokowaru and Te Kooti, took over. Most wars were small-scale, but the Waikato War of 1863–64 was not. This conflict, fought at the same time as the American Civil War, involved armoured steamships, ultramodern heavy artillery, telegraph and 10 proud British regular regiments. Despite the odds, the Maori won several battles, such as that at Gate Pa, near Tauranga, in 1864. But in the end they were ground down by European numbers and resources. Maori political, though not cultural, independence ebbed away in the last decades of the 19th century. It finally expired when police invaded its last sanctuary, the Urewera Mountains, in 1916.

Welfare & Warfare

From the 1850s to the 1880s, despite conflict with Maori, the Pakeha economy boomed on the back of wool exports, gold rushes and massive overseas borrowing for development. The crash came in the 1880s, when NZ experienced its Long Depression. In 1890, the Liberals came to power, and stayed there until 1912, helped by a recovering

History Online

For a thorough overview of NZ history from Gondwanaland to today, visit www.history-nz.org. The Ministry for Culture & Heritage's history website (www.nzhistory.net.nz) is also an excellent source of info on NZ history, including the New Zealand Land Wars.

1893
NZ becomes the first country in the world to grant the vote to women.

1914–18
WWI: 100,000 NZ troops suffer almost 60,000 casualties, mostly in France.

1939–45
WWII: 200,000 NZ troops participate; 100,000 Americans arrive to defend NZ from the Japanese.

economy. The Liberals were NZ's first organised political party, and the first of several governments to give NZ a reputation as 'the world's social laboratory'. NZ became the first country in the world to give women the vote in 1893, and introduced old-age pensions in 1898. The Liberals also introduced a long-lasting system of industrial arbitration, but this was not enough to prevent bitter industrial unrest in 1912–13. This happened under the conservative 'Reform' government, which had replaced the Liberals in 1912. Reform remained in power until 1928, and later transformed itself into the National Party. Renewed depression struck in 1929, and the NZ experience of it was as grim as any. The derelict little farmhouses still seen in rural areas often date from this era.

In 1935, a second reforming government took office: the First Labour government, led by Michael Joseph Savage, easily NZ's favourite Australian. For a time, the Labour government was considered the most socialist government outside Soviet Russia. But, when the chips were down in Europe in 1939, Labour had little hesitation in backing Britain.

NZ had also backed Britain in the Boer War (1899–1902) and WWI (1914–18), with dramatic losses in WWI in particular. NZ, a peaceful-seeming country, has spent much of its history at war. In the 19th century it fought at home; in the 20th, overseas.

Treaty House (p316), Waitangi

1975
Waitangi Tribunal is set up to investigate grievances of Maori people in relation to the Treaty of Waitangi.

1981
Rugby tour by South African Springboks divides NZ; many Kiwis take a strong anti-apartheid stance.

1985
Greenpeace antinuclear protest ship *Rainbow Warrior* is sunk in Auckland Harbour by French spies.

The Best...
Historic Atmosphere

1 Napier, Hawke's Bay (p179)

2 Waitangi Treaty Grounds, Bay of Islands (p316)

3 Dunedin, Otago (p296)

4 Devonport, Auckland (p63)

Better Britons?

British visitors have long found NZ hauntingly familiar. This is not simply a matter of the British and Irish origin of most Pakeha. It also stems from the tightening of NZ links with Britain from 1882, when refrigerated cargoes of food were first shipped to London. By the 1930s, giant ships carried frozen meat, cheese and butter, as well as wool, on regular voyages taking about five weeks one way. The NZ economy adapted to the feeding of London, and cultural links were also enhanced. This tight relationship has been described as 'recolonial', but it is a mistake to see NZ as an exploited colony. Average living standards in NZ were normally better than in Britain, as were the welfare and lower-level education systems. New Zealanders had access to British markets and culture, and they contributed their share to the latter as equals. The list of 'British' writers, academics, scientists, military leaders, publishers and the like who were actually New Zealanders is long. Indeed, New Zealanders, especially in war and sport, sometimes saw themselves as a superior version of the British – the Better Britons of the south.

'Recolonial' NZ prided itself, with some justice, on its affluence, equality and social harmony. But it was also conformist, even puritanical. Until the 1950s, it was technically illegal for farmers to allow their cattle to mate in fields fronting public roads, for moral reasons. The 1953 American movie, *The Wild One,* was banned until 1977. Sunday newspapers were illegal until 1969, and full Sunday trading was not allowed until 1989. Licensed restaurants hardly existed in 1960, nor did supermarkets or TV. Notoriously, from 1917 to 1967, pubs were obliged to shut at 6pm (see the boxed text, p337).

There were also developments in cultural nationalism, beginning in the 1930s but really flowering from the 1970s. Writers, artists and film-makers were by no means the only people who 'came out' in that era.

Coming In, Coming Out

The 'recolonial' system was shaken several times after 1935, but managed to survive until 1973, when Mother England ran off and joined the Franco-German commune now known as the EU. NZ was beginning to develop alternative markets to Britain, and alternative exports to wool, meat and dairy products. Wide-bodied jet aircraft were allowing the world and NZ to visit each other on an increasing scale. NZ had only 36,000 tourists in 1960, compared with more than two million a year now. Women

1992
The government begins reparations for land confiscated in the Land Wars and confirms Maori fishing rights.

2004
Maori TV begins broadcasting, committed to NZ content and Maori language and culture.

2005
Helen Clark is returned in NZ's third successive Labour government. The Maori Party takes four seats.

The Six O'Clock Swill

From 1917 to 1967, NZ liquor laws dictated that pubs shut their doors at 6pm – a puritanical concession aimed at preserving morality in Kiwi society. In the cities, after-work hordes would storm the pubs at 5.05pm, chugging down as many beers as possible before 6pm – the 'Six O'Clock Swill'. In the country, however, the dictum was often ignored, especially on the South Island's marvellously idiosyncratic West Coast.

were beginning to penetrate first the upper reaches of the workforce and then the political sphere. Gay people came out of the closet, despite vigorous efforts by moral conservatives to push them back in. University-educated youths were becoming more numerous and more assertive.

From 1945, Maori experienced both a population explosion and massive urbanisation. In 1936, Maori were 17% urban and 83% rural. Fifty years later, these proportions had reversed. The immigration gates, which until 1960 were pretty much labelled 'whites only', widened, first to allow in Pacific Islanders for their labour, and then to allow in (East) Asians for their money.

In 1984, NZ's third great reforming government was elected – the Fourth Labour government, led nominally by David Lange and in fact by Roger Douglas, the Minister of Finance. This government adopted an antinuclear foreign policy, delighting the left, and a more market-driven economic policy, delighting the right. NZ's numerous economic controls were dismantled with breakneck speed. Middle NZ was uneasy about the antinuclear policy, which threatened NZ's ANZUS alliance with Australia and the US. But in 1985, French spies sank the antinuclear protest ship *Rainbow Warrior* in Auckland Harbour, killing one crewman. The lukewarm US condemnation of the French act brought middle NZ in behind the antinuclear policy, which became associated with national independence. Other New Zealanders were uneasy about the economic policy, but failed to come up with a convincing alternative. Revelling in their new freedom, NZ investors engaged in a frenzy of speculation, and suffered even more than the rest of the world from the economic crash of 1987.

The early 21st century is an interesting time for NZ. Like NZ food and wine, its film and literature are flowering as never before, and the new ethnic mix is creating something very special in popular music. There are continuities, however – the pub, the sportsground, the quarter-acre section, the bush, the beach and the bach (holiday home) – and they are part of the reason people like to come here. Realising that NZ has a great culture, and an intriguing history, as well as a great natural environment, will double the bang for your buck.

2008
John Key's National Party ousts Clark's Labour after nine years in government.

2011
New Zealand hosts the Rugby World Cup: the All Blacks (only just!) win the final.

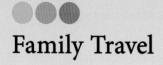

Family Travel

Overlooking Lake Tekapo (p251)

PHILIP & KAREN SMITH/LONELY PLANET IMAGES ©

New Zealand is supereasy to tackle with the kids in tow. Accommodation is usually kid-friendly, the public health care system is world class, and Kiwi food doesn't usually have chilli in it! Baby formula and disposable nappies (diapers) are widely available in cities and towns, most of which have public rooms where mothers (and sometimes fathers) can go to nurse a baby or change a nappy.

Practicalities

For helpful general tips on getting around with the kids, see Lonely Planet's *Travel with Children*.

Accommodation

Many motels and holiday parks have playgrounds, games and DVDs, and occasionally fenced swimming pools and trampolines. Cots and highchairs aren't always available at budget and midrange accommodation, but top-end hotels supply them and often provide child-minding services. B&Bs aren't usually amenable to families – many promote themselves as kid-free. Most hostels focusing on the back-packer party demographic don't welcome kids either, but some of the bigger operators do (including YHA hostels).

Babysitting

For specialised childcare, try www.rockmybaby.co.nz, or look under 'babysitters' and 'child care centres' in the *Yellow Pages* directory.

Car Hire

Procuring a kiddie car-seat for your rental car is no problem with the larger companies (Avis, Budget, Europcar etc), but some smaller car-hire companies struggle with the concept. Double-check that the company you choose can supply and fit the correctly sized seat for your child. Some companies may legally require you to fit the seat yourself. Note that kids under six months old may require a baby 'capsule' instead. To avoid delays on arrival, have this conversation with your car-hire company when you're booking.

Discounts

Child concessions (and family rates) are often available for accommodation, tours and attraction entry fees, along with air, bus and train transport, with discounts of as much as 50% off the adult rate. Do note, however, that the definition of 'child' can vary from under 12 to under 18 years; toddlers (under four years) usually get free admission and transport.

Eating Out

There are plenty of family-friendly restaurants in NZ with highchairs and kids' menus. Pubs often serve kids' meals and most cafes and restaurants (with the exception of upmarket eateries) can handle the idea of child-sized portions.

Sights & Activities

Fabulous kids' playgrounds (with slides, swings, see-saws etc) proliferate across NZ; local visitor information centres can point you in the right direction.

Some regions produce free information booklets geared towards kids' sights and activities; one example is **Kidz Go!** (**www.kidzgo.co.nz**), which details child-friendly activities and restaurants in the larger urban centres.

Other handy websites for families include www.kidspot.co.nz, with lots of kid-centric info from pregnancy through to school-age, and www.kidsnewzealand.com, which has plenty of activities suggestions. Finally, www.kidsfriendlynz.com has extensive links to various facets of NZ kiddie culture.

The Best...
Fun For Kids

1 Geysers, mud bubbles and stinky gasses, Rotorua (p109)

2 Auckland Zoo (p63)

3 Cable Car, Wellington (p163)

4 Shotover Jet, Queenstown (p279)

5 Punting on the Avon, Christchurch (p239)

Environment
By Vaughan Yarwood

Kiwi watching over its eggs

STEVEN VIDLER/EURASIA PRESS/CORBIS ©

One of the main reasons travellers come to New Zealand is to experience the country's superb landscapes. From snowy summits and volcanoes to glaciers, beaches and ancient forests, NZ has a wealth of natural assets. But this is also a fragile environment, and the pressures of agriculture, forestry and population growth have all taken a toll.

The Land

NZ is geologically young – less than 10,000 years old. Straddling two vast tectonic plates, nature's strongest forces are at work here: volcanoes, geothermal geysers, hot springs and mud pools abound... not to mention earthquakes.

The South Island has the higher mountains: the 650km-long, 3754m-high Southern Alps. Moisture-laden westerly winds dump an incredible 15m of rain annually on the Alps' western slopes. The North Island has a more even rainfall, snares most of the country's volcanic activity (especially around Rotorua and Taupo) and is spared the temperature extremes of the South – which can plunge when a wind blows in from Antarctica.

But on either island, the important thing to remember, especially if you are tramping at high altitude, is that NZ has a maritime climate. This means weather can change with lightning speed, catching out the unprepared.

A third of NZ – more than five million hectares – is protected in national parks and reserves, administered by the **DOC** (Department of Conservation; www.doc.govt.nz).

Environmental Issues

The NZ Forest Accord protects native forests, and NZ is also famous for its strong antinuclear stance, but to describe NZ as entirely 'clean and green' would be inaccurate.

European grazing systems have left many hillsides barren and eroded, and despite increasing demand for organic food, most NZ farming still relies on chemical fertilisers, pesticides and herbicides.

NZ's energy consumption has grown phenomenally over the last 20 years – NZ is one of the most inefficient energy users in the developed world. Public transport is often inadequate and ecological values still play little part in urban planning.

Other hot issues include *Didymosphenia geminata* (aka Didymo or 'rock snot') algae in waterways, fixed-net fishing endangering dolphins, and the curse of introduced possums, rats and stoats.

The Best...
Places to See a Kiwi

1 Auckland Zoo (p63)

2 Rainbow Springs Kiwi Wildlife Park, Rotorua (p117)

3 Willowbank Wildlife Reserve, Christchurch (p247)

4 Zealandia, Wellington (p163)

5 Kiwi Birdlife Park, Queenstown (p278)

IN FOCUS ENVIRONMENT

Flora & Fauna

NZ may be relatively young, geologically speaking, but its plants and animals go back a long way. The tuatara, for instance, an ancient reptile unique to these islands, is a Gondwanaland survivor closely related to the dinosaurs, while many of the distinctive flightless birds (ratites) have distant African and South American cousins.

Birds

The now-extinct, flightless moa was 3.5m tall and weighed more than 200kg; you can see skeletons at Auckland Museum (p67). Rumours of late survivals of this giant bird abound, but none have been authenticated. So if you see a chunky ostrichlike bird in your travels, photograph it – you may have just made the greatest zoological discovery of the last 100 years!

Kiwis are threatened and nocturnal, so it's rare to spot one in the wild. Other bird-nerd favourites include royal albatrosses, white herons, Fiordland crested and yellow-eyed penguins, Australasian gannets and dotterels. More common are tuis, bellbirds, fantails, pukeko, morepork owls and weka.

If you spend any time in the South Island high country, you are likely to come up against the fearless and inquisitive kea – an uncharacteristically drab green parrot with bright red underwings. Kea are common in the car parks of the Fox and Franz Josef Glaciers, where they hang out for food scraps or tear rubber from car windscreens.

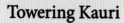

Towering Kauri

'When Chaucer was born this was a sturdy young tree. When Shakespeare was born it was 300 years old. It predates most of the great cathedrals of Europe. Its trunk is sky-rocket straight and sky-rocket bulky, limbless for half its height. Ferns sprout from its crevices. Its crown is an asymmetric mess, like an inverted root system. I lean against it, give it a slap. It's like slapping a building. This is a tree out of Tolkien. It's a kauri.'

JOE BENNETT, A LAND OF TWO HALVES, REFERRING TO THE MCKINNEY KAURI IN NORTHLAND.

Marine Mammals

Cruising the waters off NZ are whales, orcas, seals and dolphins. Kaikoura is the place to see them – sperm whales, fur seals and dusky dolphins are here year-round, and you'll also see migrating humpback, pilot, blue and southern right whales. You can swim with dolphins and seals here, too, and also at Akaroa and Tauranga.

Trees

Keep an eye out for yellow-flowering kowhai in spring, and red pohutakawa and rata in summer. Mature, centuries-old kauri are stately emblems of former days: see them at Northland's Waipoua Kauri Forest. Also look for rimu (red pine), totara (favoured for Maori war canoes), mamuka (black tree fern) and ponga (silver tree fern).

You won't get far into the bush without coming across one of its most prominent features: tree ferns. NZ is a land of ferns (more than 80 species) and most easily recognised are the mamaku (black tree fern) – which grows to 20m and can be seen in damp gullies throughout the country – and the 10m-high ponga (silver tree fern) with its distinctive white underside.

Maori Culture
By John Huria

Piupiu (beaded skirts) of *kapa haka* dancers

PAUL KENNEDY/LONELY PLANET IMAGES ©

If you're looking for a Maori experience in New Zealand you'll find it – a performance, a conversation, an art gallery, a tour. Maori are a diverse people: some are engaged with traditional cultural networks and pursuits; others are occupied with adapting tradition and placing it into a dialogue with our rapidly globalising culture.

Maori Then

Three millennia ago people began moving eastwards into the Pacific, sailing against the prevailing winds and currents (hard to go out, easier to return safely) in large, double-hulled ocean-going craft. Some stopped at Tonga and Samoa; others settled the central East Polynesian tropical islands.

The first arrival in Aotearoa (NZ's Maori name) was the great navigator Kupe, whose wife Kuramarotini gave Aotearoa its name: *'He ao, he ao tea, he ao tea roa!'* (A cloud, a white cloud, a long white cloud!)

The early settlers moved around a lot, but when they settled, Maori established *mana whenua* (regional authority), whether by military campaigns or by peaceful intermarriage and diplomacy.

Maori lived in *kainga* (small villages) with associated gardens. From time to time people would leave their home base and go to harvest seasonal foods. When peaceful life was interrupted by conflict, Maori would withdraw to a *pa* (fortified village).

Then Europeans arrived. See the History chapter, p330, for more.

Maori Today

Today's Maori culture is marked by new developments in arts, business, sport and politics. Many historical grievances still stand, but some *iwi* (tribes: Ngai Tahu and Tainui, for example) have settled historical issues and are major forces in the NZ economy. Maori have also addressed the decline in Maori language use by establishing *kohanga reo, kura kaupapa Maori* and *wananga* (Maori-medium schools). Maori radio stations abound; **Maori Television** (www.maoritelevision.com) and the Maori-language station **Te Reo** (www.tereo.tv) occupy TV screens. In late May or early June, Matariki (Maori New Year) is a time for learning, planning and preparing as well as singing, dancing and celebrating.

Religion

Christian churches and denominations are important in the Maori world: there are tel-evangelists, mainstream churches for regular and occasional worship, and two major Maori churches (Ringatu and Ratana).

But in the (non-Judaeo Christian) beginning there were the *atua Maori*, the Maori gods, and for many Maori the gods remain a vital and relevant force. They are spoken of on the *marae* and in wider Maori contexts. The traditional Maori creation story is well known and widely celebrated.

Visiting Marae

As you travel around NZ, you will see many *marae* complexes, which should only be visited by arrangement with the owners. *Marae* complexes include a *wharenui* (meeting house), which often embodies an ancestor. Its ridge is the backbone, the rafters are ribs, and it shelters the descendants.

Hui (gatherings) are held at *marae*. Issues are discussed, classes conducted, milestones celebrated and the dead farewelled. *Te reo Maori* (the Maori language) is prominent, sometimes exclusively so.

If you visit a *marae* as part of an organised group, you'll be welcomed in a *powhiri* – a process involving a ceremonial *wero* (challenge), a *karanga* (ceremonial call) between women, *whaikorero* (speech making) and a *waiata* (song). The visitors' speaker then places *koha* (a gift, usually an envelope of cash) on the *marae*. The hosts then invite the visitors to *hariru* (shake hands) and *hongi* (greet). Visitors and hosts are now united and share food and drink.

The Arts

Some of the largest collections of Maori arts (or *taonga*, meaning treasures) are at Wellington's Te Papa museum, the Auckland Museum and Canterbury Museum in Christchurch.

Traditional Maori Arts

Carving

Traditional Maori carving, with its intricate detailing and curved lines, can transport the viewer. It's quite amazing to consider that it was traditionally done with painstakingly

The Hongi

The Maori *hongi* greeting involves pressing the forehead and nose together firmly, shaking hands and perhaps offering a greeting such as '*Kia ora*' or '*Tena koe*'. Some prefer one press (for two or three seconds, or longer); others prefer two shorter (press, release, press).

made stone tools, until the advent of iron (when nails suddenly became very popular). The apex of carving today is the *whare whakairo* (carved meeting house), with traditional motifs used to interpret stories and embody ancestors.

Weaving

Weaving was an essential art that provided clothing, nets and cordage, footwear, mats and *kete* (bags). Some woven items were major works – *korowai* (cloaks) could take years to finish. Woven predominantly with flax and bird feathers, they are worn now on ceremonial occasions. Flax was (and still is) the preferred medium for weaving, but contemporary weavers use everything in their work: raffia, copper wire, rubber – even polar fleece and garden hoses!

Haka

As any All Blacks rugby fan will tell you, experiencing the awe-inspiring, uplifting *haka* – chanted words, vigorous body movements and *pukana* (when performers distort their faces, eyes bulging with the whites showing, perhaps with tongue extended) – can get the adrenaline flowing. The *haka* isn't just a war dance; it's also used to welcome visitors, honour achievement, express identity or to present strong opinions.

Ta Moko

Ta moko is the Maori art of tattoo, traditionally worn by men on their faces, thighs and buttocks, and by women on their chins and lips. Historically, *moko* were tapped into the skin using pigment and a bone chisel, but the modern tattooist's gun is more common now. Many Maori wear *moko* with quiet pride and humility.

Contemporary Maori Arts

A distinctive theme in much contemporary Maori art is the tension between traditional Maori ideas and modern artistic mediums and trends. For general information on Maori arts today, see www.maoriart.org.nz.

Writing

Key Maori authors to scan the shelves for include Patricia Grace *(Potiki, Cousins, Dogside Story, Tu)*, Witi Ihimaera *(Pounamu, Pounamu; The Matriarch; Bulibasha; The Whale Rider)*, Keri Hulme *(The Bone People, Stonefish)*, Alan Duff *(Once Were Warriors)* and James George *(Hummingbird, Ocean Roads)*. Poetry buffs should seek out anything by the late, lamented Hone Tuwhare *(Deep River Talk: Collected Poems)*.

Theatre

Theatre is a strong area of the Maori arts today. Instead of dimming the lights and immediately beginning the performance, many Maori theatre groups begin with a stylised *powhiri*, with space for audience members to respond to the play, and end with a *karakia* (blessing or prayer) or farewell.

The Best...
Places to Experience Haka

It's worth looking out for **Taki Rua** (www.takirua.co.nz), a prominent theatre group and veteran independent producer of Maori work.

Film

Barry Barclay's *Ngati* (1987) was NZ's first nondocumentary, feature-length movie by a Maori director. Mereta Mita was the first Maori woman to direct a fiction feature: *Mauri* (1988). Other films with significant Maori input include the harrowing *Once Were Warriors* and the uplifting *Whale Rider*. Oscar-shortlisted Taika Waititi wrote and directed *Eagle vs Shark* and *Boy*.

The **New Zealand Film Archive** (www.filmarchive.org.nz) in Auckland and Wellington is a great place to experience Maori film, with most showings either free or inexpensive.

Dance

Contemporary Maori dance often takes its inspiration from *kapa haka* (group cultural dance) and traditional Maori imagery. The exploration of pre-European life also provides inspiration.

NZ's leading specifically Maori dance company is the **Atamira Dance Collective** (www.atamiradance.co.nz), which produces critically acclaimed, beautiful and challenging work.

Active New Zealand

Shotover River jetboat (p350)

JOHN ELK III/LONELY PLANET IMAGES ©

New Zealand's astounding natural assets encourage even the laziest lounge lizards to drag themselves outside. Outdoor activities across the nation are accessible and supremely well organised. Commercial operators can hook you up with whatever kind of experience floats your boat – from bungy jumping off a canyon to sea kayaking around a national park – but don't miss the chance to engage with nature one-on-one, a million miles from home – just you and the great void.

Tramping

Tramping (aka bushwalking, hiking or trekking) is the perfect vehicle for a close encounter with NZ's natural beauty. There are thousands of kilometres of tracks – some well marked, some barely a line on a map – plus an excellent network of huts enabling trampers to avoid lugging tents and (in some cases) cooking gear.

Before plodding off into the forest, get up-to-date track and weather info and maps from the appropriate authority – usually the **Department of Conservation** (DOC; www.doc.govt.nz) or regional i-SITE visitor information centres. If you have your heart set on a summer walk along one of the Great Walks, check out the booking requirements and get in early. If you want to avoid the crowds, go in the shoulder season. DOC staff can also help plan tramps on lesser-known tracks.

The Best...
Other Tracks: Long & Short

1 Tongariro Alpine Crossing (p146)

2 Queen Charlotte Track (p202)

3 Coast to Coast Walkway, Auckland (p68)

4 Banks Peninsula Track (p247)

5 Mauao Base Track, Mt Maunganui (p121)

Online, www.tramper.co.nz is a fantastic website with track descriptions and ratings. For safety tips, see www.mountainsafety.org.nz.

The Great Walks

NZ's nine official Great Walks (one of which is actually a river trip!) are the country's most popular tracks. Natural beauty abounds, but prepare yourself for crowds.

On the North Island, the 46km, three- to four-day **Lake Waikaremoana Track** in Te Urewera National Park is easy-to-medium in difficulty, offering lake views, bush-clad slopes and swimming. Through the volcanic landscape of Tongariro National Park, the **Tongariro Northern Circuit** is a medium-to-hard three- to four-day tramp over 41km. The easy **Whanganui Journey** is a 145km, five-day canoe or kayak down the Whanganui River in Whanganui National Park.

Down south, the hugely popular, two- to five-day **Abel Tasman Coast Track** is rated easy and takes in 51km of beaches and bays of Abel Tasman National Park. The 78km **Heaphy Tack** in Kahurangi National Park is a medium-hard-rated walk over four to six days. The easy-to-medium 60km **Kepler Track** in Fiordland National Park passes lakes, rivers, gorges, glacial valleys and beech forest over three or four days. Also in Fiordland are the easy, four-day **Milford Track** over 54km, and the medium-difficulty **Routeburn Track** over three days and 32km. On remote Stewart Island, the **Rakiura Track** (36km over three days) is a medium-difficulty track with bird life (kiwi!), beaches and lush bush.

Passes & Bookings

To tramp these tracks you'll need to buy **Great Walk Tickets** before setting out. These track-specific tickets cover you for hut accommodation (from $10 to $51.10 per adult per night, depending on the track and season) and/or camping ($5 to $20.40 per adult per night). You can camp only at designated camping grounds; note there's no camping on the Milford Track. In the off-peak season (May to September), you can use **Backcountry Hut Passes** (per adult $92, valid 6 months) or pay-as-you-go **hut tickets** (camping $5, huts $10-15) instead of Great Walk tickets on Great Walks except for the Lake Waikaremoana Track, Heaphy Track, Abel Tasman Coast Track and Rakiura Track. Kids under 18 camp and stay in huts for free on all Great Walks.

There's a booking system in place for Great Walk huts and campsites. Trampers must book their chosen accommodation and specify dates when they purchase Great Walk tickets. Bookings are required year-round for the Lake Waikaremoana Track, Abel Tasman Coast Track, Heaphy Track and Rakiura Track. Bookings are required for peak season only (October to April) on the Kepler Track, Milford Track, Routeburn Track, Tongariro Northern Circuit and Whanganui Journey.

Bookings/ticket purchases can be made online (www.doc.govt.nz), by email (greatwalksbooking@doc.govt.nz) or via DOC offices close to the tracks. Bookings open in mid-July each year.

Guided Walks

If you're new to tramping or just want a more comfortable experience than the DIY alternative, several companies can escort you through the wilds, usually staying in comfortable huts (showers!), with meals cooked and equipment carried for you.

Places on the North Island where you can sign up for a guided walk include Mt Taranaki, Lake Waikaremoana and Tongariro National Park. On the South Island try Kaikoura, the Milford Track, Heaphy Track or Hollyford Track. Prices for a four-night guided walk start at around $1500, and rise towards $2000 for deluxe guided experiences.

Skiing & Snowboarding

NZ is an essential southern-hemisphere destination for snow bunnies, with downhill, cross-country and ski mountaineering all passionately pursued. Heliskiing, where choppers lift skiers to the top of long, isolated stretches of virgin snow, also has its fans. The NZ ski season generally runs from June to October, though it can go as late as November.

NZ's commercial ski areas aren't generally set up as 'resorts' with chalets, lodges or hotels. Rather, accommodation and après-ski carousing are often in surrounding towns, connected with the slopes via daily shuttles.

Some people like to be near Queenstown's party scene or Mt Ruapehu's volcanic landscapes; others prefer the quality high-altitude runs on Mt Hutt, uncrowded Rainbow or less-stressed club skiing areas. Club areas are publicly accessible and usually less crowded and cheaper than commercial fields, even though nonmembers pay a higher fee. Many club areas have lodges you can stay at (subject to availability).

Visitor information centres in NZ and **Tourism New Zealand** (www.newzealand.com) have info on the various ski areas and can make bookings and organise packages. Lift passes cost anywhere from $40 to $95 per adult per day (half-price for kids). Lesson-and-lift packages are available at most areas. Ski and snowboard equipment rental starts at around $40 a day (cheaper for multiday hire).

Online, see www.brownbear.co.nz/ski and www.snow.co.nz.

North Island

The key North Island ski spots are Whakapapa and Turoa on **Mt Ruapehu** (www.mtruapehu.com) in Tongariro National Park, and **Tukino** (www.tukino.co.nz) on the eastern side of Mt Ruapehu. **Manganui** (www.skitaranaki.co.nz) on Mt Taranaki offers volcano-slope, club-run skiing.

South Island

Most of the South Island action revolves around the resort towns of Queenstown and Wanaka. Iconic ski fields near here include **Coronet Peak** (www.nzski.com), the

Heliskiing

NZ's remote heights are tailor-made for heliskiing, with operators covering a wide off-piste area along the Southern Alps. Costs range from around $800 to $1200 for three to eight runs. **HeliPark New Zealand** (www.helipark.co.nz) at Mt Potts is a dedicated heliski park. Heliskiing is also available at Coronet Peak, Treble Cone, Cardrona, Mt Hutt, Mt Lyford, Ohau and Hanmer Springs.

Remarkables (www.nzski.com), Treble Cone (www.treblecone.com) and Cardrona (www.card rona.com). NZ's only commercial Nordic (cross-country) ski area is Snow Farm New Zealand (www.snowfarmnz.com), near Wanaka. Snow Park NZ (www.snowparknz.com), also near Wanaka, is NZ's only dedicated freestyle ski and snowboard area.

In South Canterbury there's Ohau (www.ohau.co.nz) on Mt Sutton, Mt Dobson (www.dobson.co.nz), Fox Peak (www.foxpeak.co.nz) and Roundhill (www.roundhill.co.nz), which is perfect for beginners and intermediates.

In Central Canterbury, try Mt Hutt (www.nzski.com), Mt Potts (www.mtpotts.co.nz), Porters (www.skiporters.co.nz), Temple Basin (www.templebasin.co.nz), Craigieburn Valley (www.craigieburn.co.nz), Broken River (www.brokenriver.co.nz), Mt Olympus (www.mtolympus .co.nz) or the family-friendly Mt Cheeseman (www.mtcheeseman.co.nz) near Christchurch.

Northern Canterbury opportunities include Hanmer Springs (www.skihanmer.co.nz) and Mt Lyford (www.mtlyford.co.nz). In the Nelson region is the low-key Rainbow (www.ski rainbow.co.nz), with minimal crowds and good cross-country skiing. Awakino (www.ski awakino.com) in North Otago is a small player, but good for intermediate skiers.

Extreme Stuff

The fact that a pants-wetting, illogical activity such as bungy jumping is now an every-day pursuit in NZ says much about how 'extreme sports' have evolved here. Bungy, skydiving, jetboating and white-water rafting are all well established, all against the laws of nature, and all great fun!

Bungy Jumping

Bungy jumping (hurtling earthwards from bridges with nothing between you and eternity but a gigantic rubber band strapped to your ankles) has plenty of daredevil panache.

Queenstown is a spider-web of bungy cords, including a 43m jump off the Kawarau Bridge, a 47m leap from the top of a gondola, and the big daddy, the 134m Nevis Highwire. Other South Island bungy jumps include Waiau River (near Hanmer Springs) and Mt Hutt ski field. On the North Island, try Taupo, Taihape, Auckland and Rotorua. Varying the theme, try the 109m-high Shotover Canyon Swing or Nevis Arc in Queenstown, both seriously high rope swings: swooosh...

Skydiving

Ejecting yourself from a plane at high altitude is big business in NZ. There are plenty of professional operators, and at most drop zones the views on the way up (not to mention on the way down) are sublime.

At the time of writing, safety concerns had sparked a wholesale review of skydiving in NZ, with operators having to comply with stringent new Civil Aviation Authority regulations. Ask your operator if they have CAA accreditation before you take the plunge.

Check the website of the New Zealand Parachute Federation (www.nzpf.org) for info and operator listings.

Jetboating

Hold onto your breakfast – it's passenger-drenching 360-degree spins ahoy! On the South Island, the Shotover and Kawarau Rivers (Queenstown) and the Buller River (Westport) have fab jetboating. On the North Island, the Whanganui, Motu, Rangitaiki and Waikato Rivers are excellent for jetboating, and there are sprint jets at the Agrodome in Rotorua. Jetboating around the Bay of Islands in Northland is also de rigueur.

White-Water Rafting

There are almost as many white-water rafting possibilities as there are rivers in the country, and there's no shortage of companies to get you into the rapids. **Whitewater NZ** (www.rivers.org.nz) covers all things white-water. The **New Zealand Rafting Association** (NZRA; www.nz-rafting.co.nz) has an online river guide, and lists registered operators.

Mountain Biking

NZ is laced with quality mountain-biking opportunities. Mountain bikes can be hired in towns such as Queenstown, Wanaka, Nelson, Picton, Taupo and Rotorua, which also have repair shops. Some traditional tramping tracks are also open to mountain bikes.

Various companies will take you up to the tops of mountains and volcanoes (eg Mt Ruapehu, Christchurch's Port Hills, Cardrona and the Remarkables) so you can hurtle back down. Rotorua's Redwoods Whakarewarewa Forest offers famously good mountain biking, as do the 42 Traverse (close to Tongariro National Park), the Alexandra goldfield trails in Central Otago, the new Queenstown Bike Park, and Twizel near Mt Cook. Also try Waitati Valley and Hayward Point near Dunedin, Canaan Downs near Abel Tasman National Park, Mt Hutt, Methven and the Banks Peninsula.

Aerial Sightseeing

Small planes and helicopters circle the skies on sightseeing trips (called 'flightseeing' by the locals) all over NZ, operating from local aerodromes. It's a great (but not particularly environmentally friendly) way to absorb the country's contrasting landscapes and soaring mountains, plus some seldom-viewed terrain deep within national parks. Some of the most photo-worthy trips take place over the Bay of Islands, the Bay of

Snowboarding, a popular sport in New Zealand
PHOTOGRAPHER: CAVAN IMAGES/GETTY IMAGES ©

Cycle Touring

If you're only in NZ for a short time, you mightn't have considered doing any cycle touring, but with good roads and even better scenery, it's a magical way to see the country. Most towns offer touring-bike hire at either backpacker hostels or specialist bike shops, and there are repair shops in the bigger towns. Anyone planning a cycling tour (particularly of the South Island) should check out the self-guided tour options at www.cyclehire.co.nz as well as Lonely Planet's *Cycling New Zealand*.

Plenty (especially Whakaari Island), Tongariro National Park (from Taupo), Mt Taranaki, Aoraki/Mt Cook, the West Coast glaciers and Fiordland (from Te Anau).

Sea Kayaking

Sea kayaking is a fantastic way to see the coast, and get close to wildlife you'd otherwise never see.

Highly rated sea-kayaking areas around NZ include the Hauraki Gulf, the Bay of Islands, Coromandel Peninsula, Marlborough Sounds, Abel Tasman National Park and Fiordland. The **Kiwi Association of Sea Kayakers** (KASK; www.kask.org.nz) is the main NZ organisation. The **Sea Kayak Operators Association of New Zealand** (www.skoanz.org.nz) website has a map of paddling destinations with links to operators.

Surfing

NZ has a sensational mix of quality waves perfect for both beginners and experienced surfers. Point breaks, reefs, rocky shelves and hollow, sandy beach breaks can all be found.

NZ water temperatures and climate vary greatly from north to south. For comfort while surfing, wear a wet suit. In summer on the North Island you can get away with wearing a spring suit and boardies; on the South Island, a 2mm to 3mm steamer can do the job. Steamers are essential in winter.

Top North Island surf spots include Raglan, Mt Maunganui, Taranaki's Surf Highway 45 and the East Coast around Mahia Peninsula. Down south try the Kaikoura Peninsula, Dunedin and the Punakaiki on the West Coast.

Online, www.surfingnz.co.nz lists surf schools, while www.surf.co.nz provides information on many great surf spots.

Horse Trekking

Unlike some other parts of the world where beginners get led by the nose around a paddock, here you can really get out into the countryside on a farm, forest or beach. Rides range from one-hour jaunts (from around $50) to week-long, fully catered treks.

For equine info online, see the **Auckland SPCA Horse Welfare Auxiliary Inc** (www.horse talk.co.nz) website. For trek-operator listings, see www.truenz.co.nz/horsetrekking or www.newzealand.com.

Survival
Guide

Sea kayaking at Cathedral Cove (p92), Coromandel Peninsula
PHOTOGRAPHER: DAVID WALL/LONELY PLANET IMAGES ©

A-Z

Directory

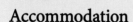

Accommodation

Across New Zealand, you can bed down in historic guesthouses, facility-laden hotels, uniform motel units, beautifully situated camp-sites, and hostels that range in character from clean-living to tirelessly party-prone. Accommodation listings are in order of authorial

preference, based on our assessment of atmosphere, cleanliness, facilities, location and bang for your buck.

○ **Budget** Up to $100 per en-suite double

○ **Midrange** $100 to $180 per en-suite double

○ **Top-end** More than $180 per en-suite double

Price ranges generally increase by 20% to 25% in the largest cities (Auckland, Wellington and Christchurch). If you're travelling during peak tourist seasons, book well in advance. Accommodation is most in demand (and priciest) during the summer holidays from Christmas to late January, at Easter and during winter in snow resort towns such as Queenstown.

Visitor information centres provide reams of local accommodation information,

often in the form of folders detailing facilities and up-to-date prices; many can also make bookings on your behalf.

For online listings, visit **Automobile Association** (AA; www.aa.co.nz) and **Jasons** (www.jasons.com).

B&BS

Bed and breakfast (B&B) accommodation is a growth industry in NZ, popping up in the middle of cities, in rural hamlets and on stretches of isolated coastline, with rooms on offer in everything from suburban bungalows to stately manors owned by one family for generations.

B&B tariffs are typically in the $120 to $180 bracket (per double), though some places charge upwards of $300 per double.

Online resources:

○ **Bed & Breakfast Book** (www.bnb.co.nz)

○ **Bed and Breakfast Directory** (www.bed-and -breakfast.co.nz)

FARMSTAYS

Farmstays open the door on the agricultural side of NZ life, with visitors encouraged to get some dirt beneath their fingernails at orchards, and dairy, sheep and cattle farms. Costs can vary widely, with B&Bs generally ranging from $80 to $120. Some farms have separate cottages where you can fix your own food, while others offer low-cost, shared, backpacker-style accommodation.

PUBS, HOTELS & MOTELS

○ **Pubs** The least expensive form of NZ hotel

Practicalities

○ **News** Leaf through Auckland's *New Zealand Herald*, Wellington's *Dominion Post* or Christchurch's the *Press* newspapers, or check out www.stuff.co.nz.

○ **TV** Watch one of the national government-owned TV stations (TV One, TV2, TVNZ 6, TVNZ 7, Maori TV and the 100% Maori-language Te Reo) or the subscriber-only Sky TV (www.skytv.co.nz).

○ **Radio** Tune in to Radio National for current affairs and Concert FM for classical and jazz (see www.radio nz.co.nz for frequencies). Kiwi FM (www.kiwifm.co.nz) showcases NZ music; Radio Hauraki (www.hauraki .co.nz) cranks out classic rock.

○ **DVDs** Kiwi DVDs are encoded for Region 4, which includes Mexico, South America, Central America, Australia, the Pacific and the Caribbean.

○ **Electrical** To plug yourself into the electricity supply (230V AC, 50Hz), use a three-pin adaptor (the same as in Australia; different to British three-pin adaptors).

○ **Weights & measures** NZ uses the metric system.

accommodation is the humble pub. As is often the case elsewhere, some of NZ's old pubs are full of character (and characters), while others are grotty, ramshackle places that are best avoided, especially by women travelling solo. In the cheapest pubs, singles/doubles might cost as little as $30/60 (with a shared bathroom down the hall), though $50/80 is more common.

○ **Hotels** At the top end of the hotel scale are five-star international chains, resort complexes and architecturally splendorous boutique hotels, all of which charge a hefty premium for their mod cons,

Book Your Stay Online

For more accommodation reviews by Lonely Planet authors, check out http://hotels.lonely planet.com. You'll find independent reviews, as well as recommendations on the best places to stay. Best of all, you can book online.

snappy service and/or historic opulence. We quote 'rack rates' (official advertised rates) for such places throughout this book, but discounts and special deals often mean you won't have to pay these prices.

○ **Motels** NZ's towns have a glut of nondescript, low-rise motels and 'motor lodges', charging between $80 and $180 for double rooms. Most

are modernish (though decor is often mired in the '90s) and have similar facilities, namely tea- and coffee-making equipment, fridge, and TV – prices vary with standard.

Business Hours

Note that most attractions close on Christmas Day and Good Friday.

○ **Shops & businesses** 9am to 5.30pm Monday to Friday, and 9am to 12.30pm or 5pm Saturday. Late-night shopping (until 9pm) in larger cities on Thursday and/or Friday nights. Sunday trading in most big towns and cities.

○ **Supermarkets** 8am to 7pm; often to 9pm or later in cities.

○ **Banks** 9.30am to 4.30pm Monday to Friday; some city branches also open Saturday mornings.

○ **Post offices** 8.30am to 5pm Monday to Friday; larger branches also 9.30am to 1pm Saturday. Postal desks in newsagencies open later.

○ **Restaurants** Food until 9pm, often until 11pm on Fridays and Saturdays.

○ **Cafes** 7am to 4pm or 5pm.

○ **Pubs** Noon until late; food from noon to 2pm and from 6pm to 8pm.

Climate

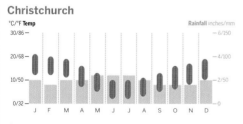

Auckland

Christchurch

Queenstown

Customs Regulations

For the low-down on what you can and can't bring into NZ, see the **New Zealand Customs Service** (www.customs.govt.nz) website. Per-person duty-free allowances:

- 1125mL of spirits or liqueur
- 4.5L of wine or beer
- 200 cigarettes (or 50 cigars or 250g of tobacco)
- dutiable goods up to the value of $700.

It's a good idea to declare any unusual medicines. Biosecurity is another customs buzzword – authorities are serious about keeping out any diseases that may harm NZ's agricultural industry. Tramping gear such as boots and tents will be checked and may need to be cleaned before being allowed in. You must declare any plant or animal products (including anything made of wood), and food of any kind.

Discount Cards

- **International Student Identity Card** The internationally recognised ISIC is produced by the **International Student Travel Confederation** (ISTC; www.istc.org), and issued to full-time students aged 12 and over. It provides discounts on accommodation, transport and admission to attractions.
- **New Zealand Card** This is a $35 discount **pass** (www.newzealandcard.com)

that'll score you between 5% and 50% off a range of accommodation, tours, sights and activities.

Electricity

230V/50Hz

Food & Drink

The NZ foodie scene once slavishly reflected Anglo-Saxon stodge, but nowadays the country's restaurants and cafes are adept at throwing together traditional staples (lamb, beef, venison, green-lipped mussels) with Asian, European and pan-Pacific flair.

For online listings:

- www.dineout.co.nz
- www.menus.co.nz

On the liquid front, NZ wine is world class (especially sauvignon blanc and pinot noir), and you'll be hard-pressed to find a NZ town of any size without decent espresso. NZ

microbrewed beers have also become mainstream.

COSTS

Eating listings in this book are classified either as budget ($), midrange ($$) or top-end ($$$). Listings are in order of authorial preference, based on our assessment of ambience, service, value, and of course, deliciousness.

- **Budget** Under $15 for a main course
- **Midrange** $15 to $35 for a main course
- **Top-end** More than $35 for a main course

VEGETARIANS & VEGANS

Most large urban centres have at least one dedicated vegetarian cafe or restaurant. See the **New Zealand Vegetarian Society** (www.vegsoc.org.nz) restaurant guide for listings. Also look for the vegetarian icon in Eating listings in this book, as it indicates a good vegetarian selection.

Gay & Lesbian Travellers

The gay and lesbian tourism industry in NZ isn't as high-profile as it is in neighbouring Australia, but homosexual communities are prominent in the main cities of Auckland and Wellington, with myriad support organisations across both islands. NZ has relatively progressive laws protecting the rights of gays and lesbians; the legal minimum age for sex between consenting persons is 16. Generally speaking,

Kiwis are fairly relaxed and accepting about homosexuality, but that's not to say that homophobia doesn't exist.

RESOURCES

There are loads of websites dedicated to gay and lesbian travellers. **Gay Tourism New Zealand** (www.gay tourismnewzealand.com) is a good starting point, with links to various sites. Other worthwhile queer websites include the following:

- www.gaynz.com
- www.gaynz.net.nz
- www.lesbian.net.nz
- www.gaystay.co.nz

Check out the nationwide magazine *express* (www.gay express.co.nz) every second Wednesday for the latest happenings, reviews and listings on the NZ gay scene.

Health

New Zealand is one of the healthiest countries in the world in which to travel. Diseases such as malaria and typhoid are unheard of, and the absence of poisonous snakes or other dangerous animals makes this a very safe region to get off the beaten track and out into the beautiful countryside.

MEDICATIONS

Bring medications in their original, clearly labelled containers. A signed and dated letter from your physician describing your medical conditions and medications, including generic names, is also a good idea. If carrying syringes or needles, be sure to have a physician's letter documenting their medical necessity.

VACCINATIONS

NZ has no vaccination requirements for any traveller, but the World Health Organization recommends that all travellers should be covered for diphtheria, tetanus, measles, mumps, rubella, chickenpox and polio, as well as hepatitis B, regardless of their destination. Ask your doctor for an International Certificate of Vaccination (or 'the yellow booklet'), which will list all the vaccinations you've received.

Insurance

A watertight travel insurance policy covering theft, loss and medical problems is essential. Some policies specifically exclude designated 'dangerous activities' such as scuba diving, parasailing, bungy jumping, white-water rafting, motorcycling, skiing and even tramping. If you plan on doing any of these things (a distinct possibility in NZ), make sure the policy you choose covers you fully.

You may prefer a policy that pays doctors or hospitals directly rather than you having to pay on the spot and claim later. If you have to claim later, make sure you keep all documentation. Some policies ask you to call back (reverse charges) to a centre in your home country where an immediate assessment of your problem is made. Check that the policy covers ambulances and emergency medical evacuations by air.

It's worth mentioning that under NZ law, you cannot sue for personal injury (other than exemplary damages). Instead, the country's **Accident Compensation Corporation** (ACC; www.acc .co.nz) administers an accident compensation scheme that provides accident insurance for NZ residents and visitors to the country, regardless of fault. This scheme, however, does not cancel out the necessity for your own comprehensive travel-insurance policy, as it doesn't cover you for such things as loss of income or treatment in your home country or ongoing illness.

Worldwide cover for travellers from over 44 countries is available online at www.lonelyplanet.com/bookings/insurance.do.

Internet Access

INTERNET CAFES

Internet cafes in the bigger urban centres or tourist areas are usually brimming with high-speed terminals. Facilities are a lot more haphazard in small, out-of-the-way towns, where a so-called internet cafe could turn out to be a single terminal in the corner of a DVD store.

Many public libraries have free internet access, but there can be a limited number of terminals.

Internet access at cafes ranges anywhere from $4 to $6 per hour. There's often a minimum period of access, usually 10 or 15 minutes.

WIRELESS ACCESS & INTERNET SERVICE PROVIDERS

Increasingly, you'll be able to find wi-fi access around the country, from hotel rooms to pub beer gardens to hostel dining rooms. Usually you have to be a guest or customer to access the internet at these locations – you'll be issued with a code, a wink and a secret handshake to enable you to get online. Sometimes it's free; sometimes there's a charge.

The country's main telecommunications company is **Telecom New Zealand** (www.telecom.co.nz), which has wireless hotspots around the country. If you have a wi-fi-enabled device, you can purchase a Telecom wireless prepaid card from participating hotspots. Alternatively, you can purchase a prepaid number from the login page and any wireless hotspot using your credit card. See the website for hotspot listings.

If you've brought your palmtop or notebook computer, you might consider buying a prepay USB modem (aka a 'dongle') with a local SIM card: both Telecom and **Vodafone** (www.vodarent .co.nz) sell these from around $100. If you want to get connected via a local internet service provider (ISP), there are plenty of options, though some companies limit their dial-up areas to major cities or particular regions. ISPs include the following:

○ **Clearnet** (☎ 0508 888 800; www.clearnet.co.nz)

○ **Earthlight** (☎ 03-479 0303; www.earthlight.co.nz)

○ **Freenet** (☎ 0800 645 000; www.freenet.co.nz)

○ **Slingshot** (☎ 0800 892 000; www.slingshot.co.nz)

Money

NZ's currency is the NZ dollar, comprising 100 cents. There are 10c, 20c, 50c, $1 and $2 coins, and $5, $10, $20, $50 and $100 notes. Prices are often still marked in single cents and then rounded to the nearest 10c when you hand over your money.

ATMS & EFTPOS

Branches of the country's major banks, including the Bank of New Zealand, ANZ, Westpac and ASB, have 24-hour ATMs that accept cards from other banks and provide access to overseas accounts. You won't find ATMs everywhere, but they're widespread across both islands.

Many NZ businesses use electronic funds transfer at point of sale (Eftpos), a convenient service that allows you to use your bank card (credit or debit) to pay directly for services or purchases, and often withdraw cash as well. Eftpos is available practically everywhere, even in places where it's a long way between banks. Just like an ATM, you need to know your personal identification number (PIN) to use it.

CREDIT CARDS

Credit cards (Visa, Master-Card etc) are widely accepted for everything from a hostel bed to a bungy jump. Credit cards are pretty much essential if you want to hire a car. They can also be used for over-the-counter cash advances at banks and from ATMs, depending on the card, but be aware that such transactions incur charges. Charge cards such as Diners Club and Amex are not as widely accepted.

DEBIT CARDS

Apart from losing them, the obvious danger with credit cards is maxing out your limit and going home to a steaming pile of debt. A safer option is a debit card, with which you can draw money directly from your home bank account using ATMs, banks or Eftpos machines. Any card connected to the international banking network (Cirrus, Maestro, Visa Plus and Eurocard) should work, provided you know your PIN. Fees for using your card at a foreign bank or ATM vary depending on your home bank; ask before you leave. Companies such as Travelex offer debit cards (Travelex calls them Cash Passport cards) with set withdrawal fees and a balance you can top-up from your personal bank account while on the road – nice one!

MONEYCHANGERS

Changing foreign currency or travellers cheques is usually no problem at banks throughout NZ or at licensed moneychangers such as Travelex in the major cities. Moneychangers can be found in all major tourist areas, cities and airports.

TAXES & REFUNDS

The Goods and Services Tax (GST) is a flat 15% tax on all domestic goods and services. Prices in this book include GST. There's no GST refund available when you leave NZ.

TIPPING

Tipping is completely optional in NZ – the total at the bottom of a restaurant bill is all you need to pay (note that sometimes there's an additional service charge). That said, it's totally acceptable to reward good service – between 5% and 10% of the bill is fine.

TRAVELLERS CHEQUES

Amex, Travelex and other international brands of travellers cheques are a bit old-fashioned these days, but they're easily exchanged at banks and moneychangers. Present your passport for identification when cashing them; shop around for the best rates/lowest fees.

●●●

Public Holidays

NZ's main public holidays:
- **New Year** 1 and 2 January
- **Waitangi Day** 6 February
- **Easter** Good Friday and Easter Monday; March/April
- **Anzac Day** 25 April
- **Queen's Birthday** First Monday in June
- **Labour Day** Fourth Monday in October
- **Christmas Day** 25 December
- **Boxing Day** 26 December

In addition, each NZ province has its own anniversary-day holiday. The dates of these provincial holidays vary – when these dates fall on Friday to Sunday, they're usually observed the following Monday; if they fall on Tuesday to Thursday, they're held on the preceding Monday.

Provincial anniversary holidays:
- **Southland** 17 January
- **Wellington** 22 January
- **Auckland** 29 January
- **Northland** 29 January
- **Nelson** 1 February
- **Otago** 23 March
- **Taranaki** 31 March
- **South Canterbury** 25 September
- **Hawke's Bay** 1 November
- **Marlborough** 1 November
- **Chatham Islands** 30 November
- **Westland** 1 December
- **Canterbury** 16 December

SCHOOL HOLIDAYS

The Christmas holiday season, from mid-December to late January, is part of the summer school vacation. It's the time you'll most likely to find transport and accommodation booked out, and long, grumpy queues at tourist attractions. There are three shorter school-holiday periods during the year: from mid- to late April, early to mid-July, and mid-September to early October. For exact dates see the **Ministry of Education** (www.minedu.govt.nz) website.

●●●

Safe Travel

Although it's no more dangerous than other developed countries, violent crime does happen in NZ, so it's worth taking sensible precautions on the streets at night or if staying in remote areas. Gang culture permeates some parts of the country; give any black-jacketed, insignia-wearing groups a wide berth.

Theft from cars is a problem around NZ – travellers are viewed as easy marks. Avoid leaving valuables in vehicles, no matter where they're parked; you're tempting fate at tourist parking areas and trailhead car parks.

Don't underestimate the dangers posed by NZ's unpredictable, ever-changing climate, especially in high-altitude areas. Hypothermia is a real risk.

NZ has been spared the proliferation of venomous creatures found in neighbouring Australia (spiders, snakes, jellyfish...). Sharks patrol NZ waters, but rarely nibble on humans. Much greater ocean hazards are rips and undertows, which can quickly drag swimmers out to sea: heed local warnings.

Kiwi roads are often made hazardous by speeding locals, wide-cornering campervans and traffic-ignorant sheep. Set yourself a reasonable itinerary and keep your eyes on the road. Cyclists take care: motorists can't always overtake easily on skinny roads.

In the annoyances category, NZ's sandflies are a royal pain. Lather yourself with insect repellent in coastal areas.

Shopping

NZ isn't one of those countries where it's necessary to buy a T-shirt to help you remember your visit, but there are some unique locally crafted items you might consider.

CLOTHING

Auckland, Wellington and Christchurch boast fashion-conscious boutiques ablaze with the sartorial flair of NZ designers. Check out www.fashionz.co.nz for up-to-date information. Keep an eye out for labels such as Zambesi, Kate Sylvester, Karen Walker, Trelise Cooper, NOM D and Little Brother.

From the backs of NZ sheep come sheepskin products such as footwear (including the much-loved ugg boot) and beautiful woollen jumpers (jerseys or sweaters) made from hand-spun, hand-dyed wool. Other knitted knickknacks include hats, gloves and scarves.

Long woollen Swanndri jackets, shirts and pullovers are so ridiculously practical, they're practically the national garment in country areas. Most common are the red-and-black or blue-and-black plaid ones; pick up 'Swannies' in outdoor-gear shops.

MAORI ART

Maori *whakairo rakau* (wood-carving) features intricate forms such as leaping dolphins, as well as highly detailed traditional carvings. You'll pay a premium for high-quality work; avoid the poor examples in Auckland souvenir shops.

Maori artisans have always made bone carvings in the shape of humans and animals, but nowadays they cater to the tourist industry. Bone fish-hook pendants, carved in traditional Maori and modernised styles, are most common, worn on a leather string around the neck.

PAUA

Abalone shell, called paua in NZ, is carved into some beautiful ornaments and jewellery and is often used as an inlay in Maori carvings. Be aware that it's illegal to take natural paua shells out of the country – only processed ornaments can be taken with you.

POUNAMU

Maoris consider *pounamu* (greenstone, or jade or nephrite) to be a culturally invaluable raw material. It's found predominantly on the west coast of the South Island – Maori called the island Te Wahi Pounamu (The Place of Greenstone) or Te Wai Pounamu (The Water of Greenstone).

One of the most popular Maori *pounamu* motifs is the *hei tiki,* the name of which literally means 'hanging human form'. They are tiny, stylised Maori figures worn on a leather string or chain around the neck. They've got great *mana* (power), but they also serve as fertility symbols.

The best place to buy *pounamu* is Hokitika, which is strewn with jade workshops and gift shops. Rotorua also has its fair share of *pounamu* crafts.

Traditionally, *pounamu* is bought as a gift for another person, not for yourself. Ask a few questions to ensure you're buying from a local operator who crafts local stone, not an offshore company selling imported (usually Chinese or European) jade.

Telephone

The major service provider is **Telecom New Zealand** (www.telecom.co.nz). **Vodafone** (www.vodafone.co.nz) is also a key player in the mobile (cell) phone market.

INTERNATIONAL CALLS

Payphones allow international calls, but the cost and international dialling code for calls will vary depending on which provider you're using. International calls from NZ are relatively inexpensive and subject to specials that reduce the rates even more, so it's worth shopping around – consult the *Yellow Pages* for providers.

To make international calls from NZ, you need to dial the international access code (📞 00), the country code and the area code (without the initial 0). So for a London number, you'd dial 📞 00-44-20, then the number.

If dialling NZ from overseas, the country code is 📞 64, followed by the appropriate area code minus the initial zero.

LOCAL CALLS

Local calls from private phones are free! Local calls from payphones cost $1 for the first 15 minutes, and 20c

Important Numbers

NZ country code	☎64
International access code from NZ	☎00
Emergency (ambulance, fire, police)	☎111
Directory assistance	☎018
International directory	☎0172

per minute thereafter, though coin-operated payphones are scarce – you'll need a phonecard. Calls to mobile phones attract higher rates.

LONG DISTANCE CALLS & AREA CODES

NZ uses regional two-digit area codes for long-distance calls, which can be made from any payphone. If you're making a local call (ie to someone else in the same town), you don't need to dial the area code. But if you're dialling within a region (even if it's to a nearby town with the same area code), you do have to dial the area code.

INFORMATION & TOLL-FREE CALLS

Numbers starting with ☎0900 are usually recorded information services, charging upwards of $1 per minute (more from mobiles); these numbers cannot be dialled from payphones.

Toll-free numbers in NZ have the prefix ☎0800 or ☎0508 and can be called free of charge from anywhere in the country, though they may not be accessible from certain areas or from mobile phones. Telephone numbers beginning with ☎0508, ☎0800 or ☎0900 cannot be dialled from outside NZ.

MOBILE PHONES

Local mobile phone numbers are preceded by the prefix 021, 025 or 027. Mobile phone coverage is good in cities and towns and most parts of the North Island, but can be patchy away from urban centres on the South Island.

If you want to bring your own phone and use a prepaid service with a local SIM card, **Vodafone** (www.vodafone.co.nz) is a practical option. Any Vodafone shop (found in most major towns) will set you up with a SIM card and phone number (about $40); top-ups can be purchased at newsagencies, post offices and petrol stations practically anywhere.

Alternatively, if you don't bring your own phone from home, you can rent one from **Vodafone Rental** (www.vodarent.co.nz) priced from $5 per day (for which you'll also need a local SIM card), with pick-up and drop-off outlets at NZ's major airports. We've also had some positive feedback on **Phone Hire New Zealand** (www.phonehirenz.com), which hires out mobile phones, SIM cards, modems and GPS systems.

PHONECARDS

NZ has a wide range of phonecards available, which can be bought at hostels, newsagencies and post offices for a fixed dollar value (usually $5, $10, $20 and $50). These can be used with any public or private phone by dialling a toll-free access number and then the PIN number on the card. Shop around – rates vary from company to company.

Time

NZ is 12 hours ahead of GMT/UTC and two hours ahead of Australian Eastern Standard Time. The Chathams are 45 minutes ahead of NZ's main islands.

In summer, NZ observes daylight-saving time, where clocks are wound forward by one hour on the last Sunday in September; clocks are wound back on the first Sunday of the following April.

Tourist Information

LOCAL TOURIST OFFICES

Almost every Kiwi city or town seems to have a visitor information centre. The bigger centres stand united within the outstanding **i-SITE** (www.newzealand.com/travel/i-sites) network, affiliated with Tourism New Zealand (the official national tourism body). i-SITEs have trained staff, information on local activities and attractions, and free brochures and maps. Staff can also book activities, transport and accommodation.

Bear in mind that many information centres only

promote accommodation and tour operators who are paying members of the local tourist association, and that sometimes staff aren't supposed to recommend one activity or accommodation provider over another.

There's also a network of **Department of Conservation** (DOC; www.doc.govt.nz) visitor centres to help you plan activities and make bookings. Visitor centres – in national parks, regional centres and major cities – usually also have displays on local lore, flora, fauna and biodiversity.

TOURIST OFFICES ABROAD

Tourism New Zealand (www.newzealand.com) has representatives in various countries around the world. A good place for pretrip research is the official website (emblazoned with the hugely successful 100% Pure New Zealand branding), which has information in several languages, including German and Japanese. Overseas offices:

o **Australia** (✆ 0415-123 362; L12, 61 York St, Sydney)

o **UK & Europe** (✆ 020-7930 1662; L7, New Zealand House, 80 Haymarket, London, UK)

o **USA & Canada** (✆ 310-395 7480; Suite 300, 501 Santa Monica Blvd, Santa Monica, USA)

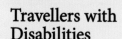

Travellers with Disabilities

Kiwi accommodation generally caters fairly well for travellers with disabilities, with a significant number of hostels, hotels, motels and B&Bs equipped with wheelchair-accessible rooms. Many tourist attractions similarly provide wheelchair access, with wheelchairs often available.

Tour operators with accessible vehicles operate from most major centres. Key cities are also serviced by 'kneeling' buses (buses that hydraulically stoop down to kerb level to allow easy access); taxi companies offer wheelchair-accessible vans. Large car-hire firms (Avis, Hertz etc) provide cars with hand controls at no extra charge (advance notice required). Mobility parking permits are available from branches of **CCS Disability Action** (✆ 0800 227 200, 04-384 5677; www.ccsdisabilityaction.org.nz) in the main centres.

For good general information, see NZ's disability information website **Weka** (www.weka.net.nz), which has categories including Transport and Travel.

Visas

Visa application forms are available from NZ diplomatic missions overseas, travel agents and **Immigration New Zealand** (✆ 0508 558 855, 09-914 4100; www.immigration.govt.nz). Immigration New Zealand has over a dozen offices overseas; consult the website.

VISITOR'S VISA

Citizens of Australia don't need a visa to visit NZ and can stay indefinitely (provided they have no criminal convictions). UK citizens don't need a visa either and can stay in the country for up to six months.

Citizens of another 56 countries that have visa-waiver agreements with NZ don't need a visa for stays of up to three months, provided they have an onward ticket and sufficient funds to support their stay: see the website for details. Nations in this group include Canada, France, Germany, Ireland, Japan, the Netherlands and the USA.

Citizens of other countries must obtain a visa before entering NZ. Visas come with three months' standard validity and cost NZ$110 if processed in Australia or certain South Pacific countries (eg Samoa, Fiji), or around NZ$140 if processed elsewhere in the world.

Women Travellers

NZ is generally a very safe place for women travellers, although the usual sensible precautions apply: avoid walking alone late at night and never hitchhike alone. If you're out on the town, always keep enough money aside for a taxi back to your accommodation. Lone women should also be wary of staying in basic pub accommodation unless it looks safe and well managed. Sexual harassment is not a widely reported problem in NZ, but of course it does happen.

See www.womentravel.co.nz for more information.

Transport

●●●

Getting There & Away

ENTERING THE COUNTRY

Disembarkation in New Zealand is generally a straightforward affair, with only the usual customs declarations to endure and the uncool scramble at the luggage carousel. Recent global instability has resulted in increased security in NZ airports, in both domestic and international terminals, and you may find customs procedures more time-consuming. One procedure has the Orwellian title Advance Passenger Screening, a system whereby documents that used to be checked after you touched down in NZ (passport, visa etc) are now checked before you board your flight – make sure all your documentation is in order so that your check-in is stress-free.

PASSPORT

There are no restrictions when it comes to foreign citizens entering NZ. If you have a current passport and visa (or don't require one), you should be fine.

AIR

There's a number of competing airlines servicing NZ and a wide variety of fares to choose from if you're flying in from Asia, Europe or North America, though ultimately you'll still pay a lot for a flight unless you jet in from Australia. NZ's inordinate popularity and abundance of year-round activities mean that almost any time of year airports can be swarming with inbound tourists – if you want to fly at a particularly popular time of

Climate Change & Travel

Every form of transport that relies on carbon-based fuel generates CO_2, the main cause of human-induced climate change. Modern travel is dependent on aeroplanes, which might use less fuel per kilometre per person than most cars but travel much greater distances. The altitude at which aircraft emit gases (including CO_2) and particles also contributes to their climate change impact. Many websites offer 'carbon calculators' that allow people to estimate the carbon emissions generated by their journey and, for those who wish to do so, to offset the impact of the greenhouse gases emitted with contributions to portfolios of climate-friendly initiatives throughout the world. Lonely Planet offsets the carbon footprint of all staff and author travel.

year (eg over the Christmas period), book well in advance.

The high season for flights into NZ is during summer (December to February), with slightly less of a premium on fares over the shoulder months (October/November and March/April). The low season generally tallies with the winter months (June to August), though this is still a busy time for airlines ferrying ski bunnies and powder hounds.

AIRPORTS

A number of NZ airports handle international flights, with Auckland receiving the most

Departure Tax

An international departure tax of NZ$25 applies when leaving NZ at all airports except Auckland, Christchurch and Dunedin, payable by anyone aged 12 and over (NZ$10 for children aged two to 11, free for those under two years of age). The tax is not included in the price of airline tickets, but must be paid separately at the airport before you board your flight. Pay via credit card or cash. Departing Auckland, Christchurch and Dunedin, a NZ$12.50 Passenger Service Charge (PSC) applies, which is included in your ticket price.

traffic. You can fly internationally from:

○ **Auckland International Airport** (AKL; ☏09-275 0789, 0800 247 767; www.aucklandairport.co.nz; Ray Emery Dr)

○ **Christchurch Airport** (CHC; ☏03-358 5029; www.christchurchairport.co.nz; Memorial Ave)

○ **Dunedin Airport** (DUD; ☏03-486 2879; www.dnairport.co.nz; Miller Rd)

○ **Hamilton International Airport** (HIA; ☏07-848 9027; www.hamiltonairport.co.nz; Airport Rd)

○ **Palmerston North International Airport** (PMR; ☏06-351 4415; www.pnairport.co.nz; Airport Dr)

○ **Queenstown Airport** (ZQN; ☏03-450 9031; www.queenstownairport.co.nz; Sir Henry Wigley Dr)

○ **Rotorua International Airport** (☏07-345 8800; www.rotorua-airport.co.nz)

○ **Wellington Airport** (WLG; ☏04-385 5100; www.wellington-airport.co.nz; Stewart Duff Dr)

● ● ●

Getting Around

✈ **AIR**

Those who have limited time to get between NZ's attractions can make the most of a widespread network of intra- and interisland flights.

AIRLINES IN NEW ZEALAND

The country's major domestic carrier, Air New Zealand, has an aerial network covering most of the country. Australia-based Jetstar also flies between the main cities. Beyond this, several small-scale regional operators provide essential transport services to outlying islands such as Great Barrier Island in the Hauraki Gulf, Stewart Island and the Chathams. Operators include the following:

○ **Air Chathams** (☏03-305 0209; www.airchathams.co.nz)

○ **Air Fiordland** (☏0800 107 505, 03-249 6720; www.airfiordland.com)

○ **Air New Zealand** (NZ; ☏09-357 3000, 0800 737 000; www.airnewzealand.co.nz)

○ **Air West Coast** (☏03-738 0524, 0800 247 937; www.airwestcoast.co.nz)

○ **Air2there.com** (☏04-904 5130, 0800 777 000; www.air2there.com)

○ **Fly My Sky** (☏09-256 7025; www.flymysky.co.nz)

○ **Golden Bay Air** (☏03-525 8725, 0800 588 885; www.goldenbayair.co.nz)

○ **Great Barrier Airlines** (☏09-275 9120, 0800 900 600; www.greatbarrierairlines.co.nz)

○ **Jetstar** (JQ; ☏0800 800 995; www.jetstar.com)

○ **Salt Air** (☏09-402 8338, 0800 472 582; www.saltair.co.nz)

○ **Soundsair** (☏0800 505 005, 03-520 3080; www.soundsair.co.nz)

○ **Stewart Island Flights** (☏03-218 9129; www.stewartislandflights.com)

○ **Sunair** (☏07-575 7799, 0800 786 247; www.sunair.co.nz)

AIR PASSES

With discounting being the norm these days, and a number of budget airlines now serving the trans-Tasman route as well as the Pacific Islands, the value of air passes isn't as red-hot as in the past.

From Los Angeles return, **Air New Zealand** (NZ; ☏09-357 3000, 0800 737 000; www.airnewzealand.co.nz) offers the Explore New Zealand Airpass, which includes a stop in either Wellington, Queenstown or Christchurch plus three other domestic NZ destinations. Prices at the time of research started at around US$1150.

Star Alliance (www.staralliance.com) offers the coupon-based South Pacific Airpass, valid for selected journeys within NZ, and between NZ, Australia and several Pacific Islands, including Fiji, New Caledonia, Tonga, the Cook Islands and Samoa. Passes are available to nonresidents of these countries, must be issued outside NZ in conjunction with Star Alliance international tickets, and are valid for three months. A typical Sydney–Christchurch–Wellington–Auckland–Nadi pass cost NZ$1050 at the time of research.

 BICYCLE

Touring cyclists proliferate in NZ, particularly over summer. NZ is clean, green and relatively uncrowded, and has lots of cheap accommodation (including camping) and abundant fresh water. The roads are generally in good nick, and the climate is generally not too hot or cold. Road traffic is the biggest

Nga Haerenga, New Zealand Cycle Trail

The Nga Haerenga, New Zealand Cycle Trail (www.nzcycletrail.com) is a major nationwide project that has been in motion since 2009, expanding and improving NZ's extant network of bike trails. Funded to the tune of around NZ$46 million, the project currently has 18 'Great Rides' under construction across both islands, most of which are already open to cyclists in some capacity. See the website for info and updates.

danger: trucks overtaking too close to cyclists are a particular threat. Bikes and cycling gear (to rent or buy) are readily available in the main centres, as are bicycle repair shops.

By law all cyclists must wear an approved safety helmet (or risk a fine); it's also vital to have good reflective safety clothing. Cyclists who use public transport will find that major bus lines and trains only take bicycles on a 'space available' basis and charge up to $10. Some of the smaller shuttle bus companies, on the other hand, make sure they have storage space for bikes, which they carry for a surcharge.

If importing your own bike or transporting it by plane within NZ, check with the relevant airline for costs and the degree of dismantling and packing required.

See www.nzta.govt.nz/traffic/ways/bike for more bike safety and legal tips.

HIRE
Rates offered by most outfits for renting road or mountain bikes range from $10 to $20 per hour and $30 to $50 per day. Longer-term rentals are often available by negotiation.

 BOAT

NZ may be an island nation but there's virtually no long-distance water transport around the country. Obvious exceptions include the boat services between Auckland and various islands in the Hauraki Gulf, the interisland ferries that chug across Cook Strait between Wellington and Picton, and the passenger ferry that negotiates Foveaux Strait between Bluff and the town of Oban on Stewart Island.

 BUS

Bus travel in NZ is relatively easy and well organised, with services transporting you to the far reaches of both islands (including the start/end of various walking tracks), but it can be expensive, tedious and time-consuming.

NZ's dominant bus company is **InterCity** (☎ 09-583 5780; www.intercity.co.nz), which also has an extra-comfort travel and sightseeing arm called **Newmans Coach Lines** (☎ 09-583 5780; www.newmanscoach.co.nz). InterCity can drive you to just about anywhere on the North and South Islands.

Naked Bus (☎ 0900 625 33; www.nakedbus.com) is the main competition, a budget operator with fares as low as $1 (!).

SEAT CLASSES
There are no allocated economy or luxury classes on NZ buses; smoking is a no-no.

RESERVATIONS
Over summer, school holidays and public holidays, book well in advance on popular routes. At other times a day or two ahead is usually fine. The best prices are generally available online, booked a few weeks in advance.

BUS PASSES
If you're covering a lot of ground, both **InterCity** (☎ 09-583 5780, 0800 222 146; www.intercity.co.nz) and **Naked Bus** (☎ 0900 625 33; www.nakedbus.com) offer bus passes that can be cheaper than paying as you go, but they do of course lock you into using their respective networks. All the following passes are valid for 12 months.

Nationwide Passes

○ **Flexipass** A hop-on/hop-off InterCity pass, allowing travel to pretty much anywhere in NZ, in any direction. The pass is purchased in blocks of travel time: minimum 15 hours ($117), maximum 60 hours ($449). The average cost of each block becomes cheaper the more hours you buy. You can top up the pass if you need more time.

○ **Flexitrips** An InterCity bus-pass system whereby you purchase a specific number of bus trips (eg Auckland to

Tauranga would count as one trip) in blocks of five, with or without the north-south ferry trip included. Five/15/30 trips including the ferry cost $210/383/550 (subtract $54 if you don't need the ferry).

○ **Aotearoa Adventurer**, **Kiwi Explorer**, **Kia Ora New Zealand** and **Tiki Tour New Zealand** Hop-on/hop-off, fixed-itinerary nationwide passes offered by InterCity. These passes link up tourist hot spots and range in price from $645 to $1219. See www.travelpass.co.nz for details.

○ **Naked Passport** (www.nakedpassport.com) A Naked Bus pass that allows you to buy trips in blocks of five, which you can add to any time, and book each trip as needed. Five/15/30 trips cost $157/330/497. An unlimited pass costs $597 – great value if you're travelling NZ for many moons.

North Island Passes

InterCity also offers 13 hop-on/hop-off, fixed-itinerary North Island bus passes, ranging from short $43 runs between Rotorua and Taupo, to $249 trips from Auckland to Wellington via the big sights in between. See www.travelpass.co.nz for details.

South Island Passes

On the South Island, InterCity offers 11 hop-on/hop-off, fixed-itinerary passes, ranging from $43 trips between Christchurch and Kaikoura, to $583 loops around the whole island. See www.travelpass.co.nz for details.

SHUTTLE BUSES

Other than InterCity and Naked Bus, regional shuttle-bus operators include the following:

○ **Abel Tasman Coachlines** (☏ 03-548 0285; www.abeltasmantravel.co.nz)

○ **Alpine Scenic Tours** (☏ 07-378 7412; www.alpinescenictours.co.nz)

○ **Atomic Shuttles** (☏ 03-349 0697; www.atomictravel.co.nz)

○ **Cook Connection** (☏ 0800 266 526; www.cookconnect.co.nz)

○ **Dalroy Express** (☏ 06-759-0197, 0508 465 622; www.dalroytours.co.nz)

○ **East West Coaches** (☏ 03-789 6251, 0800 142 622; eastwestcoaches@xtra.co.nz)

○ **Hanmer Connection** (☏ 0800 242 663; www.atsnz.com)

○ **Go Kiwi Shuttles** (☏ 07-866 0336; www.go-kiwi.co.nz)

○ **Knightrider** (☏ 03-342 8055, 0800 317 057; www.knightrider.co.nz)

○ **Southern Link Travel** (☏ 0508 458 835; www.southernlinkbus.co.nz)

○ **Topline Tours** (☏ 03-249 8059; www.toplinetours.co.nz)

○ **Tracknet** (☏ 03-249 7777, 0800 483 262; www.tracknet.net)

○ **Waitomo Wanderer** (☏ 03-477 9083, 0800 000 4321; www.travelheadfirst.com)

○ **West Coast Shuttle** (☏ 03-768 0028; www.westcoastshuttle.co.nz)

🚗 CAR & MOTORCYCLE

The best way to explore NZ in depth is to have your own wheels. It's easy to hire cars and campervans at good rates; alternatively, consider buying your own vehicle.

AUTOMOBILE ASSOCIATION (AA)

NZ's **Automobile Association** (AA; ☏ 0800 500 444; www.aa.co.nz/travel) provides emergency breakdown services, maps and accommodation guides (from holiday parks to motels and B&Bs).

Members of overseas automobile associations should bring their membership cards – many of these bodies have reciprocal agreements with the AA.

DRIVING LICENCES

International visitors to NZ can use their home country's driving licence – if your licence isn't in English, it's a good idea to carry a certified translation with you. Alternatively, use an International Driving Permit (IDP), which will usually be issued on the spot (valid for 12 months) by your home country's automobile association.

FUEL

Fuel (petrol, aka gasoline) is available from service stations across NZ. LPG (gas) is not always stocked by rural suppliers; if you're on gas, it's safer to have dual-fuel capability. Aside from remote locations such as Milford Sound and Mt Cook, petrol prices don't vary much from place to place (very democratic): per-litre costs at the time of research were around $2.10.

Freedom Camping

New Zealand is so photogenic, it's tempting to just pull off the road at a gorgeous viewpoint and camp the night. But never just assume it's OK to camp somewhere: always ask a local or check with the local i-SITE, DOC office or commercial campground. If you are freedom camping, treat the area with respect – if your van doesn't have toilet facilities, find a public loo. See www.camping.org.nz for more freedom camping tips, and www.tourism.govt.nz for info on where to find dump stations.

HIRE

Campervan

Check your rear-view mirror on any far-flung NZ road and you'll probably see a shiny white campervan (aka mobile home, motor home, RV) packed with liberated travellers, mountain bikes and portable barbecues cruising along behind you.

Most towns of any size have a campground or holiday park with powered sites for around $35 per night. There are also 250-plus vehicle-accessible **Department of Conservation** (DOC; www.doc.govt.nz) campsites around NZ, ranging in price from free to $19 per adult: check the website.

You can hire campervans from dozens of companies, prices varying with season, vehicle size and length of rental.

A small van for two people typically has a minikitchen and foldout dining table, the latter transforming into a double bed when dinner is done and dusted. Larger 'superior' two-berth vans include shower and toilet. Four- to six-berth campervans are the size of trucks (and similarly sluggish) and, besides the extra space, usually contain a toilet and shower.

Over summer, rates offered by the main rental firms for two-/four-/six-berth vans start at around $160/260/300 per day, dropping to as low as $45/60/90 in winter for month-long rentals.

Major operators include the following:

- **Apollo** (☎09-889 2976, 0800 113 131; www.apollocamper.co.nz)

- **Britz** (☎09-255 3910, 0800 831 900; www.britz.co.nz)

- **Kea** (☎09-448 8800, 0800 520 052; www.keacampers.com)

- **Maui** (☎09-255 3910, 0800 651 080; www.maui.co.nz)

- **Pacific Horizon** (☎09-257 4331; www.pacifichorizon.co.nz)

- **United Campervans** (☎09-275 9919; www.unitedcampervans.co.nz)

Backpacker Van Rentals

Budget players in the campervan industry offer slick deals and funky, well-kitted-out vehicles for backpackers. Rates are competitive (from $35 per day May to September; from $80 per day December to February). Operators include the following:

- **Backpacker Campervans** (☎0800 422 267; www.backpackercampervans.co.nz)

- **Backpacker Sleeper Vans** (☎03-359 4731, 0800 325 939; www.sleepervans.co.nz)

- **Escape Rentals** (☎0800 216 171; www.escaperentals.co.nz)

- **Hippie Camper** (☎0800 113 131; www.hippiecamper.co.nz)

- **Jucy** (☎0800 399 736; www.jucy.co.nz)

- **Spaceships** (☎09-526 2130, 0800 772 237; www.spaceshipsrentals.co.nz)

- **Wicked Campers** (☎09-634 2994, 0800 246 870; www.wicked-campers.co.nz)

Car

Competition between car-rental companies in NZ is torrid, particularly in the big cities and Picton. Remember that if you want to travel far, you need unlimited kilometres. Some (but not all) companies require drivers to be at least 21 years old – ask around.

Most car-hire firms suggest (or insist) that you don't take their vehicles between islands on the Cook Strait ferries. Instead, you leave your car at either Wellington or Picton terminal and pick up another car once you've crossed the strait. This saves you paying to transport a vehicle on the ferries, and is a pain-free exercise.

International Rental Companies

The big multinational companies have offices in most major cities, towns and airports. Firms sometimes offer one-way rentals (eg collect a car in Auckland, leave it in Wellington), but there are often restrictions and fees. On the other hand, an operator in Christchurch may need to get a vehicle back to Auckland and will offer an amazing one-way deal (sometimes free!).

The major companies offer a choice of either unlimited kilometres, or 100km (or so) per day free, plus so many cents per subsequent kilometre. Daily rates in main cities typically start at around $40 per day for a compact, late-model, Japanese car, and around $75 for medium-sized cars (including GST, unlimited kilometres and insurance).

○ **Avis** (☎09-526-2847, 0800 655 111; www.avis.co.nz)

○ **Budget** (☎09-529 7784, 0800 283 438; www.budget .co.nz)

○ **Europcar** (☎03-357 0920, 0800 800 115; www.europ car.co.nz)

○ **Hertz** (☎03-520 3044, 0800 654 321; www.hertz.co.nz)

○ **Thrifty** (☎03-359 2720, 0800 737 070; www.thrifty .co.nz)

Local Rental Companies

Local rental firms dapple the *Yellow Pages*. These are almost always cheaper than the big boys – sometimes half the price – but the cheap rates may come with serious restrictions: vehicles are often older, and with less formality sometimes comes a less protective legal structure for renters.

Rentals from local firms start at around $30 per day for the smallest option. It's obviously cheaper if you rent for a week or more, and there are often low-season and weekend discounts.

Affordable, independent operators with national networks include the following:

○ **a2b Car Rentals** (☎0800 666 703; www.a2b -carrentals.co.nz)

○ **Ace Rental Cars** (☎09-303 3112, 0800 502 277; www.acerentalcars.co.nz)

○ **Apex Rentals** (☎03-379 6897, 0800 939 597; www.apexrentals.co.nz)

○ **Ezy Rentals** (☎09-374 4360, 0800 399 736; www.ezy .co.nz)

○ **Go Rentals** (☎09-525 7321, 0800 467 368; www.go rentals.co.nz)

○ **Omega Rental Cars** (☎09-377 5573, 0800 525 210; www.omegarentalcars.com)

○ **Pegasus Rental Cars** (☎03-548 2852, 0800 803 580; www.rentalcars.co.nz)

Motorcycle

Born to be wild? NZ has great terrain for motorcycle touring, despite the fickle weather in some regions. Most of the country's motorcycle-hire shops are in Auckland and Christchurch, where you can hire anything from a little 50cc moped (aka nifty-fifty) to a throbbing 750cc touring motorcycle and beyond. Recommended operators (who also run guided tours) with rates from $80 to $345 per day:

○ **New Zealand Motorcycle Rentals & Tours** (☎09-486 2472; www.nzbike.com)

○ **Te Waipounamu Motorcycle Tours** (☎03-377 3211; www.motorcycle -hire.co.nz)

INSURANCE

Rather than risk paying out wads of cash if you have an accident, you can take out your own comprehensive insurance policy, or (the usual option) pay an additional fee per day to the rental company to reduce your excess. This brings the amount you must pay in the event of an accident down from around $1500 or $2000 to around $200 or $300. Smaller operators offering cheap rates often have a compulsory insurance excess, taken as a credit-card bond, of around $900.

Most insurance agreements won't cover the cost of damage to glass (including the windscreen) or tyres, and insurance coverage is often invalidated on beaches and certain rough (4WD) unsealed roads – read the fine print.

ROAD HAZARDS

Kiwi traffic is usually pretty light, but it's easy to get stuck behind a slow-moving truck or campervan – pack plenty of patience. There are also lots of slow wiggly roads, one-way bridges and plenty of gravel roads, all of which require a more cautious driving approach. And watch out for sheep!

ROAD RULES

Kiwis drive on the left-hand side of the road; cars are right-hand drive. Give way to the right, including when you're turning left and an on-coming vehicle is turning right into the same street (this particular rule is rumoured to be changing at some stage).

At single-lane bridges (of which there are a surprisingly large number), a smaller red arrow pointing in your direction of travel means that *you* give way.

Speed limits on the open road are generally 100km/h; in built-up areas the limit is usually 50km/h. Speed cameras and radars are used extensively.

All vehicle occupants must wear a seatbelt or risk a fine. Small children must be belted into approved safety seats.

Always carry your licence when driving. Drink-driving is a serious offence and remains a significant problem in NZ, despite widespread campaigns and severe penalties. The legal blood alcohol limit is 0.08% for drivers over 20, and 0% (zero!) for those under 20.

LOCAL TRANSPORT

BUS, TRAIN & TRAM

NZ's larger cities have extensive bus services but, with a few honourable exceptions, they are mainly daytime, weekday operations; weekend services can be infrequent or nonexistent. Negotiating inner-city Auckland is made easier by the Link and free City Circuit buses. Hamilton also has a free city-centre loop bus; Christchurch has a free city shuttle service and the historic tramway (closed post-earthquake at the time of research). Most main cities have late-night buses on boozy Friday and Saturday nights.

The only city with a decent train service is Wellington, which has five suburban routes.

TAXI

The main cities have plenty of taxis and even small towns may have a local service.

🚌 TRAIN

NZ train travel is about the journey, not about getting anywhere in a hurry. **Tranz Scenic** (📞 04-495 0775, 0800 872 467; www.tranz scenic.co.nz) operates four routes:

- **Overlander** Between Auckland and Wellington.

- **TranzCoastal** Between Christchurch and Picton.

- **TranzAlpine** Over the Southern Alps between Christchurch and Greymouth.

- **Capital Connection** Weekday commuter service between Palmerston North and Wellington.

Reservations can be made through Tranz Scenic directly, or at most train stations (notably *not* at Palmerston North or Hamilton), travel agents and visitor information centres. Discounts on the *TranzCoastal* and *TranzAlpine* apply for children and seniors (30% off) and backpacker card-holders (20% off).

TRAIN PASSES

Tranz Scenic's **Scenic Rail Pass** (www.tranzscenic.co.nz) allows unlimited travel on all of its rail services, including passage on the Wellington–Picton Inter-islander ferry. A two-week pass costs $528/402 per adult/child. There's also a seven-day *TranzAlpine* and *Coastal Pacific* pass for $307/215.

Behind the Scenes

Our Readers

Many thanks to the travellers who used the last edition and wrote to us with helpful hints, useful advice and interesting anecdotes:

Mark Gibson, Julian Porter

Author Thanks

CHARLES RAWLINGS-WAY

Thanks to the many generous, knowledgeable and quietly self-assured Kiwis I met on the road, especially the i-SITE staff in Hamilton, Waitomo and New Plymouth. Thanks to Errol Hunt for the gig, and the ever-impressive Lonely Planet production staff (including the Lords of SPP). Humongous gratitude to my tireless, witty and professional co-authors: Sarah, Brett, Peter and Lee. Thanks also to Warren for Wellington, and to Meg, Ione and Remy for holding the fort while I was away.

Acknowledgments

Climate map data adapted from Peel MC, Finlayson BL & McMahon TA (2007) 'Updated World Map of the Köppen-Geiger Climate Classification', *Hydrology and Earth System Sciences*, 11, 163344.

Cover photographs: Front: Milford Sound and Mitre Peak, Fiordland National Park, Travel Pix Collection/AWL ©; Back: Champagne Pool, Wai-o-Tapu Thermal Wonderland, Gareth McCormack/Lonely Planet Images ©.

This Book

This 2nd edition of Lonely Planet's *Discover New Zealand* guidebook was coordinated by Charles Rawlings-Way, and was researched on the ground by Charles, Brett Atkinson, Sarah Bennett, Peter Dragicevich and Lee Slater. We would also like to thank the following people for their contributions to this guide: Professor James Belich (History), John Huria (Maori culture) and Vaughan Yarwood (Environment). This guidebook was commissioned in Lonely Planet's Melbourne office, and was produced by the following:

Commissioning Editor Errol Hunt
Coordinating Editor Kate Whitfield
Coordinating Cartographer Hunor Csutoros
Coordinating Layout Designer Lauren Egan
Managing Editors Barbara Delissen, Brigitte Ellemor
Managing Cartographers Mark Griffiths, Corey Hutchison
Managing Layout Designer Chris Girdler
Assisting Editors Pete Cruttenden, Kate Evans, Samantha Forge, Catherine Naghten, Sam Trafford, Amanda Williamson
Assisting Cartographers Joelene Kowalski, Samantha Tyson, Chris Tsismetzis
Cover Research Naomi Parker
Internal Image Research Rebecca Skinner, Nicholas Colicchia
Thanks to Ryan Evans, Larissa Frost, David Kemp, Valentina Kremenchutskaya, Anna Lorincz, Alison Lyall, Kate Mathews, Trent Paton, Alison Ridgway, Suzannah Shwer, Gerard Walker

SEND US YOUR FEEDBACK

We love to hear from travellers – your comments keep us on our toes and help make our books better. Our well-travelled team reads every word on what you loved or loathed about this book. Although we cannot reply individually to postal submissions, we always guarantee that your feedback goes straight to the appropriate authors, in time for the next edition. Each person who sends us information is thanked in the next edition, the most useful submissions are rewarded with a selection of digital PDF chapters.

Visit **lonelyplanet.com/contact** to submit your updates and suggestions or to ask for help. Our award-winning website also features inspirational travel stories, news and discussions.

Index

000 Map pages

000 Map pages

How to Use This Book

These symbols will help you find the listings you want:

◉	Sights	⟳	Tours	🍷	Drinking
🏄	Beaches	🎉	Festivals & Events	☆	Entertainment
🏄	Activities	🛌	Sleeping	🛍	Shopping
🎓	Courses	✕	Eating	ℹ	Information/Transport

These symbols give you the vital information for each listing:

☎	Telephone Numbers	📶	Wi-Fi Access	🚌	Bus
☺	Opening Hours	🏊	Swimming Pool	⛴	Ferry
P	Parking	🥗	Vegetarian Selection	Ⓜ	Metro
⊖	Nonsmoking	📋	English-Language Menu	Ⓢ	Subway
✳	Air-Conditioning	👶	Family-Friendly	⊖	London Tube
@	Internet Access	🐾	Pet-Friendly	🚊	Tram
				🚆	Train

Reviews are organised by author preference.

Look out for these icons:

FREE	No payment required
🍃	A green or sustainable option

Our authors have nominated these places as demonstrating a strong commitment to sustainability – for example by supporting local communities and producers, operating in an environmentally friendly way, or supporting conservation projects.

Map Legend

Sights
- 🏖 Beach
- 🛕 Buddhist
- 🏰 Castle
- ✝ Christian
- 🕉 Hindu
- ☪ Islamic
- ✡ Jewish
- 🗿 Monument
- 🏛 Museum/Gallery
- 🏚 Ruin
- 🍇 Winery/Vineyard
- 🦁 Zoo
- ◎ Other Sight

Activities, Courses & Tours
- 🤿 Diving/Snorkelling
- 🛶 Canoeing/Kayaking
- 🎿 Skiing
- 🏄 Surfing
- 🏊 Swimming/Pool
- 🚶 Walking
- 🏄 Windsurfing
- ✛ Other Activity/Course/Tour

Sleeping
- 🛏 Sleeping
- ⛺ Camping

Eating
- ✕ Eating

Drinking
- ☕ Drinking
- ☕ Cafe

Entertainment
- ☆ Entertainment

Shopping
- 🛍 Shopping

Information
- ✉ Post Office
- ℹ Tourist Information

Transport
- ✈ Airport
- ⊗ Border Crossing
- 🚌 Bus
- 🚠 Cable Car/Funicular
- 🚲 Cycling
- ⛴ Ferry
- Ⓜ Metro
- 🚝 Monorail
- P Parking
- Ⓢ S-Bahn
- 🚕 Taxi
- 🚉 Train/Railway
- 🚊 Tram
- ⊖ Tube Station
- Ⓤ U-Bahn
- • Other Transport

Routes
- Tollway
- Freeway
- Primary
- Secondary
- Tertiary
- Lane
- Unsealed Road
- Plaza/Mall
- Steps
-)═(Tunnel
- Pedestrian Overpass
- Walking Tour
- Walking Tour Detour
- Path

Boundaries
- ─ ─ ─ International
- ─ · ─ State/Province
- ─ ─ Disputed
- ─ · ─ Regional/Suburb
- Marine Park
- Cliff
- Wall

Population
- ★ Capital (National)
- ◉ Capital (State/Province)
- ● City/Large Town
- • Town/Village

Geographic
- 🏠 Hut/Shelter
- 🔦 Lighthouse
- 👁 Lookout
- ▲ Mountain/Volcano
- 🌴 Oasis
- 🌳 Park
-)(Pass
- 🏕 Picnic Area
- 💧 Waterfall

Hydrography
- River/Creek
- Intermittent River
- Swamp/Mangrove
- Reef
- Canal
- Water
- Dry/Salt/Intermittent Lake
- Glacier

Areas
- Beach/Desert
- Cemetery (Christian)
- Cemetery (Other)
- Park/Forest
- Sportsground
- Sight (Building)
- Top Sight (Building)

CONTRIBUTING AUTHORS

Professor James Belich wrote the History chapter. James is one of NZ's pre-eminent historians and the award-winning author of *The New Zealand Wars*, *Making Peoples* and *Paradise Reforged*. He has also worked in TV – *New Zealand Wars* was screened in NZ in 1998.

John Huria (Ngai Tahu, Muaupoko) wrote the Maori Culture chapter. John has an editorial, research and writing background with a focus on Maori writing and culture. He was senior editor for Maori publishing company Huia and now runs an editorial and publishing services company, Ahi Text Solutions Ltd (www.ahitextsolutions.co.nz).

Vaughan Yarwood wrote the Environment chapter. Vaughan is an Auckland-based writer whose most recent book is *The History Makers: Adventures in New Zealand Biography*. Earlier work includes *The Best of New Zealand, a Collection of Essays on NZ Life and Culture by Prominent Kiwis*, which he edited, and the regional history *Between Coasts: from Kaipara to Kawau*. He has written widely for NZ and international publications and is the former associate editor of *New Zealand Geographic*, for which he continues to write.

Our Story

A beat-up old car, a few dollars in the pocket and a sense of adventure. In 1972 that's all Tony and Maureen Wheeler needed for the trip of a lifetime – across Europe and Asia overland to Australia. It took several months, and at the end – broke but inspired – they sat at their kitchen table writing and stapling together their first travel guide, *Across Asia on the Cheap*. Within a week they'd sold 1500 copies. Lonely Planet was born.

Today, Lonely Planet has offices in Melbourne, London and Oakland, with more than 600 staff and writers. We share Tony's belief that 'a great guidebook should do three things: inform, educate and amuse'.

Our Writers

CHARLES RAWLINGS-WAY

Coordinating author, Rotorua & the Centre, Best of the Rest English by birth, Australian by chance, All Blacks fan by choice: Charles considers himself a worldly lad, but his early understanding of Aotearoa was less than comprehensive (sheep, mountains, sheep on mountains...). He realised there was more to it when a wandering uncle returned with a faux-jade tiki in 1981. He wore it with pride until he saw the NZ cricket team's beige uniforms in 1982... But Wellington's bars, Mt Taranaki's snowy summit and Raglan's point breaks have helped him forgive: he's once again smitten with NZ's phantasmal landscapes, disarming locals, and determination to sculpt its own political and indigenous destiny.

BRETT ATKINSON

Christchurch & the Central South, Queenstown & the South, Best of the Rest On his third research trip to the 'mainland', Brett explored Maori rock art, stayed in a historic cottage in the Gibbston Valley, and negotiated a penny-farthing bicycle around Oamaru. Two weeks researching earthquake-damaged Christchurch left him even more impressed with the resilience and determination of the people of Canterbury. Brett has covered ten countries for Lonely Planet, and more than 40 countries as a freelance travel and food writer. See www.brett-atkinson.net for his latest writing and travel plans.

PETER DRAGICEVICH

Auckland, Best of the Rest After nearly a decade working for off-shore publishing companies, Peter's life has come full circle, returning to West Auckland where he was raised. As Managing Editor of Auckland-based *Express* newspaper he spent much of the nineties writing about the local arts, club and bar scenes. This is the third edition of the New Zealand guide he's worked on and, after dozens of Lonely Planet assignments, it remains his favourite gig.

SARAH BENNETT & LEE SLATER

Wellington & Lower North Island, Marlborough & Nelson Raised at the top of the South, Sarah migrated to Wellington at 16 and has lived there ever since, except for various travels and a stint in London working at Lonely Planet's UK office. An arguably flawed guidebook writer due to eternal optimism and irrepressible patriotism ('New Zealand...what's not to like?'), she nevertheless strives to find fault, particularly in relation to baked goods and beer selection. Sarah is joined in this endless quest by her husband and co-writer, Lee. English by birth and now a naturalised New Zealander, Lee's first career as an engineer has seen him travel extensively around Europe, the Middle East, North Africa and the Caucasus. Sarah and Lee are co-authors of *Let's Go Camping* and *The New Zealand Tramper's Handbook*. They are also freelance feature writers for newspapers and magazines, including the *Dominion Post* and *Wilderness*.

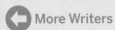

More Writers ....

Published by Lonely Planet Publications Pty Ltd
ABN 36 005 607 983
2nd edition – Nov 2012
ISBN 978 1 74220 120 7
© Lonely Planet 2012   Photographs © as indicated 2012
10 9 8 7 6 5 4 3 2 1
Printed in China